SteveHogarth

The *Invisible* Man

diaries 1998 - 2014

Steve Hogarth: The Invisible Man - **Diaries 1998-2014**

This edition first published November 2014 by Miwk Publishing Ltd.
Miwk Publishing, 12 Marbles Way, Tadworth, Surrey KT20 5LW.

ISBN 978-1-908630-85-8

Copyright © Steve Hogarth 2014.

The rights of Steve Hogarth to be identified as the author of this work has been asserted in accordance with the Copyright, Designs and Patents Act 1988.

All rights reserved. No part of this publication may be reproduced, stored in or introduced into a retrieval system, or transmitted, in any form, or by any means (electronic, mechanical, photocopying, recording or otherwise) without the prior written permission of the publisher. Any person who does any unauthorised act in relation to this publication may be liable to criminal prosecution and civil claim for damages.

A CIP catalogue record for this book is available from the British Library.

Cover and book design by Robert Hammond.
Front cover photography courtesy of Benoît Mahé.

Typeset in Utopia and Bembo.

Printed in Great Britain by TJ International, Padstow, Cornwall.

This book is sold subject to the condition that it shall not, by way of trade or otherwise, be lent, re-sold, hired out, or otherwise circulated without the publisher's prior consent in any form of binding or cover other than that in which it is published and without a similar condition including this condition being imposed on the subsequent purchaser.

www.miwkpublishing.com
This product was lovingly Miwk made.

contents

Introducton ... *7*

Acknowledgements ... *9*

1998 ... *13*

1999 ... *23*

2000 ... *39*

2001 ... *51*

2002 ... *73*

2004 ... *75*

2005 ... *115*

2006 ... *143*

2007 ... *157*

2008 ... *163*

2009 ... *167*

2010 ... *197*

2011 ... *227*

2012 ... *235*

2013 ... *273*

2014 ... *297*

introduction

Back in 1992 I went back to Doncaster to visit my mum and dad.

"What have you been up to then, son?" my dad said

"I've been on top of a mountain on a glacier in Iceland, dad. I was dropped from a helicopter..."

My dad thought for a minute before replying. "Would you make me a promise?"

"Sure," I said

"Would you begin to keep a diary? What's happening in your life doesn't normally happen to people."

And so I did.

This isn't a "sex, drugs and rock 'n'roll tabloid 'rockstar tells all'" book – this diary is about what it's like to be a 'famous' (whatever that is) touring musician travelling the world, and also how it is to go home, do the garden and plumb the dishwasher in, before popping into London to rub shoulders with Princess Stephanie of Monaco (see volume 1). Having a bath with the kids, and having lunch with Neil Armstrong.

I didn't write the diary every day. Sometimes I was too busy, too bored, or in no frame-of-mind to write anything. Some years are almost ignored, or totally absent – probably because I was holed up on a farm or in a castle writing an album and didn't have the brain-space to think about anything else. Some days are detailed moment-by-moment chronicles, while some are sketchy. Some start with detail and then remain unfinished, probably because I was called away on some errand or other – a gig, or having to get in a car and drive somewhere else. Or sleeping.

Some days, of course, weren't worth remembering.. and some are best forgotten.

This diary is simply whatever I managed to write on certain days. It also occasionally reminisces.

I apologise if I repeat myself in these pages. Often, I'm recalling the same things from the vantage-point of entirely different years, so it's only natural that a town or a gig will remind me of the same things each time I'm there. Also, there's a tendency for me to switch from the past tense to the present tense from one sentence to another. This is often because I am arriving in the present as I write.

I am in the habit of giving nicknames to the people I love and also using their real names, so I must point out that the following people are one person. (Listed here in approximate order of appearance):

Sue – Dizzy Spell, Dizzy, Diz
Sofi – Fi Fi, Hargreaves
Nial – Nially, Crompton
Linette – L
Emil – Vibes, Vibesy, Em

Mark (Kelly) – Mad Jack, Jack
Pete (Trewavas) – Trousers
Steve (Rothery) – Rothers
Ian (Mosley) – Mosley, The Cat, The Count

Over and above these are the many names of management and crew who vary from tour to tour, but the principal players will be

Lucy (Jordache): Co-Manager
Michael Hunter (Mike): Producer and Recording Engineer
Stewart (Every): Sound Engineer
Roderick (Brunton): Sound Engineer
Phil (Brown): Sound Engineer
Nick (Todd): Monitor Engineer
Rich Lee (Frenchie): Tour Manager
Jasper (Johns): Lighting Designer
Steve (Finch): Lighting Designer
Yens (Nyholm): Lighting Designer
Erik (Nielsen): Web Design, Keyboard tech
Jon Cameron: h tech
Nial Hogarth: h tech
Pete Harwood: Guitar tech
Marcus (Lee): Drum tech

acknowledgements

I would like to thank the following:

Linette for love and light, and for making me happy again.

Sofi, Nial and Emil for giving me something to be truly proud of.

The Europeans, Colin Woore, Fergus Harper and Geoff Dugmore.

Marillion: Ian Mosley, Mark Kelly, Pete Trewavas and Steve Rothery for taking me into them and allowing me to become someone whose diaries might be of interest somewhere.

Michael Hunter for music, art, science and comedy.

John Arnison for help, guidance and putting up with our phone calls 24/7, back in the day…

Richard Barbieri for allowing my voice and words into his music.

Luigi Colasanti Anonelli for his art and his love.

Frenchie for quiet help and knowing where everything is.

Bryan Leitch for his brilliance and unfailing generosity of spirit.

Paul Lewis, Nick Belshaw, Smick Hardgrave, Tim Bricusse, Dee McLoughlin for getting me into, and out of, trouble.

Benoît Mahé, Jill Furmanovsky, Niels Van Iperen, Jon Super, Steve Rothery, David Grden, Matt West and Laurent Guiraud for their photographs.

Lucy Jordache for advice and care.

Robert Hammond for wanting to publish this diary and for putting it together.

Any lyrics reproduced herein with permission of Rondor Music and Knowmore Music.

publisher's note

Minor grammatical amendments have been made to the text of this book. Everything else remains unchanged to preserve h's personal style, and to reflect the circumstances in which the diaries were written.

Happy Birthday
Mr h
Eric M
David B
Jack B
Cate B
Siân P
George L
Mark Z
Tim R
Sofia C
Tessa S
Bobby D
Thomas G
and, apparently, Jesus

1 9 9 8

Saturday 10 January *Home – Barcelona (Web Convention)*

One of the great myths of rock n'roll is that it's a process that goes on after nightfall or, at the very worst, no earlier than mid-afternoon. If only...

And so it was that, at 5.45 am, my alarm clock demanded I should go downstairs, decide which trousers to take to Barcelona, shower, pack my smalls, check I'd assembled the necessary technology (DAT player, floppy disc, reference CD of the forthcoming ambient album) and be ready for the car which would take Stewart Every (our engineer) and me to Luton airport.

At 6.45 the driver arrived at the front door looking flustered – "I've driven all over North Aston and I can't find Stewart's house!" he bellowed. Stewart doesn't live in North Aston, so it was hardly surprising. Every trip starts with a fuck up – I've come to expect it. We were going to be late. I told him I'd show him the way, and could he please keep his voice down before he woke the entire village. Trust me to get a driver who whispers at the same volume as Richard Burton doing **King Lear**. I couldn't find my wallet. It turned out to be outside in the car. I crept upstairs to say bye-bye to Sue, Sofie and Nial. Sofie was awake and had turned on her bedroom light. She was already climbing out of bed in case I left without remembering her. Nial was still fast asleep and I wouldn't have woken him, but he'd asked me to when he went to bed last night. I stirred him halfway out of sleep and kissed him goodbye. He probably won't remember it happening. I said goodbye to Sue and made my way outside before remembering my passport. Phew. That was close... I directed the driver back to

Stewart's place to find a little pile of guitar cases already outside his house. We loaded it all into the Estate Merc in the darkness and set off at high speed. Luton beckons!

As we made our way across Buckinghamshire and Bedfordshire, the dawn began to break in spectacular magenta and pink hues over the hills. Stewart and I chatted about Mo Molam, Colonel Gadaffi, Princess Di, MI6, Waddesdon Manor and what a long way from Barcelona Dunstable seems to be. I bemoaned the fact that I hadn't had a cup of coffee yet this morning, although time was much too tight to consider stopping for refreshment.

We made good time and arrived at Luton Airport at 8.15 where Pete T and Steve R were already waiting. We checked in courtesy of the unfriendly Debonair rep and made our way through to the Departure lounge for the long awaited first-coffee-of-the-day. By some miracle no one had forgotten their passport. I would have lost money on the bet.

The flight was uneventful, if not a little cold. We disembarked onto the tarmac at Barcelona airport to discover quite a chilly day – more or less the same temperature as England. When we came through into the Arrivals lounge we were greeted by a small gang of Spanish fans, who had come to welcome us and to escort us to the Hotel Gaudi. I checked into room 319, unpacked and called home to discover that it's warm and sunny in England! I returned downstairs to meet up with Pete, Steve, Stewart and the fan club to go to lunch. By now it was approaching 2.00 in the afternoon and I still hadn't had breakfast, so I was looking forward to something to eat.

We drove down to the waterfront area - modernized for the Olympics in '92 - and walked along by the crowded yacht marina to a restaurant among a line of many restaurants, bars and nightclubs, where we had a pleasant lunch of avocado and seafood. Everything seems to have been organized by two chaps called Ivan and Gabriel, and they seemed to be well on top of things. This would later be borne out by the smooth running of events at the gig. They're a friendly bunch, these Catalonians – nothing seems to be too much trouble, and they're helpful and respectful without being too 'in your face' (a common phenomenon with fan clubs – only natural n'all, but it can get a bit wearying).

After lunch we popped back to the hotel for 15 minutes so that Steve could phone home. I had a quick hot bath to remove the chill from my bones. It did the trick – I wasn't cold for the rest of the day.

We assembled once again downstairs and were taken to Radio Catalunya to perform a couple of songs with the acoustic guitars and have a chat with the local DJ who, apparently, is into the music. While he interviewed us he watched two TV's both tuned in to the Man United v Tottenham game. While we were talking, Ryan Giggs put one in to make it 1-0, but I don't know the final score. The radio studio was on the ground floor with two corner windows to the street outside where a small crowd of fans had gathered, so while we talked and then performed we were silently cheered on by them through the double glazing. From inside it was like playing to an aquarium of people. I had no monitors or headphones – I just sang in the room which was studio-dead, so I really had no idea what it might sound like. It all seemed to have gone okay, although Stewart later said the compression on the broadcast sound was so severe that everything was 'squashing' like mad when I sang louder.

We said bye-bye and signed a couple of things out in the street before the 20-minute drive to return to the venue. When we arrived there was already a local band called Arcane on-stage soundchecking. We dropped our bags in the dressing room downstairs which smelled distinctly of sewage. There's some unexplained relationship between the Spanish language and the distant aroma of drains – you'll find the two seem to coincide wherever you go in the world. I used to think it was something to do with the heat, or a failure to bother with u-bends in the plumbing, but in Barcelona today it's as chilly as England and I had a good look around the dressing room and all the sinks and toilets appear to be correctly installed. Maybe there's no mains drainage. Maybe they pump everything into the space above the suspended ceiling (it certainly smelled like it in the opening band's dressing room).

Back upstairs on stage I got to grips with the hired T3 keyboard. I had brought a disc with my sounds in it. The internal battery was flat, so it wouldn't retain any information in the event of a mains failure. Scary... Also, the keyboard wasn't weighted and the keys were sticking so it was an awkward machine to deal with, as my later performances would bear out (I might as well get my excuses in). The monitors were, however, very good so I could hear myself singing really clearly. We soundchecked for quite a while, trying to remember the arrangements of all the songs. In retrospect, a second day's rehearsal wouldn't have gone amiss. After soundcheck we returned to the dressing room for back-to-back interviews until stage-time at 10.30. I was answering questions, smiling for the camera, trying to write set lists, rehearsing my "hello, how are you's" in Catalan (which is markedly different to Spanish (e.g. Moltes Gracias as opposed to Muchath Grathiath (phonetically)) and trying to get changed, all at the same time. 5 minutes off at this point in the day would have been handy.

Well, we hit the stage around 10.40 and felt our way through the show like three blind men crossing a familiar room after someone had rearranged the furniture. The crowd forgave all the mistakes, even applauding Steve R's clanger during *Made Again* and the room was packed to the sides and rear with a standing crowd of around 700. I was glad that we'd not come here with a ten-minute set! Top marks to the crowd for not booing my appalling mess of an attempt at the keyboard tinkles in *Runaway*. We returned to the stage for three encores including a piano and voice version of *Easter* and an acoustic of Marvin Gaye's *Abraham, Martin and John*, which I dedicated on this occasion to Michael Hutchence. After the show we sat in the corner of the room and signed tickets ('Steve Dogarth on vocals') and albums. We were at it for a couple of hours – I think we met *everyone*.

We left the venue around 2.30 and were taken to a couple of clubs, the first being underground and packed so tightly that after one drink we escaped for our lives. The second was down by the sea and called the Tropicana. There were three Brazilian dancers up on a narrow stage – a boy and two tall black girls in glittery bikinis, samba-ing and salsa-ing to the music. It took me back to Rio in a flash. There's nothing compares to the spirit and the rhythm of this art-form, I'm totally into it, although, being a white English boy, I'm not connected up in the right way to be able to do the dances. I wish I'd been born Brazilian.

When the dancers took a break I decided to return to the hotel, walking back with Pete T. I fell into bed around 5.30. It had been a 24-hour hard day's night!

Sunday 11 January   *Barcelona (Web Convention)*

Enjoyed a much needed lie-in, after waking up the first time with no idea where I was. It's normal. We were to resume the schedule with the Bright Light fan club at 12.00 midday, so I got up, showered, packed and made my way down to the reception bar in desperate need of coffee, arriving at around 12.15. The bar was full of fan club folk and fan club folk's friends. Steve R sat at the bar drinking coffee, eating croissants and reading a book as though he was in the room alone. No one ignores people quite as convincingly and unselfconsciously as Steve. He seems to live in the bubble of his own universe. I ordered and drank three cappuccinos in quick succession from the peculiar twin bar girls, who were the most serious and ill-humoured bar staff I've ever experienced.

The plan was to meet up and go sightseeing whilst being filmed by a couple of chaps from Barcelona TV. We didn't get going until 2.00 in the afternoon. I stood out in the street for a while next to the phenomenal Guel Palace, one of Antoni Gaudi's creations - a massive gothic/psychedelic facade of wrought iron - opposite the hotel. It's not so cloudy today, so I was enjoying the sunshine and the blue sky (still not warm though). At 2.00 we walked across Las Ramblas, a wide avenue with market stalls down its centre, full of street performers, tourists and Barcelonans, Sunday-promenading with their families – and down an adjoining street into the old part of the town, where steep medieval walls reach upward overlooked by remarkably well preserved gargoyles.

Saturday 19 September   *Home – Göteborg*

I had to do an internet chat to the USA at 3.00 in the morning. I also had to be up at 6.00 to be ready for the car at 7.00, which would take me to Heathrow for the flight to Göteborg. I reasoned that it was all going to be very difficult, but that I could minimize the damage by going to bed early and setting my alarm for 2.45. Good plan.

Went to bed at 9.30 and lay awake until around 1.00 when Sofie began to cry with an upset tummy. Sue got up and took her downstairs for half an hour or so. I lay there wondering if she was okay, still unable to relax. Sue eventually came back to bed and the house became quiet again... for almost five minutes before Nial appeared at the bedroom door. "I've had a bad dream!" he said, and climbed into the bed next to me. "I want to go in the middle..." I hauled him across my body into the space between Sue and me, and lay awake for another hour listening to him sleeping and feeling him flailing around. By 2.00ish I'd had enough and I picked him up and carried him back to his bedroom where he returned to bed and slept peacefully. I went back to bed and, after a few more minutes, Sofie began to whimper quietly. She was obviously still in pain. I could hear her moving about and when I hauled myself back out of bed, I found her sitting on the floor next to her bedroom door, crying quietly to herself. I took her downstairs and into the lounge where she loaded a video to take her mind off her pain. I went to my room and read a couple of emails before returning to watch **Blackadder** with her.

By 2.45 she was nodding off, so I sent her back upstairs to try and sleep while I dialled the phone for the internet chat. It got off to a slow start while Melinda, somewhere in Grand Rapids, Michigan, wrestled with the technical ramifications of getting the software up and running. We were away and I was fielding questions by 3.15. It all went okay, but it's surprising how quickly the time passes when you're doing this sort of thing and, before I knew it, we were finishing up at 5.00am. I fell back into bed immediately and was finally asleep for one hour when my alarm clock roused me at 6.00 for the departure to Heathrow and to Sweden.

The management had arranged a car to take me to the airport at 7.00. I had been most specific in giving details of my address to the car company – they always get lost. Sure enough, at 7.00am, the phone rang with a driver on the other end saying he was just outside Wargrave and couldn't find my house. I'm not surprised – he was about 40 miles away. I couldn't believe it. It was to take him another 40 minutes to get to me. 40 minutes I could have spent in bed, thereby doubling my sleep for the night.

He arrived at around 8.45 and promptly drove to Heathrow at speeds in excess of 120-mph while I cowered in the back of the car, observing the fact that in an old Sierra on wet roads there was more than a fighting chance that we would shortly both be dead. Luckily, it wasn't to be, and he deposited me, exhausted and in shock, at Terminal 1 at 8.15. I found the check-in desk where Ian was having some trouble with the excess baggage. We are carrying the bare essentials – guitars and a rack full of samplers, but it was all weighing in at 300+ kilos. Excess baggage is one of those things where you're totally at the mercy of the check-in clerk. 9 times out of 10 they let you off, but today we had a jobsworth and she was determined to weigh everything and presented us with a bill for £600! If that happens on the way back we're looking at £1200 that isn't in the budget! Oh well.

When we eventually got it all sorted out and made our way to the plane, it was only half full... The flight was uneventful – I sprawled across a window seat and managed to sleep for ten minutes, waking up feeling considerably better for the power-nap. At Göteborg airport we were met by a chap with a minibus who took us first to the gig - a theatre/club in the city centre - to drop off the equipment, and then on to the hotel. For some reason, they'd put us in the Scandic which was a 15 minute drive out of town on an industrial estate. This meant we had no chance of a walk round the town, which had looked quite interesting through the bus window.

The weather was cold and grey and the record company guy was arriving in 30 minutes to start the interview schedule, which would continue to deprive me of sleep for the rest of the day. I checked into room 513 and relaxed for twenty minutes. I could really have done with a hot bath but there was only a shower. I returned to the hotel lobby to start the interview schedule. The promoter had supplied the wrong keyboards, so Mark had gone down to the gig to try to sort out the technology... I would be doing the interviews alone. There was much standing about while the record company rep tried and failed to organize a cab to a radio station. You could almost hear his one brain-cell creaking under the strain of this simple task. Nobody seemed to know who was responsible for the hotel being out of town. Nobody seemed to know who had organized the trip or why. I was tired out so not in a very forgiving frame of mind. I worked my way through the interviews and the meetn'greet of a posse of Norwegians who had come over on a mission. One of them works for BMG records in Norway, but is such a fan he intends to promote our record there anyway. Another one is an independent promotions guy who feels the same. Yet another is a marketing manager at Proctor & Gamble in Oslo and says he can print posters. Curiouser and curiouser (this lot turned out to be none other than the band Gazpacho).

At 5.00 we returned to the venue to soundcheck. The drive took us along the waterfront where we could see large ferries on the docks and an ocean-going dry-dock where a ship was being overhauled. This was the first foreign city I ever came to, when I was about twenty-one. I was playing in the band in the disco on the Tor Scandinavia – a cruise ship. It docked here before sailing on to Amsterdam. I threw snowballs at my mates on the docks here, not knowing that I was soon to be attacked by one of them and would very nearly bleed to death out in the open sea during the voyage. I was stitched back together on the ship by a Swedish naval officer with a Danish sailor assisting. It was all a distant memory now. I stared at the docks waiting for some trigger that would take me back and dig out some vivid recollection of those days as we rattled our way towards soundcheck. It never happened.

Technically, soundcheck was straightforward, although the empty room sounded very harsh. There were only a small number of people hanging around outside so I was beginning to feel nervous that no one knew the gig was happening. Soundcheck dragged on until 7.00 when I managed to find a phone to call Tom Gagliardi - a radio DJ in America - for a previously scheduled interview. After that, Steve, Pete and I drove to Goteborg's only rock radio station to be interviewed and perform a couple of acoustic songs - *The Answering Machine* and *Now She'll Never Know*. We returned to the hotel by 9.00 and I had a heavenly 30 minutes off before leaving for the show at 9.30.

On the way back to the venue I quizzed Peter (the record company rep) a little more about why we were here and whose idea the whole thing was. It was all beginning to feel like an expensive waste of time. He said there would be journalists at the show and that many people would come. It seemed unlikely to me. I was proved wrong, however. When we got back to the club I peeked into the hall. The 400 capacity room was packed with people cheering and impatiently slow-hand clapping. There was a cheer as someone spotted me enter the balcony area behind the stage, so I scurried away to get changed. Things were looking up!

The show was brilliantly received and I managed to persuade Pete to accompany me in a short acoustic rendition of *Estonia* for the second and final encore. Naturally, I have always wanted to play this song in Sweden where the loss of the Estonia ferry is still keenly felt. It was a magical couple of minutes and a meaningful way to finish what had been a pretty raucous show. Afterwards we relaxed backstage while the crew loaded the backline and while Ian waited for a certain Mr. Maloney from the promoter who was to pay us. He never showed up.

We all returned to the hotel for a couple of beers. It's amazing how potent alcohol becomes if you haven't had any sleep for a couple of days. I got drunk and staggered about a lot before returning to my room and entering a coma.

Sunday 20 September   *Göteborg – Home*

I awoke at 11.30 and, while stark naked, cleaning my teeth, I answered the ringing phone to discover we were supposed to have left already for the airport. Packed and dressed in no time and hightailed back to the airport where we weren't charged for excess baggage! I bought a Pippi Longstocking doll for Sofie and a stuffed moose for Nial during the 90 minute wait to fly back to Heathrow. Hungover and exhausted, I felt somewhat subdued – like I hadn't been to Sweden at all.

Back in England, summer had returned. The sunshine reflected brightly from the jumbo jets waiting at their Terminals like enormous cattle being milked.

Erik Nielsen, our American keyboard tech and website designer, was refused entry by immigration who wanted to put him on the next plane back to Göteborg. After much discussion, they allowed him into the UK for 24-hours to pack. They're deporting him tomorrow. It's his birthday.

Saturday 14 November   *Köln Music Hall*

Slept well on the bus, thanks to a couple of pints of Guinness in the Irish pub last night in Hannover. Woke at 11.00 to discover, somewhat confusedly, that we were standing still on the autobahn! We left Hannover at 3.00am and it should only have been a three-hour drive. I was to discover that there'd been a big traffic accident around 5.00am and that we'd been stuck on the motorway ever since.

We finally arrived at the Live Music Hall at midday. Fortunately the truck was already unloaded, so the crew hurried to try to make up the time and have the production up and ready for soundcheck at 4.30.

I hung around in catering, drinking coffee and wandering back to the bus to bring in my bags. Around 1.00pm I realised my laptop had gone missing! This had a number of dire consequences: my life is in this thing – my numbers, my diary, my lyrics, business stuff, accounts etc. To make matters worse, Mark is currently using my laptop for all the keyboard program changes in the show and he doesn't have a current safety copy!! My worst fears were that I had left the computer in the street last night while stopping to write autographs for fans hanging about. A couple of nervous hours ensued while Johnny Allan (tour manager) tried to contact the Hannover gig and see if they had it; meanwhile Mark and I tried to form contingency plans to get around doing the show without it! Eventually the good news came through that the cleaners had found it and that it was still in Hannover, but safe! Johnny arranged for it to come to Köln on a train and it was due in at 6.50 this afternoon. Deep joy! ...and what a relief!

Somehow, I'd got it into my head that the gig was in the centre of Köln, so I decided I'd go for a walk and go shopping. I'd ran out of socks and underwear. The weather was dreadful – raining and grey. I walked round the block and realised we were in the middle of some kind of industrial area and a rain-soaked five-mile walk into town wasn't really an option, so I returned to the gig to await the return of the runner, who would give me a lift into the town centre. The shops in Köln close at 4.00 on a Saturday and he didn't turn up until 3.00. We drove into town and after getting stuck in thick traffic, he finally dropped me off at 3.45, so it was all a bit of a rush. I went to a currency exchange desk in the Hauptbanhof (railway station), and when I tried to buy some marks with my Visa card I was asked for i.d. I didn't have any. I was asked for a passport, then a driving-licence, then, as a last resort, a bicycle-licence!

"We don't need a licence for a bicycle in England! Do you need a licence for a bicycle here in Germany?" I said.

"No," said the old lady behind the counter. By now we were into surrealism, so I ran with it and asked her if Beethoven had ever called in to change up some marks and had he been able to hear her through the glass? This seemed to do the trick – she relented and gave me some money.

Couldn't find socks apart from black and grey wool things. I remember thinking I'd give my right arm for a Marks and Sparks as I wandered around the busy shopping street adjacent to the Cathedral. I tried my luck in one of the department stores but could only find women's underwear and, after a couple of weeks on the road, I found this deeply psychologically unsettling, so I made my way back out into the street and in desperation bought two pairs of expensive Hugo Boss briefs in an upmarket men's boutique. I continued in vain on the quest for socks until 3.47, when I turned a corner to see Marks & Spencer standing before me as though it had been beamed down from the sky. Men's socks were on the third floor, where I jumped off the escalator at exactly four o'clock to be told that the cash registers were closed and the store also. These Germans never bend the rules, even if it means not taking the cash out of your extended hand!

I returned back towards the Hauptbanhof, stopping to wander around an antiques auction-house full of sculpture, furniture and Tiffany lamps. I took a shine to a beautiful standard lamp with a cascading stained glass Tiffany shade. I could imagine it at home in Sue's 'Indonesian' lounge. However, I have a bit of a history of buying overpriced objects-of-desire when out on the road, and I didn't want to spend money we haven't got on my now-legendary weakness for light fittings. Shame, though.

I rendezvoused back at the hotel day-room at 4.30 where the runner had arranged to take Ian and I back to the gig. Dined on goulash (urgh) in catering and soundchecked, chatting to staff of the Dutch, French, German and English fan clubs, along with Ann-Sofie Prevot who is making a short piece about us for French TV.

After soundcheck I went to bed on the bus for forty minutes before returning to try my luck in the 'interesting' gig shower. Not stone-cold but not far off. Decided on-balance to go without underwear and socks for a couple of days in order not to run out before the end of the tour. Regular showers are a more hygienic option anyway – you just have to be extra careful with your fly zip...

The show was well-received and the sound on stage was good. There was a strict curfew at 10.30 – the club became a disco later. Unfortunately this encroached on the encores and we had to cancel encore 2. I made a speech about money, greed, the state of modern capitalism etc, and realised half-way through that I was in the process of inciting a riot, so I asked the people to do us a favour and leave peacefully. I'm sure we were being heftily charged for hire of the venue, not to mention the obvious bar-profits, so it seems unnecessary to me to throw everyone out and sell the hall again. As though they weren't already making enough money. I wrote a stiff note in the guest book: "Disco is the scourge of the twentieth century", etc. I never mentioned all the nights I'd leapt around in Camden Palace in the 80's...

Mingled a little after the show with record company reps. Someone bought me one of those little boxes that bahs like a sheep when you turn it upside down. Thanked them very much and asked whether they could get me one of those boxes that laughs. I've always wanted a laugh box...

Climbed aboard the bus and probably had a beer before vanishing to my bunk ... although, to be honest, I can't remember. Tomorrow, a day off in the lovely Hotel New York, Rotterdam. Hooray!

the *invisible* man

1999   APRIL

Friday 30

1 9 9 9

Friday 30 April *Padstow, Cornwall*

Arrived home from the studio at around 6.00 and spent an hour fiddling about in the back of the jeep, trying to fasten the rear speakers down a bit better – they're buzzing around whenever any loud bass frequencies come through them. I eventually calmed them down in-between defrosting Marks & Sparks chicken curry in the microwave.

    Today is the last day of April, and I was still trying to decide whether or not to go to Cornwall – there's a town called Padstow, which has an old pagan fertility ritual on the first of May – a celebration of the coming summer. It's customary for the children and the young women of the town to wear white. The streets are decorated with coloured flags and with the branches of sycamore trees, which are fastened to the lamp-posts and buildings. A street parade goes on all day consisting of drums and accordions, which play an old traditional summer song, "Let's all unite! Summer is a comin' today," round and round, the same song, all day long. Amid the banging of drums and the wheeze of the accordions dances the 'oss (from 'obby 'oss or hobby horse). The creature consists of an apparatus attached to a strong and fit Cornishman. Around his shoulders he carries a horizontal wooden disc, which drapes a skirt from its circumference down to the floor. This skirt conceals the dancing puppeteer within. Above the disc, his head is concealed by a conical hat and mask. At opposite sides of the discs circumference is a stylized horses-head and tail. The whole thing is shiny black apart from the mask, which looks tribal and slightly African. As the 'oss creature dances, the horse's jaw makes a wooden snapping sound - more like a 'clacking' noise actually, and somehow unnerving. It is traditional for the maidens of the town to dance before the 'oss to tease him and to tempt him, and, should the 'oss capture a maiden beneath his skirt then she will fall pregnant within the year! So the May Day festival here works on a number of levels from the 'fun for all the family street party' concept all the way down to strange pagan goings on, ancient magic and bestiality. Not being initiated into the more intimate Cornish customs, I am happy to be carried along on the vibe and to be at the seaside with the pubs open all day. We came here as a family last year and had a good time. This year I am alone, as Sue and the kids are visiting her parents in South Africa, and the weather forecast's good so - around 8.00pm - I made my mind up and decided I might as well have a small adventure.

I hurriedly ate my chicken curry and threw a few things in a bag, and by 8.30 I was on the motorway. I was planning to be outside the Golden Lion in Padstow in time for the first singing of the song at midnight. Unfortunately, I underestimated the journey time and I had to slow down a little when I ran into some fog on the road through Bodmin Moor. I suppose three and a half hours was a little optimistic, and so I arrived, too late, at 12.30 where the streets were still thronging with people who were all drunk and staggering about. I wandered the streets hoping to avoid a fight and it soon became apparent that the B&B's were all closed for the night, and silent. No matter, I was mentally prepared for sleeping in the jeep and had come prepared with pillow and Nial's duvet. I found a car park and spent an uncomfortable but bearable night squashed into the rear space of the jeep. I slept fairly well until around 3.00 am, when a local vagrant arrived in the car-park and started a drunken rant, telling us we were all fucking tourists and that we should fuck off out of it, etc. I imagined the occupants of the various motorhomes and caravans parked in the car park, cowering in the dark like me, and hoping they weren't going to have to get up and have a scrap with him. He eventually lost interest and I went back to sleep and didn't bother to stir until around 9.00 am.

Saturday 1 May *Padstow*

I walked down into the town which was already humming with the sound of drums and accordions. I bought coffee and rolls in one of the little shops and had breakfast down on the harbour wall. The sky was shrouded in a grey mist which took the whole morning to clear, but now (at 12.30, as I write this) the sun is just beginning to break through and we may yet see some blue sky and sunshine before the day's out.

At 11.00, I watched the red 'oss emerge from his 'stable' at The Golden Lion amid the clamour of the tourists and the singing of the locals. I also did a little shopping at Rick Stein's delicatessen, where I bought a crab pasty for the journey home and a teapot for Diz. I treated myself to another fleece at the surf shop, and only just resisted a couple of paintings in the local gallery. Wandered up to the Ship Inn and bought a pint of lager. People must be constantly pouring into the town, because the whole place is heaving now and you can hardly move in some of the narrow streets. Getting served wasn't easy. I get the feeling some of the locals might not have stopped drinking at all since yesterday. Occasionally brilliant characters wander by – just now, a man with bushy beard wearing a peaked captain's cap which is decked with spring flowers. Children pass by me carrying balloons which occasionally burst and make me jump, mindful of the three recent nail-bomb attacks in London (last night in a gay pub, the Admiral Duncan in Soho, killing two and seriously injuring many more). We're living in violent times. As I sit here in this beautiful and beautifully sozzled Cornish fishing-town, our air-force is dropping bombs on Kosovo and Belgrade while, on the ground, Serbian troops busy themselves systematically murdering and burning their way across Kosovo to rid the region of non-Serbs. I thought it couldn't have happened again in Europe. It's chilling to think that we're all much closer to the abyss of war and the obscene spectre of genocide than we ever imagine.

Well, the sun broke through and we had a sunny blue afternoon. I returned to the jeep to drop my shopping and then back down to the harbour where I ate fish and chips out of newspaper and found a place to sit where I could catch the sunshine and watch the party. All the young people were either in love or drunk or both or lying around feeling sick from the night before. People of my generation were out with their children, trying to perform that rare balancing act between having a good time and giving the kids what they want. I, on the other hand, could do just as I pleased but, ironically, I began to feel there was nothing here for me to do. I had a short but pleasant conversation with a couple who recognized me and said they were at The Walls gig (h Band, Oswestry) last year. They invited me to come over tonight for a barbecue but I declined as I was beginning to wish I was at home. I made my way back once again to the jeep, stopping to watch the 'oss and the drums which were now beneath the maypole (a large mast in the centre of the square decorated with flags and hoops of flowers – a wonderful sight against the blue sky). The song was still being sung. I watched for a while more before stepping into a record shop, where I bought The Beach Boys **Pet Sounds** and **The Best of Prefab Sprout** CDs to play in the car on the journey home.

As I stood in the car park on the hill I took a last look down at the town below – the thumping revelry still echoing upward from the walls of the flint cottages. The buildings looked drunk too, seemingly jostling for position and crookedly-crowded onto the hilly streets, and beyond them, the quiet sea.

I drove back worrying about the stereo which still doesn't sound quite right and taking painkillers to ease a developing headache. I arrived home at 8.00 in the evening and sat down on the sofa with a beer, Rick Stein's apple pie, and a dollop of clotted cream.

On my way to bed I realized I hadn't checked the answering machine. There were two messages – one from my mum to see if I was okay and one from Nick

Belshaw's wife, Debbie, saying, "Guess where I am?" I could hear the sounds of drums and accordions in the background. "I'm in Padstow! You missed it!!"

Saturday 29 May *Geneva, Le Fete d'Espoir*

Some weeks ago I had begun to receive cryptic emails from Swiss journalist Pierre-Michel Meier ('PiMi'), inviting me to a self-promoted event in Geneva called Le Fete d'Espoir, or Feast of Hope. He was offering to cover my expenses and provide a room in The Hotel Richemond – one of the better Geneva hotels. When I told him I would like to bring Sue along too, he promptly insisted on paying her airfare also. I agreed to sing one or two songs with a local band who, he informed me, were top-class players and would have no problem learning the tunes. A couple of days before we were to travel, I received an email from PiMi, saying, "Oh, by the way, Fish will be there... Do you mind?"

Woke up at 7.00 to shower and pack for the flight to Geneva at 9.30. We set out with some nervousness as there was a power-failure in the Terminals at Heathrow yesterday which had cancelled most flights out. Power was resumed now, but there was a backlog of passengers stranded overnight so we were expecting some level of chaos upon our arrival at Terminal 2.

The journey to Heathrow was most pleasant – it was one of the finest mornings so far this year with wide-open morning skies projecting a certain light, which added depth to the fresh, spring-green hues across the fields and woods of Buckinghamshire as we travelled South-East along the M40. Today Sue's with me (for a change), and we were both hoping for some fine weather in Geneva and perhaps an early taste of summer after a long and chilly English spring. We arrived at the airport and parked at the long-stay car park before boarding the courtesy bus into the Terminal.

Inside it was pretty busy, as we expected. I found the Swissair desk and queued for ages to pick up our tickets. In front of me stood a tall, gangly figure who looked like he could only be some sort of French rock star, complete with shades perched on top of his head and bandana at the neck. I wondered if he was on his way to the same place as us. Finally managed to collect our pre-paid tickets and check in our bag only 20 minutes to take-off and made our way to the gate. As we arrived I was tapped on the shoulder by none other than John Wesley, our ubiquitous old chum, opening act and guitar tech, currently playing guitar with Scottish rock star Derek William Dick, perhaps better known as Fish, my predecessor. I knew that Fish was playing at the gig in Geneva, but didn't realise he would be complete with his own band. Pi-Mi's playing his cards close to his chest, n'est-ce pas? Wes seemed cheerful and relaxed despite receiving recent news that Fish's forthcoming US tour had to be cancelled, thereby taking out a substantial period of paid employment for the guitar man. Fish was already in Geneva, having flown in the previous evening. We said we'd see Wes on the plane and, in the meantime, I called my sister on the new mobile phone so that she could dial 1471 to find out what the number was and then call me back to let *me* know. I have since forgotten it again.

Sue and I boarded the plane but were unable to sit together as we had checked in so late. I was actually in the seat behind her so we could still chat, but Wes was up at the back so I didn't get chance to talk to him during the flight. We were delayed almost an hour waiting to take off as a consequence of yesterday's backlog of flights, so we arrived in Geneva around 2.00 where we were met at the airport by Claude Baumann, a friend of PiMi, along with Swiss promoter Mark Lambelet and his wife Janna. In arrivals I met more members of Fish's band – Tony on keyboards and Liz on additional vocals. It turned out that the gangly French rock star was Mark Tschanz (...no, neither had I...) and is, as I guessed, on the bill tonight.

We were all taken to a café where we were originally scheduled to have lunch before departing to soundcheck. As we were an hour behind schedule, it was decided I should go straight to soundcheck while Sue checks into the hotel and relaxes for a couple of hours. We had chance to say a quick hello to "hit" French band Zebda - already well and truly ensconced at a long café table - before climbing back into the minibus.

The gig had a peculiarly familiar feeling about it. I think I may have played here before, perhaps with How We Live, but I wasn't sure. PiMi showed me first to my dressing room which was a school classroom up a couple of flights of stairs. I dropped my things and followed him down to the stage, where my band for the evening (keyboards - Nicolas Hafner; guitar - Dany Ruchat; bass - Xavier Hafner; drums - François Torche) were already soundchecking. I was somewhat nervous about everything as I was supposed to be doing three songs, which the boys had supposedly already learned, and I was anxious to see if they had managed it. *Hope for the Future* is full of key changes and there was much potential for error...

We ran through the three songs (*No One Can* and *Waiting to Happen* also) and the band were note perfect. I thanked them and, much relieved, went out in the sunshine to wait for the minibus to return me to the Richemond hotel in the centre of Geneva. As I sat in the sunshine PiMi sauntered over and explained that one year ago he was diagnosed with a cancer which he feared would kill him. He had received treatment for this, and during that time he had taken solace in certain music and certain songs. Fortunately he was recently pronounced to be clear and 100% healthy, so he had decided that he would invite those artists who he felt had helped his recovery, to appear at a show which he would promote for charity; and so, half way through the day, I finally fully understood why I was here in Geneva.

I returned in the minibus to the centre of town, where we were delayed at length owing to a parade by Geneva's fire brigade (must be a Swiss thing!) which had stopped all traffic in Geneva town centre. I sweated in the gridlocked heat for twenty minutes, watching the Saturday afternoon shoppers as we edged ourselves around the block to the Richemond. I finally got out, walked the last 100 metres and ducked out of the bright sunlight into the hotel lobby – a stately affair of old wood, leather, chandeliers (and even an old sedan chair), vulgarised here and there by little glass cabinets containing discreet presentations of diamond-encrusted watches and other Emelda Marcos fripperies, for the purpose, I suspect, of shaming rich blokes into shelling out the Brazilian national debt to impress their mistresses, or appease their wives.

I was politely told that Mrs Hogarth had checked in and was across the street taking coffee in the park café. Sounds good to me.

I dropped my bag in the room (not huge, but very nice... the room, I mean) and got into a pair of shorts (I mean clothes), before returning down to the lobby and across the street into the little park where Sue sat at a table chatting to Claude, our perfect host. I ordered a beer and at last was able to relax for a couple of hours before the return to the gig. We finished up at the café and returned to the room to relax and get ready. I was on stage around 9.30 but, as this was no ordinary gig, I had agreed to go over to the event and hang-out and catch the other artist's performances. We met up in the lobby at 8.30, and were mini-bussed back to the action. By now the gig was a hum of activity, and we were hustled into the VIP artist area where the immediate search for beer began.

And sure enough, there he was – resplendent in his army trousers, scraggy grey vest proclaiming the crest of British Armed Forces in Bosnia, and topped off by a red beret. In black silk jacket and white shirt I suddenly felt terribly overdressed, like Julio Iglesias sitting down at a table with the Sex Pistols. I told him so, by way of apology, and he said "Nah! C'mon and join us! Sit down and have a beer! You look great!" And so the ice was broken – Sue and I joined Fish's band at a large round table and caught up on each other's news (ten years' worth I suppose). Sue was introduced to Tammi, Fish's wife, and the evening passed as any evening might when acquaintances enjoy a chance meeting in the pub and end up making 'a bit of a night of it'. Not long after I sat down I asked Wes whether or not he could summon up a few extra voices to sing the choruses of *Hope for the Future* with me. Fish overheard the conversation and jumped straight in: "I'll sing on it," he said. I wasn't expecting him to want to do this. His set was later in the evening than mine. This meant that the first time he would appear that night was to sing backing vocal for me. Nonetheless he was up for it and, moreover, asked me if I would return the favour by singing something with him during his set. We decided that if he were to do *Lavender* with his band I could sing *The Blue Angel* on the end of it. So that was that.

Fish seemed very keen to talk to me about the old days when the band were enjoying major league success, but the focus of his attention was always the business issues. He felt the band had been mismanaged during that time, and that had effectively led to the break-up. As far as I could tell, he no longer bears any animosity towards anyone within Marillion; the same cannot be said for John Arnison however (our ex-manager), whose very name seems to induce ear-steaming rage.

The problem with arriving at a show at 7.30 when you're not on stage until 10.00 is a predictable one. You end up sitting around drinking a little more than you should. This effect is multiplied somewhat if those hours are spent in the company of large, sociable Scotsmen, and multiplied further if the large Scotsman happens to be Fish. He doesn't try to drink a lot, and he doesn't try to get his friends drunk – he just does. By stage-time everyone at our table was a few sheets to the wind. Even Dizzy Spell had decided ("Aah c'mon, it'll be fine, it'll be a good laugh!") to sing a BV on *Hope for the Future* with Fish and Wes. My stage-time slipped back about an hour, which is invariably the case in festival situations, so I decided to go out into the hall and have a look at the show. "I'll come with you!" said Fish. At 6'3", with a scarlet beret, he literally sticks out like a sore thumb in any crowd. It was amusing to witness the side glances by various members of the audience and to watch the faces register recognition, doubt, confirmation, confusion, alarm, and eventually excitement at the prospect of Marillion's singers standing together in the crowd, affably swapping observations. People inevitably began drifting over to ask us what was happening and we soon realised we weren't going to be allowed to simply stand and watch the show, so we escaped backstage again and I went upstairs to get myself together for my set.

    I eventually made my way centre stage and looked out onto a packed room of 1000+ people. The reception was warm, although I suspect half the crowd hadn't a clue who I was. I sang *Easter* alone at the piano, and then the band joined me for *No One Can* and *Waiting to Happen*. Next up was *Hope for the Future*, so I beckoned to my unlikely backing vocalists, Fish, Wes and Dizzy Spell, and introduced them to an incredulous audience. Musically, it all went pear-shaped from here on... My fault really – after the first chorus, I let the verse run for an extra 4 bars before singing verse 2. This completely threw the house band, who had learned the arrangement mathematically and continued accordingly, 4 bars out. This, in turn, threw me and my new backing vocalists who seemed determined to sing as many choruses as they could. The many key changes in the song were shifting the accompaniment to the voices into an overall musical chaos, but nobody much seemed to mind, and I suppose it was appreciated by the crowd as a 'spirit thing', rather than anything that made musical sense. I'm sure those in the crowd who were familiar with the song must have wondered what was going on – I know I was! No real harm done however. I thanked all concerned and left the stage to much enthusiasm from the wings. "Ach it was great! I really enjoyed that! It was a blast! Y'gonna c'mon and sing with me, aren't ye?" It was turning into a fun evening...

    I don't remember what happened during the following hour or so during the seemingly interminable wait for Fish's set. When the band finally mounted the stage, I realised he'd put together a much longer set than mine and it was another hour or so before his encore, which was my cue. No doubt about it – he knows how to work a crowd. He was getting a great response right across the spectrum of age groups present. When he returned to the stage, he introduced *Lavender*: "This is no longer my song. It belongs to me and another guy, now. Please welcome him to the stage. Steve Hogarth!" I was touched. He sang the song, and I sang the *Blue Angel*, and then we both sang choruses out together – he with his bare arm around my shoulders and me tucked underneath, still feeling overdressed for the occasion; an unlikely double act really. I suppose this moment represents a crossroads at the end of a long and winding road for both of us. Life is strange. There were precious few hardcore Marillion fans in the audience to witness this event (although I did recognise Judith Mitchell from Liverpool in the front row snapping away with her camera). Everything in showbusiness exists on two levels: the event, i.e. the story, and the actuality, i.e. what we, the performers, do and remember. I remember it as a bit of fun, which I suspect is how Fish remembers it too. I'm glad it happened, and I'm glad it happened the way it happened, with no planning and no big build up, i.e. no politics, no marketing opportunity, nothing to live up to... or to live down!

Fish was a total gentleman throughout, and said and did more than he needed to. If he reads this, I'd like to say thanks for his generosity of spirit. Ironically, from my point of view, the best of the evening was yet to come. After the show was over we all went downstairs to a dressing room where Zebda were having a bit of a sing-song. One of the band plays accordion and, to the strains of the most French of all sounds, they seemed to be singing some old French drinking songs (although I suspect they might have written a couple of them). They encouraged Fish and I to join in on the choruses, and Sue and I hollered away along with all present without really knowing what the words meant. Zebda, who are more like a gang than a band, are easily as entertaining off-stage as on, and it was a shame that we didn't have more time around them to get to know them better. They insisted we sing a couple of English songs too, so we roared through a couple of old Beatles songs which, to my mind, didn't work nearly so well as the French tunes, which were all the more fun because we didn't know what we were singing! This rounded off the day perfectly, and we eventually dispersed in various vehicles back to the centre of Geneva and to bed. I asked Fish and Tammi if they were planning to go on to a club. He replied, "Ach I can't stand the pace anymore, man – I need my early nights these days!" It was 2.00 am.

Sunday 30 May *Geneva*

We had a lie-in and met up with PiMi and Isabelle around lunchtime. PiMi had reserved a table outside a café round the corner for about 12 of us, and so we wandered round in the sunshine and sat down, along with Fish, Tammi, Wes, Tony, Liz, Mark, Janna, Claude, PiMi and Isabelle. We had a pleasant light lunch during which I chatted to Fish about the pros and cons of self-management and the general trials and tribulations of the music business. Claude told me that he owns a small boat and that, if we were interested, we might like to join him and his wife Elizabeth on Lake Geneva this afternoon. I said we'd love to, and so he left lunch early and went home to fetch his boat. We eventually said bye to Fish, Wes and all, who had another acoustic gig in Switzerland tonight as part of a small acoustic tour. PiMi doesn't like the water, and so he and Isabelle said they would see us back at the hotel around tea-time for our departure to the airport.

We walked around the corner to the promenade by the lake and a short distance to a little jetty, where a bikini-clad Elizabeth was waving to us from a speedboat. Claude was the very picture of continental high-living at the wheel of the little motor-launch in his wrap-around shades. We climbed aboard, and I sat up-front with Claude while the girls reclined at the back. Suddenly I felt wealthy. We cruised across the lake, taking in the view of the expansive lakeside houses and chateaux, the green valleys and snow-peaked mountains beyond. The weather was still sunny and the sky was open and blue. Many of the lakeside buildings are Embassies or owned by impossibly rich Arabs, Claude informed me. It really was a vision of alpine paradise. There was only one thing missing – beer! Claude and I were unanimous in this, but the problem was short-lived; he said he knew of a café where we could moor the boat and he could get some refreshments. We pulled up to a little jetty alongside yet more postcard-pretty houses surrounded by flowers and hung with climbing roses, and Claude hopped off the boat, looking like Yves Saint-Laurent, to return with beer and sodas. We motored back to the centre of the lake, cut the engine and drifted in the sunshine, swapping life stories and drinking beer. One of those 'good as it gets' moments that have been absent for quite a while now.

All too soon it was time to return, so Claude wound up the revs and we set off back at high speed, which involved everyone getting soaked in the spray. We wished Claude and Elizabeth well (could it get much better?) and returned along the promenade, where we bought ice-creams before arriving back at the Richemond. There was still enough time for fruit juices on the terrace with PiMi, Isabelle, and some of the boys from Zebda. PiMi told me he had interviewed Catherine Deneuve at this very table a few years back. Hard life here in Geneva.

We returned in a Mercedes to Geneva airport (which is a bit of a disappointment of an airport considering Switzerland's wealth... not a patch on Heathrow, or the brilliant Barcelona) where I went to the gents to change out of my shorts and back into trousers for England. I can't remember the flight back at all, which I guess is a sure-sign of a job well done by Swissair. "This is your Captain speaking. Please fasten seatbelts as we have commenced the descent into London Heathrow, where the weather is raining and we have a ground temperature of a chilly six degrees. We have low cloud all the way down. Thank you for flying Swissair." Perhaps Swiss restraint prevented him from adding that he couldn't, for the life of him, understand why we had left Geneva to come here.

Looking back, I am reminded of a moment on the boat in the middle of that perfect Sunday afternoon on Lake Geneva when Elizabeth gazed out across the water, across the green valleys, and up through the wispy cirrus clouds to the faraway snowy peak of Mont Blanc, and innocently enquired of us, "Have you ever thought of living in another country apart from England?" Now why ever would we want to do that?

Thursday 18 November *Manchester Academy*

Slept quite well, but couldn't manage a repeat of yesterday's marathon lie-in, so I emerged from the bus around 10.00 and spirited my way into The Academy through a side door - toilet bag in hand - in search of the dressing rooms and much needed ablutions. Cleaned my teeth in the dressing room, but made my way to catering to interrupt the washing-up girls in order to have hot water to wash my face. Elaine and Vanessa, our caterers for this short tour, provided me with poached egg on toast and I sat with Erik who made me an espresso before joining me for breakfast. I returned to the production office and called home. Dizzy answered the phone and listened patiently to my apologies for not calling yesterday. I was relieved to hear everyone's okay at home.

I had been meaning to call Aziz Ibrahim - my guitar-playing chum from the h tour - who lives here over on Longsight estate, a mainly Pakistani area of Manchester. I was expecting him to be away somewhere, so I was surprised to find that he answered the phone. He said he would come over and pick me up. He wanted to show me his new Gretsch guitars. I'm always up for a gander at an interesting guitar; although piano was always my first instrument I find guitars much more fascinating as objects, so I said I'd see him in a little while. I went to the stage to check out everything was okay with my equipment. Erik's going to switch through my Kurzweil programs tonight as I have proved to be incompetent in this regard during the initial shows! We arranged a little run-through of the cues when I return to the venue at 3.30. Aziz arrived and Mark K, after some persuasion, decided to accompany us over to his house.

We made our way to his home – he had bought the house next door to his parents and had an access door put in; this way he retains his independence whilst getting his washing and cooking done! We arrived in a quiet terrace-house, decorated in a simple working-class fashion and not unlike the house I grew up in. We said hello to his mum, Rashida, who was courteous and seemed a little shy but this was probably because she has few English words. Aziz spoke a few words to his mother in Kasmiri before he led us through a doorway into the adjoining house, which was effectively a recording studio – all ash-wood paneling, and tungsten lighting and full to the ceiling with shop-new technology. Quite a shock. (A bit like that scene in "Help" where the Beatles all go through those terrace front-doors into their opulent sixties bachelor-pad). In addition to his impressive collection of electric and acoustic guitars he showed us a tabla drum-machine which he had bought in Hounslow. It plays all the raag rhythms and has pretty authentic sounds. He also has a little black box, about four inches square and covered in knobs and switches, which simply creates drone chords – everything for do-it-yourself Indian composition. My mind was yet to be broadened and blown further when he demonstrated the new Roland V-Guitar Synthesis system – not a sampler but a synthesizer which can be any guitar from Jimmy Hendrix's strat to Jeff Beck's strat, to Rickenbacker electric 12-string and even acoustic guitars. All you need is a guitar with a midi output interface and you're away. You'd never need to change guitar during a show and you could mix several different guitars together at will. You can alter tuning too, to different open strings and capo tunings – perfect for a guitar-idiot like me! While I was still recovering, Aziz led us back through to his parents' house where we sat down to lunch. His mum had prepared a sumptuous meal of rice and various curries, chicken and meatballs. Lovely. Thanks, Rashida x. It seemed most rude to rush off after all this hospitality, but it was time for me to return to the Academy and have a chat with Erik before soundcheck. Aziz gave Mark and I a lift back into town where we re-entered the gig.

Soundcheck was pretty uneventful. Aziz had given me a pair of earplugs which are a new design and which, in theory, don't remove the high frequencies disproportionately, and therefore make the sound quieter without changing it. In the end I came to the conclusion that they worked best if I just wore one.

I returned to the bus to relax for a little while before the show. Tonight we are to come on-stage and play the first two songs behind a sort-of-a net curtain. Jasper, our lighting designer, will project images onto it and onto the back screen, while picking up the band with individual lights. This way we will appear between two planes of projected images. Interesting in theory, but we had yet to try it. I have to stand on a little plinth which shines a circle of light upward, so there was much commotion during soundcheck while we tried to work out how to remove it later so that I didn't risk more twisted ankles or dislocated knees. I have only just recovered from a knee-cartilage repair so I'm having to be careful.

After soundcheck I retired to the bus where I watched a programme about survival skills in the Arctic. All very interesting, but there was a bit of a **Blue Peter** aspect about it: "You can tie this together with some lampwick which you might well find left behind in an old log cabin..." Hmm.

The show was delayed slightly by Mark Kelly doing his disappearing act, and he had to be paged across the gig's tannoy system before he finally appeared in the dressing room. When we got on stage we played the first two songs (*Go* and *Under the Sun*) behind the mesh-curtain. I could see the crowd faintly through the gauze and wondered two things:

1. Could they see the band? And...
2. Was that burning smell coming from beneath me simply because the tungsten lights were being used for the first time, or was I about to go up in a circle of fire like Joan of Arc? It turned out that I remained alive and nothing went up in flames. It also turned out that Jasper's projections looked fantastic, so it was all worthwhile. The band really started to sound like a class act tonight for the first time this tour, and the audience responded accordingly. I made a little speech about the Irish peace process before we played *Easter*, and it really seemed to strike a chord with the crowd. I'd forgotten about the bomb which exploded in Manchester's main shopping mall a couple of years back. Whatever I said seemed to be met with affectionate approval because, after that, the spirit of the gig climbed vertically and we could do no wrong. I must say it was one of the best audience atmospheres I can remember, made more so by memories of this same venue a year ago on the *Radiation* tour, when the audience were in a

less enthusiastic mood. I read some bad criticisms of the Manchester show back then, so I was especially relieved to see tonight's crowd so unanimously 'into it'. I finished the show buzzing with excitement. It was a relief to feel this, and a reminder of what we're capable of when it all comes together. I felt now that we had 'played the songs in' and that we were ready for London.

Tuesday 30 November *Stuttgart, Longhorn*

Up around 1.30. Last time we played here it was cold, grey and rainy. Irrationally I expected it to be the same, but was surprised to find a sunny day and blue skies. The gig is situated in the middle of nowhere on a light industrial estate next to a railway line and a motorway – not the most uplifting of vistas in any weather...

Inside, the Longhorn hasn't changed – it's a typical rock-club; dark, cold and grubby. Catering and the dressing rooms are raised up on a mezzanine which runs along the right-hand side of the hall, overlooking everything. It's pretty dirty up here too, and an aroma emanates from the plumbing which isn't exactly conducive to the atmosphere.

There's this strange German thing with the toilets. Most flush toilets here are now of a similar design to those in England, but it wasn't always so, and when I came to Germany for the first time, fifteen or-so years ago, I was amazed to see that the lavatory pans were designed in such a way so that whatever falls into them remains presented to you on a dry slab of porcelain for further visual inspection before flushing. Further aromatic inspection is unfortunately inevitable, and so these lavatories possess a fairly potent and rancid smell during (and after) use. I have often pondered the intentions of the designers of such a system... the medical profession's interest in the stool is well documented – maybe it's something to do with that. Such lavatories would also be a Godsend to diamond-smugglers and customs men, I'm sure. I can't help wondering though where this strange Germanic inclination to be intimate with one's own doings comes from. Over to you, Freud. Needless to say, the lavatories in the Longhorn are of the old design and after an overnight busload of roadies have worked their way through their morning ablutions in them... Oh my God!

And so it was that, with bulldog clip firmly attached to my nostrils, I washed and cleaned my teeth, drank several cups of coffee, and called home to be informed that Nial had mysteriously had a violent allergic reaction to substances unknown last night. He had broken out in a violent red rash and his temperature had soared. Dizzy was forced to put him in a cold bath and, after a dose of antihistamine syrup, he went to bed and woke up feeling fine. He answered the phone when I called (he had come home for lunch) and sounded his usual bright and dreamy self. Nial's one of those human beings who has always needed a lot of maintenance, and I often sympathise with Dizzy Spell who must bear the burden of this, both in my absence and my presence. He's well worth the trouble of course, and I'm sure a time will come when he assumes the same independence as Sofie and needs our attentions much less. I don't look forward to it, if I'm honest; I want to be needed.

I said I would call again later and returned to the catering area in search of a runner who could take me to town. Stuttgart is 15km from here. Last time I was in Stuttgart I found a music shop which sells hammered-dulcimers and I wanted to return there to make *absolutely sure* I couldn't afford one. I have wanted a dulcimer for years now, but have never quite got round to finding one. I found a somewhat stoned chap in a woolly hat who said he was the runner, and could take me into town. So off we went in his camper van, which also seemed strangely stoned. Stuttgart is the home of Mercedes Benz and everywhere the three-forked logo abounds. Paradoxically however, the city is situated within a steep valley and hills rise upward all around, many bearing terraces on which vines are cultivated – a surprisingly rural landscape to contain Germany's famous home of the Merc and the Porsche.

When we arrived in the centre I arranged to be picked up in an hour's time, and made my way randomly through the town, trying to dredge up distant memories of the place in order to navigate the streets. I walked through the shopping area in search of the old square where the music shop is situated. Beneath an archway I heard the strident Gothic sounds of Bach's church-organ masterpiece *Toccata and Fugue*, and was amazed to find a busker with a large accordion. I never heard anything come out of an accordion quite like it. It's a very complex piece of organ music, and the busker gave a very passable performance of it. His accordion was a substantial deep-throated instrument and not at all the effete French reed sound I have come to expect. Amazing. I gave him ten marks and exchanged enthusiasm with an old German onlooker (he in German, and I in English – neither of us understanding each other's words, but we both felt the need to express astonishment and respect) before walking on. I found the shop (whose name escapes me!) and made my way upstairs, eventually persuading the shopkeeper to lift down an odd-shaped case from the top shelf, and there inside was a beautifully made (in Munich) hammered dulcimer – obviously a quality instrument, consisting of a flat tray-like soundbox over which a great many strings are laid horizontally between three bridges. The strings are hit with small wooden 'hammers' which are really fairly short sticks, edged at the striking ends in suede in order to soften the sound, which can best be described as half way between a clang and a tinkle. A clinkle. There was a little delay while I established the minimum price I could pay for it. This turned out to be about 1500 marks – about five hundred pounds. No small amount of money... I was reminded of a time in San Francisco when I was persuaded to part with several thousand dollars for an oriental rug which, to date, has remained rolled up in a cupboard at home. Since then, I don't really trust myself with money when I'm on tour, so, once again, I reluctantly passed up my chance of buying a dulcimer in Stuttgart. I knew I would regret not buying it (and I do).

I emerged empty-handed into the square, where a handful of fairground-rides and stalls were set up for the Christmas season. Across the square was an open-air ice-rink decorated by a surrounding cardboard castle. I could see people skating over in the distance. Our South-African film-makers, Paul and Jayce, are in town interviewing Mark today. If I were a film-maker I would be drawn here like a magnet, so I was half expecting to bump onto them as I crossed the square. Spookily, there they were, exactly where I had imagined them to be... I told them I had arranged a ride back to the gig with the runner and offered them a lift. We walked back through the shopping area in search of a quick cup of coffee, and I took them to a place I had spotted above the Benetton store – a coffee bar with a wide expanse of glass with a view of the street below (thoroughly recommended, by the way – the coffee's great, the service friendly, and the view of Stuttgart's shoppers excellent, especially if you enjoy watching the world go by without the world watching you!) There's a famous studio in London called the Townhouse and they have a café right next to Goldhawk Road in Shepherds Bush - the window is floor-to-ceiling and, from the outside, looks like a big mirror. I used to love sitting in there, watching people checking themselves out as they walked by, not knowing that they were staring straight into the faces of maybe Phil Collins or Eric Clapton only inches from the end of their noses. And – being as I'm digressing - another thing that used to really appeal to me was when I was about seventeen. I had some soft shoes - baseball boots or something - and I used to go out at night and walk around the back alleys of my hometown. I wasn't up to anything dodgy, I just used to get a thrill out of walking around alone at night in the 'secret' places of the town knowing that <u>nobody</u> knew I was there. I think it was a way of enjoying being "separate" from everyone. Nowadays, I don't have to go *looking* for that feeling.

The four of us spent a little too much time in the Benetton café, and we had to hurry to meet up with the runner who took us all back to the Longhorn in his minibus. I asked the driver what the strange bunker-like buildings were at the side of the road. He informed me that they are spa-baths accommodating the natural springs here. Next time I'm here I think I'll go and have a session – I should imagine it would be most beneficial for the relief of a tour-fatigued body. I have spent every tour we've done feeling like I've been run over by a train.

Back at the gig we soundchecked and said hello to our German opening act, Blackpool – an easy-going bunch, with some good songs in their set. I have been catching their show from the side of stage for the past few nights and I'm into it. I think they all started out the tour questioning the wisdom of opening for us, but after the first night in Hamburg they declared themselves Marillion fans - I think much to their own surprise - and our audiences seem to have appreciated *their* music also.

After our soundcheck I hung around upstairs, watching Blackpool soundcheck and watching the audience drifting into the gig. It's amazing how easy it is to stand close to people and remain unnoticed when you're above their heads. I got away with it for quite some time before being spotted, then I thought I'd better go and hide in order to spare everybody the neck-ache.

I remembered the audience here from last time as being a particularly warm-hearted bunch, and they lived up to my expectations tonight. The show at the Longhorn was just the way I like them – hot, close and tight. The band played well and the crowd really stayed with it every second of the show. The boys in Blackpool sat at the side of stage, egging us on good-naturedly throughout the evening and didn't budge until all three encores were over with. For encore 3 we played *80 Days* which I preceded with a sudden impulse to sing a verse of Janis Joplin's *Mercedes Benz*. Worth doing again sometime - it worked really well!

After the show I took a much-needed shower in the functional-but-not-decorative (better than the other way round!) shower. The toilet smell was still hanging around, but had calmed down somewhat since the morning... maybe we'd all got used to it. I dressed and made my way to the bus, stopping to talk to a few people still hanging around next to the Web Germany's merchandising stall, before climbing into the bus for the long journey to Dresden. Thankyou Stuttgart – I'll look forward to returning.

In a few hours from now, Sofie and Nial will be opening door number 1 of their Advent calendars before going off to school. Just another little magic moment of their childhood I'll miss. I'll be asleep on a bus in central Europe.

the *invisible* man

2000   JANUARY

Saturday 1

THIS IS THE 21st CENTURY   (:|)

2000

Friday 26 May *Geneva   h Band, Le Fete d'Espoir*

Up at 6.00 for much staggering about, trying to decide which clothes to take to Geneva while bumping into other members of the family, all sleepwalking with a sense of puzzled purpose. Felt like a heel when I shook Nial out of a deep sleep at 6.30 – the kids are spending the weekend with the neighbours, and we had to get them round there before our departure at 7.15. I hate packing, and always leave it until the very last minute - something I always regret - and this morning was no exception. Experience has taught me to remember passport, tickets, money, keys and then leave everything else to fate.

We managed to get out of the door on time at 7.15 and I drove 50-metres down the street to the B&B where we picked up Mike Wilson who had literally just made it down the stairs. Pippa, the landlady, seemed genuinely sorry to see him go. "The other evening, darling, he took a bath and I could smell his WONDERFUL scented oils wafting down the staircase! It was all I could do to stop myself bursting in on him!"

"Blimey!" said Mikey, "…I think I got out just in time! Lovely people though, lovely people…" he muttered to himself in the back seat of the car as I sped up the road. While we're on the subject of speeding, I had to appear in Stratford-on-Avon Magistrates Court a couple of weeks ago, where I narrowly escaped a six-month driving ban, so I had my hair cut for the occasion and am now sporting a much shorter barnet. So far it's gone down quite well. Something had to be done – I'd started getting mistaken for Alice Cooper!

Arrived on time at Heathrow and sent Dizzy off to stick the car in the long-term car park so that I would be around to help Andy (guitar tech) unload the van when he arrived at 8.30. Mike hung around outside so he could have a smoke while I made my way to the Swissair desk where I found Aziz waiting for me. It's always a relief when Aziz puts in a punctual appearance - he's occasionally a little "casual" in this department (and that's compared to ME!). I queued up and collected our air tickets. Full marks to Isabelle in Switzerland - everything was there in the right names, ready and waiting. I checked that Dave's ticket would be waiting for him when he arrives here this afternoon. Dave G decided he'd rather have a few more hours in bed in Swindon than have an afternoon to kill in Geneva, so he'll be travelling alone later. Still no sign of Andy in the red van so I borrowed Aziz's phone and called his mobile to discover that he was already at the far end of the terminal with Jingles (our bass player), who had already helped him unload the van. I still can't believe how much the musicians have put into this venture. Everyone involved is doing the show for expenses only. It's meant many hours work learning the songs at home followed by three long rehearsal days, just to arrive at this point. I'm more than happy to go through all this for the joy of playing my own music again, but it's a great feeling to have a band of this calibre entering into the spirit of it and playing purely for pleasure. When I get together with other top-class players outside of Marillion, they always lament how little "real" music is around anymore, and that the chance to get together and play something interesting as a band, is a breath of fresh air. When I explained to Jingles how Marillion write together by jamming, he exploded: "That's the way it ought to be! You're so lucky! No one gets to create like that anymore - it's all guys with machines trying to write hits in their bedrooms nowadays - it really is!"

Andy drove off to the long-term car park with the van while I took on the role of tour-manager. I said hello to Nick Eade from Cutting Crew and his wife Nikki (old chums - I had persuaded Nick to come along and sing his own set) and we all queued with various guitar and flight-cases to check in. Swissair opened a desk especially for us, and a most helpful check-in girl made a potentially difficult process seem very straightforward. Dizzy Spell reappeared from parking the car and we all took the fragile and oversize cases along the hall to the alternative check-in area where an assistant immediately dropped a flight case on his finger and began jumping around cursing... We managed to check everything in and there was a delay while I wrote "FRAGILE" on the Kurzweil flight case with Tipp-Ex. This one case is worth well over five thousand pounds. However, considering the weeks of programming that had gone into Richard's and mine, they were, at this moment and as far as the show is concerned, quite priceless. I watched the rack loaded on to the conveyor belt and said a silent prayer to the great and cruel God-Of-Baggage-Handling, and we all proceeded to the gate.

The flight was uneventful except for the comedic names of the Swissair stewardesses… Ms. Fuchs was closely followed at the other end of the drinks trolley by a very nice girl sporting a name-badge labelled I.Wanna. We all suppressed a schoolboy snigger, but when we were asked, "Excuse me sir, would you like some milk from the Swiss cow?" – well, it took me over the edge...

We were met in the arrivals lounge in Geneva by PiMi and his wife, Isabelle, who saw us into a minibus for the short drive to Geneva centre.

Sue and I were dropped at the Hotel Angleterre, along with Nick and Nikki Eade, and after a bit of a wait, we managed to check into a large room with two large windows overlooking the lake. The famous fountain was in full flight against a backdrop of opulent lakeside buildings advertising famous jewellers and watchmakers, with green meadows above and beyond, leading still-further upward to the horizon where the mountains meet the sky. Not a bad view then.

We made our way back down to the ground floor where lunch had been arranged for all the British artists who were to appear at the Feast. I said hello to Fish and his wife Tammy who were already seated and we joined them at a long table where twenty-or-so of us, including my band, enjoyed a pleasant lunch and some particularly fine wine, over a period of two-or-three hours. We were to leave for soundcheck at 6.30, so around 4.00 Dizzy and I decided to return to the room for a nap. Curtains were drawn against the afternoon sunshine and I left the big windows open so that I could listen to the street-noises of Geneva as we drifted into sleep. Suddenly I felt like I was on tour again - it's curious how quickly I slip into the alternative "tour" patterns of being awake and asleep.

Got up about 6.00pm, showered and met up with the band downstairs in the lobby of the Angleterre. Dave G had arrived safely from England and everyone seemed happy with their respective hotels. I felt somehow responsible for the general contentment of my band, ever-conscious of having blagged them into doing this on the basis that they would be well looked-after (despite the fact that all the arrangements were, by this time, out of my hands). As we waited for the drivers to organise themselves I wandered into the warm street and down into The English Bar beneath the hotel. It's done-out like a library, and there was a terrific jazz trio playing in the corner. I regretted not being able to stay and listen to them, but soundcheck beckoned...

We were driven by minibus to the Stade du Sport - which was to be the venue for the Feast - arriving around 7.00pm, and took our turn in the queue to soundcheck. It was from this point onwards that things started to slip a little. Everyone expects to have to hang around in these situations and the band chilled-out and chatted amongst themselves whilst one, and then another, French middle-aged crooner took to the stage singing the kind of songs that remind you of driving through Monaco on a hot summer night in an expensive car with an expensive girl. These guys tend to swan around the stage languidly whilst singing slightly flat as if the effort required to push the notes all the way up to pitch would entail a show of enthusiasm which simply isn't possible when you're this rich and this sexually-experienced. Tres chic. Tres "sexy". Tres middle-of-the-road. I was beginning to wonder if I was going to be a little out-of-place here. I couldn't see *The Last Thing* fitting in somehow. There were going to be a lot of Swiss jaws hitting the floor as I spook about in my black feather boa rattling my sleigh bells whilst Richard and Aziz's quarter-tones beat against Dave's dark wall of distortion... Not very Monaco at all, really. I couldn't help laughing.

In the event, we didn't actually get our equipment up on to the stage until around 10.00. It was at this point that we were to discover that the monitor engineer spoke no English, and that the keyboard we'd hired-in couldn't be programmed to run my Kurzweil. I'd stopped laughing. The communication problem slowed everything down and a generally unhelpful shoulder-shrugging stage-crew caused much frustration as the minutes ticked by. At 10.45 we had yet to run a song and PiMi informed us that we must end soundcheck, which should have been finished at 10.00 so that security could lock the building. I thanked my stars that I had brought Erik and Andy with me - they were really going to have their work cut out tomorrow night during the show...

As they unplugged the equipment, Nick Eade just had enough time for a quick soundcheck. As he was only singing and playing his Danelektro guitar there wasn't much to soundcheck. Nonetheless he patiently asked - at least a dozen times over a period of twenty minutes - for more guitar in the centre-wedges. God knows where PiMi found this monitor man. Nick was singing really well anyway and I was beginning to feel that perhaps I'd been a bit ambitious bringing all this technology with me. There's a lot to be said for keeping it simple.

Oh well. I began to rise above it as we were bussed back across town, two hours late for dinner at the Café du Soleil where, I'm told, Roosevelt and Kennedy used to come for unofficial meetings over coffee. We arrived minutes before midnight when the kitchen closed, and just had time to order steak and chips. I was just tucking into mine when Erik and Andy arrived from the gig to be told there was no more hot food as the chef had gone home. They weren't terribly impressed. We shared out what was left.

A girl called Valerie from the band Galliano was having a birthday and PiMi had provided a sumptuous birthday cake. We all sang Happy Birthday umpteen times during the meal for reasons I couldn't fathom. In England, once is usually enough. By now, I'd had a couple of beers and the frazzled ends of my nerves were beginning to knit back together. However, the waiters were beginning to cough by the door and it became clear they wanted to close the café and go home.

We exited through a side door into the street to discover it was raining hard and got drenched trying to find the driver who then seemed to have misplaced the bus. Back at the Angleterre, Nick, Nikki, Dizzy and I had a last drink in the English cellar-bar beneath the hotel where the excellent jazz trio were still playing! Now that's a long set...

I went straight back to the room - I'd had a pretty long day myself. I left the big windows open so that I could listen to the street noises as Geneva too, prepared to be tucked up in bed.

Saturday May 27 *Geneva h Band, Le Fete d'Espoir*

Woke around 11.00 and ordered up coffee while Sue had a bath. I found a hotel leaflet which informed me that the lake is filled from glacial water coming down from the mountains and is emptied by the river Rhone which flows from it onward into France. The impressive fountain, which is arguably Geneva's most famous and distinguishing feature, was originally conceived as a safety valve to release high-pressure spring water from underground. It certainly shoots into the air with some force. I wonder if it's still natural or whether it's pumped...

We had arranged to meet up in the lobby around 12.00 to go to lunch.

There had been a slight change of venue so we ended up in a little café in town where twenty-or-thirty of us assembled and were served lunch so slowly that I swear the chef prepared each person's plate individually from scratch by digging up the vegetables one at a time and having the meat brought to him from Argentina on foot. Sue and I were the first into the café and waited patiently (and eventually less patiently) whilst people who had arrived thirty minutes after us, were being served thirty minutes before us, and were beginning dessert before we had received starters. As far as I could tell, there were only two staff working in the entire place. It reminded me a lot of the episode of **Fawlty Towers** when the chef has the night off and the Americans arrive for dinner. I know PiMi was doing his best to make everything run smoothly. However, I think he had more important things on his mind than the arrival time of my lunch. The weather had turned, and it was trying to rain outside. He sat alone at a table near to the door, muttering nervously into his mobile phone. Heavy rain would have massive consequences for a free outdoor show. People would stay away...

The rain soon eased and Sue and I took our chance to escape rather than risk another half-an-hour waiting for ice-cream. We walked up into the old-town where the streets are cobbled and filled with antique shops. In the past, when I've been here on tour I have sometimes spent most of the day up here reading or writing my diary in one of the numerous cafés. We were, however, all café'd out, so we mooched round an exhibition of nondescript art before walking down to the main drag for a quick peek in the Armani-esque designer shops. Interesting stuff if you don't mind looking like a stained-glass window (not at all...) and have a couple of grand to spare on threads (sadly not...).

We returned to the Angleterre, walking along the lake, where I was suddenly made famous by an Italian couple who stopped us to say hello and wished us well for the show. It's a nice feeling being recognized, provided that it doesn't happen all the time... It doesn't happen to me too much really so, on the whole, when it does, I quite enjoy it. Our fans are, generally, decent level-headed types who simply want to show a bit of support and to let you know they're rooting for you. How can that be a problem during the hours of daylight?

We got back to the hotel and, once again, went straight to bed. It's good to go to bed in the afternoon. I always wanted a bed in the garden in a summer-house - on rails - so that on certain afternoons you could roll the bed out of its house on to the lawn and have a snooze in the garden. If I ever have any real success in this mad business, I'll realize my garden bed-on-rails ambition. Imagine drifting off to sleep in bed in the afternoon to the sound of birdsong and the sunshine on your face - maybe on a sunny winter's day in a fur hat. Feel free, people, to steal this idea - it's a killer. While we're at it, here's another thing to try: Next time you shower, don't stand up, sit down in the tray - it's one of life's little pleasures, especially if you're really tired or dirty. I love to do this after a show.

Didn't sleep terribly well – pre-gig nerves had started their slow build towards the evening...

By the time we assembled in the hotel lobby at 6.30, I think everyone was feeling a certain unspoken, quiet terror at the prospect of walking on stage without being quite ready to play the songs. We felt under-rehearsed and we were all more than a little apprehensive about our friend on the monitor desk. I kept reminding everyone that the purpose of the gig was simply to enjoy ourselves, and that we weren't here to feel pressured into making the ultimate artistic statement. I wasn't fooling anyone... including myself - all six of us are perfectionists by nature and wanted the set to be killer, despite any technical limitations.

When we arrived, the show had been underway for some time and we made our way to our dressing room – a sports-hall locker-room get-into-your-basketball-kit type of changing room. There was also a communal backstage artists area where we could have a buffet dinner and free drinks. PiMi and Isabelle had thought of just about everything. They hadn't quite nailed the backstage access problem though - there were a limited number of backstage passes printed and these had long-since run out. I gave my laminate to Richard Barbieri's sister, Rosemary, who had arrived from Rome and there was a bit of to-ing and fro-ing while I arranged to get various Dutch and Spanish chums to be allowed back. Poor Isabelle was trying to organise a dozen things at once, talking into the mic of her mobile phone, walkie-talkie, and to real people who, like me, queued up to say "erm... Isabelle... I have a problem..." She retained her composure throughout the evening – I guess she must have known what it would be like from past experience.

I decided I should have one beer to settle my nerves to a point where I could think straight enough to get the band ready for the show. We were told we'd be on around 11.00 so we said we'd meet up at the dressing room at 10.00 to go through any remaining doubts in the song arrangements.

Diz and I sat down with Nick and Nikki and nibbled on light snacks and talked rubbish for a while. I then wandered around a bit saying hello to my Dutch guests, Inge, Ciska and Natasja, and to Ivan from Spain. Everyone seemed happy to be there although I suspect I was probably a little too wired to make normal conversation. I said a brief hello to Rob and Alexis Crossland who, once again, had travelled half-way across Europe for a night out.

10 o'clock soon arrived and everyone assembled in the dressing room where

we more-or-less went through the whole show – Mikey drumming his hands on his thighs whilst I sang guide vocal and shouted bass cues for Jingles. Richard and Dave listened intently, chipping in the odd comment and pulling me up if I missed something while Aziz sat back and watched the spectacle. If there was anything he wasn't sure of, he wasn't admitting it. He's worked with Ian Brown too long to get up-tight and he knows that strutting the right attitude is more important than getting everything note-perfect. Having said that, I don't recall him dropping any clangers during any of the shows we've done together.

Me – I'm alright if me monitors are working and I've got something colourful to wear. One out-of-two was assured and I eventually hit the stage in an excellent embroidered jacket (which I'd bought in a café in Cropredy!) and black feather boa.

On the whole, I had a great time up on stage, mincing and skulking around shaking my tambourines and bells. My vocal sound centre-stage was good and, although I couldn't hear jaws hitting the floor, I felt pretty confident that there must be a murmur of "What the fuck's this?" – or whatever the French equivalent sounds like.

Everything went well until *Nothing to Declare*, which involved my sitting down behind the infamous hired keyboard. Fortunately it was working but, unfortunately, the drum machine (which forms the basic groove of the song, around which the drums play) was deafeningly loud all over the stage. I guess this was the monitor-man's long awaited revenge for short tempers at soundcheck yesterday (either that or my last words to Erik as we walked on stage, which had been to make sure the drum machine was well loud during NTD). The monitor man had obviously decided to over-interpret this request as, when the song started, the drum machine was so loud in my monitors that I couldn't hear much else. It's quite an introspective song, but I had no hope of achieving any intensity or tenderness vocally with the deafening thumping and booming under my chin. I closed my eyes tightly and tried to ignore it, but it got so loud during verse two that my mic began to resonate and a low booming feedback began ringing all over the stage. Any half-wit who'd ever been allowed near a monitor desk would have eliminated this quickly, but it carried on for most of the remainder of the song, killing the song stone dead. This was a shame as I had included it in the set, principally because I knew it was a favourite of PiMi - the organiser and instigator of the show. Oh well. We finished the set with *The Last Thing* which was much better and, by this time we knew we had the audience well-and-truly confused, so we left the stage feeling triumphant.

We returned to the artist's bar to drink a couple of well-earned beers. Don't really remember the details... except that several artists wandered up to me over the rest of the evening to say they'd enjoyed our set. I kept noticing people going by wearing my beads, which had no doubt flown off during sudden movements whilst on-stage. I think Jingles nicked some of them...

A high-point in the evening was when Richard B introduced me to Italian photographer Luigi Collosanti Antonelli, who had taken a dozen-or-so Polaroids of our set (really good photographs - he's obviously a talented boy) which he gave to me as a present. I have them at home and, when I get a minute, I'm going to frame them all together as a memento of the evening. What a band! Everyone wants to do another show. I wonder if I can organise something before we forget it all?..

Wandered out into the security pit to watch Nick Eade sing a couple of songs. A beautiful black girl (sorry - no name) sang a backing vocal into a mic which wasn't switched on while Aziz also added a second guitar which wasn't in the PA. I never told him... but it set me wondering just how much of my show the audience actually got to hear!

Sunday 11 June *Home – Heathrow   Lunch with Rick and Neil*

The alarm shook us both out of deep sleep at 7.15. Much too early to be getting up on a Sunday.... Our Sundays are usually fairly laid-back affairs these days - mooching round the house and waking up slowly while the kids watch a video on TV, but today, coincidence had brought us something very exciting in prospect...

Upon his suggestion, I had arranged to meet Rick Armstrong who would be on his way to Scotland from Cincinatti for a week's golfing holiday with his dad, Neil Armstrong - the internationally renowned astronaut and, of course, the first man to set foot on the moon. They were arriving at Gatwick and then taking the bus to Heathrow for the onward flight to Glasgow, so I had arranged for us all to meet up with him in Terminal 1 at 9.30. To say the Armstrong's are keen golfers would be something of an understatement... I suppose they must be, to endure an almost 24-hour journey to the first tee. (I just don't get it.)

To get to Heathrow for 9.30 we were going to have to be away from the house by 8.30 latest. Sofie was staying over with a friend in the next village so I had to drive over and pick her up. Shortly after the alarm clock sounded its quartz/ceramic squawk both Sue and I realized that neither of us knew where Sofie's friend (Alana, surname unknown...) lived and we didn't have a number for her either. A typical Hogarth hair-brained master plan developed which involved yours-truly staying in bed to "think" while Sue ransacked Sofie's room in the hope of gaining clues to her whereabouts. Fortunately, while I was "thinking" the phone rang and it was Sofie to say she would meet me at 8.00 in the high street, so I threw some rags on and jumped in the car.

When I arrived, I was greeted by seven or eight girls - still in their pyjamas with sleeping bags and duvets wrapped around them - who had come to wave Sofie off. There was much giggling as we waved bye-bye, and then we returned home.

Everyone bundled into the car and we drove to Heathrow terminal 1, parked the car and arrived on time in the terminal at 9.30. No sign of Rick and Neil though.

We hung around for half an hour or more, wondering if we'd got the wrong end of the stick with the arrangements. Eventually, and to our relief, the boys appeared in the terminal looking somewhat anxious and perspiring under the weight of the golf clubs. There was a brief nod of greeting from Rick while Neil joined the queue at the check-in desk. Time was tight and they might not make the flight. Everything about this seemed bizarre to me. Neil Armstrong for heaven's sake! Flying to Gatwick then sitting on a shuttle bus and THEN queuing up to board a flight from Heathrow to Glasgow! I would have expected him to be carried around like the Pope, but nope – he just lives like an ordinary chap. When he got to the front of the queue, I watched a disinterested check-in girl open his passport, read his name, look at his face, and check-in the golf-clubs and bags without raising an eyebrow. I felt like running over there and saying "Have you any idea who this man is?!!!!" Fame sure is a funny thing.

Rick and Neil came over to us with bad news (for them), and excellent news for us. They had missed the connection and the next flight wasn't for another 2 hours. "Does anyone fancy brunch?" said that same voice which I had heard say "One small step for a man.." all those years ago, so we went up onto the mezzanine balcony and sat down at a table in Garfunkel's restaurant. I sat next to Rick, and Nial sat next to Neil. We ate pizza and salad while Nial told the old man all about his new bicycle. Neil seemed genuinely fascinated by my little boy's story. What a lovely chap. I decided I'd be the first stranger he's met NOT to say "So what was it like then?!" although every fibre of me was bursting to hear the Moon-shot first-hand. I'm a little proud that we didn't grill the guy – we just chatted away about the journey from Cincinnati to Gatwick and allowed everybody to relax.

Eventually Neil got around to reminiscing a little – not about Apollo 11, but about the picnic on the North Pole. The test-pilots in the astronaut program were an elite within the elite and were afforded the perk of being able to "sign-out" a plane for leisurely pursuits on their days-off. Neil and his fellow astronaut-trainees decided it might be cool to have lunch on the North Pole. They requisitioned a plane with snow-skids, packed the hampers and flew there. He told us the smoothest ice is the ice nearest to water and so, having found a suitable place to land, they did so without incident and commenced unpacking and enjoying the picnic.

"At some point, we turned around to discover that the ice beneath the plane had softened and the plane had descended down into the ice. The wings were now at ground level."

He paused for a smile.

"Well, fortunately, there are research stations at the North Pole and we managed to explain our situation and hitch a ride home on another plane."

"What happened to the plane you'd borrowed?"

"Oh, it's still there. I guess it just carried on down..."

We chatted more about the barmy conspiracy theorists who don't believe Apollo 11 went to the moon.

"I think Buzz ended up punching one guy out"...

And he told us about the X15 rocket plane which, during earlier preliminary missions, he had to fly back to earth from the edge of space whilst bolted onto the underside wing of a B52 bomber.

"That was a difficult one. The wings had to be very small so that they wouldn't tear off when the rocket fired. Unfortunately that made it not terribly air-worthy. On one occasion I skipped out of the atmosphere and not only missed the landing site, but almost missed America altogether.

"Incidentally, to my knowledge, I actually hold NASA's record for farthest landing from a designated splashdown site. During the aborted Gemini 8 mission we landed in the wrong ocean."

He seemed quite proud of this fact and maintained that it was a record which was unlikely ever to be broken.

We also talked about his most dangerous moment, during training for the flight of the lunar module. He ejected from "the flying bedstead" *one second* before it crashed to the ground at Ellington Air Force base in Houston – oddly enough the closest he came to death in his professional life.

When our time was up, Neil insisted on picking up the bill for lunch. He wouldn't let us contribute. What a cool and lovely guy! He had indeed spent as much time listening to Nial's account of his new bicycle as he had regaling us with stories of his own life. Once again, I couldn't help but feel for Rick – it can't have been easy growing up in that shadow. All things considered, Rick seems a stable, self-confident chap. It's a miracle.

I never did get to hear Neil's recollections of the moon landing first-hand, although I have heard about it over the years from Rick... How Buzz overloaded the computer because he didn't turn off the rendezvous radar to the command-module as they commenced their descent to the moon. (I guess he didn't fancy "burning" the bridge to his ride home.) Unfortunately the computer (having the processing power of an old Casio watch) didn't have the memory to run the rendezvous radar AND the landing radar at the same time, so it crashed! ..leaving Neil no choice but to land the thing manually, famously (and almost tragically) nearly running out of fuel in the process.

I later heard that, during one of his many American-university lectures, a student asked Mr.A how he felt as he traversed the lunar boulder-field trying to find a spot to land and listening to mission-control counting down the seconds of available-fuel left "60 seconds... 30 seconds..."

He grinned, and in his measured, Ohio drawl said:

"Well, you know how, when the fuel gauge on your automobile says zero... there's always a little gas left in the tank."

Postscript

Before we said goodbye I offered to give the chaps a lift to Gatwick when they returned from St Andrews later in the week. I couldn't face the thought of them being bundled onto another coach. As it turned out, their flight back to Heathrow from Glasgow was delayed by a computer problem at air-traffic control and, with the connection from Gatwick to Cincinnati at risk, we raced round the M25 in the outside lane at not much under a 100mph - Rick in the passenger seat and Neil in the back with the golf clubs. I kept glancing in the rear-view mirror and thinking, "Holy fuck! I've got Neil Armstrong in the back of my car! It'd be a shame if I'm the one to kill him after all he's been through…" so I asked one of the dumbest questions I've ever asked:

"Is it okay that I'm driving this fast?"

Bearing in mind this question was addressed to a man who had calmly sat on a skyscraper full of several million litres of liquid oxygen, hydrogen and kerosene exploding beneath him and projecting him skyward into space..

After a slight pause for thought, I heard the familiar voice coolly drawl: "That's fine."

the *invisible* man

2001 SEPTEMBER

Tuesday 11

The world's gone mad

2001

Monday 12 February *Home – Bath*

And so it was that at 12.05 I began frantically packing in time for my 12.15 departure. I managed to get out of the door by 12.20 – a little late for my arranged meeting with Andy Rotherham at Oxford station. Andy will be driving my car around the UK over the next two weeks. The weather was pretty rainy once again, and I winced as I managed to set off a speed camera on the Botley road, despite driving in heavy traffic. I don't know how I do it! More trouble on the way...

I arrived at the station around 12.50 and Andy was waiting for me. I gave him the keys and, in the pouring rain, hurriedly transferred some underwear and socks into an overnight bag. At the station I bought a single to Bath Spa and boarded the train which was already at platform 1. There was a moment of panic as the train was announced departing to London Paddington. I grabbed my bag and almost leapt from the train before being told that I must change at Didcot and I was on the right train after all. Phew. Changed platforms at Didcot and, amazingly, the express to Bath arrived five minutes later, on time. I found an empty seat and strapped the Walkman on to listen to our recently mastered new record. It sounded great, but then you could construct a pretty convincing argument to show that I'm biased. My new faith in the efficiency of the rail network was to be short-lived. When we arrived in Swindon, a voice crackled in the tinny speaker above me, saying that owing to flooding on the line we would have to continue the next part of the journey at a severe speed restriction, and

I eventually arrived in Bath one hour late at around 4.00.

The rain had stopped so I walked up through the shops, stopping to buy more Walkman headphones which were 'far superior' and would be 'much louder' than those supplied with the machine. They weren't, but by then I'd removed the practically impregnable hard-moulded plastic packing which has to be destroyed in order to give up its contents (without which, of course, "'he product cannot be returned'). I also bought another pair of shoes to get me through the tour before making my way through the town to the hotel – only a Travelodge (the money's tight on this University tour!) but more than adequate, and right in the centre of town on George Street. I'm here on my own today as I'm popping over to Bristol tonight to sit in on Andy Fox's rock radio show. The rest of the band are playing with Eddie Jordan at the Albert Hall in one of those charity gig things.

I dropped my bag in room 305 (still have the key here! Oops) which was stiflingly hot, and got out of there quickly after opening the window and turning off the heating. I wandered over the road to the Moles studio in search of my old chum, Jan Brown, and managed to persuade her out of the office for a soda in the pub opposite. Jill Furmanovski had called to say that she's in town with fellow photographer Fernando Aceves (another mate I'd worked with in Mexico City), so I gave her a tinkle on the mobile and we were soon huddled round a table together. I did the introductions, and we chatted for a while until Jan had to return to do some work, and Jill and Fernando departed for the cinema.

Made my way down Broad Street to the Abbey and Browns restaurant where I had a burger for tea whilst listening to **Anoraknophobia** again on the CD Walkman. I called home and chatted to Dizzy, before making my way back to the station. I'd allowed myself 90-minutes for the 15-minute train journey to Bristol. It wasn't enough! Most of the trains were either cancelled completely or running massively late. Bought copies of **Private Eye** and **The Spectator** which contained an article by the head of Opec, regarding who was really to blame for the price of oil. He says that Western Europe's policy of ever-increasing fuel tax is at odds with Western Governments constant calling for free-trade. He says we want a free market, but we don't want freedom of movement of people from one country to another – it's hypocrisy. He's got a point. I suppose you could easily show that the massive taxation of oil by Western governments is simply a tool to bolster their own economies at the expense of the Arab economies... hmm. The rest of **The Spectator** was the usual boring old Tory nonsense, so I turned my attention to **Private Eye** and chuckled along as I waited in the cold for a train to Bristol. I took a cab to the radio station and played them some of the new record. They were well impressed, but then Andy and Ian at Eagle FM represent a dying breed of people at radio who have any time for thought-provoking music. It's all dance, tits, ass, biceps, and ecstasy at radio these days. Chop 'em out and see if you can get Britney/Kylie/Robbie to sit on your knee... Maybe I should change my name to Stevie... or "h-ie".

Well, at the end of the evening I had a pint with Andy and Ian, and Andy gave me a lift back to Bath where I went to bed and watched something-I-can't-remember on TV and fell asleep.

Tuesday 13 February *Bath*

Enjoyed the unbridled luxury of waking up alone in a comfortable bed with nowhere to go and nothing urgent to do, i.e. had a lie-in and didn't think about anything or anyone until gone 10.00 when I arose to a beautiful blue morning. It was like an antidote to the flooded, rainy grey of yesterday. Showered and made myself a coffee with the one-cup kettle perched on the shelf along with sachets of average instant coffee and several of the inexplicable, bizarre, *silly* plastic foil-covered tubs of UHT milk – a must for anyone who wants to see their drinks change colour at the splash of a whole dessert-spoonful of white watery stuff that tastes of NOTHING. I don't like them. Went down to reception and persuaded them to allow me to log on and pick up my email at the counter. Travelodge rooms don't have phones you can dial out on. Handy... but I've sworn not to complain on this tour.

Still bursting to hear the new album blasting out of some serious speakers, I went back over the road to the Moles studio, but, unfortunately, a session was already underway and I couldn't interfere, so I had a coffee and chatted with the tape-ops until Jan showed up for work. Then I left them all to their day and wandered round Bath looking at the antique shops, and trying to decide how to kill the five hours before the rest of the band showed up.

I ended up in Browns again at lunchtime and had a slow and lazy lunch reading the papers before returning to the hotel and going back to bed for an afternoon snooze. Heaven. I'm in a kind of super-relaxed exhaustive state at the moment. I have spent the last eight months fretting over the new album and breaking my head over the words. *Map of the World* almost drove me to the river, and now it's all finished and I know I don't need to think about writing ANYTHING for a few months. It's funny how the body caves in when the mind decides it's finished.

Around 4.00 the band showed up and Tim B told me that soundcheck wasn't until 6.30, so we killed time in the café over the road. Ian and Steve said they'd had a good time at the Albert Hall last night. Maybe I should have gone for the lig, but I don't really like doing that and hanging out if I'm not performing – I feel like I'm freeloading.

At 5.30 we drove over to the Bath Uni campus and hung around for a while trying to get into the student union hall, which was all locked up. When we got inside I said hello to the boys, before being directed into a strange-smelling office to be interviewed by a student for the college rag. She was understandably clueless about us and said she thought we were going to be something like Marilyn Manson. When I said absolutely not at all, I couldn't decide whether she was disappointed or relieved. She said she'd been surfing the net and found a song called *Grendel*, full of mythical lyrics. She said she liked it. I think I glazed over at that point...

Friday 16 February *Leeds Cockpit*

Checked out of the hotel at 12.00 for the drive down the M1 to Leeds. Bright sunshine again today.

Arrived at the peculiar Travel Lodge around 2.00 and checked in. We'd been here before in November last year and I left my gloves. No one at reception was admitting to ever having them though. Oh well. Dropped my bags and went walkabout in the general direction of Harvey Nichols via Call Lane where my old boss Rick Harrison still owns one of the best guitar shops in the UK, Music Ground. I had a wander round lusting after the old Fenders and Rickenbackers and particularly a hollow bodied Les Paul with F hole – yours for a couple of grand...

Carried on down the road to the Victoria Arcade - a refurbished Victorian shopping arcade full of Leeds' richer shops including the only Harvey Nichols outside London where, if you can justify it (and I can't) you can buy a Dolce & Gabbana shirt for £450! Phew. I was out of underwear (again! - a common problem on tour) so I managed to get out of there only eighteen quid lighter for three pairs of Calvin Kleins. The shirt'll have to wait...

I hadn't eaten yet today so I killed the remaining time to soundcheck in Harvey Nics caff out in the Victoria Arcade drinking coffee and munching an excellent chicken and chilli-jam sandwich. When I asked the waitress if they had anything to read, she brought me a copy of yesterday's **Sun**. Hmm... I'd have expected something more highbrow from Harvey Nics.

Well, after two slow coffees I decided I'd had enough of watching Leeds go by and I made my way over to the gig.

Not to put too finer point on it, the Cockpit ain't a beautiful thing so I didn't spend too long in there but returned to the hotel to watch Richard Whitely struggle through another episode of **Countdown**. What a peculiar television programme. Robert Powell was adjudicating!

Soundcheck was sonically extremely loud and as ugly as it will always be under a corrugated steel roof. We're doing this show, along with the Zodiac and Dingwalls, to pay for the University gigs which would otherwise lose us a lot of money, so we're gritting our teeth and doing what must be done... Rehearsed *Out of this World* and *Man of 1000 Faces* which we'll add to the show tonight.

Returned to the Travelodge where security is very tight - they must have been regularly robbed in the past. You can't get in without pressing a bell and waiting for a receptionist to buzz the door open. Opening the door requires both hands at the moment the lock is released - impossible for anyone carrying bags - and by the time you've realized this and put your bags down, you have to return to the bell press (not next to the door) to try your luck and your patience once again. Once inside, you discover that the lift won't work unless you swipe your room key through a slot inside, and when you finally get to your room with your bags you discover that the phones don't dial out, you can't pick up email, and the telephone number of the hotel isn't written on the telephone or published anywhere else, making it difficult for your loved ones to call you. Still, the beds are comfortable and the gig's right next door.

There's no dressing room in the Cockpit so we decided to get changed in our rooms and walk round to the gig in stageclothes. As we approached the "backstage entrance" – a rear door only accessible by walking through a car park in the dark – I had the misfortune to walk down a small hole in the ground – some kind of access point to a water tap with a flap cover which had broken off. My right foot dropped straight down 6 inches and my right shin scraped against the sharp metal-edge of the hole. Luckily I didn't break my leg or sprain my ankle. I could have, so easily. Went straight on stage and as I sang the opening song, I could feel the blood running down my shin on the inside of my jeans and into my shoe. It's all glamour.

The sound on stage was something of a car crash - this place is a cellar and sounds like a metal-clad cave – but the audience were terrific. Afterwards, I hung around and signed some autographs while the poor crew tried to negotiate the equipment and themselves around us. Getting the gear out of here was going to take a while...

Thursday 8 March *Coniston*

Woke up at 8.25 in room 11 of the Glenridding Hotel, Ullswater. I had booked a morning call for 8.00, which I hadn't received. No wonder – I had unplugged the phone! Doh! I was supposed to be downstairs at 8.30 to leave for Coniston with Steve Rothery. I bungled around, bouncing off the walls, trying to get dressed and shower at the same time. The hot water took an age to come through – I really couldn't face a cold shower this morning. I arrived downstairs at 8.45 and managed to make it into the breakfast room before Rothers appeared, announcing that Coniston was further away than we had originally thought and that we must leave immediately. Downed a quick coffee and smuggled a plate of toast past the receptionist and into the car. We sped away through the massive hills past sheep dyed pink and then orange, on the steep dry-stone-walled moorland of the magnificent Kirkstone pass - on our way to Ambleside (where we passed a shop called 'The home of football') before turning right for Coniston.

We arrived in Coniston around 9.30am and stopped to ask directions to the boathouse, where Bill Smith had arranged to meet us. At the top of the road that descends to the lake we were stopped by a stony-faced policeman who told us we could go no further. Tense moments passed whilst we tried to convince him that we were official guests of the dive-team. He was supposed to have a list of car registration numbers, but - if he had one - he didn't bother looking at it. Eventually he reluctantly let us through telling us we would probably be turned back at the next roadblock. Miserable bugger. We arrived at the next checkpoint and were waved straight through to the car park by the lake where Bill Smith joyfully bounced up to meet us - already inside his wet suit - saying "Hello! What kept you?" Once again, I was struck by his physical resemblance to Marillion's former singer, and the irony that he probably has a greater right to the nickname... I should explain: Bill's a Tyneside engineer with a passion for diving. He had often previously spent his spare time diving on Second World War shipwrecks and using new technologies to see and to dive at ever-greater depths. A few years ago he heard the Marillion song *Out of This World* - a song inspired by Donald Campbell's fatal water-speed record attempt on Coniston Water in January 1967 - and the song set a fire in him, a quest to go to Coniston (thought to be bottomless in the 60's) and use new remote-operated technologies to locate and, hopefully, retrieve Bluebird. He has done just that.

Down at the lakeside there were about fifty people - mostly TV, radio and press - clutching cameras and microphones, and all set back from the lake by a rope, which was being monitored by police. Bill marched through the police line beckoning us along behind him past bemused officials, to the end of a jetty, which looked out twenty metres to a large barge with a crane-arm swinging out over the water. Bill told us that he had towed the Bluebird from its original crash location this morning at 5.00 am and that they were making ready to bring her to the surface here so that she could be manoeuvred on to a trailer which would tow her to the shore. As Bill had decided to make Steve Rothery his official photographer, Steve set about making his cameras ready to capture the amazing events about to unfold, crouching low on the end of the jetty while I leant against a post, occasionally scanning over my shoulder at the media scrum roped-off up the beach. I'm sure a few of them were wondering who the hell we were. Little did any of them know that I was the one who had started all this, having written the words, which led to the song, which led Bill to spend the last four years determinedly trying to find the Bluebird.

I was introduced to Michaela - a girl in green Doc Marten boots - who was the roving reporter for the **Westmoreland Gazette**. Bill had obviously decided she was groovy enough to be allowed forward from the throng of national media to the end of the jetty. The **Westmoreland Gazette** is based in Kendal, where I was born. I told her I was born at Helme Chase hospital which she told me is under threat of closure at the moment. It's not the same place I was born – that was a maternity hospital ran, at the time, by nuns. Helme Chase was now a ward within the main area hospital. Indeed, the newspaper was campaigning to save the Helme Chase ward. Perhaps we could help, I suggested... auction something off perhaps... Michaela said yes, that would be nice, but she was too wound up in the immediate proceedings to discuss it further.

Around 10.00am it became apparent that a technical hitch had happened - the Bluebird had drifted beneath the barge and the barge would have to be moved out of the way to avoid her colliding with the underside as she was lifted. By now, I was really feeling the cold, which had slowly crept into my bones during the hour of standing over the water on the end of the exposed jetty. I walked back up the beach - trying to avoid the gaze of the press and the police - to the Bluebird Tearooms and bought myself and Steve a cup of coffee. The view from the window of the tearoom was excellent so I ordered a toasted teacake and bought a few Donald Campbell postcards and a slab of Kendal Mint Cake (made mainly of sugar with peppermint flavouring and famous for having been taken to the summit of Everest by Hillary and Tenzing during their famous first ascent.) On any other occasion I would have stayed put and watched the rest of the morning unfold from the window of the warm tearooms, but this was too important to witness at a distance.

I returned to the end of the jetty. The barge was now in the right position and the orange float-bags, which would bring Bluebird K7 to the surface of Coniston for the first time in 34 years, were being inflated. I listened with mounting anticipation to the sound of the pumps on the barge and watched the divers in the water hauling at the blue-nylon ropes until, at 10.45, the famous blue tail-fin of the Bluebird appeared above the surface of the water. I was amazed by the fact that it was still blue - that the paint had held under the water for three decades and that the union-flag motif remained, almost intact - stubbornly evoking the patriotism of the man, and of another age. The atmosphere was oddly celebrational and sombre at the same time. Bill was grinning away as only someone can as they see four years of their own hard work come to fruition - hamming it up for the cameras and wearing a flamboyant coloured felt hat (which I'm told he always wears when "searching") He looked like a victorious buccaneer-jester, beaming away at the assembled media. I had begun to wonder whether the mood was getting a little too flippant to suit the occasion. Any light-heartedness came to a sudden stop, though, as the rest of the craft appeared above water, revealing a shocking, mangled mess of metal at the front of her - immediately behind where the cockpit (and Donald) would have been as she hit the surface of the lake at 300mph. Suddenly it felt like there were too many people witnessing this – too many of the wrong people. I include myself. I might have initiated all this but I felt I had no right to be there really – like some uninvited stranger showing up at a famous funeral looking for autographs and a mention in the media. I watched as Donald's second wife, Tonia Bern-Campbell was ferried to the barge to gain a closer presence to the crash-damaged machine, which was still half-submerged and surrounded by divers, still tugging at the flotation bags and manhandling the Bluebird in an attempt to guide her onto the tow-trailer and prevent her colliding with the barge. Tonia looked on for a while. God knows what she felt. What do you feel when you're confronted with the wreckage of a machine that killed your husband 34 years ago? Surprised by a sudden rush of grief? Guilty for not being able to feel enough? Angry for being forced to confront this in the glare of the media? 34 years is a long, long time.

The process of guiding Bluebird onto the tow-trailer was long and involved. All in all, the divers tugged and held the ropes in the cold water of the lake for a good two hours before, at last, a land-rover winched the trailer and her precious cargo slowly towards the beach.

And there she stood, much bigger than she had looked in the old photographs. Again, a certain quietness descended the scene for a time as celebration gave way to introspection and we all slowly took in the sight before us. From the rear, Bluebird is indistinguishable from a jet fighter – she is almost intact from the cockpit rearwards, as if she'd crashed head-on into a mountainside. I suppose the impact was not dissimilar.

As the press took their photographs and clamoured to interview Bill, I chatted to the divers who were very relieved to be out of the water. Even wet-suited, they must have been freezing and exhausted after all their hard physical work. They seemed to me like a really nice bunch of people - friendly, intelligent and down-to-earth free-spirited types, brought together by their enthusiasm for diving and adventure.

Bluebird was taken up the beach and locked up inside a boat-house. All the commotion died down as the journalists took their turn to interview Bill and then found a quiet corner to file their stories. Precious photographs were being e-mailed from laptop computers by cellular phone links to the worlds press offices for tomorrow's front pages. So no one really seemed to notice when one of the divers climbed from a small boat holding the nose cone of Bluebird. I recognized the remnants of the two crossed union-flags which once adorned her snout. It was badly distorted and most of the blue paint had gone but, being of aluminium, no corrosion had taken place. I was honoured to be given this to hold and a Reuters photographer, Jon Super, took a photograph of me looking along the shoreline and holding what would have been the first thing to hit the water on that fateful January day in 1967. For me, a complete circle was closed since the evening in 1967 when I watched the news with my mum and saw that lobster-like machine somersault backwards through the air and the explosion of white on the black&white TV screen as she smashed into Lake Consiton …and I wondered why my mum was crying.

By this time, my heart was heavy and my mind was well and truly blown! I retired to the tearooms for a coffee and a sandwich while Steve R wandered about outside talking into his mobile phone. On emerging into the daylight I ran into Bill who said "D'you want to have a look?"

Steve and I followed him into the boathouse and we and the dive-team suddenly had the Bluebird all to ourselves. The outside world was locked out and, for the first time I got to have a private moment with this piece of history. She was still dripping water onto the concrete floor of the boathouse and, amazingly, still oozing jet fuel! The smell of high-octane spirit was overpowering. All that time under water… maybe there were air locks, or maybe the water trapped the fuel in some way – after all, spirit is lighter than water so it would act like an air-lock, I suppose. The smell of the fuel only served to further-remove the 34 years she'd been under the lake. Suddenly it felt like no time had passed.

At the front end of the wreckage, fastened to one of the cross-members of the metal structure was a half-inch bolt – bent out of shape to almost 90 degrees. Attached to this was a short and torn remnant of seat-belt material. This would have been the harness, coming up from the floor between Donald's legs, holding him in place. It was the single most disturbing moment of the day for me. I only hope Tonia never noticed it.

Ken Norris - Bluebirds' designer - had appeared and was talking to Bill at the rear of the craft. I managed to eavesdrop parts of their conversation. Apparently Bluebird was designed for a maximum speed of 250mph! Ken was saying he was surprised at the extent to which Bluebird had withstood the crash. I couldn't catch everything he was saying, but he seemed emotionally detached and interested in the machine totally from an engineering standpoint. I guess he'd done his grieving a long time ago, but I still found it strange him seeming so unsentimental.

Steve and I emerged from the boathouse to a crowd of people hoping to catch a glimpse inside, and made our way back to the car. Our plan was to check out of our hotel and into a hotel in Coniston. We reserved a couple of rooms at The Black Bull Hotel and drove back over to Ullswater where we checked out of the Glenridding Hotel returning, once again across the hills to Coniston.

Our welcome at the Black Bull was as warm as any I've ever had. Sue, the landlady seemed genuinely pleased to have us and keen to help us. We checked in and ordered dinner in the lounge bar. The walls were adorned with photographs of Campbell's exploits. Even the beer was called "Bluebird Ale" ...and it was excellent. By now, I was pretty weary so I said I'd see Steve in an hour, and had a bath while watching Liverpool playing Porto on TV through the open door. Relaxing on the bed in a towel, I answered a knock on the door to find Steve informing me that Bill and all the divers were downstairs in the bar demanding our assistance in celebration!

I got dressed and went downstairs to be handed a beer by Bill. We all sat down and tall tales were told of diving on battleships in fjords and submarines from the war. I told them of my chance meeting with Paul Barney, sole British survivor of the Estonia, not long after she sank with almost 1000 people aboard and his account of his 5 hours in the Baltic Sea waiting to be rescued. It's quite eerie how many of the big news stories throughout my life have somehow brushed against me personally... I shudder to wonder what will be next.

The dive team had dinner at The Black Bull and then we all trooped round the corner to their hotel, The Sun Inn (where Donald himself used to stay). As it turned out, we all had a few beers and talked together quite late into the night. However, the whole affair was pleasant and good-natured, and nobody got out of hand. Around half-past eleven it occurred to Steve and I that perhaps we might be locked out of our hotel. Steve disappeared and returned to confirm that, yes indeed, the Bull was all locked up and, although one of the outside doors were accessible with a safety code, the management had neglected to tell us what it was. Oh dear. There were two emergency telephone numbers on my key fob so I went to the bar to ask if there was a payphone in the Sun Inn. I was directed through to another room and as I walked, a distinguished silver-haired lady said, "Excuse me – aren't you the chap who wrote the song?" It took me a moment to realize that this was Tonia Bern-Campbell. She held out her hand in greeting and I gently took it, telling her it was an honour to meet her. She looked much more glamorous than her appearance down at the lake that morning, and her heavily accented English reminded me of Za-Za Gabor. I asked her where she was from originally, and she told me that she is Belgian but has spent much time in Italy, England and now, San Diego in the USA. She said that she too, is a singer and quizzed me on the technical difficulties of the melodies of Burt Baccarrach and Michel Legrand! She asked if I might send her a copy of *Out of this World*. I promised I would and she gave me her address. She explained that she had objected to the raising of the Bluebird for fear of what else might be found within the wreck. Fortunately, there appears to be no trace of her husband. She seemed in a bright mood, and I had the impression that she'd recovered from the harrowing experience of the day's earlier events. During our conversation, the few people in her party rose to leave and so I wished her "goodnight" and reaffirmed my promise to send her the song.

I returned to the task of trying to find the access-code to our hotel so that Steve and I would be able to sleep tonight. Steve eventually sorted it out and I wrote the code down.

I drank a little more and chatted a little more with the divers and the BBC crew who were there making a documentary about the whole project. We would love to make the music to accompany this. I was wanting to talk to the director, Mike Rossiter, to persuade him he could trust us to provide him with a great soundtrack, but he was holed up in the corner of the bar with his friends and I didn't want to crash in on his leisure time. I managed to speak to him briefly before we were all thrown out of the bar at midnight, and he gave me his address so I could send him some music.

I made my way down the lane in the rain, back to the Black Bull – an apt name as, when I got to the door with the coded entry lock on it, it was too dark to read the letters and numbers on the buttons. I stood there like a blind man reading Braille with my fingertips for at least ten minutes, hoping my eyes would become accustomed to the pitch darkness enough to see something, but to no avail. In the end I think I got it right by fluke, and in a state of much relief, made my way through the darkness inside and upstairs to my room. Before I went to sleep I thought I'd better try and write down what had happened today…

When I finally closed my eyes and drifted into sleep it must have been nearly dawn. A sad tune hummed silently in my head,

"…*only love will turn you round …only love will turn you round...*"

Monday 23 April *Hannover*

Woken at 5.30 by the telephone by my bed at the Holiday Inn, Heathrow. Oddly enough it didn't come as much of a shock. I think I was dreaming about it happening just before it did… Phoned Mark in room 2305 to check he was up. There was a sound at the other end like someone destroying a telephone, so I think he was having a bit of trouble…

Showered, dressed and put my things together before going downstairs to the hotel reception. I must have been the first person to appear this morning as the staff started scurrying around and turning on the lights in the lobby. Well, that's a first.

At ten to six the airport bus appeared so I telephoned Mark again to see how he was doing. He was just on his way out through the door of his room. Unfortunately the bus pulled away before he showed up so we had to wait for the next bus. While we waited he suddenly realized he'd lost his flight tickets and ran off back to his room to try to find them. The next bus came during his absence and I persuaded the driver to wait until he returned. The traffic was pretty thick during the short journey to Terminal 2 and it was 6.30 by the time we arrived to check in for the 7.10 to Hannover. There was still a queue of people waiting to check in so we waited our turn and when we got to the desk the check in clerk said, "I'm afraid the flight is very busy and you won't be able to sit together..." peering into his computer screen and then picking up his telephone he listened for a moment and then said, "I'm afraid it's worse than that – the flight is overbooked and you can't get on at all."

Oh dear. The next flight to Hannover was not until 11.15 – not much use to us. We made our way across the hall to the ticket desk where a helpful girl was doing her best to offer alternatives to the growing queue of pissed-off businessmen and women. After some research she offered us the 8.55 to Hamburg, which arrives at 11.30. We rang Louise Veys to give her the bad news and she promptly set about trying to organize transport to get us from Hamburg to Hannover by road – a journey of at least 2 hours! Looks like it's going to be one of those days... By way of compensation, British Midland gave each of us a voucher for £50 which we then had to go to terminal 1 to cash... I checked my bag in and we wandered down the labyrinth of tunnels and corridors to Terminal 1 where we were handed the cash. This turn of events means that I was paid for a promo trip for the first time ever!

Mark and I had now got a couple of hours to kill so we went for coffee and a spot of breakfast while I pondered the irony of the fact that I could, after all, have slept in my own bed with my wife last night for the first time in three weeks!

Well, we made our way to the gate and hung around in an uninspiring concrete lounge for some time before boarding the plane. The flight was pleasant and uneventful and my bag showed up at the other end, unlike the last time we came to Germany for promotion when my luggage went missing and showed up in Amsterdam, three days later.

We were met at Hamburg airport by Michael and Markus who took us back to Hannover in a black VW minibus. I wandered in and out of consciousness trying to catch up on deprived sleep during the 90-minute journey and when we arrived at CMM promotions' offices we hit the ground running and were hurried into the first phone interview of the day. Now, any intelligent casual reader of this diary in years to come may justifiably wonder why a record company would go to the time and massive expense of sticking a couple of musicians in a hotel for the night before flying them to another part of Europe, whereupon they are rushed into a minibus and driven half-way across Germany to do an interview on the telephone. Well, folks – that's the music business! I always expected the music business to be insane - that's why I'm in it - but sometimes it's quite a bit more insane than I am...

Anyway, as we were now two hours behind schedule there was much work to catch up on, so the lunch break was cancelled and we worked through until 6.00 pm when we were hurried back out of the building to drive one hour to Bremen for an interview with Burghard - my favourite DJ on earth. Here's a guy who is totally into the music he plays. He plays an imaginary drum kit along with the music and you can tell he's simply loving it. He played a few of our new songs during the interview, playing *This is the 21st Century* alongside an excellent cover of The Beatles' *I'm Only Sleeping* by Suggs (of Madness). He then surprised me by broadcasting a live recording of The Europeans *Writing for Survival* which I didn't know existed. He told me that it was Radio Bremen's own recording of a gig we had done in the town in 1984 (which, try as I might, I can't remember doing.) We left the radio station to go to a restaurant for dinner at 10.00 in the evening. The kitchen was on the point of closing when we arrived so I ordered something and then asked if I could be taken to check in at the hotel so that I could at last have a wash and change of clothes for the first time in 17 hours. I quickly called home to say hello before running back downstairs to return to the restaurant where, finally, we could relax. Dinner was pleasant enough and we talked rubbish and put the world to rights with Michael and Markus. There was much debate about whether Kohl had been right or wrong in his mission to re-unite Germany. Ever the idealist, I admire him for acting on pure principle and doing something about it on such an enormous scale. The Germans don't really see it that way though. In the West, they have to live with the reality of high taxes and falling currency values and living standards, while in the Eastern sector the people feel like they have been "bought" by the West, only to lose their jobs and now find it impossible to afford the rich goods that surround them, or to keep up with their well-educated and better-motivated western counterparts. Massive social or political changes are never straightforward whether they're based on sound principles or not. Personally, I still think the re-unification of Germany was the right and proper thing to do.

I gradually mellowed out after a couple of beers and we returned to the hotel where Mark suggested a 'nightcap' in the bar. I knew it was a bad idea, but agreed anyway and so we ended up staying up far too late and drinking far too much. Michael said he would give me a call at 9.30 in the morning as we must leave at 10.15 for the flight to Munich. Went to bed and spent most of the night wrestling with the German pillows - soft square things that refuse to assume the right shape to support one's head no matter how they're manipulated.

Woken by the ringing telephone. "Good Morning Steve! Michael here. Are you ready to leave? It's five past ten!" Oh my God. Ran around like a headless chicken trying to shower, dress and pack in five minutes. My watch had completely vanished and I had to practically dismantle the room before finding it under the mattress in the middle where I absolutely had not left it. It was going to be another one of those days...

Postscript 1

I'm convinced that the only way my watch could have arrived beneath my mattress - in the middle of the area of the mattress – was if it had been carefully placed there. I can only conclude that a member of the hotel staff, or cleaning staff, had taken a shine to it and decided to stash it where it could later be stolen. If I noticed it gone and made a fuss, the room could be searched and the watch found. If I checked out and left it then called to ask if the hotel had found it, they would search the room and deny it was there. Dodgy...

Postscript 2

It turns out that it was Burghard's last broadcast on Radio Bremen. He's been made redundant to make way for restructuring of the station format. That'll teach him to play music he enjoys. If you ever wonder what's wrong with radio, bear in mind that the likes of Bob Harris and Burghard struggle to remain at radio. And it seems to be the same everywhere in the world. They are eventually kicked out in favour of DJ's who play music from a strict playlist dictated by "the parent company" which usually owns entire strings of radio stations nationwide. So next time you hear Tina Turner sing "*What's love got to do with it?*" on Radio Hush, you can be sure she's asking the right question.

Friday 25 May *Amsterdam Heinekenhalle*

Woke at the Holiday Inn Amsterdam. Showered and ordered coffee on room service. Forgot to ask for milk or sugar, so it came with neither. Had sugar and milk sent up. The simplest things can take ages when you live in hotels. Checked out. Hung around in the bar finishing Steve Rothery's lunch. Took the bus to the Heineken Halle and arrived in the maze which is the backstage area. Everything's painted white and grey and very disorientating. It's a brand new building and some of the details (like which floor you're on) have yet to be finished.

Soundchecked and was impressed by the acoustic quality of this enormous hall. It has been purpose-designed for electric music, and you can tell. Wandered aimlessly around backstage trying not to get lost. Chatted to Phil Harrison who had flown in from England and made my way to the VIP balcony to watch the Porcupine Tree's set. They sounded and looked great - like a mini-Pink Floyd. With the basic light rig that they were using the volume of colour was impressive so I could see that our show was going to look even better with the additional intelligent light sources, which were not yet being used. I returned to the dressing room and told the boys that our show was going to look great out front.

Now the Dutch can be a funny bunch. We're very popular here in Holland, but I've done shows here where the response from the crowd has been distinctly icy. I've also done shows where the reception has been really great. You never know which way they're going to go...

Well, it turned out to be one of those nights where everything just goes right from the moment you strike up. My sound was great and I was singing well, but in addition to that, I had a vibe going with the 5000 strong crowd and everything I said to them seemed to be the right thing at the right time. I'm not someone who has ever developed a "patter" for the shows (saying the same things every night - being "professional" so-to-speak...) so my introductions and chat are pretty hit and miss. Tonight though it all felt right. Before *80 Days* I made up a little song about Holland and the Dutch fans and it all rhymed as it came out. Improvised things like this are fantastic when they work and really fire an audience up, but I have to be in the right frame of mind... As I hit the last note of the intro, Steve R hit the first chord of *80 Days* and to my joy it was completely in the right key for my improvised tune. This was pure chance but sounded like a masterstroke! It was good to be on a big stage playing to a large crowd again. I think if we ever made it really big, I could be very comfortable doing the Freddy Mercury thing and strutting and stomping about, working the stadium crowds... Shame, really. We'd need to write a dozen hit singles first, of course, and that's not really what Marillion are about.

At the end of the set we came off-stage to prepare for encore 1. By chance, a man went by wearing a huge beer-dispenser – a tank of Heineken with a tap and a load of plastic glasses so that he could sell beer to the people in the crowd. We managed to persuade him to part with it and I strapped it on and returned to the stage where Pete and I handed out much-needed free beer to the front row. This raised the vibe higher still and so the encores were played in a great atmosphere. After the show I showered before making my way to a bar area at the front of the gig and I really never have been mobbed in quite the same way in my life. I must have kissed and been kissed by over a hundred women and men in ten minutes. I signed a whole lot of autographs before I could get upstairs to the bar where I was mobbed all over again. It was terrific, but James Fishwick who was playing the role of temporary minder seemed to find it well-scary... I think it could have been, if I didn't know our fans the way I do. There's never anything to fear from genuine affection.

Tuesday 29 May *Strasbourg, La Laiterie*

The bus stopped... and remained still for some time, so I opened one eye, pulled back my little curtain and tried to focus my eyes on the blinding light that assaulted me. I couldn't see much to start with, but then, out of the haze came several psychedelic cows painted on a large end wall of a building. This must be La Laiterie, Strasbourg, then. It was a beautiful sunny morning - and I suddenly felt like I was in Southern Europe, after Lille in the north of France, yesterday. I rolled out of my bunk, threw on a pair of shorts and climbed downstairs and out into the street. We were parked opposite some kind of Conservatoire and there was the mute sound of a bassoon drifting from an open window somewhere. Occasionally, a young girl would emerge from a door, cross the quiet street in the sunshine and disappear into the building opposite. Ian M appeared in the open doorway of the bus, looking particularly cadaverous and grumpy this morning and announced that he'd had about 3 hrs sleep. I know Ian well enough to leave him alone at times like this… He climbed out of the bus and slumped down against the wall in the sunshine next to the truck, which was being unloaded. This is Ian's way of letting our tour manager, Tim, know that he would like to be taken to a hotel VERY SOON. From an otherwise empty street a kid in his early teens appeared - dressed in rapper fashion – waistline round his arse, baseball cap at 3 o'clock, shoes undone etc, carrying a substantial blaster, and sat down next to the truck also. As I walked into the building I began to chuckle to myself in anticipation of the scene which would surely unfold outside. "If he turns that blaster on, Mosley's reaction will be swift, measured and extremely violent," I surmised. (Note: he did… and it was.) Still chuckling, I entered La Laiterie, which seemed dirtier and smaller than I had remembered from last time. The dressing rooms were covered in the usual "rock club" graffiti – I never worked out what it is that drives grown-men to scrawl ejaculating penises on the walls of rooms that they're then going to have to sit in for hours on end… I showered and emerged, still sweating - it's so hot today!

   Last time we were here, we stayed at a great hotel on the river in the stunningly beautiful old centre of town. I went looking for it. I walked into town, stopping to change up some cash, and mooched along the river where I eventually found Le Petit Regent Hotel. I have fond memories of the room I had last time above the weir on the River Ill – having breakfast, gazing out over the rushing water at the medieval buildings that border the river as it winds through the old town.

   I decided to set up camp on the terrace of the Petit Regent's little Brasserie, Le Pont Tournant. A few tables were set outside by the river so I sat down and had a slow and excellent afternoon, drinking Gerwurstraminer (my favourite wine) and spoiling myself rotten with a three hour lunch. A friend, Chris Brockwell, had given me a copy of Ian Dury's biography before I left England and so I chilled out in the sunshine reading my book, enjoying lunch, and listening to the river flow. Boats occasionally went by, in and out of the lock below me. Across on the far bank, was a little square where people were sitting out. There was a little midget-man - impeccably dressed in a top hat and tuxedo – who arrived in the square with a small hand-wound barrel organ which set up a pleasant reedy tune in amongst the sound of the flowing river. All in all, I decided this was about as good as life gets. Eventually, around 3.00 the staff began to clear cutlery, glasses and table cloths from the tables and I put my book down and paid the bill.

   I wandered back through town (muttering "Reasons to be cheerful… part 3," to myself as I walked) in search of a music shop (my tambourines are disintegrating - it seems they are not designed to be shaken...) and a wine shop, in the hope of finding a bottle of Gewurztraminer Grains Noble – you can't really get it in England down at the offy. Managed to find two bottles at £17 a pop; not cheap, but then it really does taste like sweet orange-marmalade...

Wandered back towards the railway station and eventually found a little music shop. There was a semi-acoustic Telecaster hanging in the window which caught my eye. Sunburst with an f hole. Lovely. Went in and managed to buy a tambourine - not really what I was looking for, but it'll do. I was about to leave when I found myself asking if I could have a feel of the Telecaster in the window. (Quick chorus of "How much is that telly in the window" – altogether now...) It was second-hand and priced at 3000 francs - about £300... I tried it through a couple of amps and it sounded fine, so I knocked him down to 2700fr and bought it! By now the time was approaching 4.30 and I would be needed at soundcheck so I returned in the general direction of the station – bottles clanking and tambourine tinkling in various carrier-bags, and a guitar-bag strap cutting into my shoulder. At the station I tried to hire a taxi to take me to La Laiterie but there was much amusement and shaking of heads amid volleys of unfathomable French. I think the cabbies were telling me it was only a short walk, and not worth their trouble. I have never got on well with French taxi-drivers. I was once nearly murdered by one in Paris with a lead cosh...

As there didn't seem to be much choice, I set off again on foot in the scorching heat with my carrier bags tinkling and my new guitar getting heavier with each step. I asked the way to La Laiterie from passers-by who all sent me for long walks in the wrong direction, before eventually staggering sweating, limping and jangling into the gig.

I plugged the new guitar in at the soundcheck and it sounded very nice... Hooray!

After soundcheck we all had to hang around in the cartoon-orgasm-festooned "d(ep)ressing rooms. I was very conscious of the fact that I could be enjoying a beer by the river in the early evening sunshine - only half a mile down the road - but we were trapped. No-one had a car and I didn't fancy my chances of making it through the many fans who were outside waiting for the doors to open.

The sun blazed in through the windows of the depressing room as the boys in the band hung around, totally absorbed in their laptops and palm-pilots. (Choose life, I say...) Meanwhile I became increasingly frustrated. Strasbourg's River Ill continued to beckon.

And so showtime edged slowly towards us while I read every pathetic declaration on every square-inch of the four walls and ceiling. I went to have a listen to Robin Boult - our opening act - who was playing brilliantly as usual down on stage. He finished his set and came upstairs commenting that the sound on stage was very dead. He wasn't wrong.

We descended to the stage. The heat was very intense down there.

At centre-stage my sound had altered completely from soundcheck. Totally dry – like being in a wardrobe full of feathers. During the show I struggled with the sound of my voice and tried to improve it by singing harder – eventually singing myself hoarse. The heat was exhausting. Every now and again a combination of influences in a show can bring-about the downward spiral into frustration, self-loathing and general irritation. Unfortunately, tonight was to be "one of those"... I had to fight myself to remain on stage. There was nothing wrong with the crowd – I was just having a bad night and my voice wasn't working properly. Didn't feel much like going back on for the first encore so the band jammed while I was getting my head together. It was a good jam and I had half a mind to leave 'em to it, but after a while it sounded like they were waiting for me so I went on to sing *Waiting to Happen* and *Between You and Me*, and things started to pull in an upward direction. By the end of encore 2 I think I'd gone some way towards redeeming myself, but I came off stage in a bit of a state and sat in the shower tray with my head between my knees for almost an hour. At least the water was warm.

The problem with touring is that, after a few weeks, every aspect of the performance has a tendency to feel automatic and mechanical. I start to feel like a performing dog and I worry that all sincerity and inspiration has been "repeated" out of it. This paranoia sometimes stifles me mentally and physically and I have to find ways of keeping it real and getting a vibe going. At Strasbourg I failed totally. C'est la vie. So, all in all, it had been a great day ruined by a bad show from yours truly. You can't win 'em all... but you can try. Must try harder.

Got back on the bus around 2.00 and went to bed under a cloud. It was still too hot...

Tuesday 11 September *Coniston, 9/11*

Got up around half-seven and saw Sofie and Nial off to school before packing my things and climbing into the car around 9.00 for the drive North to the Lake District and Coniston. I have been invited by Gina Campbell to sing at the funeral of her father, Donald Campbell, tomorrow. Today Stewart and I will head North and set up our sound-equipment in the church, so that I can have a run-through and check everything will work okay on the big day.

It was a pleasant drive – the weather was fine and the traffic, even on the terrible M6, was fairly mobile. I arrived in Coniston village around 1.00 and saw the red van already unloaded in the churchyard. Stewart said he needed a little more time before he would be ready for me, so I wandered across the road for a half in the pub opposite. The bar-girl asked me what brought me to Coniston and I explained that I was here for tomorrow's funeral of the great man. "Personally, I fink it's not right," she said, "I fink they should of left him alone in the lake instead of draggin 'im around like this."

I returned to the church where Stewart was all ready to go. He had set up a mic at the front of the church on the raised steps leading to the altar. He played the track and I sang over it while he ran around the church, listening and adjusting levels and eq. It was all sounding pretty good so we thought we'd have another run-through for luck. Half-way through the song, Gina appeared at the back of the church and I felt my emotions surge as I realized the importance of this song in her presence. I fought the tears down and finished the song whereupon she clapped and told me she thought it was perfect. So far, so good – I still have the real thing to get through tomorrow with a packed church full of the "great and good", and, of course, the few mortal-remains of the man himself. Gina said she'd see us back at the Windermere powerboat Club and departed.

I suggested to Stewart that we pop back over the road for a pub-lunch, so the two of us ordered sausage and Yorkshire pudding and sat down to wait for it to arrive. When it came it was great, and we chomped our way through excellent sausage while Stewart told me he had the flu and felt dreadful. We were about to get up and leave when I overheard a voice coming from the television in the adjoining room:

"People are jumping from the windows of the upper floors..."

At first I thought it must be a movie or some work of fiction, but the tone in the narrator's voice sounded too real. Oh God, I thought – the stock-market has crashed... Stewart and I got up and walked into the adjoining room to look at the TV...

Well, the rest is history. We stood open-mouthed and unbelieving at the sight that greeted us. The World Trade Centre in New York stood in the centre of the TV screen belching black smoke from its upper floors as a TV caption beneath read "Plane crashes into World Trade Centre". As we looked on, a second passenger airliner banked at an impossible angle over the city, and hit the sister-tower like a guided missile, which, of course, is exactly what it, and its passengers and crew, had become. Heaping disbelief upon disbelief we watched as the caption read "south tower has collapsed" and shortly after, "north tower has now also collapsed". Then there appeared a close up of the upper floors and the tall roof mast descending into a cloud of thick dust as we watched the tower descend vertically down into itself and the ground. The TV now announced unconfirmed rumours of attacks on the Pentagon and more aircraft hi-jacked. Despite the feeling that reality was slipping away, I felt an appalling rational train of thought take over me... "I'm too old to be conscripted, and my children are too young. Thank God." Could this be the beginning of the third world war? Nostradamus's "...third, and most terrible, war" which "will come from the East"?

I really wanted to go home. But today, I can't.

We emerged into the street in a daze and drove to Hawkshead where a ferry takes you across Lake Windermere to the Windermere-side where the Powerboat Club is situated. I'm not sure that I should have been driving. I was in something of a daze. Richard Crichlow - head of BBC news - called to say that he wouldn't be coming to Coniston after-all and that he was making a U-turn on the M6 to return to London. Looks like Donald Campbell's funeral won't make it onto tomorrow night's news bulletins. Oh well. It would have been churlish in the extreme to reflect on the fact that I had lost yet-another rare chance to sing on prime-time national television, but it was hard to push the thought away, no matter how despicable it seemed.

We arrived at the Windermere Powerboat Club and were allocated a room by John, the manager. Gina had arranged a twin-room for Stewart and me. It was simply furnished but had a huge bay window with a fantastic view of the lake and the hills beyond. We moved our things in, before making our way downstairs to the bar for a much-needed drink. Despite tomorrow's singing, I broke a sacred rule and ordered a large Scotch – I needed it.

Gina's chums from Leeds started arriving. We all sat outside on the terrace overlooking the banks of the lake and talked incredulously about the mad events of the day, whilst getting increasingly well-oiled. This only added to my sense of the surreal. Around 6.00 Gina and her partner, Marshall, arrived and we all came inside to the bar. Red wine was ordered and, despite my efforts to take it easy, everything began to slip further away. We asked if there was any chance of a spot of dinner and John said that his wife (an excellent cook, we were to discover) could prepare us some cod. When it was ready we were led through to the dining room where we were served an excellent evening meal. My sense of the truly-bizarre deepened still further when Marshall produced a ukulele-banjo and led us all in a sing-song of some old music-hall tunes.

So there I was, in a Power-Boat Club, overlooking Lake Windermere, singing *You Are My Sunshine* to the accompaniment of a ukulele in the full-knowledge that there was now a pile of rubble in Manhattan where the World Trade Centre used to be, preparing myself for the following day when I would sing *Out Of This World* in church at Donald Campbell's funeral service, and contemplating the fairly real possibility that World War 3 was imminent. I'm afraid that was as much of a day as I could cope with, so I made my excuses and retired to bed.

On TV in the room were endless images of carnage, fire-balls, dust clouds, and long shots of Manhattan enveloped in what looked like a nuclear explosion, while horrific fact and conjecture vied for my attention. Enough. I slept fitfully, woken periodically by nightmares which were true when I woke up, and panic-attacks at the thought that maybe I wouldn't have a voice in the morning. I kept getting up and staggering around in the darkness, trying to drink water from a glass which I couldn't find, and not wanting to wake-up Stewart who seemed to be having much less trouble sleeping than I.

What an awful day.

Wednesday 12 September   *Coniston, Donald Campbell's Funeral*

For the umpteenth time I had woken and stared into space. It was 7.45. Stewart had set an alarm clock for 8.00, so I waited until 8.00am rolled around and then I sang "beep, beep, beep, beep!" so that he could switch it off before it started. I hate alarm clocks, especially those quartz beepy ones. We both staggered around, shaving and showering and cleaning teeth, while I tried to decide whether to get my posh clothes on for the funeral, or wait until I'd had breakfast.

I was still in a considerable state of reality-slip as I arrived at the breakfast-table to find most of Gina's chums already seated. There was a selection of morning papers laid out on the table. All my previous night's bad dreams captured in technicolour stills. I couldn't read them. I wondered by what percentage newspaper-sales have increased this morning. On days like these, newspapers should be free. It seems wrong to charge people money to read reports of devastation on this scale. I ordered poached-egg on toast and tried my damnedest (successfully – for once!) to consume it without spilling egg down my white shirt.

Stewart and I were first to leave, around 9.30, returning to Coniston again via the Hawkshead Ferry. Radio 5 Live crackled away on the medium wave as my car-radio struggled to receive the signal amid the hills. More horror, more conjecture. Much talk of prime-suspect Osama Bin-Laden who, despite denying his part in yesterday's massacre, seems to be the man they all blame. How do they know?

Drove off the ferry in the pouring rain wondering whether the cruise-missiles are already on their way to Afghanistan. In Consiton, there was nowhere to park so I left the car in a side-street so that I could get to the church without getting my clothes totally drenched. An old dear opened a bathroom window to warn me: "You'll get a ticket if you leave that there!" I daresay she'd be on the phone to the police as soon as I'd walked away. Oh well. Today, parking-tickets aren't even on my radar.

Inside the church, Stewart and I managed to make a quick and final soundcheck. To my immense relief the voice was working. Well, we've prepared enough! It's all down to my nerve holding now, and to Don't ghost not fiddling with the controls... (Dave Meegan (producer, *Afraid of Sunlight*) was quite certain Don's ghost fiddled constantly with the technology when we originally recorded the song).

I managed to borrow a brolly from a chap called Novvy and walked up the steep lane to the Sun Hotel where I had arranged to meet Bill Smith for a drink at 10.45. I was a little late, and seemed to have missed everybody, but at least I found a space in the car-park, so I returned to the car and drove back to the Sun where I knew it would be safe from Supergran and the long-arm of the law.

As the rain lashed down I returned to the church under Novvy's brolly. A crowd had started to gather outside and policemen huddled and chatted together amongst a riot of umbrellas. I made my way into the church and to my place on the left-hand end of the third pew from the front. Now came the long wait as Stewart played Mozart's 17th and 21st concerti for piano and orchestra. The congregation arrived in two's and three's. In front of me, various Lords and Lord-Lieutenants. To my side, the family of Robbie Robinson – Donald's closest surviving friend. Gina had organized a male-voice choir and they arrived, noisily shuffling seats and pews until they were comfortable and prepared. Mike

Rossiter (who directed the BBC's documentary about Bill's search for the Bluebird) arrived and sat down in the pew behind me. I said hello and we exchanged insincere pleasantries. I never asked him why there was no mention of our song in his documentary, or why he failed to reply to, or acknowledge my letter to him.

Time passed, and around 1.30, the cortege arrived. Donald's coffin, draped with the Union flag, had come to us first by launch across Coniston via the crash-site, and then by horse and carriage. Bill Smith and the rest of the pall-bearers were visibly soddened by the heavy rain as they slowly brought Donald to rest before the altar before taking their places. Behind came Gina and Marshall along with Donald's widow, Tonia. The service commenced with a succession of hymns – all very traditional and churchy, and a minute's silence in honour of yesterday's victims of what was becoming known as "9/11". More hymns and a recital by the male choir followed. I began to feel that a performance of a rock epic might seem terribly out of place here and my nervousness multiplied as the seconds passed. I was to follow the tribute to Donald's life, which was to be made by Robbie. And what a perfect tribute it was, a heartfelt and sincere acknowledgement of Donald's life's work and character, by a man not normally given to public speaking, who portrayed his friend as a modest and decent bloke - his voice only cracking towards the end, when he said "I'm sure that Donald has finally found his bluebird of happiness. No one deserves it more."

The vicar then introduced me, and I was up. I managed not to fall over the flowers or the step, and I stood at the mic, with Donald's coffin at my side and Donald's lovely daughter before me. I thought, "Better get it right, then!" as the intro-music of *Out Of This World* came up through the monitors and my heart pounded.

I held it together all the way to the last line ("…everything that she said") which I choked on a little. My, my, it was a relief to have finished. No one clapped, of course, so it was impossible to know the feeling from the people. Stewart gave me an encouraging nod as I passed him to sit back down, so I figured it must have been at least okay.

The remainder of the service passed by in a bit of a dream until it was over, and the coffin was carried down the aisle once more. I was heartened and touched by the number of people who later went out of their way to tell me they had enjoyed my song – one woman saying she had goosebumps throughout.

I emerged into the street and followed the cortege through Coniston village to a graveyard some distance from the church. It was raining hard now, and amidst the crowd of umbrellas, the scene before me couldn't have been more poignant and funereal if it had been carefully scripted and designed for a feature film. At the graveside the umbrellas clashed together and water dripped into the collar of my jacket as the flag was removed from the coffin to reveal a dark blue casket, which was lowered into the ground. I had the honour of being among those to cast a handful of soil onto the casket. I privately said goodbye and wished him well as I did so. All this to a man I never knew.

And so, for me, another strange cycle was complete. I wrote some words inspired by a childhood memory, which were to result in a woman being able to bury her lost father, and in a national-hero finding his way to rest. I felt like going home now, but I had promised to return to Windermere to have tea with Gina, and to attend a dinner in the evening. I phoned home as I walked back into Coniston. Sue still seemed shaken by the events yesterday in America, so I decided I would return home after tea in Windermere. Back at the boat-club I drank tea and ate scones while a great many people, including the Lords and Ladies, had the decency to shake my hand and thank me for singing. Most memorable was old Ken Norris, who designed the Bluebird K7 (to run at speeds up to 250mph on water - not 300!) who shook my hand and said a somewhat-distracted thank you. I said a brief hello/cheerio to Tonia.

I waited nervously to apologize to Gina for my early departure. It was difficult to catch her alone, of course, but I eventually butted in and explained why I felt I must go. She hugged me in thanks and told me the song had been "just right".

Well, I was only there for Gina and Don, so I went away happy.

Magically, the weather had changed totally and the sun was shining from a clear blue sky as I drove away from the boat club for the long journey south, and homeward.

2 0 0 2

Thursday 28 November *Studio – Manchester*

Arrived at the studio at 9pm with a jeep full of clothes.

No sign of a bus, but the doors were open and there were flight cases and equipment of various shapes and sizes strewn about outside the open workshop door. Said hello to Erik, Colin and Rod and wandered inside to the lounge where monitor man Phil Brown was watching Liverpool FC on the telly. Exchanged greetings and chatted for a while, before going upstairs in search of a few more items of stage-wear. The bus was running late so I decided to go to the pub, have a pint and read the newspapers. Interesting reading about MI5 documents declassified today. Oswald Mosley married his wife Diane in Goebells front room! Now there's something I didn't know. Aren't the British aristocracy a bundle of laughs?

Returned to the Racket Club at 10.45 where the bus was now parked. Transferred all my bits and bobs and had a beer whilst not really watching the remake of **Ocean's Eleven** on the video in the upper back lounge.

Found a copy of Vogue and a copy of Jane Austen's **Pride and Prejudice** in the cupboard above my bunk - must have been girls on this bus before us, then... I can't really see most rock n'roll bands getting off on Mr. D'Arcy coming out of a pond with his shirt all wet. Still, y'never know with artists – I went through a phase of reading Vogue and the classics mi-self.

Chas and Roy (Cry No More) are with us for this short Xmas tour and it was good to see them again. Roy confessed to never having been on a tour bus before... I bet he doesn't sleep! Action-movies tend to bore the pants off me so I didn't hang around for very long before turning in. Didn't sleep terribly well - it always takes a couple of nights to get into the swing of bus life. We're only travelling to Manchester. There's something wrong with the gearbox of the bus and there's a grinding juddering sound whenever the driver changes gear. Not conducive to a good night's sleep...

Friday 29 November *Manchester Academy*

Woke up for the 105th time outside Manchester Academy. I think I felt the bus park up before I was properly asleep. Forgot to bring a pillow! Aaargh! I'll buy YET ANOTHER one tomorrow. That's three in two months! Soon you won't be able to get into our house for pillows...

Outside it wasn't raining (unusual for Manchester!) and I could see the crew stamping around waiting for the venue to open the doors and let us in. Normally you'd expect to be inside a venue by 9.30 am, and it was long-past ten. In the end no-one showed up 'til 11.00. Great. I wandered round the corner and found a café where I had a couple of coffees and chatted to Rothers who was already ensconced with his nose behind a magazine. Steve devours technology mags with a voracity way-beyond obsession. I often take the mickey...

2004

Monday 19 April *(or thereabouts...)*

Went to bed and watched Al Pacino who had made a film about Shakespeare, and Richard the third. You can't help liking him. (Pacino, that is). Woke up several times in the night – too hot, too cold and wondering what time it is until I decided to get up and shower at 8.30. I hadn't had chance to shower yesterday - I had a train to catch and I'd left it all too late - so it felt good to be under the water and feel wholesome again before the rigours of the day.

We're supposed to be in Aylesbury in production rehearsals for the **Marbles** tour, but we're in Hilversum, Holland doing **Top of The Pops**. Great things are happening here at the moment. We're number 8 in the chart – Marillion's biggest hit single ever here. I was on the front page of the **Telegraaf** yesterday and Radio 2 here have just added our single *You're Gone* to the playlist. There's a good chance that the single will carry on up the Dutch chart and be even higher next week! I had breakfast with Steve and Ian. Steve's on the Atkins diet and is complaining that he is now living almost entirely on eggs. I have therefore christened him Cool Hand Luke. We left the hotel at 9.30 in two separate cars and got half way to the TV station before we realized we'd left Steve at the hotel. Each car assumed the other had him! We decided to carry on and then send a car back for him later... When we arrived at the TV station it became apparent that most of the hired equipment had failed to turn up. No drum-kit, no bass guitar and no amplifiers. Oh well... We were shown downstairs to a dressing room and then on to make-up where Monique from Eindhoven, used an airbrush on my face. Well that's a first. I've heard of having your imperfections airbrushed out but this was literal. The sensation of cold air and a fine liquid spray was really pleasant and must be particularly so on a hot day. I also persuaded Monique to lend me some black greasepaint to put on my boots, which were in need of a polish after scuffing them round London yesterday.

We hung around waiting for equipment to come together before we could soundcheck. I'm singing a live vocal while the band mime to a playback of the single. Through the dressing room wall I could hear the sounds of an orchestra rehearsing somewhere so I set off in the general direction of the music to see if I could sit in and watch them play. Up a few flights of stairs and along a few of the corridors in this maze of a place, after a few wrong turns I found the source of the music and opened a door into a large studio where, sure enough, an orchestra was playing. They finished playing just after I sneaked in and so I clapped. Everyone stared and the reaction was mixed. Some of the players smiled while some gazed at me in a nonplussed fashion. The conductor stared for a moment over his glasses before turning back to his sheet music in order to ready himself for the next piece. Everyone was now practicing different things at once and there was a quiet anarchy of strings, woodwind and muted brass as the conductor shuffled his manuscripts. After a few minutes he tapped his baton and all fell quiet apart from a clarinet player who was duly admonished in Dutch by the lead violinist. Discipline has to be tight when there's 40 or more people involved. I shudder to imagine how anyone could ever make sense of the process if they were all as wayward as the five of us. (I have often likened our creative process to five 5-year-old's building a nuclear reactor). The orchestra once again began to play the most exquisite introduction to another piece of music. Being unaware of all but the most popular classical works, I have no idea what they were playing except that it was beautiful but at the same time, not terribly memorable. I didn't hear a melody that I could carry away in my memory. I listened til the end and then decided against risking anyone's wrath by clapping again. I slipped out and back to our dressing room where it was soon time to go down to the TV studio to soundcheck.

We were shown the way to studio 4 which was a huge space with two different **TOTP** stages in it and a mass of big TV lights hanging up in the high, dark ceiling. We were being recorded alone as they had moved the recording time from evening to morning in order to fit us in today, so there were no other artists around.

Soundcheck was uncomplicated – sound man, René introduced himself and gave me a good balance between the backing track and my voice. I'm singing okay despite the hour of day – I'm not usually at my best before mid-afternoon. We returned to the dressing room for a little more hanging-around, which I used up by listening to the backing track of *You're Gone*. It's been edited for TV, so I was double-checking I knew the arrangement so I sang in the right places. When we were asked to return to the stage for camera-check, I was just commenting to the band that it was a shame there was no audience in the studio when about 25 of our Dutch fans snaked into the studio and were herded to the back of the room beyond the cameras. I waved at them from a distance before studio-floor-manager Jean-Marc told us that they were happy to record the song now. They made one run through and then they took one take, and that was that. By now it was 12.40 and time was getting tight for our return flight to England, so we wasted no time in getting our bags together and leaving the building. Said hello to the fans on the way out and then climbed aboard the mini bus where driver, Patrick, was waiting to take us back to Schipol airport.

Back at Schipol we queued to check in at the Easyjet counter (the band's paying for the flights!) as I pondered once again how many times I have been in this place in the grip of terrible hangovers. It made a nice change to be here feeling healthy. The check-in girl must have been having one of those days as she insisted on weighing our hand-luggage and then refused to let me or Pete carry on our bags. We reluctantly checked them in after removing our laptops – you wouldn't want baggage-handlers anywhere near those... We went through security and then straight down to gate D04. Schipol is HUGE and I've learnt to go to the gate in plenty of time for the flight as it can often take up to 20 minutes to walk there. Once at the gate, there was time to kill so I went to a nearby bar with Pete for a sandwich and a cup of tea. Ian eventually appeared and told us that the gate had now been changed to gate 20. Went to Gate 20 to discover that it doesn't exist! After more wandering around, we were told that the gate was D04 after all. Returned to D04 to be told it was Gate 22. Ah, the joys of flying – give me a tour bus any day. Having finally established that we were at the right gate, I began work on today's diary until the flight was boarding.

Slept most of the flight. Well, not exactly "slept" – nodded around like a zombie in the upright position, while the plane buffeted around in turbulence caused by some pretty thick rain-clouds. Back in lovely Luton airport, we walked across the tarmac in the rain and into the terminal to pick up bags. Ian offered to give me a lift to Aylesbury, so we made our way to the car park and eventually took our place in a traffic jam on the A41. Ian wanted to drop in at his house in Tring on the way to Aylesbury as he was concerned about reports of water coming through the kitchen ceiling... When we got there, all looked fine – no flooding and the kitchen ceiling hadn't fallen in. I felt pretty tired by now so I persuaded him to make me a quick coffee before we set-off again for Aylesbury. We arrived behind Aylesbury Civic around 5.00pm and we bumped straight into our old chum and truck-driver for the tour, Simon Lake. I gave him a cuddle and made my way into the building.

I had had the bright idea of opening today's production rehearsals to The Front Row Club (our ultra-fan club for the really hardcore fans) so there were already a number of people hanging around and generally milling around in the building. I found my way to a dressing room and then onto the stage. We are using in-ear monitors for the first time ever today. These are moulded devices, which are placed inside the ear canal. They contain small diaphragms which project the sound directly to the ear drum, much like walkman earphones, only better and, of course, *much* dearer. The user wears a radio receiver belt-pack, which receives the signal from the monitor desk, so a mix of the entire band can be fed to the in-ears. Using this system for the first time was going to take some perseverance and care so I worked with Phil Brown - our monitor engineer - to try and set up a mix that I could work with. Everything gradually came together and the band and I slowly worked our way through the new set of songs from **Marbles**. This was to take the rest of the evening until around 10.30 when we moved on to the older songs. There was an 11 o'clock sound curfew so we had to stop at 11.00, which was just as well, really. It had been a LONG day.

I was given a lift home by Adrian Tredinnick, who had been hanging out at the gig and was going to stay over at our house. He took me to King's Sutton station so I could pick up my car, which had been left there yesterday when I took the train to London for my interviews at Broadcasting House, and then the long journey to Holland.

Sunday 2 May   *Tilburg 013*

Woken many times in the middle of the night by the colossal roar of someone snoring very close to me. "Snoring" doesn't really describe the sound adequately – I lay in the darkness trying to articulate the noise that was rattling the entire bus in an almost **Looney Tunes** cartoon fashion. I settled on: A water-buffalo in labour, with a bad adenoidal problem. This, however, remains an understatement. As I lay there trying to believe what I was hearing, a general chorus of more snoring, groaning, wheezing and occasional distant farting was added to the symphony. I was reminded of the "beans round the camp-fire" scene from Mel Brooks' movie **Blazing Saddles**. My amusement was tempered somewhat by the desire to be asleep and the worrying fact that we have many nights ahead of us in this situation... I screwed my fingers into my ears and tried to put the zoo-symphony out of my mind, but it was no good. In the end I gave up and got up. It was 5.45. I went downstairs and put the kettle on. It wasn't long before other people started appearing. Tour manager Quinner arrived first, closely followed by drum-tech Rich. We all marvelled at the intense snoring above and discussed the amazing fact that it was possible for a human being to generate such sound pressure levels without actually stripping the skin from their throats during the night.

Outside in Tilburg it was already light and already a nice day. The sky was clear and the streets deserted. It seemed unusually quiet, even for 6am, until I remembered that this is Sunday and hardly anyone would be going to work. I further remembered that yesterday had been Queen's Day (not a huge gay-parade but a Dutch national holiday and annual celebration day) and that the nation would probably be a little slow off the mark this morning. This was a shame for me as I really wanted to wander into town and find a nice café to have breakfast and write my diary which was already getting a little behind. Keeping this thing going is a bit of a chore and takes up my few precious spare hours during each day.

Around 9.00 I got off the bus to make my way into the centre of town only to discover that the bus was locked into a secure area of the venue surrounded by a high fence and all doors to the outside were securely locked. I contemplated climbing over but was discouraged by the pointed anti-personnel spikes at the top. Normally, I'd have gone for it, but it's too risky to chance a twisted ankle or sprained wrist on the first day of a long tour, so sense prevailed (for once). As I stood at the railings contemplating (once again) a caged existence, our huge silver "Stage Truck" arrived out in the street and Simon Lake glided the articulated lorry into place on the pavement – always an impressive feat to see trucks and trailers reversing and manoeuvring into tight spots. He jumped out and we exchanged greetings and I asked him if he'd had a good journey. He'd been here since yesterday when the celebrations were raging. He had to park the truck out of town, so he'd missed the revelry. Quinner went back to the bus to get him a cup of tea, which was duly passed through the bars of the railings. It was like visiting day in prison. Simon phoned the guy who was to open up the gig for us to load in and he arrived ten minutes later with a large bunch of keys. After a brief examination of the big metal gate to the compound he mused "Oh! It's open!" and slid the gate soundlessly sideways. Mirth ensued as we all realized we hadn't been locked in at all and had spent the last hour conversing between the bars of an unlocked gate. "*These chains are all your own... This cage was never locked*" tee hee. Suddenly free, and a little embarrassed, I wandered into town.

I like Tilburg. It's very modern, but it's designed for people to enjoy outdoor café life. There's a large square where you can sit out and drink coffee, have a bite to eat and enjoy the fresh air. Between the square and the 013 (gig) is a pedestrianized street lined with bars and cafés where people meet and relax. I thought perhaps just one of these might be open for breakfast... Wrong. I walked all over Tilburg and couldn't find any signs of life at all so I returned to the gig. By now the truck was being unloaded. I chatted more with Simon Lake who showed me pictures of the canal-boat he lives on when he's not on the road. He has abandoned his regular gig as head truck driver for the big Peter Gabriel tour in order to come and do what he "likes doing best" – us. What a top chap. I'm very flattered.

I left it another hour and then tried again to find a bar, which would make me breakfast. I eventually succeeded and ordered Outsmeiter - fried egg, ham and cheese on bread - and coffee. Just what the doctor ordered. I wrote the diary until the battery was low on the laptop and then returned to the show to wash some shirts and have a shower. Said hello to the support band, Gazpacho, who had arrived from Norway and then returned to the bus to catch up on much-needed sleep following last night's barnyard 'entertainment'. Woke up in time for soundcheck, which passed without incident. Rothers says he's heard from someone that our single is now number 2 in the Dutch charts! Couldn't believe it. Just as well; it later turned out that this is the Free Records/Pepsi Chart, not the official national chart. Either way, it's still great to be number 2 somewhere in something! Discovered a great photograph of us outside the catering room downstairs – something the kitchen staff had taken last time. Had dinner (pork and potatoes) and went back to bed again.

Woke at 8.30 and got into my stage-clothes for the gig.

Gig went pretty well for the first half. For the second set, Erik re-plugged a couple of leads round the wrong way which meant that the loops channel and the effects channel of Mark's samplers were swapped around. This caused Mosley-the-cat untold monitor trouble and he was deeply unimpressed at the end of the show. At one point I thought he was going to punch Mark... I mediated and tried to calm him down. I think he'd be better off with in-ears and anti-depressants – works great for me!

Monday 3 May *Utrecht Muziekcentrum*

The bus had been stationary for most of the night after a pretty short journey from Tilburg. I woke about 10.00 and pulled back my little curtain to confirm we were in fact in Utrecht outside the Vredenberg Muziekzentrum. We've played here many times before and never been disappointed with the experience - it's a great sounding venue and we can always rely on a good crowd, Utrecht being home to a great hardcore Marillion following. I made my way down to the dressing room and did a bit of laundry. I had the idea of bringing a tumble-drier out on the road this tour. This means we can wash our clothes in the sink and they'll be dry after one hour. Something as insignificant as this can completely transform the touring experience. When you're constantly travelling and sleeping on a bus, an endless supply of clean clothes - especially underwear and socks - becomes a great luxury and makes the whole process much more pleasant. Being able to wash stage clothes is also terrific. In the past, I would go on stage some nights wearing the same unwashed shirt that I'd worn for the previous three nights and feeling rather grubby and grateful that the front row wasn't close enough to share the pong. The alternative was to send laundry out with the 'runner' who would return later to declare that the launderettes were all closed, or (even worse, but fairly often...) would return with one of my precious £200 white shirts now died a dirty grey or pink colour. I have now learned that - as in all things in life - if you care for it, you'd better not let anyone else look after it. Our careers are living proof of this also. But I digress...

We installed the tumble-drier in a neighbouring dressing room and I loaded in my wet laundry with a glow of pride. It's the little things...

Dizzy txted me earlier to say that there was torrential rain in England so I hardly had the heart to tell her that the weather is beautiful here in Utrecht – mild and sunshiny. I decided to go out, don my sun specs and have a beer and a spot of lunch by the canal. I prefer Utrecht to Amsterdam – it has the same quintessentially Dutch system of canals, which snake through the town, but it's smaller, cleaner, and a little more peaceful. On a sunny day you can watch the world go by in the street and on the water, and the Dutch are a little more colourful than the English, so there's always something to catch the eye and to amuse.

I returned to the gig for an interview at 3.30 and as I arrived I bumped into a man with a surreal and mad painting. It all suddenly made sense. He's called Mark and he wrote an email to me a while back saying his paintings had been inspired by our music and also enclosing his web address where I could go and view his work. I had a look and I liked it. It's abstract and slightly mad in a very primitive way. Quite aboriginal, in fact. I had replied and told him I liked his stuff and he had promptly written back and said he'd like to make us a present of one of his paintings, so I arranged for him to come to the Utrecht show. Since then, of course, I'd completely forgotten all about it until now when the sight of the painting titled *Welcome To Your First Afterlife Party* had reminded me of all this. I think it'll look great on the studio wall.

Made an interview with the Web Holland before soundchecking. I'm slowly getting used to the in-ears. Everyone says I'm singing better than ever. I've also found that I'm not getting nearly as vocally strained as I used to and that I'm hitting all the high notes. After the show, I still feel like I have plenty left, and I don't wake up in the morning feeling hoarse either. Now I know why so many singers have used in-ears for so long.

Well, the show went brilliantly. I'm starting to communicate more with the audience now that I'm settling down with the new show, and the response from them was marvellous. After the show I mingled for a bit with the aftershow guests and with Sjaak from the Dutch distribution company, but I felt pretty washed out so I made excuses and left for an early-ish night. Sleeping a lot better since I started using earplugs to filter out the colossal snoring!

Tuesday 4 May *Zwolle Ijsselhallen*

Enjoyed a lie-in for the first time in months. Slept almost uninterrupted until 1pm. What a luxury! Looking out of my little bus window, I could see an uninviting car park, seemingly in the middle of nowhere, so I was in no particular hurry to explore the area.

Eventually rose and made my way into a huge hangar of a place where the equipment was already up and running on a large stage at one end. It was colder inside than outside and, like most empty buildings of this type and size, pretty gloomy and depressing. Had a coffee, showered and said a few words to an interviewer from Holland's Radio 1, before persuading someone to give me a lift into town so I could find a café and catch up with the diary. I'm now sitting in an upstairs tea-room above a pastry shop – the kind of place favoured by old-ladies for hot-chocolates and cream cakes in the afternoon. I'm overlooking the main square and shopping street. This is an infinitely preferable experience to hanging around in a shed out of town, and yet I'm sure it won't occur to the rest of the band to go anywhere else. I just don't understand this particular characteristic of 'em. Over the years we have travelled to many different places on earth and I have walked the streets and haunted the cafés whilst most of the band remained firmly anchored to some depressing dressing room somewhere, happy to spend the day reading or playing on some computer-game. Perhaps it's the fear of getting lost. Or tiring yourself out… Oh well, to each, his own.

I spent an hour in the café before meeting up with the runner who took me back to the gig for soundcheck. Up on the stage the band were debating a change of set. *Estonia* was added, and also *Cover My Eyes*. It was one of those soundchecks that drags on for hours and re-established the unique Marillion tradition of soundchecking for longer than the show itself…

Afterwards we had a buffet dinner. All the big plates had gone so I spread my meal across two small plates …and that's the most interesting thing that happened to me all day!

Until the show, that is. We're still improving steadily at this stage of the tour and as I start to feel secure with the music I can turn my attentions more to remaining close to the crowd. I believe that an audience is a kind of energy-ball and that my most important job is to connect to it and to sustain it. This may sound a bit "hippy" as a concept, but experience has shown it to be true. I can feed the energy simply by performing into it. When I'm distracted, I perform into myself and then the audience can only witness what I do, instead of feeling part of it. When I connect to it, then everyone becomes part of it, and so they connect to each other through me and that's when a really great vibe happens in the room. Unfortunately, the connection can be broken at any moment when something distracts me, and I now have so much to do, that the potential for distraction is huge. Little things - like knowing the running order of the set – and having a "second nature" understanding of the chords I need to play on the piano and guitar, make it much easier to stay 'in the energy'. This is why it takes a few shows to get it all going. I'm playing acoustic guitar on a few songs including *Don't Hurt Yourself* where I provide the backbone of the song. The fact that I'm not really a guitarist, and that the change from E-minor to B-minor is fairly tricky, means I need every last ounce of concentration (and luck) to get through it. But each night I feel it getting better and easier. The Zwolle show was great. I was in and out of the energy, but, for the final encore, *Cover My Eyes* gave me the chance to concentrate solely on it and the response was like a tidal wave. I forgot to put my in-ear monitors in, and this was to be a happy accident as I could suddenly hear the massive sound of everyone in the room singing the intro as one voice. Every hand was raised and clapping, all the way to the back. This is what it's all about.

Wednesday 5 May *Berlin:* Day Off

Woke up around 10.00 and made my way to the front of the bus where Paul Rowlston was already sitting. It was a beautiful blue day as the bus edged its' way along one of Berlin's main Boulevards (Strasse des 17 Juni – yes, I know it's French – apparently something to do with cannon that were captured from

Napoleon...) towards the Brandenburg Gate. We chatted and Paul filmed the interesting monuments that passed on our way past the B Gate and the "new" Reichstag on our way to find the hotel. Today is a day off so I agreed to meet up with Paul and Jayce for an interview later. We decided to do it at the famous Berlin zoo. I said I'd call Paul when I was ready... ("ready for what's next", eh, Bono?)

When we arrived at the hotel we were told that rooms *weren't* ready so I sat myself down in the hotel-bar and ordered up coffee while writing this diary. Time passed and Quinner kept appearing to say that my room still wasn't ready, but it didn't really matter as I had much catching up to do with the diary anyway.

Around 2pm I finally entered room 427 and took a much-anticipated shower before trying to find something in English on the TV. The choices were CNN News (American propaganda channel) or BBC World (something approaching the truth with anything too contentious edited out). Incidentally, I'm told that most Americans consider CNN to be dangerously left wing... Many consider Fox news (or George Bush TV, as its better described) to represent the "balanced" view. Blimey!

I relaxed for a while on the bed but in the end I didn't really have time to sleep as I'd arranged to meet Paul and Jayce at 3.00pm. We took the train to the zoo station and walked through the corridors with U2's song of the same name buzzing around in my head ("I'm ready, I'm ready for the laughing gas... I'm ready for what's next..."). Just outside the station was a stall selling fresh fish. Paul wondered whether they might have some "fantastic plaice" ...Funny at the time. Fish jokes abounded for a further 10 minutes...

Berlin zoo came as a pleasant surprise – it's really beautiful – a big late-nineteenth century park, full of flowers and trees. Many of the animals aren't caged, but simply separated from the public by wide, deep, ditches. This gives the place a very natural atmosphere. The dangerous cats are caged, of course, but one look at the Jaguars and Leopards and I was very grateful for the bars. I marvelled at the Indian Rhinoceros – bigger and more heavily "armour plated" than it's African counterpart according to Paul and Jayce... and they should know – they've seen em coming up the street (or so they said...).   Not long after we arrived, the weather took a turn and it began to rain pretty hard, so we retired to the restaurant where I ordered up what turned out to be bright-green beer and sour-cherry ice-cream. We set up under a parasol outside by the duck pond and I was interviewed by Paul as Jayce rolled the camera. The green beer tasted of beer with a slight undercurrent of pickled onions and asparagus... Hmm. The ice cream was better. While Jayce changed tapes, Paul returned to the restaurant to buy me something more conventional and returned with a bottle of Pilsner lager, which tasted slightly of fish! ...Must be a Berlin thing. Or maybe they left it too near to the penguin food.

The weather gradually improved during the interview so we went for a wander through the zoo. I don't think I've ever seen a giant-panda before in the flesh. What an amazing creature - a look of pure madness in its eyes (I don't suppose I'd have been too sane if put in the same position...). We passed flamingos so orange-pink that they glowed in the daylight, and on past American bison (more U2 imagery – you can tell they recorded Achtung Baby here alright). Around 6.30 it was chucking-out time so we made our way back to the station and then took another train back to the hotel. I returned to my room and decided to have a snooze. Big mistake, I woke at 10.30pm – too late to eat, too awake to go to bed, nothing on the telly except **Intolerable Cruelty** – a Coen brothers attempt to make George Clooney funny. They failed. I turned it off after half an hour.

Went downstairs and found Ian, Mark, Quinner and Ian Bond, just finishing dinner. Hung out with them for an hour over a beer and then ordered a hot chocolate to try and get myself back in the mood for going to bed.

Returned to the room and wrote the diary for another hour before forcing myself back to sleep. Days off on tour are always a bit of a struggle.

Thursday 6 May *Berlin Columbiafritz*

Woke up at 9.00 and decided that, lovely as it is, I'd had enough of room 427, so I showered, packed and left the hotel at 10.00 with the crew. It was good to be back on the bus where I feel more comfortable. All my things are within reach and the scenery constantly moves. If I'm sleepy I can hit my bunk and sleep. If I'm not, I can chat to the excellent boys in the crew who are all interesting characters in their own way. We arrived at the Columbiafritz and I chatted to Simon Lake (truck) as we loaded in. He'd been hit by falling rocks during last night's journey! What are the chances of that happenin', eh? I returned to the bus and spent an hour replying to an email interview for Spain somewhere. All's going well – we're getting great reviews in Spain and Italy at the moment and I was told we were on the cover of the main Norwegian newspaper yesterday. Reviews – good or bad – don't mean much to me anymore, but good reviews help the marketing of the album so it's good that they're good.

Hung around at the gig all day. We're out of the centre of town here so there was little point in going walkabout. This is only a little gig – stage space is well tight, but it'll all be fine. No more drum-problems for me now I'm on in-ears. Everything's manageable. Whoopee.

Soundcheck was good. We rehearsed the end of *Neverland* again and – for the first time – I think we all knew what we were doing. I had a spot of food, which had been cooked by local girls and was the best food I'd had for ages. Chicken satay and the best cauliflower I've ever had! They'd also made some kind of stewed apple desert, which was almost like baby food. Being quite a fan of baby food I found it totally delicious. Andy Rotherham appeared and reminded me I'd promised him a beer in Berlin. He introduced me to his German pen-friend and four or five us walked down the road - me with my hood up to avoid detection – and found a dodgy kebab bar which sold beer. It seemed to be all there was on offer, locally. As we entered the bar I was immediately "nobbled" by a crusty looking chap who shook my hand and then soon reappeared with a special-edition of **Marbles** for me to sign. We had a beer and Andy told me about how he was stationed over here when he was in the RAF during the tense times of the cold war. He said the general public had no idea how close the world was to letting all the nukes off. He said he honestly thought he'd never see the end of his 3-year tour of duty. He used to sit outside a hangar, which contained a bomber already loaded with an atomic bomb for The Warsaw Pact. He used to have a key round his neck, which was to open the hangar and admit the pilot for take-off. He was on 24hour "2-minute notice". He thought it was going to happen. Jesus... Makes you wonder what's going down right now that we may never know about. Live for the day. Live for the day!

Afterwards he insisted on showing me the Templehof airport – right across the road. I'd wondered what the monstrous **1984** Orwellian building opposite the gig might be. I'd never imagined it was an airport – looked more like the ministry of Truth. We walked into the enormous concourse. Designed by Hitler's master architect, Albert Speer it really is a huge edifice, built to intimidate all who saw it. Not my cup of tea really, but impressive nonetheless. Andy marvelled at the fact that the entire structure is faced with marble. Closer inspection revealed that it would appear to be, in fact, solid marble... I guess money was no object to Mr Speer. Andy tells me the Zeppelins used to fly from here. Gazing across the main entrance hall, it was easy to hallucinate 1930 Berlin's aristocracy making their way in furs and sharp suits to board the first ever passenger flying machines on their way to Paris or New York. We returned to the gig and I got myself into the undertaker's garb and little spectacles that I currently wear for *The Invisible Man*.

The gig was great. Every night we're improving and settling into the new technology. We played this place on the **Anoraknophobia** tour and I remember the crowd being distinctly cool. I put it down to Berlin being an art capital and not so easy to impress, but there were no such problems this time. The reaction was much more expressive and when I took out my oysters (in-ear monitors) at the end of the show for *Cover My Eyes*, everyone sang the song as one and the noise was huge. Something's definitely happening... Maybe it's a combination of things, I dunno. Airplay, staying power, the internet, the new album, who knows? But something's definitely happening.

Friday 7 May *Hamburg Markthalle*

Didn't seem to take long to get to Hamburg. The bus seemed to be still for most of the night. I rose around 12.00 and alighted the bus to find Col and Rich standing around outside. "What's happening?" I said. "Dunno, the gig's locked and the truck's not here!" they said. Oops... I walked around the building to discover the truck double-parked on a busy stretch of dual carriageway. Parked cars prevented the truck from being able to park. The equipment was already being loaded into the street. The access to the Markthalle is via a lift. All hellishly tricky for the crew. I made my way into the gig (over an art gallery bearing the slogan "Look after your private parts" – well why wouldn't you?) and remembered being here with the Europeans 22 years ago. Wow. And I'm still doing it. And still loving it too. I could tell at a glance that the gig would be good for the crowd. The space is a system of terraces so that everyone has a good view of the stage, and everyone feels close to the stage even if they're not. Sometimes you just a get a good feeling from a room, and this is one of them. Quinner told me that today's day-rooms have been booked in a very tasty hotel overlooking Hamburg's famous inner-city lake so I opted to go there for a shower and to relax.

The local promoter gave us a lift over there in a brand new leather-upholstered BMW 5 series. That boy's making too much money... We arrived at the Atlantic Kempinski Hotel, checked in and I made my way to room 217, which was on the front face of the hotel with double-doors opening onto, and overlooking the lake. Beautiful. I ordered a Club Sandwich (an indulgence, considering that I could have eaten for free back at the gig, but you have to treat yourself now and again when you're touring...) and showered. They have a health spa in the hotel so I wandered along the corridor to see if I could use the solarium. It was available, and a beautiful health-spa receptionist in a white uniform showed me the way. It was one of those stand-up ones which only takes 10 minutes to give you a fair old cooking.

Returned to the room and watched under-sea creatures on TV with the sound down whilst also writing this diary. I was supposed to telephone a Czech journalist at 3.30 and Quinner had said that he'd txt me the number. However, I noticed that my mobile was no longer working. There was some problem between my Orange phone and the local network and it didn't work for the rest of the day. Managed to get hold of Quinner with the landline in the room and he gave me the number, but when I called, there was no answer anyway. Oh well. I rested on the bed for a while until 4.30 when I made my way back down to reception and into a taxi back to the gig.

The band was already on the stage rehearsing *The Uninvited Guest* which we'd decided to add to the set in order to "up" the energy-level in the encores. I joined them and we checked all was okay. The band and crew sat down to dinner, but I was still full from the club sandwich so I didn't bother. Massive Attack's **Mezzanine** was playing out in the gig through the PA so I went into the hall to listen to it. It's a sonic masterpiece. I sat at the back of the empty room, listening, when people started flooding in through the doors. I decided to sit still and keep my head down. It was quite good fun being unnoticed in a gig full of people who would have recognized me at a glance. A few clocked me but they smiled and left me alone - bless 'em. One or two discretely shook my hand or asked me to sign something, but I remained mostly unnoticed in the dark. Gazpacho, our opening act took to the stage and I stayed out-front to listen to them. They're not bad at all and this was the first chance I had to watch their set. Roderick seemed to be doing a good job sorting out their sound, which improved steadily as their show progressed. The crowd responded well to them and I could feel the temperature rising in the room. It was getting pretty hot in here. We've pre-sold 800 tickets and it's a Friday night so we might pick up a hundred more walking up. 900 people in this room was going to be pretty packed, and as Gazpacho played, the crowd gradually swelled. I caught most of their set before being summoned by Quinner to meet and greet a couple of competition winners, so went back stage and said hello. Soon it was time to get changed for the show. I got into my stage clothes and we wished each other a good show before taking to the stage.

I'm pretty comfortable with the in-ear monitors now and I was much more able to stay with the crowd tonight. The heat was intense and I could feel the sweat running down my back, legs and arms. I like it hot – rock n'roll's supposed to be about sweat. The new music was going down really well – I felt a surge of enthusiasm from the crowd as we played *You're Gone* – a sure sign that it's been picking-up a little airplay here, and probably thanks to BFBS radio which can be heard easily in this area. The second half of the show was even better received and the new encores worked a treat – we are now encoring with *Estonia*, *The U.Guest* and finishing with *Cover My Eyes,* which everyone in the room sang at a deafening level. Brilliant. After the show the crowd was baying for further encores well-after the equipment was unplugged and the drums dismantled. We've played Hamburg many times over the years but I've never known a reaction like this in this city. When I removed my shirt after the show it was as wet as if it had been thrown into a river. What a great and memorable night.

Monday 10 May *Oslo:* Day Off

Woken suddenly by a prod from tour manager Quinner. It was the middle of the night i.e. 9.00 in the morning. Everyone had to get off the bus to go and get on the ferry from wherever we were (never found out) to Göteborg. I rolled out of my bunk into the half-lit chaos of 18 unwashed blokes all trying to grab boots and bags from a confined space at once. It was like a slow motion replay of a crisis in a submarine. We all bundled out of the bus into a ferry-terminal and wandered around like sheep for a while until we gradually discovered where we should be going. I cleaned my teeth as I crossed the car park and felt slightly, just slightly, better for it. Our destination appeared to be a steel corridor on a raised pedestrian-bridge. In the side of the corridor was an exit, which was closed but would eventually lead to a ferry, which hadn't arrived yet. This wasn't going to be quick... ugh... We sat on the floor and generally hung around mumbling to each other like zombies. Everyone had had about 4 hours sleep at this point so our mood was subdued, but affable. Ian Mosley lay on the floor like a murder victim and asked if anyone could draw a chalk line round him. There was a party of seven or eight 14 (I'm guessing) year-old schoolgirls next to us who had all had much more sleep than us and, I suspect, had a somewhat more wholesome lifestyle too. They were all singing some inane romantic pop song, which they re-started whenever they got to the end. It's always heart-warming to see the fairer sex having a good time, but at this point in the day it was wearing a bit thin with us lot, to say the least (some old cynic in our entourage observed it would only be a matter of time before they grew up and set about the serious business of being tense and miserable around some poor bloke for the rest of their lives. A bleak view, I thought).

By the time the gate was finally opened to let us on to a high-speed ferry (which had now reversed (!) into the dock), we were all twitching from a need to escape the Von Trapp family singers and get hold of a cup of coffee. We bought coffee and Danish pastries (which turned out to be the best I've ever tasted) and set about the process of achieving respiration. Cold-blooded species have to sit on a rock for some time after the break of each day in order that the sun can warm their bodies up to a point where they can function. A touring band and crew possess similar characteristics.

The ferry journey took two hours, which felt like five. I went out to the rear deck to watch the raging white torrent of the boat's wash stretching back to the horizon and chatted to Ian Bond about Richard Barbieri's amazing toilet bag/first-aid kit which included most available prescription-drugs and even extended to the inclusion of emergency-fillings! Much more hanging around ensued until we were finally docking in Göteborg. I mused that the last time I was on a ferry in these waters, I was bleeding to death while a couple of Scandinavian sailors sewed my right hand back together (see the last verse of *This Strange Engine*). We returned to the car deck, boarded the bus and I was back in bed before Charlie – our busdriver – had even started the engine. Woke up around 2.00 and made my way to the back lounge to write the diary. Downstairs, some of the crew were watching **Schindler's List** and as I typed, horrified screams of men, women and children drifted up the stairwell. Lovely. Top marks to Spielberg for making a movie which HAD to be made. I've never seen it and I don't suppose I ever will. I'm not the kind of person who needs man's inhumanity to man spelled out and re-enacted before my eyes. I guess I'm sensitive enough to it already. The fact that it happened at all serves as a reminder to all of us that it can happen again. Anywhere. And, interestingly enough, neither religious men, nor religious institutions will lift a finger to stop it. We must all guard against the human weakness of forming into tribes in order to lift our self-esteem. We can feel good about ourselves without having to find someone else to classify as inferior. It's the slippery slope down into that same abyss.

I tried to blot out the bleak noises and concentrate on remembering Hamburg and Berlin in infinitely better times. Our gigs there last week had been great and attended by many seriously lovely Germans. Stereotyping is, of course, part of that same slide down into tribalism and is as accurate a concept of "sin" as I can think of. We all do it, and we must all guard against it. Right – I'll climb down off my high-horse! Here endeth the sermon.

Outside, the scenery was beautiful, pine forests and untouched Nordic countryside, occasional lakes, and then eventually opening out onto a vista of water, islands and fjords as we made our way into Oslo. I couldn't remember crossing the border from Sweden into Norway – maybe I was asleep.

We arrived in the centre of town and checked into a hotel. Opposite I could see a great many Edwin Shirley trucks parked up. It turns out that Britney Spears is playing here tonight. I'm told she's on the road with 17 trucks! That's a serious amount of space for frocks, make-up and a CD player, eh?

I dropped my bags in room 323 (later labelled 'THE ZONE' by drunken crew, in white insulating tape across the doorway) and went down into the street, which had many cafés with outdoor seating. I perched myself down, ordered a steak and a beer (I hadn't eaten since this morning's Danish pastry) and set about writing the diary. Ian M joined me after a few minutes, then Steve R, then Ian Bond and we sat and watched the Norwegian world go by for a couple of hours when Jan-Henrik Orme (the singer from Gazpacho) showed up with his partner, Anelie, and announced he was going to take us somewhere better. You've just got to love the Nogs! He hailed a cab and took us down to the harbour-front where there were many restaurants and bars. After some deliberation we decided on a traditional Norwegian place right at the end of the waterfront. There were pictures on the walls of old Oslo as well as crusty old sea-fearers. There were also some genuine old whale harpoons – heavy-duty stuff. The bar had draught Guinness and it was just what I fancied, so I ordered a pint and, to my surprise, it was the best pint of Guinness I've had in or out of Ireland. Everyone was ordering dinner, but I'd eaten so I stuck to the drink apart from an ice-cream sundae with egg-nog. Different... Roderick ordered smoked whale-meat which arrived garnished with sour cream, red onions and accompanied by strange popadom-like things. I had a taste and, although I'm not sure where I stand on the subject of murdering such intelligent mammals, whaling IS and has been a part of Norwegian culture for centuries and I guess I should either become an outright vegetarian or stop wringing my hands. Well, it was delicious. Chatted with Erik, Quinner, Roderick, and the Gazpacho family and drank Guinness til midnight, when we thought we should really call it a day before it all got out of hand... Jan-Henrik wouldn't let us pay for anything and despite much discussion, I couldn't get him even to accept money for the return journey in the cab.

When we arrived at the hotel, Erik suggested a last beer in his room, so I went upstairs with him, and Jan and Anelie came too. Had one last beer and talked drunkenese for an hour before returning to 'The Zone' and to bed.

Tuesday 11 May *Oslo Rockerfeller*

Woke around 11.00 to a txt from Dizzy and spent most of the morning txting her. Checked out at 1.00 and found Mosley the cat and TM Quinner sitting in hotel reception. We walked over to the gig, Rockefeller, which was only a few streets away. Hung around for a while and tried to see if Lars, who did monitors for us last time, was around. He wasn't – the locals said he was working in his own studio. I'm not surprised. It was obvious last time that he knew what he was doing. They have a wireless internet thing going here at the gig so I connected to it and enjoyed using the Mac Airport thing for the first time. You either know about this or you don't. If you don't, then I won't bore you to tears by explaining it, but it's the kind of thing that comes in really handy if you're on the road, and it works like magic!

My customary "Oh my God! I've lost..." panic of the day came about as I realized I'd left my laptop charger plugged into the hotel room wall, so I hightailed back over there in the rain to see if I could find it. I made my way back up to room 323 and it had gone. I then asked the Chinese cleaners if they spoke English. They didn't, but through a process of sign language I saw eyes light up in recognition of my desperate mimes, and one of the girls found the power supply carefully wrapped in a bag on one of the trolleys. Naturally I thanked her profusely in my best Chinese-Norwegian and returned to the streets of Oslo. I decided to wander round the town for a bit, get a flavour of the place and see if I could make my way to the main square where we had stayed last time at the Grand Hotel. Eventually found it and returned to a café-bar which called itself Woodstock and was playing live concert footage of Lenny Kravitz on the TV's. Seemed like a reasonably vibey place to write the diary so I wandered in and was politely told by a pretty waitress that I could only sit there if I was eating. If I only wanted coffee, there was a coffee bar attached through in the next room. Fair enough... I wandered through into a less vibey coffee bar and hid around the corner out of sight. It wasn't waitress-service so I never actually got round to ordering a drink – I just opened up the laptop and got on with it for an hour, and no-one seemed bothered. After a while I looked up and recognized a familiar t-shirt coming toward me. It was one of our Carlsberg spoof t-shirts. "*Marillion. Probably the best band in the World*" proudly nicked from Carlsberg's own design and slogan. It was a fan from Trondheim in the north of Norway – 500km from Oslo. He and his friends had driven the 5-hour drive to see us tonight. He asked if I'd mind if they joined me, and I said sure. Two more people – a boy and a girl – joined me. (I can't remember their names as I write this in Stockholm, so apologies. Forgive me - I'm a cabbage). He noticed I didn't have a drink and insisted on buying me a beer. We chatted about why we hadn't played Trondheim and I tried to explain the economics of routing a tour – we'd need a day-off either side of the show to make it possible. We chatted til I realized it was past 5.00 and I should be soundchecking, so I said bye-bye and made my way back to the gig, getting lost for a while, before ending up back at the hotel we'd stayed at. It was a bit of a circular route to the gig but I arrived back in time.

Soundcheck was peculiar. Nothing sounded quite right and no one was admitting to anything having changed. My Kurzweil (one of the machines I use for piano sounds) seemed quiet in the in-ears so I had it turned up quite a lot. Now whenever you do things like this, you're asking for trouble... More often than not, the fault sorts itself out during the show... and blows your head off. So it's always with a wary reluctance that you change anything radically at this point in a tour. Anyway, there's not much choice if you can't hear something. Mark K was having problems with his in-ears and it was decided that the transmission mast should be moved to a place more centre-stage so that he could get a better signal. While the crew were sorting this out, the band dispersed and soundcheck was never really finished properly. This was to prove a mistake. I suggested we return to the stage to play the beginning of *The Invisible Man* but no one felt it necessary. (I really hate being proved right). I returned to the bus and descended into a deep sleep until I awoke automatically at 9.00. Tonight we were on stage at 10.00pm. I was met at the door by Quinner, who reminded me of a "meet n'greet" arranged for competition winners before the show. Still waking up I was ushered into a dozen or so Norwegians, some of whom had no concept of shyness and got straight into my face telling me about their lives and asking me searching questions about mine. One of them burst into some kind of deafening Jewish-sounding lament at one point and insisted that I sing along in order to warm up my voice. I politely declined whilst casting around the room for an escape route, but there wasn't one. Another fan began rounding us up for a band photograph while barking instructions at us about where, and how, to stand. By this time I was almost awake.

To our relief the "meet n'greet" was eventually disbanded so that we could get ready for the show. "Shock n'Rock" or maybe "Stun n'Run" would be a more fitting expression for it. Gazpacho were coming off stage having played to their home-crowd and gone down extremely well, so I congratulated them. They're a pleasant and generous bunch and deserve good things.

Then we hit the stage and my earlier instinctive worst fears all materialized in sequence as the keyboard sample sounds for *The Invisible Man* were all mixed up with sounds which should be in other songs. The guitar sounds were too loud in my monitors, and as the show wore in, the Kurzweil returned to its former level and, as predicted, blew my and everyone else's heads off. Things like this phase us all no small amount, and we all played like idiots, queuing up to drop clangers. Oh shit. The first half of the set couldn't end too soon and we went backstage to regroup and try not to perform a post-mortem. We duly performed a post-mortem and generally complained and squabbled. Sense prevailed in the end and we decided to return to the stage with teeth gritted to salvage what we could of our reputations. The second set went much better and although getting into "the zone" wasn't really on the cards, I think we repaired whatever damage we'd done in the first set. Afterwards John (Gazpacho's guitarist) declared it was the most enthusiastic response he'd ever seen from an Oslo audience, so that cheered us all up a lot. Showered and then chatted to Jan Henrik's girlfriend, Anelie, for a while.

Returned to the bus and was sitting in the back lounge when a girl popped her head round the door and said "Hello! Who are you, then?" All the boys lit up (as boys do when pretty blonde Norwegian girls suddenly say hello) and duly started a conversation. They've got a lot of front these Norwegian girls... I was too tired to talk to people I don't know so I slid upstairs and into bed. Slept fully clothed. Again. Woke up in the early hours to remove my shoes. Really must get round to getting undressed.

Wednesday 12 May *Stockolm Chinese Teatern*

Pulled back my little curtain and recoiled as the white light of a sunny day blasted my retinas through my wide-open irises. As the blurs cleared and the white calmed down to colours and shapes, I could see that we were parked on the Stockholm waterfront in the centre of the poshest part of town. Tonight we play the Chinese Theatre which is situated next to (and co-owned by) the fabulous Berns Hotel (*the* place to currently hang out and be seen in Stockholm). I love this city. All Ingmar Bergmann's ghosts are here. The old town and the waterfront are so beautiful and haunting. I have sometimes walked alone through the old town late at night to discover it almost completely deserted, and I've felt like a time-traveller wandering through an empty city during the day, it's bustling and as glamorous as Mayfair.

It had been arranged for us to have lunch in the café of the Berns hotel. I threw some clothes on (no underwear – I seem to have run out...) and wandered into the conservatory where most of our scruffy band and crew were already assembled – bleary eyed and decompressing from yet another night on the bus. The interior of the adjoining room is among the most ornate interiors I've seen anywhere – a rococo frenzy of amazing plasterwork, paintings, frescoes and chandeliers. It could be the interior of a palace. Two immaculately uniformed and beautiful waiters (one female, one male) were coming and going, taking orders and providing desperately needed coffee to band and crew. The waiter was young, blond, tall, elegant and never stopped smiling. Can't imagine why... Having grown up here, tall and good-looking and surrounded by a seemingly endless supply of the most beautiful girls on earth, it must have been a struggle to stop grinning even in the most worrying of situations.

Quinner had asked us all yesterday what we'd like to eat here today and it had all been ordered in advance. I thought I was ordering dinner so I'd opted for the roast pork and mashed potato. Bizarre then to watch it arrive in front of me so soon after rolling out of bed. Pork for breakfast? Oh well... no different to bacon and egg really. It's all in the mind. The food was lovely but I couldn't relax as there were interviews to do. Quinner took me to a room in the hotel where I had a couple of radio phone-interviews – one to Göteborg and another to Greece. Managed to squeeze in a lightning shower before the phone rang and there was a DJ from Göteborg on the other end of the line. "Can you hold on please for 2 minutes?" she said.

"Sure! I'll go and put some clothes on." I said. She probably thought I was joking.

After that I had to hang around til 2.00 pm (too much time to sit and wait/not enough time to go anywhere) for the Greek phoner. Shame really, as it was a gorgeous day out and I wouldn't have minded a wander round the old town... True to form, the phone never rang at 2.00 so I let the Quinner know and he managed to sort things out - the phone rang at 2.10 and I spoke to a guy from the Greek radio station who told me there was a power cut at the moment and maybe they could do the interview at 2.30 when the power was restored. There goes another precious hour out of the day then... Bugger. How the hell are they going to organize the Olympics?! It'll run about as smoothly as a nativity play in an infants school (sorry, Greece. As I read this now from the vantage point of November 2004, I couldn't have been more wrong. It was one of the best-organised and most impressive Olympics ever.) "I'll give em til 2.30 and then I'm off!" I thought. The phone rang at exactly 2.30 (!) and it was the Greeks saying that power was restored and they could now do the interview. The radio station is in Thessaloniki (I think) on the Greek mainland and our single, *You're Gone* is currently no.3 on their playlist. We had a pleasant chat – I think the DJ's were fans. Makes a change.

Whoopee, it's 3.00pm and I am now FREE til 4.30! Went outside to discover that the sun had gone in and the temperature had dropped ten degrees – it was now pretty damned chilly. Apparently at this time of year, if the wind comes in off the sea, the temperature drops like a stone because there's still a lot of ice out on the Baltic, so it's like having a huge refrigerator waiting off the coast. I crouched freezing in the street while Freddie Bilquist took a few photographs, before hurrying back into the Berns Hotel to write the diary in the café. Bumped straight into Ian and nattered to him for a while instead... Managed to write a few words before I was needed at the gig. Wandered over the road to the Chinese theatre where soundcheck was already getting underway.

The Chinese theatre is a lovely old art-deco place, designed for drama and musicals rather than rock n'roll, but Marillion's live show works as well in this environment as it does in a rock club. The sit-down audience situation, combined with the natural reserve of the Swedes was going to make for a pretty low-energy audience-vibe, so I adjusted my psyche accordingly for the show ahead. Sometimes you need a reaction, and sometimes you can decide it's art and forget about the crowd completely. This was to be one such night. Soundcheck went by without incident although the vertical 5-floor climb to the dressing rooms deserves a mention. (After a 150 minute show, you need oxygen...).

I returned to the room at the Berns to relax for one whole, blissful hour before wandering down to the bar where I walked straight into our ex-personal-assistant, Smick Hardgrave who emigrated to Sweden after falling in love with his (now) wife, Helen who used to work at Stanbridge Farm where we wrote **Holidays In Eden**. I haven't seen Helen for many years. Another Stanbridge girl, Ulrike had also come along. No-one had aged even a day in the 10 years that have passed (must be the fresh air or something in the Swedish water) and it was great to see them and catch up and reminisce about drunken japes in fancy dress, etc, all those years ago.

Showtime arrived and off we went. I remained well and truly inside the music throughout and this was to be one of my favourite shows of the tour to date. By the end of the show, the audience gave us an ovation. This is equivalent to full-blown hysteria for Swedes, so I knew we'd hit the spot. Afterwards I had a drink in the Berns with my old chum Per Thöresson, who works for the UN in Sweden and once showed me round the UN building in New York. He's now based back here in Stockholm and something of a big wig. It was good to see him. His meteoric rise up the diplomatic ranks hasn't altered him at all. We eventually said bye-bye to our chums who were, by now, the right side of several sodas, and returned to the bus where I climbed into bed for the relatively short trip to Malmö in the south of Sweden.

Friday 14 May *Malmö – Prague*

It's my birthday. 40 again. And never been kissed. 2 of the previous 3 statements are lies.

As I got out of the shower after the Malmö show, I noticed it was 12.20. Officially now May 14. Hooray. Quinner magically produced 2 bottles of Champagne and the band clinked glasses and wished me happy birthday. Much looning about ensued including a brief reappearance of Jack's wilder side – something not seen too often these days – but as soon as he started juggling with and orange, an apple and his cellphone, the memories came flooding back. Eventually wobbled onto the bus. I sat at the front for a while and drank a beer before crashing into bed. Woke up at various points of the morning to the jingling of my phone as txts just kept coming in. Kept going back to sleep as I had decided to have "God's own lie-in". Got up around 12.45 to realize that I had now slept through more than half of my birthday. I vaguely remembered the sounds of the bus pulling onto and then departing a ferry at some point in the middle of the night. When I went to bed I was in Sweden. Now we're somewhere on one of Germany's autobahns...

Not long after I rose, the bus pulled into a motorway services. Great – I could wash and clean my teeth and have a little breakfast/lunch. Oh dear. Turns out that this particular facility is undergoing renovation. The toilets were round the back, and of the temporary building-site type. One of the cubicles contained something so vile that anyone entering it immediately spun round and left again. I wasn't going to look... Cleaned my teeth and hurried out in the hope of sitting down to a spot of birthday lunch. The restaurant was closed and the only hot food on offer was to be found in a little kiosk where a steely-eyed woman was selling sausages and coffee. There was a choice of two kinds of sausage – both of identical German-sausage shape, but one of a slightly darker complexion than the other. I went for the darker one which was served with a little dry bread and mustard, and sat down at a formica table with a coffee. I was joined by our truck-driver, Simon Lake, who had, by coincidence, arrived at the same place. "These German sausages – they're the wurst!" he quipped to all-round groans from band and crew. Oh well – not exactly a slap up birthday feast, then. Half way down the sausage, my phone rang. It was none other than Dave Meegan, our producer, friend and all round top-bloke. He'd called from England to wish me a Happy Birthday. He says he's going to try and make the Dublin show. I hope he can. Most of our music owes its sound and character as much to him as it does to us.

We returned to the bus around 2pm and, on the way across the car park I chatted with Simon who told me about the film **A Beautiful Mind** which he'd recently watched on DVD. He said it was great and went off to the truck to lend it to me. Climbed onto the bus, stuck it on the DVD player in the upstairs lounge and watched it for the next 3 hours or so. He was right – it's a great and compelling movie with an extraordinary and brilliant lead performance from Russell Crowe throughout. Highly recommended. Half way through the movie, my phone rang and it was my old chum Dave Crawshaw from Doncaster (now Sheffield) calling to wish me Happy Birthday. That was sweet of him. I probably sounded a bit distracted by the movie. Sorry Dave.

As the film drew to a close, I had a look out of the window where the stunning sight of old Dresden presented itself. We were on a bridge over the river and overlooking the old ornate buildings. This place must have rivalled Paris and Vienna, until the last war, when much of the city and its inhabitants were incinerated by the RAF in a single night. War. What is it good for? Absolutely nothing. When will we ever learn that violence only leads to obscenity, sorrow and a mess which takes decades to recover from? Oh well. Here in 2004, Dresden is subject to more mundane and universal problems like Friday-evening traffic-jams. And we were in the mother of traffic jams. It took us nearly 2 hours to get from one side of Dresden to the other, pushing our original ETA of 5.30 in Prague, to 7.30. I texted Sue who was already there, and had been waiting for me all day, to let her know the bad news. She took it well, understanding that there really was nothing I could do except sit on a hot bus with 17 similarly sweaty blokes and wait until we got there.

After a seemingly unending journey along winding narrow roads through hilly and beautiful countryside – sometimes looking like Devon, sometimes looking like Switzerland – we finally arrived in Prague and made our way across the most enormous flyover which literally "flew over" the rooftops of much of the city, far below. The flyover spans a huge valley and the feeling looking out of the bus window was exactly that of looking out of a light-aircraft at the city below. Sods law dictates that as we stumbled into the reception area of the hotel at 7.45, we were just beaten to it by an entire coachload of Japanese tourists who a hapless receptionist was unsuccessfully trying to check-in in front of us. Fortunately for me at least, Sue already had a room. Unfortunately, I didn't know the number. Fortunately I could call her on the cellphone. Unfortunately, she wasn't answering it. Kept trying and eventually got hold of her and took the lift up to my room where all I really wanted to do was take a shower and give her a long overdue cuddle. Not an option of course, as I had been told that an interview with a Prague radio station was imminent. I was supposed to have already been at the radio station between 7.30 and 8.00 for a special show dedicated to the band. Dresden had put paid to that, and so Quinner had rescheduled the interview by phone and the DJ was already on the line. I tried to sound intelligent and give the impression that I was having a great birthday in Prague... but it involved a lot of imagination and less than total honesty. The interview finally ended and I made it into the shower. Sue had ordered ice-cream in honour of my birthday arrival at 5.30, which was melted into luke-warm mush. Ate it anyway and it was LOVELY. She'd also brought me a load of birthday cards from home. Typically Nial's was the funniest – a long declaration of love and the fact that I was undoubtedly the best dad in the world, and then signed, "From your deluded son, Nial". I'm still laughing about it... He'd also bought me a pair of Manchester United underpants several sizes too small. "If they don't fit, can I have 'em?" he said as I called to thank him! What a top boy. Sofi had gone out for the night and had vanished off radar. Tried several times in vain to call her.

Sue and I later went out into Prague to have dinner. We took the metro into the old town and found a little old restaurant where the food turned out to be excellent. Afterwards we walked across the famous old Charles Bridge across the river, past the fire-eaters and beggars who kneel down with their heads bowed to the ground... It must hurt. I didn't have any polish currency at all and I don't suppose they'd have had much use for the Norwegian krones that, inexplicably, I've ended up with. The view in both directions from the bridge is totally stunning and as Gothic a dream as you could have. Floodlit cathedrals hover in the sky on the dark hills and ornate domes and spires abound in every direction. We stopped and had coffee at the little open restaurant on the far side of the bridge where the naked flames of old Gothic lanterns dance into the night. The staff were welcoming and friendly despite the lateness of the hour. As we drank our coffee in the candlelight, we marvelled at the medieval waterside buildings. I could see an old waterwheel in the darkness set alongside huge old stone castle walls. What a place. Unfortunately, Prague has become something of a haven for the "Brit stag and hen party weekend" crowd since the budget airlines began flying here. Food and drink are cheap if you've got pounds sterling, so it's now common to encounter gangs of our lary fellow countrymen staggering around demonstrating England's "lad culture" to the bemused Czechs. Aah, I'm so proud...

Saturday 15 May *Prague Lucerna Hall*

Woke at 11.30. The phone rang and it was the dulcet tones of Lord B who was making sure I was going to make the 12.30 departure from reception. Dizzy seemed even more tired than me and didn't stir as I rolled out of bed. There was a txt on my phone from none other than Andy Gangadeen which simply said "Fancy a spot of breakfast, love?" He was here in the hotel! What a prince! I hurried downstairs and discovered him at the bar with his girlfriend, Louise, having a spot of breakfast and beer. These kids know how to drink! They insisted I join them in a beer and so I accepted whilst realizing this was the first time I'd ever rolled out of bed in a morning and opened a beer. It's come to this! Better watch myself... I don't suppose you're a proper artist til you're a confirmed alcoholic and registered drug-addict with a string of divorces behind you but, so far, I've been hoping to avoid the stereotype...

It was such a nice gesture for Andy to come out. Andy drummed on my third h-band tour and we have become good friends. If only the world were made of such people, there would be unimaginable and brilliant art everywhere. Everyone would have a big heart, humility, a sense of humour to match their sense of honour... and everyone would be as cool as fuck. God bless you Andy G.

We had to rush off to a record store in town where we were booked for a signing session. We made our way into the building and were announced to the stage by a guy who sounded exactly like a horse race commentator – a bit like listening to the Grand National in Czechoslovakian (you'd have to have been there...) Signed record sleeves for an hour or so and then walked through the town to another curious small "mall"-type place where there is the most amazing and bizarre centre-piece of a sculpture which consists of a horse suspended upside down in the air by its hooves, with its neck curling backwards and downwards and it's head lolling lifelessly open mouthed and tongue out. Sitting astride the underside of the horse, the right way up, is a knight in full battle armour. Mighty surreal, and probably inspired by some ancient Czech folklore... I was so enthralled by this that I didn't realize the band had already been announced to the "VIP reception" in a nearby bar. I was hurried along and projected at high speed into a place where everyone was clapping. I recognized most of the assembled throng as they were nearly all UK fan club members and familiar US fans. Out of the few unfamiliar faces, one particular guy with a grand countenance and a millionaire's beard, stood out as the obvious "VIP". I said hello to him and he quipped something in return. Seems to be a character... Turns out he was the promoter.

The show that night was great-if-sparsely-attended. At one point I thought someone had said we hadn't got paid for it. 'Could have done the joke: "Does anyone know how to get cash out of a Czech?" Anyway, the man with the millionaires beard DID pay us (and it's a crap joke anyway).

Tuesday 15 June *Le Rockstore Montpelier*

Rolled out of bed and made my way in the gloom to the bright light of the upper front deck of the tour bus. We're parked in a VERY French-looking back street – a little run-down, but unmistakably French. I can't even define it, but one glance and you know you're in France (if you'll pardon the rhyme).

Today we have an "early start" as I have promotion to do from 2pm. I also want to go looking for new maracas – the ones I brought with me are beginning to disintegrate. I bumped into mad Jack who'd already been up the street and he told me that if I walk a little way up the hill, the gig's on the left. I soon found it (called Rockstore) and watched a team of grinning local crew boys literally lifting parked cars and bumping them down the street to make way for our truck.

Inside the gig I was introduced to local promoter Chantal and catering girl ("Hello I'm Aurelie, but you can call me 'Queen of the Sandwich' – I'm in charge of the food"). I wasted no time in quizzing them both about possible maraca shops and Chantal said she'd make a couple of calls. It was declared that a shop had been found and that the sandwich-queen should show me the way. We walked back down the hill and along some tram-lines. Montpellier has a really modern tram-system which would be the envy of any town in England and as we walked, brand new blue trams glided almost silently past. Everywhere vibrated with that stylish ambience so often found in the South of France. The sun shone and I decided I was very nearly awake. Aurelie – all dressed in black despite the sunny day – led me into a shopping mall called Polygon or Octagon or something like that and we soon found a music shop at the far corner. Yes, the man said he has maracas, and a pair promptly appeared. They weren't really what I was looking for – they were a bit crunchy and low-pitched, but I thought they'd do for *This Is the 21st Century*. He sold them to Aurelie at a "special reduced price" in return for future favours promised (she could get him into the gig any old time, I'm sure) and we returned to the venue via the huge main square. Only in France would such attention and space be allocated to the centre of a town. Beautiful grand buildings surround a massive open area. There's an old carousel and at one end a beautiful old opera house. Cafés abound and there were people everywhere enjoying the day. I made a mental note to come up here after the show and have a beer.

Back at the venue, I thanked the queen-of-the-sandwich and she promptly returned to her sandwiches. French journalist and friend, Bertrand Poucheron, had arrived from Marseille with his Japanese wife, Sayaka. Bertrand's generosity knows no bounds and he was quite insistent that he take us to lunch. I didn't have much time, but I quickly took a shower at the gig and we wandered back up the hill where a table had been booked on the terrace of a fine restaurant. Hard life, eh? I only had half an hour – not much time for lunch in France – but Bertrand explained to the waiter and a minute steak arrived in, well, not much more than a minute! I seem to be famous here – I was constantly being pestered for autographs throughout the day, including during lunch, where I had to keep jumping up to have my photograph taken with various well-meaning French folk. It sometimes gets a bit much when you're eating... Still, I can't complain – God knows what it's like for Bowie, Jagger, Bono and Britney! I guess you just end up having to be rude to people, or hide. Must be a shame...

After lunch I rushed back to the show where a somewhat untogether French camera-crew interviewed me and then suggested the band soundcheck so that they could film it. Ian Bond wasn't ready with the sound and much headscratching and cursing took place all round. We eventually had a knock through *Fantastic Place* and got rid of 'em, so that Ian could finish eq-ing the PA and we could soundcheck properly.

After soundcheck a fairly disastrous meal happened in a restaurant up the road. The staff seemed incapable of feeding anyone in less than 4 hours and one by one, band and crew got pissed off and left. Oh well. I returned to the bus for the only 10-minutes I really had to myself all day. Sometimes you just need 5 minutes alone or you get hatchy. Returned to the dressing room – 2 floors up a spiral staircase. Keeps you fit...

The show was pretty damned packed and would turn out to be the most enthusiastic of the tour. The crowd were absolutely amazing. Ian Bond metered the crowd noise at the end of the show and the crowd alone registered 109dB. This is way beyond illegal and also well into the pain barrier. I never heard a noise like it at a show. Thank you so much Montpelier. Afterwards, I showered and went downstairs to sign a few autographs. Dizzy rang and we had a nice chat and I told her all about it.

Went up the road with the boys from Gazpacho and had a beer in a bar on the square – we couldn't sit out... it was too late. Returned to the bus and hit the bed running. Woke up at 6, fully-clothed (again) and still wearing my shoes (again) – always a sign of a good night...

Sunday 4 July   *Belfast   The Empire*

Woke at the sound of Quinner saying, "Lucy – you better get up... We can't do the gig. It's impossible!"

I thought I'd better get up... Pulled on my trousers and fell out of the bus into a Belfast side street where half-a-dozen local crew were loitering about waiting for something to happen. Made my way into the gig through a backstage door and into the main room. 'Sure is beautiful – all wooden railings and a balcony, Lautrec-style paintings – like an old time music-hall or a circus. Huge murals on the wall of pre-raphaelite women beneath crossed union flags and scrolls bearing the word Empire. Jeez – you can tell we're in amongst the loyalists... The only problem was that the stage was VERY small. Erik was having a nervous breakdown at the prospect of getting the band and its equipment on this stage. Well, that wasn't actually the ONLY problem. There was also the fact that it was impossible to bring in our lights... and pretty damned impossible to bring in sound too. There was just nowhere to put ANYTHING. The house PA was four flown "Martin" full-range cabinets. I reckon this is about half the size of the minimum amount of PA we'd need for a room of this size. There was a nice Midas mixing desk driving the whole thing though, so we were in with a chance. By the time I'd sized up the situation, most of the rest of the band were in the room – like me, they'd been panicked out of bed by Quinner's earlier declaration. We were all unanimous that we shouldn't cancel the show and that we should do whatever must be done to make some kind of show happen. There were 2 mirror-balls hanging from the roof, along with one or two moving lights. Steve Finch (our lighting designer) was going to have to program the entire show from scratch. Fortunately for us, he seemed prepared to do it and did us the favour of not huffing and puffing and making a drama out of it. He just set about getting on with it. Top chap, Steve Finch. Having made the decision to go ahead with the show, the truck was opened and I watched while its contents were emptied into the street. All the lighting and sound flight-cases had to come out to gain access to our backline equipment. Eventually there were so many flight cases in the road that Charlie had to move the tour-bus round the corner in order to fit them into the street! Unfortunately my wallet was on the bus, which had now departed, so I asked Erik to lend me a tenner so I could go and get a coffee. Walked round the corner and found a little café, *Maggie May's*, where I ordered coffee. A newspaper had been left at my table. I use the term newspaper in the loosest sense - all the usual stuff about David Beckham, Wayne Rooney, etc., surrounded by as many pictures as possible of girls not wearing much. A substitute for news. A substitute for thought. A distraction from a crap life, for the masses. Drank a fairly dodgy coffee and then ordered 2 poached eggs on toast, and bacon, which soon arrived with hard yolks. Oh well. Cheers Maggie.

Returned to the gig and Quinner pointed me in the direction of the day-rooms which had been booked in the hotel opposite the gig. Rang the doorbell and was greeted by a friendly receptionist called Helen. What an accent they have here in Belfast! Sounds great on a girl but a bit hard on a boy. Anyway Helen was lovely and pointed me "street op the steers thar" to room 417. It turned out to be more-or-less a vertical 4-floor climb. Arrived knackered at room 417 and dropped my toilet bag on the bed. There was a modern hi-tech flat lcd TV which I tuned into some program about the Olympics. Cycling and boxing. This was followed by a program about Sport Relief – a charity, raising money for poor kids in various struggling parts of the world – Peru, India, Zambia. Victoria Beckham was digging around on a rubbish dump in Peru with a little 9 year-old girl who lives on the dump and digs around for glass every day of her life in order to sell it for recycling and scratch a meagre living. Harrowing stuff. Probably did Posh the world of good. Probably would've done me the world of good too. I wonder who paid for the flights... I bet she didn't, and I bet she didn't fly economy either. I hope I'm wrong. I showered and cleaned my teeth and changed the dressing on my splinted little finger while the celebs asked us all for money to take the children out of poverty. It's all a drop in the ocean of course, but one kid taken off a rubbish dump is exactly that. If you read this, send something to Sport Relief, even if it's only a quid.

I had heard from the local crew that the shops in Belfast open at 1 o'clock on a Sunday so I figured if I mosied into town, I'd arrive on time. I'm in need of more sticky tape for my ailing little finger. I'm suffering from a detached tendon following a bizarre incident with a balloon in Turin... Helen told me that the walk into Belfast city centre was "street op the streeut thar" (straight up the street, there) and only about a ten-minute walk. I phoned home on the mobi and chatted to Sue as I wandered along the streeut. All's well back in England and everyone's looking forward to seeing me on Wednesday in Leeds. I was still chatting to Sue as I arrived outside Boots the chemist, which soon opened its doors to a small throng of early customers. I made my way in through the heady aroma of the perfume counters and over towards the medical section where I eventually found what I was looking for, and emerged with micropore tape and finger bandage. Spent another half-hour wandering around the city centre trying to find Hugo Boss underwear. No luck. I'll remain "commando" for another couple of days.

Returned to the gig along the long road out towards the Botanical Gardens area of Belfast and bought an ice-cream in a shop full of organic remedies. Arrived back at the gig having thoroughly run out of things to do and installed myself up on the little balcony at the back of the Empire so I could watch the crew making final preparations for soundcheck. Inconceivably, all the equipment was on the stage! There were no security measures here whatsoever and the front doors of the venue were open to the street, so people kept wandering in and up the stairs to chat. Fair enough – it's not as though I'm here very often, and I was looking forward to the gig immensely, simply to sing *Easter* here. I wrote *Easter* back in 1987 for the people of Northern Ireland caught up in the troubles". When I joined Marillion we finished the song together and recorded it on our first album (the band's fifth) **Seasons' End**. We've never played in Northern Ireland, so I have waited 17 years to sing this song here. It was going to be an honour to sing these words to these people. What's particularly uplifting is the fact that the "troubles" look like they're now all but over and many of the old rivalries are dissipating as the political process of the new Irish Assembly slowly, slowly bears fruit.

Soundcheck was long as there was much to do but we eventually got through it. Afterwards I got back on the bus for a nap before returning to the gig. We changed in an upstairs room full of upturned chairs and tables. There seemed to be a kitchen up here too and as I changed my trousers – naked from the waist down, a waitress came along the corridor to be greeted by the sight of me bending over. She must have had one hell of a view. She made a small involuntary shriek and disappeared quickly into a side-room. It was probably a cupboard.

The show wasn't a disappointment. I found an old ecstacy tablet in the bottom of my toilet bag and I thought, "What the hell!" so I was flying throughout the gig. During *Easter*, a guy clambered up on stage, threw his arm round me, and sang the song with me down the mic. No one's ever done this before and it seemed perfect to have a Belfast boy sing the song with me. I don't know which side of the sectarian divide he was from and I don't care. There we all were, singing for, and celebrating peace. It was an amazing and heartwarming memory and well worth the long, long wait. Didn't really want to go through the charade of leaving the stage and returning for encores as it was almost impossible to get on and off stage, so we just kept going 'til we ran out of music.

Marvellous. Thank you to all who showed up and may the Lord, in his mercy, be kind to Belfast.

Tuesday 14 September *Paris Elysee Montmartre*

Roused by the TM to be told that the bus would only be able to park briefly outside the Elysee Montmartre, so we'd all better be ready to run. Rolled out of bed into the familiar gloom of a bus deck in submarine-scramble mode – bodies pushing past and falling over each other – and pulled my bits and pieces together so as not to have to get through the day without something crucial. Out in the street it was sunny and I stumbled out of the bus into the familiar bustle of Montmartre's busy streets. Straight up the hill I could see the gold painted carousel, and above it, the surreal white enormous glow of Sacré Coeur.

Elyssee Montmartre was open for access so I climbed the steep stairs into the main hall which looked like it had been hit by the world's biggest litter bomb. The floor looked like the immediate aftermath of a pop festival – ankle deep in rubbish – particularly squashed plastic beer-beakers. I tiptoed through the mire into the dressing room where a guy was mopping the floor. Decided against an immediate shower and wandered back into the hall looking for coffee... At the back of the hall a middle-aged woman had arrived and had set up a buffet and an urn. I remembered her from last time we played here. She's been serving breakfasts to bands and crews here for years and deserves a name-check. Thank you, Francoise Michelet. Coffeed up, and sat chatting to the crew and band. Pete's reading a book about Elvis and keeps coming out with interesting and little-known facts. Elvis used to use three different types of hair gel at once: One for the front so it would flex when he shook his head, one for the sides which must be stiff so nothing would move, and yet another one at the back, to achieve the all-important "D.A." (my Dad told me about this... it stands for "Duck's Arse"). He'd done this since before he was famous. As with all success, attention to detail is vital...

While I drank coffee at the back of the hall, an amazing transformation was taking place as a small but highly effective team of guys (all black) swept and then mopped the floor of the hall, leaving it immaculate in well-under an hour.

I decided I'd pop outside and try to wake myself up a little, so I wandered down the street where – already – I spotted a guy in a Marillion t-shirt waiting at the road junction. I kept my head down and managed to avoid getting into conversation – it was a little too early in the day... Found a couple of music shops and eyed up a powder-blue Fender Jaguar which I wouldn't have minded owning... It wasn't particularly expensive, but I'm a bit skint at the moment, so it wasn't really an option.

Returned to the gig and showered before venturing back out with Paul Rowlston, who was still keen to interview me further about the songs on the new album. We headed up the hill to Sacré Coeur. By this time it was a glorious day and there were many people sitting out on the grassy slopes below the cathedral, sunning themselves. We climbed the wide steps up towards the church and I was immediately accosted by a dodgy bloke from Senegal who hustled me mercilessly into allowing him to weave a cotton braid for my wrist. I acceded while his companions hustled Paul who was much more experienced at refusing. I was declared to be "a good man" while Paul was reviled as "a Nazi and a fascist!" I was then relieved of ten euros for the character reference, but I must admit he made a nice job of the wrist braid, which I'm still wearing. We arrived at Sacré Coeur and walked around it while Paul marvelled at its' design and then I suggested Place du Tertre - the little square to the left of the church where all the artists paint and sketch for the tourists. We settled on a street café where we ordered vin-rouge and I spent the next couple of hours being interrogated on camera by Paul. As I talked, we occasionally paused while I signed autographs for passers-by. On show days I become famous! "It's our honeymoon," said one couple. Another memorable moment was when a French guy with his hair tied back came up to me and asked me if he could shake my hand. As he did so, he said nothing, but he held my gaze and the expression in his eyes was so meaningful that I felt tears welling up in my own. This might all sound a bit "luvvie" ish, but you'd have had to be there really to feel it. As he walked away I turned to Paul who was already shaking his head in response to the gravity of that unspoken moment. My words have reached deep inside some people, and sometimes they just want to let me know. Some people can say more with their eyes than their mouths. And I can listen with my eyes – often better than with my ears.

By the time the interview was over it was almost 3.30 in the afternoon. Today's an early show – 8pm – and soundcheck is set for 3.30, so we hurried back down the steps for the short downhill walk to the Elysee. When we returned, I ran straight into Bertrand Poucheron – journalist and long-time supporter of the band – who had brought me a bottle of wine. The French seem to set great store upon the giving of gifts and I've never walked away from a Paris show empty-handed.

Soundcheck progressed fairly quickly and we were done by 4.45 so I figured there was still time to get a cab across town to La Bastille where my favourite sock shop, Bexley, is situated. I always buy my socks from here – they're 100% cotton and reasonably priced if you buy 10 pairs at a time, so whenever I'm in Paris, I try to pop in. This time it would be more of a saga than a "pop" but it's not every day I'm here and I had a couple of hours to kill. I made my way back outside on to the Boulevard Rochechouart where I was told I'd get a cab "no problem". Hmm… As it turned out, it was 5pm on a Friday afternoon and taxis were pretty scarce. Empty taxis were non-existent and I walked up and down until about quarter-past before persuading a (notoriously reluctant and usually deliberately "difficult") Parisian taxi driver to take me. The traffic was hellish as it is in all the world's cities at 5 on a Friday afternoon, and so we arrived over at the Bastille around 5.40. To my relief, the shop was still open. I dived in to this lovely little shop – all wood panelling and dedicated solely to handmade shoes and socks (if you pardon the pun) - and selected 20 pairs of socks in various colours. I waited for about 10 minutes while a particularly delicate and slightly fraught debate took place between the shopkeeper and a lady customer in front of me. As far as I could tell, it had something to do with the exchanging of a pair of her husband's shoes. Her husband meanwhile stood courteously behind her as if to say "She's much better at this kind of thing than me…" The delicate debate finally concluded to the customer's satisfaction and the evident relief of the shopkeeper, and the couple exchanged the shoes and made an exit. I managed to pay for the socks in a couple of minutes, (i.e. roughly how long it would have taken his previous client to ask the way to the door) and emerged onto the sunny Paris street proudly clutching a bulging bag, with the satisfied grin of a mission accomplished against all odds. For some reason, it was much easier to find a cab for the return journey. Maybe I just got lucky. Back in Montmartre there was a large crowd outside the Elysee so I kept my head down and negotiated my way up the side streets unnoticed. I don't feel the need to avoid our fans, but in this situation I would have been stuck for an hour signing autographs and this would involve me missing dinner and not being able to chill-out before the show.

Popped up the side street to the Café Montmartre (believe it or not, they have a picture of me on the wall! I don't think they have the faintest idea why – but the owner took a shine to me last time I was here!) and had minute-steak and chips for dinner before returning to the show. The club was packed by now so I had to hide in the dressing room until showtime. In the meantime, Paul R filmed me doing a quick, "Hello – I'm sorry I can't be there" message for Willie Robertson's birthday next week. Willie* owns Robertson-Taylor Insurance Brokers who insure the whole of rock n'roll. We've been friends for many years and I was invited to his birthday bash at Shepherds Bush Empire on the 8th June. I'll be on tour so I'll have to miss it – Shame.

*Now, sadly, the late Willie Robertson. Much loved and much missed. (h, 2014)

Tuesday 21 September *"Oh Baby Baby, It's a Wild World"* – Air Rage...

Woke up at 7.30 after one of those bad nights of waking up repeatedly and wondering what time it was. Rolled out of bed and downstairs where I showered before making my first crucial coffee of the day. The house was slowly coming to life as Nial, first, and then Dizzy appeared in the kitchen. Nial went to shower and I drank coffee, kissed good morning to Sofie and tried to gather my thoughts and possessions together. I leave for Mexico City this morning. There's a car collecting me at 8.30. It arrived early at 8.10 so I maintained my old tradition of not actually packing until the car arrived. Threw all my things together and said bye bye to Nial and Sofie who went off to school happily. Dizzy shed a few tears – she's not looking forward to me going away. I'm sure I'd feel the same if the boot were on the other foot – I'll be away for about three weeks, and I guess I'll be the centre of attention more or less throughout. There's much can happen to place a wedge between us, but we've come this far and we've both fought to keep our marriage together despite some colossal pressures. If anything was going to split us up, I think it already would have*. As with everything else in life, we've both learned from years of previous experience and, believe me, there's much to learn from living this way. (*h note: spoke too soon...)

I left at 8.30 on a bright sunny morning and the taxi made fairly good time, depositing me in Heathrow Terminal 3 around 9.45. I met up with Steve, Pete, Ian and tour manager Quinner (Mark's flying in tomorrow) and we checked into flight UA 919 to Washington DC for the first leg of the journey. Check-in was pretty straightforward, much to my surprise as I was expecting security procedures to be pretty heavy. Security at International Departures was thorough however and a pair of scissors and Swiss Army Knife (which was a present from EMI Switzerland and bears the "His Master's Voice" logo on it – it's been in the bottom of my toilet bag for years) were confiscated and checked into lost property so that at least I can claim them back upon my return. I made my way to the gate and we boarded the 747, which took off on time without a hitch. Amazing.

For most of it, the flight was fairly uneventful. I spent much of it chatting to Roderick, our sound engineer and trying to read his Sound-on-Sound magazine over his shoulder. The stewardesses must have been around since the 60's, and are now, well, in their sixties by the look of them. Personally I think the shine had long since faded in terms of their enthusiasm for the job, and it's a shame they didn't retire when they ceased to enjoy it. I'm sure I remember a time when cabin crew were young, glamorous, pleasant and had at least the pretence of a sense-of-humour, but those days are gone now as far as many global carriers are concerned, and I think UA must actually have put this lot through some kind of passenger aversion-therapy. I felt like I was back at school under the gaze of disapproving teachers.

We were due into Washington around 14.45 and thankfully around 14.45 we were told to fasten our seatbelts for landing... I was looking forward to getting away from the surly uptight stewardesses and stretching my legs. As we landed, a voice came over the PA. "Ladies and Gentlemen, this is the purser. I have to inform you that we are not landing at Washington Dulles airport as we have been redirected to Bangor International Airport in Maine."

As I listened to this, I looked out of the side window to see a line of four or five large military aircraft – this place looks like a USAF airbase... The purser continued:

"The flight crew are too busy to speak to you right now but I can tell you that this diversion is due to bad weather over Washington and the need to refuel the aircraft."

Hmm... well that sounded plainly untrue to me and I began to fear the worst. Jesus... a hijack? A suspected bomb? I asked the nearest stewardess what was going on. Why do we need to refuel when our time in the air has been as scheduled? She seemed neither concerned nor interested and told me that she had only been in the job for two years and didn't understand the intricacies of re-fuelling. I asked her, politely, whether there was any chance of speaking to a stewardess who DID understand the intricacies of re-fuelling then. The tension I already felt was heightened when the purser came back on to the PA to tell us we were not allowed to use our cellphones at this time. 15 more confused and nervous minutes passed before the captain finally deigned to speak to us.

He told us that "a few people at the back of the aircraft have been asking questions" and he could now tell us that the diversion had been requested by the FBI and security forces and at the moment he was advised that he was "forbidden to fly to Washington in this aircraft with these passengers and this crew at this time." A strange choice of words...

We were told we could now use our cellphones to call home if we should require, and that we should remain in our seats with seatbelts fastened until further notice. An hour passed while the 747 stood on the runway until the captain came back on the PA to tell us that we must now "de-plane" and take all our hand-baggage with us.

On the way through the door of the 747 I was told by a stewardess that two "suits" from the FBI had boarded the plane and already escorted two people from the aircraft. Wow. Let's hope nothing's about to go bang, then...

We were led into a bleak hall where several lines had formed to pass through immigration and into the USA... The unfortunate chap in front of me was questioned at length, delaying the queue I was in, as all the others seemed to move along smoothly (you know the feeling). 'Turns out his only crime was to be holding a Pakistani passport, but that was enough to warrant him being taken into a side-room from which I never saw him emerge. I had bought a little digital camera on the flight over, so I was trying to snap some kind of visual record of what was going on. I was tapped on the shoulder by the guy behind me who said I risked arrest if I was caught taking photographs in the immigration-hall. I told him I thought this was the land of the free. "Not any more." he said, ruefully.

I was fingerprinted and asked a few routine questions by a female immigration officer who was actually very pleasant, especially so when compared to UA's bitter old trolly-dollies. After immigration I went through to a baggage hall where I picked up my hideous and beautiful pink suitcase before crossing the hall to Customs where an old female Customs officer had a good rummage through my cases. Having done this I was asked to put my pink suitcase on another conveyor where it disappeared into a hole in the wall. Now we were free to wander down into the main lobby of the airport via a descending escalator. At the bottom of this stood a uniformed airport-attendant who asked me, smilingly, if I had any questions.

"Yes." I said, "Do you know what's EXACTLY going on here?"

"Yes." He said, in a hushed tone "The FBI just took Cat Stevens and his daughter off your flight... but I haven't told you!"

Bloody Hell! All this for a singer/songwriter who has claimed to be a pacifist his entire life and wrote a song called "Peace Train". A good job Lennon wasn't on the plane – they'd have taken him out and shot him! (*if some other nutter hadn't already done it.)

This was quite a story and would be particularly so back in England where Cat was a big star in the 60's and 70's so I called Lucy and Lord B (our publicist) to let them know what had happened. Leave it to us, they said... I hung up the phone, conscious of the fact that I'd just broken a pretty big news story. Strangely we now had to retrieve our checked-in baggage AGAIN from a conveyor on this level so there was more hanging around until the hideous pink bag showed up. This enabled us all to go and form ANOTHER queue across the hall and begin checking in all over again. The pink bag was checked in afresh but not before being examined by yet another security guy who swabbed the handle before placing the swab in a machine – checking for trace elements of explosives, no doubt. Aah, them singer/songwriters can go off bang at any moment... (I was beginning to feel like I might explode myself, however, this was only just the beginning...) Having checked my pink bag back in, we were pointed back up the stairs to a gate where (see if you can guess?) our hand baggage was put through a scanner along with the contents of our pockets etc... etc...

So now we were all back at a departure gate where we waited yet another hour before being allowed back on the plane. If this makes tedious reading, it made bloody tedious doing!

Back on the plane we waited a further hour while the captain explained that the airport at Bangor Maine was not equipped to load 747's so all baggage was being reloaded into the hold by hand which would take a long time, but that the airport staff were "doing a great jarb". He then informed us that, for similar reasons, the plane was unable to re-stock food or drinks and that the staff would only be able to give us limited supplies of water, and nothing else, during our onward flight to Washington. He thanked us all "on behalf of America, himself, his crew, his children and his grand-children for our patience and understanding". This seemed a bizarre statement, but 'bizarre" was beginning to be lost on me as a concept. I think he was trying to imply that by being patient (we had a choice?) and subjecting ourselves to a 7-hour diversion (and much arsing about while our bags were repeatedly examined by various different people and machines) we had somehow saved him and his entire family tree from annihilation at the hands of a mad Muslim intent on bloody mass-murder. It was good to know that the man entrusted to fly our 747 was such an easy-going rational guy... So now we were all super-heroes too... Well that's nice.

After a private pause to contemplate whether the runway was long enough to take off, I crossed my fingers and, at last, we thundered down the tarmac clearing the perimeter fence by what looked like a few feet. The journey to Washington was refreshingly straightforward although a little spartan. After an hour or so, water was passed round sparingly. I tried to look grateful so as to avoid the evil eye of the headmistress.

When we arrived it was 10pm local time. We had missed the last flight of the day to Mexico City and we had been booked on the 8.40am flight in the morning, which was not direct, but via Chicago – once again, hundreds of miles in the wrong direction. The crowning news of the day, however, was that there was not one single hotel room available anywhere in Washington DC. Apparently there's some hot new exhibition of Native-American history at the Smithsonian Institute (Museum) and the city is packed solid with visitors. This means that our only choice was to sleep in the airport and, after frantic phone calls, which failed to secure any hotel rooms at any price, we settled down beneath the white fluorescent lights which (UA staff said) could not be switched off "for security reasons" (ah, America's new answer to every rational query). Small aeroplane-pillows and thin blankets were found in an attempt to fall just short of treating us like farmyard animals, and we lay down one by one on the seats of the airport terminal. I think I managed an hour of fitful sleep before my phone started ringing and the UK's radio and TV news started asking me what was happening. First came BBC Radio 5 live, then after a brief show of interest from **Good Morning America**, which waned, Channel 4 news. I was still talking to Channel 4 news when our 8.40 flight to Chicago began boarding. Quinner our tour manager, attempted to negotiate us an upgrade to business-class as a compensation for the delay and the sleepless night, but UA would have none of it. They said that any liability was not theirs as the diversion had been a security-issue.

What's particularly tricky in all this, is that I have to sing live at The National Auditorium (capacity 9000) tonight (Wednesday), it's being broadcast live on Mexican television and I haven't slept since Monday. No pressure then. When I got on the plane I saw that I had been given a seat in the middle of a row of three occupied seats. I got back off the plane and threw a minor fit into the face of a Customer Relations supervisor, eventually being offered a row of 3 empty seats at the rear of the plane so that I could sleep. I spent a valuable hour horizontal before disembarking for the connecting flight to Mexico City, which was leaving almost immediately.

We rushed to the gate and made it in time to check in and make our way onto the plane. No empty row of seats for me any more. The checked in baggage had been checked right through this time, so we were kind of resigned to maybe not getting our luggage for a day or two. Made our way onto the plane and settled down to be told, after a while, that the pilot's seat was faulty (!?!?!) and that another one must be found and assembled in it's place. You couldn't make this stuff up, and sadly, I'm not. That was about an hour ago, and there's still no sign of it. As I write, I'm further from Mexico than I was this morning and going nowhere fast. The longest journey of my life was the ludicrous one from Rio to Boston via Heathrow, back in 1996 and at 37 hours, I thought it couldn't be beaten. At the moment I've been travelling for exactly 33 hours and we still have to get down to Mexico City. I get the feeling we're going to break our own record.

The new pilot's seat finally arrived and was installed in around 2 hours. At 11.45am, we set off to Mexico, exhausted, mindful of tonight's live TV performance, and resigned to whatever happens next. Soundcheck at The National Auditorium is noon. I think we'll probably miss it...

After we were airborne food was served. I wasn't really hungry but my game-plan was to have a couple of beers and lapse into coma so that at least I could chip away at some of the 6-hours jet-lag and general exhaustion and perhaps be in with a chance of being in a fit state to sing tonight in Mexico City. When the steward came round with the drinks I asked for two beers. I figured this would save him the hassle of having to serve me twice. On British Airways they'd have probably given me two without me asking (they often have). However, on United Airlines, this proved an insurmountable problem.

"I'm sorry sir I cannot give you two beers"

"Why not?"

"I can't legally provide you with more than one beer."

"What?! How is it illegal? I have been flying all over the word for years and I have never heard of that!"

"US law, sir. I cannot provide you with more than one beer but if you let me know when you have finished this one I will provide you with another." He said in the slightly terse manner I've come to expect from UA's cabin crew. He then asked Steve Rothery, seated next to me, what he would like to drink? I said he would like a beer.

"Is that true sir?" the steward said to Rothers.

"Yes." Said Steve.

"I'm sorry – I cannot give you a beer because I have reason to believe that this beer would not be for you, but would be for your *friend* here."

I'm talking about little less-than-half-pint cans of Heineken here. I sighed and saw little point in debating the issue - it's no-doubt a "security" thing. I sipped at the little can as slowly as possible whilst casting an eye over the in-flight movie **The Alamo** – the usual Hollywood American legend dressed up as heroic fact, which, strangely I wasn't in the mood to watch. When I had finished the beer I pressed the button to ask the steward for another. He arrived and told me tersely that he was still serving passengers further down the plane and that he would get back to me when he was finished. Jesus, what a country this is! I've been travelling for 37 hours and I'm being ticked off for doing as I was told in the first place. I hung on another ten minutes or so, after which the seat-belt signs were turned off, so I thought I'd just walk down the plane and ask him for a beer, then he could simply reach into the trolley and give me one. This I did but he refused, became shirty and told me that he didn't like my attitude. I told him I wasn't crazy about his attitude either and asked to speak to his superior. He directed me to the front of the plane where I tried and failed to complain about the situation to the purser. He listened whilst visibly bristling and then said "You've had your say, now let me have mine..." I was accused of harassment and the so-called superior told me that if I persisted in "causing trouble he would have the plane landed at the nearest airport and have me escorted from the aircraft". Now in an extreme state of derision, I resisted the urge to reach out and strangle him, remained calm and asked him how difficult it would have been for his colleague to simply reach down into a trolley and pass me a beer, and how this question constituted harassment of the cabin crew? ...but it was a waste of breath. I was so very tempted to call his bluff and tell him to go ahead and ground the plane, but that would have put an end to tonight's acoustic show in Mexico and would have also further buggered up the lives of all the passengers on this flight (not to mention getting me banned from ever entering the U.S. again). In the end he said he would bring me a beer when he had finished serving the first class passengers if I could assure him that there would be no "problem". I resented the implication that I was some kind of troublemaker and I told him I failed to understand the question but that, no, there would be "no problem". I was given a second beer some 15 minutes later. Gosh! I'd consumed (almost) an entire ¾ of a PINT of lager in an hour! Call in the marines - madman on board! For the rest of the flight I kept my head down and - too stressed to sleep - tried to faithfully reproduce the events of the day here in this diary.

The steward in "economy" ($1400 return from Heathrow) never did bring me a beer.

We FINALLY arrived in Mexico City around 4.00 pm and were met in the arrivals lounge by two friendly and helpful Mexican girls – working for the promoter – who escorted us speedily through immigration and customs, and we were soon in a minibus with our good friend Andrea Escobar who said "Hey – there's some beer in the cooler if anyone's thirsty."

It felt good to be back in a sane, civilized country.

Sunday 3 October *Cincinnati Bogarts*

Woke up late around 12.45 and realised we'd crossed another time-line East so it was already 1.45. Quinner was asking if I had any laundry as he'd found a Laundromat across the street. This was no ordinary launderette – it was "Sudsy Malones" launderette and bar! An inspired name for an inspired idea. You can go along with your dirty washing and load up the machines, then go and have a couple of beers while you're waiting. Don't know why it hasn't caught on in the UK. Probably illegal on the grounds that it would make life better for the people...

After Q had gone off with the laundry I found a few more garments in desperate need so I wandered into Sudsy's myself. It was all dark in the front – and a few motley types were on bar stools at the bar. It reminded me a little of Moe's in *The Simpsons* or that bar in space in Star Wars. At the back it was lighter and, sure enough there was the Laundromat. I lifted the lid on a few washers before finding our load and added my bits and bobs to the assembled soups. Made my way back across the road wondering whether or not it's a crime to lift the lid on someone else's laundry... it had felt like a violation.

Returned to the gig on this perfect blue sunny day and sat in the dressing room trying to work up the energy to clean my teeth and get in the shower. I was still stuck to the sofa at 2.30 when Rick Armstrong arrived in the dressing room. Cincinatti is Rick's town and we had arranged a special "swap the band" session for him, his brother Mark, and his niece Kali. This weekend, the Armstrongs were coincidentally having a family reunion and there was a rumour that Neil was going to pop in and watch. Rick is the son (and spitting image) of Neil Armstrong, test pilot, astronaut and, of course the first man to walk on the moon. I'd met Neil before at Heathrow airport a couple of years back and he had bought my family lunch.

Rick and I chatted down in the bleak dressing room of Bogart's club until finally I could put it off no longer and I excused myself so I could shower and "get up". Feeling much better, I went upstairs to the stage where the crew were trying to trace the source of a mains crackle. This process dragged on for about an hour and involved much jumping up and down to make the crackle happen, followed by much scratching of heads.

Rick's family arrived and there was the sudden chaos of the three small children, Kyle, Lilly and Bryce – all strumming guitars and blowing harmonicas. They were certainly in the mood for a musical occasion. Back up on stage I began checking out my monitors in amongst the persistent mains crackle. Time was running short and we had to get on... I noticed from the stage that Rick's brother, Mark had arrived along with his wife Wendy and their daughter Kali, who was walking on crutches. They have recently discovered that she has ligaments missing from her knees, and has had to have an operation involving grafts. Poor thing. Must be bloody painful, but she's a spirited girl and seems to be toughing it out. When she's recovered, she has to go through the whole thing again with the other leg. Nice...

Then, there he was, the great man himself looking very relaxed in chinos and a Hawaiian shirt along with his wife, Carol. I said hello and we chatted for a while. Someone had arranged for Rick to get up at soundcheck and play a song, so we organised that and we all played *Waiting To Happen* together. Kali got up too. She seemed already perfectly at home on a stage and sang well and with great energy. Neil patiently and graciously posed for photographs with the band, and Steve R snapped an impromptu shot of he and I in conversation. At this point he has laid his hand upon my shoulder. Being a restrained and measured man by nature, I was touched by this gesture of affection and whenever I look at the photograph I feel doubly privileged to have known him.

The mains crackle was finally laid to rest and the rest of the soundcheck proceeded without incident.

Can't remember much about the show. I guess it must have been eclipsed by Sudsy's, and the Armstrong family soundcheck.

Wednesday 13 October   *Quebec La Capitole*

At some point in the middle of the night I realised I was awake and with a certain feeling in the back of my neck. It was the slow internal movement that I remembered from the last time it ricked and, sure enough as I held perfectly still in the darkness, I felt it go. It's a feeling that can hardly be described. It's like something slides inside and then there's an intense pain like cramp which can only be eased by finding a certain body position, but any attempt to move head or body results in a return of the intense cramp – like a spear stuck in it. Now I'm in trouble... I spent the rest of the night trying to find a position where there was no pain, but it's impossible to lie in the same position all night and every time I moved the pain returned. There was nothing much I could do but try and get back to sleep. Eventually I must have dozed off, but when I next woke, the pain was even more intense as I had, no doubt, moved around in my sleep. I carried on like this until I could hear signs of life in the bus and people moving around, and then I asked tour manager Quinner to see if he could find me some kind of physiotherapist as I certainly couldn't perform tonight in this state. I know from experience that it normally eases up during the day, but how much was anybody's guess. It took me some time to find a way out of the bus bunk. The pain was severe whenever I moved and I found myself letting out involuntary yelps as I attempted to get into my clothes and on to my feet.

Out in the street it was evident that we were parked in Quebec's old town – just by the city walls (the only walled city in the North American continent). It was a gorgeous day and I alighted the bus with Wes and saw Lise out in the street, sitting on some steps with a coffee. I asked her where she'd got it and she pointed at an adjacent coffee shop so Wes and I wandered in where we found Steve Rothery already sat down with a coffee and some kind of cake. I killed time with the boys until Quinner returned to say that the hotel had found me a sports physio, Dr Blaise Dubois (no less.) and I must take a cab to a surgery about 20 minutes away. Annie, the hotel manager took me over the road and spoke to the taxi driver on my behalf (my French isn't quite up to the intricacies of explaining directions to far-flung surgeries), she even gave me 40 Canadian dollars to get me there and back. "I'll put it on the room" she said. What a girl – most hotel staff wouldn't have bothered moving from the front desk.

The taxi eventually arrived at a kind of mall somewhere and the driver helped me find the surgery, locate the doctor, and gave me a number so that I could call him back when I was finished.

After waiting a while I was shown in to see Dr Blaise Dubois. I was expecting a Belgian looking man with a dark curly moustache, but instead I found a short-haired young Scandinavian-looking guy with sculpted blonde Frank Zappa face-fuzz. Tres-chic, and a very pleasant and knowledgeable chap. His English was patchy but not as patchy as my French, yet we managed to communicate in both languages at once. He soon found the places in my neck and upper spine and I winced with admiration at the ease with which he inflicted colossal pain upon me. After much exploratory prodding he concluded that it was probably unwise to manipulate me as it would probably render me in even more pain for the show tonight, so he applied a hot pack to my neck to relax the muscles a little and I was left alone to 'cook' for 20 minutes. When he returned he stretched me a bit to see if this might help and by the time he'd finished I did have a little more freedom of movement. He prescribed 600mg of ibuprofen every 4 hours and so, after being relieved of 70 dollars, I went round the corner to the pharmacy to buy some.

I returned to the gig in the taxi. The taxi driver seemed most keen that I should use his company to get to the airport in the morning so I booked him to come to the hotel at 4.00 am. I fly at 6.05 to Honolulu, Hawaii. There's a chap called Daniel Allen who lives in Hawaii and he left a note on my stevehogarth.com guestbook saying he would like to thank Marillion for the many years of music, and to show his appreciation, he is offering to fly all five of us to Hawaii for an all-expenses-paid holiday! Too good to be true? Well, the boys thought so... but I made a few enquiries and thought "What the Hell!". He seems to be sincere and says he is wealthy and can easily afford it – that it would be his pleasure and a privilege. I contacted him and, as I was the only taker, he offered to fly my wife from London so we could meet up in Hawaii and enjoy his treat together. He has booked her flight (and she's probably already en route) along with mine from Quebec tomorrow morning at dawn! What an extraordinary and generous chap.

I returned to the hotel around 3.15, still not having checked in... The Hotel du Capitole is physically adjoined to the Theatre du Capitole – tonight's gig – and the building in which it's housed is one of the most beautiful buildings in Quebec. I checked in to room 321 (321 for the second time this tour...) which had a beautiful view over old Quebec to the seaway beyond, and Annie persuaded the chef to make me a chicken club-sandwich which was brought up to me in my room (another bending of the rules...) so that I could have time to have a bath AND eat breakfast before the soundcheck at 4pm. By now the ibuprofen was working and I felt much improved as I lowered myself into a heavenly hot bath. The sandwich eventually turned up just before 4.00 so I ate it on the run as I got ready to go down to soundcheck.

The Capitole Theatre is a beautiful old cabaret-theatre accessible directly from the hotel. I arrived on stage still clutching the club-sandwich plate as I finished "breakfast" at 4.15. The whole place is a good size for us, although it was slightly disconcerting to see tables and chairs about the place. There'd be little chance of equalling the vibe of last night's Montreal show at the Spectrum. Time was tight as we had to leave to do an in-store appearance and signing session at 5pm. The stage sound was good though – Mike's really on top of my monitor-needs now and I rarely have to ask him for anything. Luckily we managed to grab 5-minutes back in our rooms before leaving for the signing session so I got time to take some more tablets. Having been in pain all day, I was beginning to feel physically tired and I briefly contemplated cancelling the signing session, but I figured it wouldn't take long. Wrong.

Unlike the quick journey across town I was expecting, we were bundled into cars which drove out of town for 20 minutes to a suburban mall in the Ste Foy area. By the time we arrived I was hurting, tired and worried about the show. At least it's the last one – if I'd ricked my neck 2 weeks ago in LA the whole tour would have been a struggle. We made our way through the underground car-park and up through a maze of tradesmen's corridors into the back of a large music store and then out on to the shop floor where a queue had formed to see us. A little cheer went up as we sat down at a trestle table and Quinner saved the day by sorting me out with a beer. Most of the girls and all of the guys wanted to shake my hand as they filed past for signatures. Every handshake hurt my neck, especially the firm no nonsense-grip favoured by the Canadian men. They all mean well, of course, but after an hour of this I was praying silently for it to stop. The queue finally came to an end and then everybody wanted their photographs taken with us so, just when I thought it was over... it wasn't. I must confess I gave it 5 minutes and then went back to the back of the shop to hide until the boys caught up. We returned to the hotel – another 25 minutes – to be told that we must meet on the 4th floor at 8pm for a meet and greet. This gave me just enough time to shave. I still don't know why, or who we met. They were all very nice but I wasn't really introduced to anyone. We arranged to meet back up in hotel reception at 9pm to go next door for the 9.30 stage time. This gave me the best part of 45 minutes alone WITH NOTHING TO DO. Heaven. I found a miniature bottle of Grand Marnier in the minibar and slugged that down. The only way to get through tonight's performance was to drink LOADS and FAST so I set about doing just that. Quebec was lit up outside my window now in the darkness – really a beautiful sight – as I relaxed in the dark on my bed.   At 9.00 I made my way down to reception and then over to backstage where a leopard-skin patterned chaise-longue seemed to be the centrepiece of the room. A shame we couldn't have got it in the truck... Got ready for the show in between gulps of Canadian beer and hit the stage feeling not too bad! The show was pretty intense but not in the same league as yesterday. To be honest, I wasn't at my most lucid and sober so it may have been better or worse than I remember.

After the show the band immediately got down to the serious business of having an end of tour celebration drink in the hotel bar. This was a pretty chaotic affair with a mixture of band, chums, fans and eventually crew. The proceedings were made more colourful by the presence of Andy, a transvestite in full-drag, including fishnet stockings and miniskirt. I'm all for it. By now, I was the wrong (or right...) side of a few tequilas and feeling no pain whatsoever, which was just as well. A minimum of two people were trying to talk to me at any one time, all of the time, and I tried mostly in vain to understand or respond with anything lucid or articulate. My master plan was to stay up until 3.30 and then take the taxi to the airport. However, around 2.00 I hit a wall of exhaustion and party-overload and snuck off upstairs to my room to crash. I had arranged a wake-up call for 3.45 – this would give me a cosy 15 mins to shower and get out to fly to Honolulu via Newark, NY at 6.05am.

Thursday 14 October *Quebec*

Woken by the pink dawn-light streaming in through the window. I noticed two things:
    The phone was off the hook – I must have knocked it off getting into bed.
    It was 7.05am.
    Bugger.

2005

Friday 10 June *Home – NYC*

Woke at 6.30 and couldn't really get back to sleep. Today we fly to NYC to begin a small acoustic tour. Unfortunately Dizzy's dad had a heart attack last Thursday and was rushed to hospital so she flew out to Pretoria last Friday. (I dropped her at Heathrow before heading up the M4 to Bristol for the first warm up show.) My departure to New York today means that we'll be leaving Sofi and Nial to fend for themselves for a week. This is a first, and I'm sure it was contributing to my nervousness as I lay there contemplating the day ahead. I wanted to be sure I would leave them with everything they need. The fridge is full of food, I've left loads of change for school dinners and Sarah, our next-door neighbour, has kindly offered to take them to the supermarket if they should run low on supplies. Nonetheless, not having done this before, I couldn't help fretting that I'd clear off to America and forget something crucial and fundamental. I had also decided to glaze the wardrobe before my car arrived to take me to the airport at 10.30 am. We've had some glass panels made and they arrived yesterday. Didn't want to leave a load of glass around the house under the circumstances so I tried to fit them last night before running out of silicon sealant. Couldn't get any more 'til 9.00am so it was all a bit tight... Got up at 6.45 and decided to get the pink suitcase out and pack. Was just about ready when Nial got up at 8.00. I said I'd take him to school (normally he gets the school-bus) as I won't be seeing him for a couple of weeks. We left at 8.20 and drove the 5 miles to Brackley where I dropped him off. "Bye Dad. You're the best dad" he said as he wandered off in the direction of the school building. I love him so much. As luck would have it, the hardware shop didn't open til 9.00 and it was only 8.40 so I decided to drive to the doctors (15 miles away in the wrong direction) and pick up a prescription before returning to buy silicon sealant at the hardware shop. Went home and began fitting the glass panels. When it got to 10.15 I roused Sofi who isn't at school today and she pointed out that my car had already arrived. Better finish packing. Was still finding shirts and socks as I climbed into the car on what was a fine sunny morning.

Spent the journey to Heathrow writing on the computer and it seemed to pass quickly. At Terminal 3 I met up with Lucy and the boys and a fairly chaotic check-in followed but we got away with only £60 on the excess baggage. Not bad considering we have 4 guitars and a load of audio gear. Got frisked at Security even though the machine didn't go beep when I walked through it. "Just a quick random search," he said. Well I've heard it called some things... Maybe it was the trousers... I wasn't wearing underwear so the search was a bit more intimate than I suspect either of us had hoped... Walked away whistling, "Getting to know you," and found a seafood bar where I had a breakfast of salmon and brown bread before making my way to gate 18 where the Virgin 747 to JFK was already boarding. The flight seemed unusually quick at 6hrs 45mins and the cabin-crew were pleasant and friendly, we didn't get diverted, nobody got arrested, the plane didn't need any fundamental components replacing, and nobody threatened to arrest *me* for ordering a second drink. Marvellous. Not United Airlines then.

Took a cab into Manhattan with Lucy and Steve R and arrived at the Marcel hotel on the corner of E23rd St and 3rd Ave in pretty good shape apart from the need to shower. Checked in and helped the boys with the heavy equipment which was stored in a back room before going up to room 605 in the slowest lift in NYC. Showered and spent a couple of hours in the bar downstairs drinking beer and discovering the delights of Patron Tequila care of the Dublin barman, Mark. Invited him to the show on Sunday and toddled off to bed.

Saturday 11 June *NYC*

Slept well and woke up at 6.00 but managed to slip in and out of sleep until 9.00. A good effort. Opened the curtains expecting the same sunny weather of yesterday but was surprised to see it raining. I realized that I hadn't packed one single item of outer clothing. Shirts in plenty, but no jackets. There's always something...

I decided to brave the weather and go and buy an American SIM card for my mobi then I can use it with a phone-card and I'll be able to call England more cheaply. As I walked down E23rd St the rain got heavier until I was fairly well-soaked. All the phone shops were closed so I figured they must open at 10.00. Got further drenched trying to find a Starbucks so I could pick up some email, and after the usual wrangling, managed to open an account and log on. I'm expecting a transcript of an interview I did with a couple of guys in America last week, which I'd promised to correct and return. They hadn't sent it anyway. The AC in Starbucks was bloody freezing after coming in from the hot street all wet-through. Not a good thing to do to yourself at the beginning of a tour. Pneumonia. Bring it on! A girl from Israel asked me to watch her bags while she went to the loo. They never exploded and when she got back we got talking about the continuing war with the Palestinians. I had to tread carefully. She, after all, lives there, and I've never even been. How can you make peace though with people who were born and grew up in forced-isolation camps? And how can you make peace by bombing them? She says it's not like it is in the news reports. She says they're one-sided. Hmm... She said Israeli politicians are self-seekers who aren't really representing the feelings of the people. Well, knock me down with a feather.

By now it had stopped raining so I wandered down the street and found a phone-shop where a man relieved me of $60 and I emerged with a new US number. I returned to the hotel but couldn't resist popping into a little book store on E24th to buy a book which had caught my eye in the window. It's called **On Bullshit** and was worth the money for the title alone. When I got back I changed out of my damp clothes and soon it was time to meet downstairs to go to lunch. We were meeting a couple of guys called David and Stuart who are marketing men. They are also fans and had contacted Lucy to see if they could help us with anything and have subsequently secured us an interview with Sirius Radio – quite a big deal here. We met at a restaurant called St. Andrews which has a massive selection of drinks. I ordered a bottle of Young's "Dirty Dick" bitter (well, you have to) which is brewed in Wandsworth which, when you're in Manhattan, feels ten times further away than it actually is. I ordered a salad and watched open-mouthed as huge portions of spare-ribs and fish and chips arrived at our table. I'd never have managed any of it. (Oddly enough, there are very few overweight people on the streets of Manhattan.) Nice caff though.

In the evening we played a short acoustic set at Tower Records in Greenwich Village. The shop staff all seemed excited to have us there. My sound wasn't great, but stuff like this isn't really about the quality of what you do – it's just the fact that you showed up and made a noise. Still, you can't help but want it to be classy. Sometimes, that just aint an option. Seemed to go down okay.

Afterwards we went to a couple of tequila-bars and drank Margharitas. A most pleasant and relaxing evening before the hard work begins.

Sunday 12 June *NYC Bowery Ballroom*

Unfortunately, I didn't write this one up. I remember it being a good night though. A Los Trios romp in front of a good sized and "up for it" crowd. My voice was rested and I thought I sang well. The evening was notable for Rufus Wainright showing up with his entire band. I chatted with drummer, Matt Johnson for a while (notable for having played and co-written *Dream Brother* with Jeff Buckley on the classic **Grace** album), with the lovely Jason Hart who plays keyboards, and with Joan Wasser, who plays viola and sings backup with Rufus. Great that they all came. The following day a txt came in from Rufus saying, "I'm jealous of your range", which was all it said.

Friday 17 June   *Montreal La Tulipe*

Walked out onto the stage at La Tulipe Theatre, Montreal and the 700 capacity crowd went completely wild as one. I was alone and, for once, I could be certain it was for me. A massive wave of noise rolled over me as I looked out into a crowd of open-mouthed grinning faces. All seemed to say, "You're here. It's amazing. We have waited for you. You mean so very much to us. All you have to do is sing." I stood away from the piano centre-stage, raised my arms and let it wash over me. I never felt anything like it in my life. As my head rolled back and my eyes closed the audience responded and the cheering moved up to a new pitch of outright screaming. It wasn't hysteria though, it was raw affection. I'm finding it hard to write down because words don't do it justice. In that 3-minute outpouring of pure joy I felt that every hardship and petty frustration I have endured over the years of making music, was worthwhile – indeed, of no significance whatsoever. Thank you Montreal. You have eclipsed Le Zenith on the **Season's End** tour. Wow – what is it with the French? When they fall in love, they fall deep. One day, I'll write this city a song.

Saturday 3 September   *Home – San Diego*

Woke up at 7.00 and went downstairs to finish packing and to finish fiddling with Nial's iPod in the hope of leaving him with a working one while I'm away. Showered and drank coffee. By 8.45 there was still no sign of a car so I called Rich so he could check it was all okay. Sue got up along with Nial to say bye bye. I managed to burn a slice of toast and set the smoke alarm off in the house before departing with a spare set of house-keys having lost my own... My driving licence continues to elude me but at least I found my passport, which was tucked safely in my back pocket.

To my relief, the car showed up at 8.50 and we left on time at 9.00 for Heathrow arriving at 10.00am. Check in was straightforward although there was some commotion regarding Steve's pedal-board, which couldn't be checked through without him and he'd already gone through to departures. We had to go and find him and he had to come back out. Easier said than done. I had a spot of breakfast before walking the 40 miles to gate 46 where we boarded the 747 without incident. My usual aisle reservation had gone un-reserved and so I settled down grumpily into a middle seat between Rich and Colin. Sometimes I think I ought to pull rank a bit more than I do...

Take-off was accompanied by a massive bang from beneath us followed by intense juddering of the entire fuselage. They don't usually do that... I must own-up to some moderate fear, despite my many flights.

The flight was long at ten and a half hours but I spent most of it working on a new h song (*Oil*) and the hours seemed to pass pretty quickly. The BA crew kept me supplied with regular refills of London Pride (they'd have all gone to jail for that in America!) but sleep wasn't really an option. Next to Steve R across the aisle, there was a baby going off like it had been placed on a spike for the duration of the flight. "Colic," I thought... "The first four years are the worst." I had to feel sorry for him. He was wearing his noise-cancelling headphones (Rothers is a gear junkie) but I don't think they were quite up to cancelling a baby-on-a-spike.

At last we landed at LAX with roughly the same grace as we took off. The pilot threw the aeroplane in the approximate direction of the runway, which we hit hard and somewhat sideways. Maybe he was on an exchange-scheme from "Gate Gourmet".

Immigration at LA was refreshingly quick compared to the one-hour queue I'm used to at New York (and some of my previous LA arrivals), but we made up for it by having to wait ages for the bags. After that we breezed through Customs and out into the street. I'm in LA again! Love or hate this place, you can't argue with the sunshine and palm-trees. We took the courtesy bus to Alamo Car Rentals and I sat on all the equipment for half-an-hour in the late afternoon sunshine while the boys rented cars. I was surprised to find the temperature lower than in England. Who'd have thought?

After much faffing, cars were hired and off we went – a little hesitant at first – towards the freeway down to San Diego. Rothers and Pete fiddled with the radio trying to tune it in to Steve's iPod. We got it going in the end and drove to the accompaniment of Jeff Buckley, and Steely Dan's *Babylon Sisters*. ("*Drive west on Sunset to the sea...*") well, you must. All went smoothly until we hit a one-hour traffic jam for an accident, which, as we passed, seemed to involve three or four badly beaten-up cars. How does anyone HAVE a traffic accident here? Four lanes of cars - all traveling on a perfectly straight road at exactly the same 65mph speed. You can only really crash by falling asleep. I was reminded of a story my good friend David Smith told me - of the American who bought a Winnebego and was told by the salesman that it was "fully automatic". He drove to the freeway, engaged the cruise control and crashed horribly after he went up the back to make a cup of tea...

After what seemed like a year, we cleared the accident and eventually rolled into the Hilton Hotel at Del Mar (near San Diego) around 7.30 pm – i.e. 20 hours since I got out of bed. (Luxury, compared to the Cat Stevens Mexico City journey from HELL last year.)

I checked into my room 1007 (very spacious) and joined Rich and Roderick for sodas on the terrace. Got chatting to an old dear called Violet Parkhurst who said she was a painter. She said she specialized in seascapes and had sold paintings to Margaret Thatcher and Ronald Reagan. She invited me to check out her website and I said I would. (I had a look the following morning and discovered she used to go out with Clark Gable! Jeez – it's amazing who you bump into in California). I sat with the boys next to an open gas fire – a kind of high-tech posh equivalent of a camp fire – on the terrace by the hotel lobby. I was once again reminded of the beans-scene from **Blazing Saddles** but I didn't mention it – I was in mixed company. Downed a couple of beers and a Patron tequila and called it a night. A definitive Hard Day's night.

Sunday 4 September   *San Diego Del Mar Races and moving rooms…*

Thought I did rather well – slept 'til 5.00 then catnapped through to 9.00. Got up, showered up, and went down to the restaurant for breakfast. It was a buffet thing. Had to wait for a table for 5 or 10 mins so returned to my room for extra clothes – I was finding the AC a little chilly. After the buffet breakfast I decided to take the shuttle bus down to the beach and take a few photographs. The Hilton is next to the horse racetrack at Del Mar and the shuttle bus went there first to drop off a few race-goers. During the journey a woman called Michelle announced that she owned a private box in the grandstand: "If you go racing, just find box 9E by the finish-line and speak to George. Tell him Michelle says it's okay". Things have a habit of developing at speed in America. It was worth knowing although I didn't know if I wanted to go racing, really. I was dropped at the beach chanting "George, Michelle, 9E, George, Michelle, 9E…" to myself in case I needed the facts later. Mooched around and discovered a café called *The Poseidon* on the beach, where I spent the next couple of hours sipping lemon tea and later had the best Bloody Mary I've ever tasted.

There seemed to be some problem getting hold of the shuttle bus to return so I decided to walk it. Immediately got hopelessly-lost and ended up flagging down cars to ask for directions. Everyone pointed me in different directions until I asked a couple in an old car with a baby in the back. "Hop in," they said, "We'll drop you near the racecourse". I jumped in the back and the baby grinned away at me whilst chatting in unfeasibly good English. He was trying to tell me about a mouse getting in the cat food. He told me over and over again. He was very impressed by it. So would I have been. Especially when I was two years old. That's one seriously ballsy mouse. They dropped me at the Racecourse at Del Mar and I made my way in, asking everyone about box 9E, George and Michelle. No one had heard of any of it, of course, but eventually I gained access and after much general enquiry I found myself sitting in the grandstand with a perfect view of the finish line. I took several photographs of the horses and jockeys. To be honest, though, the punters were more interesting. One guy in a Stetson cowboy-hat caught my eye. He looked around 55 and was sporting a bushy droopy moustache and a pair of round reading glasses balanced on the end of his nose, looking for-all-the-world like Doc Holliday. In England he'd have stopped traffic, but here it's considered absolutely normal. He sat next to a brassy blonde (55 done up as 25) and adjacent to another guy – the other traditional American stereotype: Hawaiian shirt, reversed baseball cap, moonfaced and overweight. 'Bizarre to see the old-timers side-by-side with the junk-food generation.

I watched a few more races and noticed that a jockey called something like Carlos Venezuela (but not quite) seemed to be riding in all the races and winning most of 'em. My gran used to love the 'horses' and she taught me to bet on the jockeys – not the horse they were on. She used to know who the best trainers were too. Despite all this deep-seated nostalgia I decided against having a flutter. I hadn't so-far picked any of the winners anyway so I couldn't see the point in upping the disappointment by losing money too. I wandered around the grandstand and into Bings café. Lovely old black and white pictures on the wall of Crosby with Edward G Robinson, Jack Dempsey and even a shot of J Edgar Hoover hanging out at the course.

Eventually decided I'd had enough of the races and walked back to the hotel. Even though the hotel was next to the racecourse, I felt like a rebel by actually WALKING. It's nuts here. If people want to go next door, they take a Hummer or a Porsche Carrera. Then they go to a gym and "work-out" because they believe exercise is very important. Gotta have those abs and a tight butt! It's 25 degrees on the street but they freeze the air in this hotel so much that we all need to wear a jacket to feel comfortable. It's as if the entire nation is trying to find ways of spending a FORTUNE on stuff that could be totally free. The only POSSIBLE justification for going ANYWHERE in a Hummer is to make people notice you. And yet the windows are, invariably, tinted.

When I got back I had hit a bit of a jet-lagged slump so I lay on the bed and tuned the TV to National Geographic. I drifted in and out of consciousness during a programme about people being abducted by aliens. It was somewhat surreal to keep coming round to the eye-witness accounts: "There were four of them – very thin with huge eyes and almost no mouth. Dry powdery skin. They took me from my bed to a flying saucer where they began interfering between my legs..." The program seemed to be on some kind of half-hour rotation and every time I woke up it was repeating the same thing. The sense of the surreal was eclipsed and compounded when chaotic sounds began emanating from the adjoining room to mine. Someone was re-enacting the gimp scene from **Pulp Fiction**.

I guessed there were at least three people in the room. One was shouting obscenities associated with some kind of hardcore sex-ritual whilst I heard the sound of bodies literally bouncing off the wall. I didn't know this stuff happened in real life... or maybe I did, but I never thought I'd get this close to it. It was really horrible and very disturbing. I leapt from the bed to check that the connecting door, from my room to theirs, was securely locked on my side (!) and then called reception and they said they'd send security to talk to them. Good luck!

I asked to move rooms. There was no way I was going to sleep tonight next to that lot! I packed, and one of the porters came round to help me move. As we walked down the corridor I told him what I'd heard. He said he'd go and check it out. He was bloody welcome to.

Well this episode had certainly woken me up! I called tour-manager Rich, to let him know I'd moved rooms and to tell him why. He sounded suitably amused. He was down at the Belly Up club (where we'll play on Wednesday) with the crew. Roderick said he'd drive back and pick me up so I freshened up and went down there with him.

The gig is in the Cedras area of Solana Beach. It seemed posh and arty as we drove along the street. Roderick took a picture of me outside the gig. Well, at least they'd spelled our name right...

Inside it's a groovy little club – lots of wood and paintings of rockn'roll iconography. The staff seemed friendly. I ordered a Corona and chatted to Rich, Col and Roderick while we waited for tonight's band The Knitters to come on stage. They were good if you like indie-Country & Western. Not really to my taste but they were good at it – especially the guitar player Dave Abrahams who was brilliant. The singer could have been produced on a computer by starting with Al Pacino and morphing to Harrison Ford. Somewhere along the way you'd have got him. The other singer was his wife (I think) who reminded me of Kirstie McColl to look at. They seemed to have lots of good songs – all good-natured down-home country-rockabilly stuff. The most memorable line of the evening was "*Put another critter on the road*" – a homage to the joy of road-kill. We left half-way through as Roderick was crashing out and nobody was too fussed about staying.

I returned to my new, quiet, room in another wing of the hotel – far enough a way from the monster ménage-a-trois - and fell immediately into sleep.

Woke up to the sound of the TV: "Men who experience a continuous erection for more than 4 hours should seek immediate medical attention"

So should their girlfriends... God Bless America.

Wednesday 16 November   *Home – Bus*

Had decided to go straight to the studio from the pub. Said bye bye to Dizzy and half the village and drove to the Racket Club in Dizzy's jeep so she could hang on to my car while I'm away. Parked up and admired the big pink tour bus, which was almost ready to leave. Was greeted in the car park by Colin, who said, "Mary, the merch girl is hammered. You better humour her..." Understood. He wasn't lying. I got on the bus and said hello to Phil, Bryan, Yenz and upstairs Pete was sitting at the front. Went back down to the lower lounge. Mary appeared shortly after. I have never seen anyone so out of it. She couldn't form words but she kept lunging towards people – me included – to say things no one could understand. Whenever she left the lounge, much debate ensued about which particular cocktail of drugs could have reduced her to this state. She seemed some way beyond the effects of mere alcohol. It was all most strange because she had acted perfectly normally yesterday at the Aylesbury show and was a paragon of quiet efficiency the day before that, whilst loading the truck at the Racket Club. This was an entirely different human being. Blimey... There was much suppressed mirth from the crew with each new attempt she made to talk or stand up and move about. She seemed very concerned about my throat not getting cold and kept attempting to wrap a scarf around my neck...

Soon the bus was underway and I sat in the lower lounge talking to Phil and Quinner. As the journey progressed she became violent and began throwing punches at Quinner who eventually said, "Now if you don't calm down, I'm going to have to hit you..."

Rich came to the rescue and took her off to try and talk her down nicely. He failed, and returned a full hour later saying that, "either she goes or I do!" I asked why and he said, "Because I'm crew boss and I'll be responsible for her, and there's no way I CAN be". Fair comment. Somewhere in amongst all this she had fallen over completely rigid on her face and was now sporting a very fat lip which wasn't making it any easier to understand her. Later, I heard Quinner asking for Gaffatape to bind her wrists and ankles together. I advised against it on the grounds that if she wakes up dead (a distinct possibility considering the state she was in) we'd all be put behind bars. After a while, it went from being funny to being distinctly uncomfortable, so I went to bed. Didn't sleep very well. It always takes a couple of nights to get used to bus-sleep.

Thursday 17 November *Wolverhampton Civic Hall*

Woke up for the first time on this tour's tour bus. Regrettably, the bunks on this one don't have windows so you have to get up to know where you are. I put it off as long as possible, wondering what had become of Mary, the smashed merch girl... The bus was quiet – most of the crew were up working in the gig. I recognized the familiar side-wall of Wolverhampton Civic Hall. Dressed and wandered into the gig where I was met by the usual scurry of bodies, flight cases and the shouts from above as lights were being rigged. Found the catering room where there was a breakfast buffet set up and made myself a coffee. Sat for quite a while by the TV, half-watching, half-talking, half working. There's wi-fi here so I logged on and sent a couple of emails to Ian M who would be still at home. Eventually Quinner appeared to say that he'd fired the merch girl. After last night's display there's no way we could leave her in possession of a big bag of cash every night. Q said she'd got up, opened a bottle of beer, lit up a cigarette and gone and had a dump in the bus toilet (CARDINAL sin) only to emerge without flushing it. Wow. Pure class. I'm glad *I* didn't have to tell her.

Looks like we've got the tour off to a controversial start. We're going to need someone to sell merch then.

Told Quinner the joke about the Barbie dolls, which Sally had sent me by email and went off to find the dressing room. There are whirlpool baths in the dressing rooms here – very luxurious. Ran a bath. It took ages. When the bath was finally full, I turned off the water and noticed all kinds of flotsam – mostly dust, dead creatures and bits of grass – providing a film of scum on the surface. This kind of put me off so I pulled the plug and had a shower instead. Spent another hour or two working on my *Oil* song demo, "*One Oil-Man Deserves Another*". It's coming along nicely. Tonight's opening act, Wanderlust had put a bottle of champagne and a card in our dressing room. Nice touch.

Around mid-afternoon I was on stage checking monitors when Ian, Lucy and Steve arrived. I filled them in on Mary's antics last night to the amusement of all and slight embarrassment of Lucy who had hired her. Soundcheck seemed to pass without incident although I don't think anyone's happy with their sound yet. Even *I* don't know what to ask for to improve it. I tried placing some overall EQ across my in-ears, but I'm not sure it helped.

Went back to the bus for a power-nap and then returned to the gig to catch the end of Wanderlust's set. They gave a spirited performance although clearly not used to the situation.

Then we were up. The crowd again lived up to our expectations. It's always a great vibe here and it's a shame to have this show so early in the tour. We weren't at our best – still de-bugging the keyboard rig (will it ever end?) and not yet having arrived at a comfortable monitor situation – but I did my damnedest and I think we left with our reputation grazed but not ruined. Wanderlust helped by getting down between the barrier and the stage and collectively "getting off" on every note we played. Bless 'em. After the show I chatted with them for a while. Nice people. Seemed awfully grateful for the chance. The drummer's girlfriend was wearing a black sable Russian hat. Asked if I could have a feel. (The hat, I mean). Amazingly dense and silky fur. Worth 700 quid in London, but she said you can get them for 60 in Russia if you know people. Gorky Park... Went to bed composing a bawdy poem about a girl called Mable, but I think I nodded off before I completed it.

Friday 18 November *Middlesborough The Empire*

Got up around 7.45 and went down to the lounge. We were parked up at the side of an A-road and the bus juddered sideways as each truck and car sped past. Outside was beautiful countryside completely white-over with frost. I could see hills over to the right. The Yorkshire Dales. Fantastic. I felt like getting into some thick clothes and going for a walk across the fields. It wasn't really an option... Brian, the lighting assistant (who seems to function perfectly and hyperactively on 3 hours sleep per night – quite a handy metabolism for lighting crew...), appeared and we chatted for a while until I decided I really should go back to sleep. When I next awoke we were in Middlesbrough city centre. I got up and went and had a look in the gig. Loads of character but really shabby backstage like the Astoria in London. It's an old music-hall kind of theatre but it's been re-fitted in a kind of gothic style. Statues in the hall and gryphons on the bar. It was like being in a nightclub in Narnia. I went to the ladies toilet to freshen up and was intrigued to discover an enormous pink dispensing machine selling sex toys. Quite a range of stuff too including vibrators, knob rings and various other metal fittings, edible lube, ribbed finger attachments, and more that I can't remember – priced up to about 12 quid. Wouldn't have known what to do with half of it. Never even saw such machines in London. Looks like Middlesbrough's hardcore...

Went up 3 flights of stairs to the dressing rooms. Horrible, cold, damp, smelled like a bedsit and was similarly decorated with woodchip and crappy posters. Jesus. Places like this make me feel distinctly unsuccessful!

Walked down the street and found a café still doing breakfast. They were playing Christmas songs on the stereo. I guess it's upon us now. We certainly have the weather for it – it's bloody cold out – but there's still girls going by outside with bare midriffs like it's midsummer. They suffer for their glamour, these northern girls. I ordered bacon and eggs and toast and a mocha coffee and cheered up as I dreamed-back to my own young Christmases. In those days I didn't just believe in magic – it used to tingle inside me. Then you outgrow it and you have to wait until you have your own children so you can witness it happen again. I love Christmas. Mad Jack arrived and joined me. We're still talking! Quite unusual at this point in a tour... We returned to the bus and I tried to find him an Ethernet lead, but I didn't have one. He needed it for something or other – I long-since stopped listening to all talk of computers. He managed to get one from Quinner and strode off with his usual sense of zealous purpose. I stayed up in the back lounge and worked on mixing my demo of the *Oil* song so I could play it to Aziz and Dal in Manchester tomorrow. I was still fiddling around on the laptop when Quinner came to take me to do an interview with some chap who'd turned up. He has some kind of internet rock radio station and seemed to be a fan. I was taken back to the bedsit in the sky where I joined Rothers for the interview. The DJ said it would only take 15 minutes. They always do. It took 45 at least. They always do. He went away happy and I went downstairs to the stage to try and fix my Kurzweil levels which have been a little... er... wrong.

Soundcheck passed without hysteria although it took ages as usual. We have so much to check! I alone am generating inputs from a Yamaha P250 stereo piano, Kurzweil K2500 stereo sampler (sometimes played from the P250 and sometimes played from my radio midi cricket bat via a midi merge box), acoustic guitar (mono straight to pa) and electric guitar (mono miked up from a combo guitar amp), I must also set levels for my centre mic and the mic at the piano along with a vocal reverb which is applied to my vocal monitor mix simply to make me feel good! Then there's God knows how many drum inputs from Ian. I set an overall level for this, but sometimes I adjust kick drum and hi-hat levels within it. Steve Rothery generates separate Marshall and Roland amplifier levels plus (when he plays it) a 12-string acoustic guitar (mono straight to pa). Are you bored or mystified yet? Then there's Mark generating an overall keyboard mix (stereo) along with separate stereo loops, stereo samples, mono bass-pedals AND a vocal mic. Pete generates a mix of bass guitar (d.i) and miked amplifier (mono) along with his vocal mic. He plays various midi pedals which control audio samples managed by Mark. Occasionally he may play acoustic guitar.

No wonder it often takes longer than the show (2hours+) to soundcheck...
Sometimes I feel like I've done 2 shows each day, and I almost have!

During the soundcheck who should walk into the gig but John Otway! He's playing next door in the Town Hall with a band called The Hamsters including guest appearances by Otway and none other than Wilko Johnson and Norman Watt-Roy, the Blockheads amazing bass player. Too good to miss. I said I'd be over as soon as I got off stage and he said he'd stick us on his guest list. Tonight's an early show (8.15 – no support) so there wasn't much time to relax before we were back on stage.

I enjoyed the show – a bit chaotic and very cosy on stage, but I think we did well.   Afterwards, I stuck a jacket on and went next door. On my way I bumped into Janick Gers (Iron Maiden's guitar player) who'd popped in to see our show. He's a lovely chap and he seemed to have enjoyed it. Middlesbrough seems to be the ligging capital of rock n'roll. Who'd have thought? I arrived in the Town Hall in time to buy a beer and talk to Otway before he mounted the stage to perform The Osmonds *Crazy Horses* and then the highlight of my evening, when Norman and Wilko got up and finished the show with Ian Dury's *Hit Me with Your Rhythm Stick*. Sadly I never caught Ian and the Blockheads live but this was a glimpse of how it must have been. What a bassplayer! What a bassline! The whole song's a bass solo really, and Otway added the necessary lateral energy to the lead vocal. I hope Ian caught it from somewhere in the spiritual ether. I'm not religious but I sent him a prayer. You never know...

Afterwards, I went back to the bus and then to the hotel day-room to shower. (The shower at the gig looked like you'd catch a venereal disease if you so much as pulled back the curtain wearing rubber gloves.) Left my hideously expensive and totally fabulous Jean Paul Gaultier black-jeans in the hotel room, never to be seen again. Middlesbrough, goodnight.

Saturday 19 November   *Glasgow ABC*

Rolled out of bed around 11am and recognized the familiar sight of Sauchiehall Street. So this is where the gig is, then. Dressed and ran into Col who says it's a lovely gig. Went inside. Nice hall, the ABC. Big old iron girders splayed out massively but elegantly in the roof space, and the biggest mirror-ball you ever did see (apart from Pink Floyd's one which opens out like a Terry's Chocolate Orange to reveal another one inside...). I went to the dressing room. Nicely furnished with leather sofas and designer sink. Cleaned my teeth in the designer sink. Hadn't slept particularly well and was in need of someone to moan at. Quinner wasn't around. Marillion's anti-publicity machine had (as in "hadn't") left its mark in advance of our arrival then. There was no mention of us playing here tonight whatsoever despite many posters of other artists and forthcoming attractions in evidence outside. I know we've got a fanatical and priceless fanbase but sometimes I wish we made a bit more effort to remind the general public that we exist. Grrr...

Finally managed to get directions to the day-room. The Art House Hotel in Bath Street and walked over there. Q was already there, sorting things out. The room wasn't ready so I went walk-about in search of underwear. I bought my last batch here at the Boss shop opposite Princes Square in Buchanan St. Made my way there on what was a very cold morning past buskers playing bag-pipes. You could tell you weren't in Derby. The cold weather evokes Christmas once again. It's all so sudden. I like Glasgow. It's full of human beings. Real people with no pretence are to be enjoyed in any direction you look. Just don't stare too long – someone might take exception and it's still possible to pick up a 'Glasgow smile' here if you're in the wrong place at the wrong time. While we're on the subject, Rangers are playing Celtic here today, so I'd been advised to be a bit wary on the street from mid-afternoon onwards. I bought a coffee in Costa and managed to spill it all over the front of the white coat I was wearing. Not the height of glamour, but hey... Saw and bought a pair of black jeans in Diesel in Buchanan St before returning to the Art House Hotel where the day-room was now ready. And very nice it was too. Lovely room. Well-designed and very artsy-fartsy. I spent a while sponging the coffee off my coat and then relaxed on the bed for a couple of hours. It was blissful after two nights on the bus and a long walk round Glasgow's cold streets.

Returned to the ABC for soundcheck and couldn't help noticing a fancy dress hire shop over the street. Went back out and wandered in. Emerged shortly after with a Santa outfit, purchased for £45.00. You can't go wrong! Said hello to old Norwegian friends Gazpacho who are opening for us tonight. It was nice to see them again.

Soundcheck was long but unremarkable (i.e. I can't remember it and, like flights, "unremarkable" is good.)

Went back out to the bus and watched a DVD of Deep Purple on the **Machine Head** Tour. This was the tour that I caught "for real" at Sheffield City Hall. That was the night I decided at the ripe old age of 16 that I wanted to do this for a living. It's very therapeutic to watch old footage of rock bands. Hardly any equipment or crew – just a bunch of guys working hard, performing hard and being "in the moment". It can remind you of what's important. It reminds you that there's more to life than being super-tight and re-creating the album you just recorded down to the finest detail. No. It's all about the vibe, and what you share with the audience. So no more moaning about who missed this chord or that chord or whether the playing was perfect or the singing absolutely spot-on throughout. It doesn't matter. We're there to create a feeling and an energy. That's every bit as important as the music. Working day-in and day-out with a bunch of musos, it's easy to lose sight of the simple and fundamental truths.

I hit the stage bearing this in mind and was greeted by a big room full of Glaswegians in party mood. Really enjoyed the show and kept saying "It's great to be back after so long!" I'd forgotten that we played Glasgow only last year.

What a pillock. After the show, I went round the corner to a bar and drank beer and tequila with Gazpacho til 1.30 when I got the call to return to the bus, departing for Manchester. Wobbled onto the bus and zig-zagged to bed.

Sunday 20 November *Manchester Academy*

Slept well for the first time. It always takes a few days on the bus before proper sleep happens. Getting used to the bed and the movement. Had a lie-in and took my time before emerging into the bright sunshine of a perfect winter's morning. Bumped into Lucy and she set about the business of trying to locate the trousers I left in Middlesbrough. The hotel reception are trying to locate the housekeeping staff etc. (some hope). Left her to it, on the mobile phone out in the street and wandered inside. It's Sunday and as I helped myself to a coffee inside the Academy, one of the local crew asked me if I'd been to church. Much ironic mirth all round...

Spent much of the morning trying to do all the things that are so simple at home. Changing clothes, having a wash, cleaning your teeth, washing your clothes. On the road, every little thing is complicated. The dressing room door was locked, the toilet door has no lock, the water isn't hot. My dirty washing is in a number of different locations (bus bunk, suitcase in bus-bay, wardrobe flight-case). All this stuff is easily sorted out, but it takes 30-mins to do the things which would take two at home. I was also trying to test an effects-box with my piano – not for the show tonight, but perhaps for the one-man show I'm planning next February. As soon as it was plugged in, it lit up and then died. "It's never done that before", said Pete, who's lent it to me. Took another 2 hours to get it going. This was done by taking the lid off, doing absolutely nothing, and then putting the lid back on again. No doubt it will continue to work flawlessly now until I'm on a stage with it in front of a few hundred people...

Eventually I had my socks and pants all washed and hanging on a coat-hanger. Rich had forgotten to take the tumble drier out of the truck and the driver was now asleep in said truck so nothing could be disturbed. Not a problem as he'll be up in a couple of hours but do you see what I mean?

Left wet washing and wandered down Manchester's Oxford Road in search of breakfast. It was a choice between McDonalds and Subway, so I plumped for that. Emerged with some sort of exotic hot chicken-salad baguette and called home as I walked back. Sue says there's been a thick frost today and that it's a lovely morning there too. She's been out for a walk with the kids. Wish I could've gone too. You can't have everything. Arrived back at the venue. Lucy's not having much luck with the trousers. Went on stage to discover the effects box now working so Pete gave me a master class ("Push that button there, then push it again. Hang on a minute... maybe it's the other button. That's it... I think...") while I attempted to eat the Subway baguette, spraying breadcrumbs all over everything. I soon got the hang of it (the pedal, not the sandwich). Dunno if it's something I'd want to use on stage though... it's tricky deciding how complicated to make everything. If in doubt…

Went back into the dressing room and attempted to get on-line. Managed it after a while and picked up a few emails. Paul Lewis is coming over tonight and wants putting on the guest list (forgive the grammar – a throwback from my days in the Europeans with the Glaswegians). Lord B's wondering if he should invite Richard Curtis to say a few words at the London Forum show. I think it would be a good thing. While I'm on-line, Aziz arrives so I say hello and play him the *Oil* song. He thinks it's great. Hooray. Dal later appears and I play it to him. He's blown away. Great. Now what do I do with it? Maybe I should upload it to the world for free while it's still fresh and relevant. (PS nope – I released it on the **Arc Light** mini-album in 2013!)

The news has come through that tonight has sold out. With guests, there's going to be 2100 people in here. It'll be packed. Marvellous. Hung around and watched Aziz and Dal soundchecking. Technologically chaotic, but artistically astounding, as always. There really is no-one on earth can play the guitar remotely like him and Dal's tabla playing is in another place.

By now, the doors are open so I have to run and hide for half an hour until they're on stage. I go out to the sound desk to listen. Rod's still sorting out their sound. It's tough being an opening act. At this moment my sisters and mum nudge me so I say hello to them for a while before running off with Sue's boy, Dan, to show him the action from the side of stage. I take him up on stage and we watch the rest of Aziz's short set from behind the guitar cabinets. He goes down well but I'm reminded once again that it's not enough to be brilliant. You need that lucky break that crosses you over to the mainstream punters. And a shed load of marketing money… It happened to Marillion before I met them and we've managed to maintain a hard-core big enough to make it possible for us to function at a certain level. It's like getting an enormous rock to roll. Once it's rolling you can keep it going easier than the effort it took to get it started. So rockn'roll's not such a bad name for it. But it could have been called "momentum" instead. Doesn't have the same ring about it though… (and anything derived from Latin is very unrock n'roll).

I decided to risk half an 'e' tonight so I had one about 15 minutes before showtime. Worked a treat and I was on fire for the show. The place was as busy as I have seen it – solid to the back wall. I sang and performed with total relaxation and remained in the zone throughout. The band played well and there was no noticeable clangers or system crashes from the keyboards. Alleluya. Played five songs for the encores and then got changed into the Santa outfit for a romp through **The Erin Marbles** (joke Irish-drinking version of **Marbles** which we recorded to give away for this year's Xmas fanclub CD). A fabulous time was had by all. Talked to mum and Sue and Gill for an hour afterwards, then showered and got on the bus. Mosley got on and gave me a kebab. It doesn't get any better than this folks! Went to bed with that inner-glow which you can only get from raw-onion…

Monday 21 November *Bus*

In the dark distance I could hear people getting up. I think it was only two people I heard getting up so I must have slept through a lot of it. Everyone except me is getting off the bus today – about 15 people – and flying to Barcelona in a couple of days. I have decided, on balance, to stay on and do the drive. It will give me some time and space to write the diary and, hopefully, be creative. Well, that's the theory! I contemplated getting up – mainly because I wanted a pee – but didn't do it. I went back to sleep drifting in and out until I felt the bus vibrate into life again and move away. We must be leaving the Racket Club... I lay in the dark trying to visualize the journey – the slow trundle along the private road then the left turn, the slight bend to the right, the T-junction, the right turn onto the A41 and onwards to the M40 and the journey to Dover. Napped a little more and then got up and went to the front of the bus on the upper deck. We were on the M40 passing the big fence with the graffiti saying "Why Do I Do This Every Day?" It's the best graffiti I ever saw. I never had to commute. When I had a proper job I wrote *Going to Work* to explain how I felt about it.

This tour bus is designed so that the driver is separate from the passengers – you have to call him on a phone to talk to him. I couldn't get power for the kettle so I picked up the phone and Eddie Monk said, "Top of the morning!" I explained that I couldn't get the kettle to boil and he said it's because he'd forgotten to flick a switch when we left. He sorted it out for me and I made a coffee and watched the M25 go by until we got to Dover. I asked Eddie if he fancied breakfast (it was 2 in the afternoon...) in Langan's Brasserie once we were on the ferry. It became the plan. The ferry seemed busy but Langan's was deserted, apart from us and a couple of other customers. We sat by the window and watched the sea. I had poached eggs Florentine followed by bangers and mash. All excellent. Chatted to Eddie about the tax man, in between calls to the Jean Paul Gaultier shop... I've done it again and left a pair of expensive trousers in a hotel room in Middlesbrough (never to be seen again) and now I'm trying to find a way to buy another pair and have them FedExed to Barcelona. Also Gabriel rang to offer me free tickets to the Barcelona football match tomorrow. Unfortunately we won't arrive in Barca 'til Wednesday so I passed on the chance to Pete. Shame... I was looking forward to watching Ronaldinho play.

We were soon heading out of Calais. I pottered around the bus, plugging my piano in (it's up in the top lounge), and tweaking my song about oil, in the laptop. After a while I became drowsy so I returned to my bunk and read for a little while. I'm re-reading Le Carrés, **The Constant Gardener**. Eddie stopped the bus around 6pm when his driver-hours ran out. Now he must rest for 8 hours before we can continue. We parked at a motorway services somewhere north of Paris and I watched **24-Hour Party People** (the story of Factory Records) in the downstairs lounge before coming upstairs to write this. I'm now at the front of the bus looking out onto the silent dark lorry-park. Eddie can't run the engine so the heating is off. I'm wearing my bath-robe on top of my clothes as it's getting pretty chilly... I might go and watch another movie. I might go to bed. I'll probably write a bit more diary. I'll do the other days...

As it turns out, Dizzy called me just after the above paragraph. She sounded fine until she said, "I put the car in a ditch this morning." She said she'd hit a patch of sheet ice and it just skidded around from one side of the road to the other. Luckily, there was nothing coming the other way or she'd have crashed. She said she'd jarred her back a little but was otherwise unhurt apart from the shock. The car wasn't even damaged either, so it's a lucky escape all round. She was on her way to teach at Middleton Cheney School. She managed an hour or so but then went home feeling a bit too shaken to do more. I guess it's sod's law that I chose not to go home today or I would have been there for her, but I couldn't have known this would happen.

Found vodka and tomato juice in the bus and went upstairs to watch **Gladiator** DVD while pouring Bloody Marys. Went to bed.

Tuesday 22 November *Bus*

Slept well but woken at 11.30 by the phone ringing. Thought it might be further crisis at home so leapt out of bed to answer it. It was Mark who thinks he's left his passport in his suitcase! Of course, he's in England and is supposed to be flying to Barcelona this morning. He wanted me to have a look in his suitcase to see if his worst fears are correct. I telephoned Eddie to ask if he can stop the bus at the next possible place so that I can haul his suitcase out of the bay (luggage area beneath the back-lounge) and have a look. The phone call from Mark used up the last few pounds of credit on my phone and I spent the next 20 minutes trying and failing to re-credit it. Eddie stopped the bus at the next junction and I prepared to brave the cold and go and rummage in the bus-bay. When I opened the door, Eddie was standing there saying he'd had a call from the UK and Mark has now found his passport. Apparently, he'd had it all along. Sigh. Still, I can't talk – I do that kind of shit all the time! Even as I type, a pair of trousers are theoretically winging their way to Barcelona... I'll believe that when I see it...

Got back aboard the pink bus and made a coffee. Went upfront upstairs to continue this diary. As I write, we're south of Clermont Ferrand and must be at quite an altitude as there's a thick frost out there clinging to the trees. The bus is labouring under the climb. It looks bloody cold out there. Beautiful. Just passing an exit for St. Poncy (...more or less what my old games master used to call ME) and "Montpellier 268km". Christmas-card views. Glad I didn't miss this.

Decided to photograph it and grabbed my camera but as I returned to the front window we were descending the hillside and the frost had all-but-vanished. Spent the next hour or two, photographing the views, which were spectacular although I'm not sure I'll have done them justice. I was hoping to photograph the new Milau Bridge – the highest and longest bridge in the world. Eddie wasn't sure where it was but thought we'd probably be crossing it soon. It wasn't to be. We eventually pulled into a service station as Eddie's driving-hours have again expired for the day. We'll be here now until the early hours of tomorrow. Went into the services and had a wash and changed clothes. Loads of photographs of the Milau valley bridge adorned the restaurant. I was really hoping to cross it in daylight. Unfortunately it is south of us so we'll cross it in the dark and I'll probably be asleep. Oh well. I'll try and stay up for it anyway. Having terrible problems with my mobile phone. O2 - my service provider - only allow a total of £90 top-up in any given month and I seem to have already spent that and ran out. To put this into perspective, my one phone-call FROM Sue last night cost me £22.00, and Mark used up another £8.00 this morning asking me about passports. For some reason, calls in France are costing a fortune. Now I'm out of credit and can't top-up. Jesus. Is nothing simple in the modern world? I never saw this one coming or I could have bought a load of vouchers in England before I went away. I guess I'll just have to go back to how I did it in the old days – production office phones where possible and hotel phones when I'm in one!

So now here I am again at the front of the bus. Eddie's asleep and we can't run the engine so there's enough power for TV and video but not for heating. I'm in a French lorry park and it's slowly getting chillier. There's a frost outside now. I think I might go back over to the café and order a beer or a coffee.

Went over to the service area and they couldn't serve me beer so I ordered a coffee. After some delicate negotiation I managed to get a large one with milk in it. Here in the south of France they tend to drink only espressos. Sat at a Formica table with the laptop and continued writing up the diary til they politely asked me to leave at 10.30. "Ah'm afchéed we're closing sirr..." Nice people.

Returned to the freezer and watched **Puppet on a Chain** – Alistair MacLean story about drug running in Amsterdam. Very 60's... Recommended mainly for the haircuts.

Wednesday 23 November *Barcelona*

Got up in the night as the bus had slowed so I went up front to see if we were on the Milau Bridge as I really didn't want to miss it. The road-signs were in Spanish, so I had missed it hours ago. Went back to bed. When I next got up, the bus was trundling through the main streets of Barcelona. It doesn't look warm out there... When Eddie pulled up at the Bikini Club I remembered a Starbucks where I'd had coffee with Richard Barbieri when the h band played here, so I walked over with the laptop and wrote yet more diary while sitting in a soft chair in the window. Gabriel had texted to say that he would meet me at the gig at 12.00 so I made my way to the hotel to freshen up.

Got to the hotel around 11.20 and attempted to check into the day room. The receptionist said I had no reservation. I asked to speak to the room of Mr Quinn, who wasn't in, and then to Ian M, who was in and said sleepily, that there should be a room in my name. While he was telling me this, an attractive young lady showed up and the receptionist began checking her in and continued to ignore me completely for the next 15 minutes whilst I became increasingly agitated. As the minutes ticked away and he made charming and polite conversation with his new (and later than ME) guest, I contemplated having to go back and meet Gabriel, unshowered after a 2 day bus journey, and generally in desperate need of "facilities". I tried all the usual things - asking to speak to the manager etc - but he continued to check in the girl to my right as though I was some kind of minor irritation. I decided to throw his computer monitor across the lobby and through the front window, and was just reaching for it when Phil Brown, our monitor engineer magically appeared. He said he'd been watching from the café across the street and thought he'd better come and help. I'm glad he did – he saved me a fortune. He gave me his own hotel room key and I went upstairs and quickly showered before returning to the Bikini to find Gabriel outside waiting in the street. Took him inside so I could drop my bag back on the bus and said hello to Ivan.

Took a taxi across town with Gabriel to a recording studio to meet Kitfluss, "the most famous keyboard player in the whole of Spain!" He's also doing the charity gig in December and he's going to play the piano while I sing *Silent Night* in Catalan. Gabriel had arranged a meeting so that we could decide which key would suit my voice best. Made our way into the studio and met Mr Kitfluss who seemed very nice and didn't speak a word of English. At length, we settled upon C#. I am to be later joined in the carol by schoolchildren who will sing in G. The move to G from C# sounds really nice, so everybody's happy. We said farewell to Mr K and Gabriel took me to a little family-run restaurant nearby where we had steak and chips followed by the local hamon (thinly sliced smoked and salted uncooked ham – a Spanish speciality) with tomato bread. All excellent. Gabriel introduced me to the lady of the house (a lovely Catalan lady who was serving us) as "the best singer in the world!" She knows he's running the Palau St. Jordi (the biggest gig in Barcelona, frequented by U2, Madonna, Santana, Elton John, and all the huge Latin American and Spanish stars I've never heard of) so she was very impressed, and I daresay equally confused that she should have never heard of me. Gabriel and I chatted as best we could – his English is dreadful, but just good enough for me to follow his drift, most of the time. He told me about some big Argentinian star ("as big as Maradonna in Argentina") who had given him the tour-jacket he was currently wearing. "Do you like it?"

"Yes, it's very nice." I said, courteously.

"Then you must have it. A present from me!"

"No, really. You mustn't. I have enough jackets."

"No. This is for you. It's important to me that you have it."

What can you say to such generosity? I took it gratefully and made him promise not to give me any more presents. He duly said he would get me and Nial a Barca football shirt, autographed by Ronaldinho. Well, I couldn't really turn THAT down!

What a generous man, and what a lucky bastard I am to have him as a friend.

We walked back through the city looking for a taxi, past the place where Gabriel grew up with his mother. He told me he hardly knew his father who had been a bit of a wanderer and an alcoholic – at one point living rough on the streets. Gabriel said it was his intention someday to build a place in Barcelona for the homeless people to go. I have absolutely no doubt that he will.

Back to the Bikini for soundcheck. All okay. We're using house lighting tonight so there's not much for our lighting crew to do. Yenz will do his best, I'm sure. He's a talented chap and very attentive to the details. Just before soundcheck, my replacement JPG trousers arrived via FedEx from London. One size down from the last ones so I could do with losing a few pounds. If I can just stay off the beer... ha ha ha. Got on the bus and went to bed, sleeping like a baby 'til 8.30.

The show went well. The crowd were up for it. The gig was sold-out and all the equipment worked. There were some lovely moments. A little jam I started before *The Party* was really delicate. I'm getting to grips with the pink Les Paul now and it's begun to sound as good as it looks! Wore the Santa outfit at the end. Saw a photograph of it later. Looked bloody great. Hurrah! Afterwards, chatted to Ivan and Gabriel at length then went out into the street to sign autographs for the faithful. Lovely. Went back to the bus and put **My Cousin Vinnie** on in the upstairs lounge. Too tired to watch much. Turned it off and went to bed.

Wednesday 23 November   *Istres*

Rolled out of bed to see where we are. We seemed to be out somewhere in the French countryside. I could see signs for Istres, so we must be close. There were traces of snow on the ground. While in Barcelona I'd heard that it was snowing in the South of France. Here was proof. Strange weather we're having... Went back to bed and soon I felt the bus come to a stop. Didn't feel the need to hurry – we're in a big hall in the middle of nowhere... might as well stay in bed.

Eventually rose and made my way into the L'Usine (it means factory). Found catering and grabbed a coffee. Quinner said there was a day-room if I was interested. I was, and so the runner took me in a car for a 15 minute drive to a funny little hotel called The Comfort Inn. No one spoke any English but they seemed friendly in a provincial sort of way. Or should I say a Provencal sort of way – we are, after all, in Provence. I went up two floors to my room. It was dreadful, but I could at least have a little time to myself. I freshened up and decided to go back downstairs and see if I could have lunch in the restaurant. There were already quite a lot of people in the restaurant – all men. At one long table was a load of guys who looked like some kind of a sports team... maybe rugby – they were all big guys. I sat at a single table and ordered steak frites which I seem to be living on lately. I set up the laptop and typed up the diary while eating. The landlady seemed amused to have me there and kept nodding and smiling. Paid for lunch and then went back upstairs to fiddle about with the laptop... still working on my *Oil* song. Soon the phone rang and it was the reception saying, "Monsieur, votre rendezvous, est arrivé!" The runner had returned to take me back for sound-check.

Back in the gig, Bertrand Pourcheron was waiting. I had an interview with him, so I took him to the catering room along with his friend, Didier and spent

20 minutes or so talking. "If you were a tree which one would it be?" I like those kind of questions. They make a nice change…

Sound check went well. Not too long, for a change, although I was having trouble with radio interference. We tried switching frequencies several times but without much luck. Never mind. After soundcheck we hung around for quite a while as opening act, A Day's Work, soundchecked for hours and hours. We're not on tonight 'til 9.45, so I went back to bed for an hour on the bus.

The show went well. Everything seems to be working now musically and technically and the audience had the soulful French vibe going on. I completely forgot to announce that it was Steve R's birthday tomorrow, but the word must have got out as several choruses of Appy Berssday To Yooo seemed to break out spontaneously.

Afterwards I signed things and stood for photographs with the people who had waited behind. Very nice people. Not in any way pushy. The bus then drove us all to Marseille where we will stay tonight and then we'll have the day off there tomorrow. Seemed like a nice hotel – hard to tell in the dark, but it's right on the sea-front, just to the East side of the city. Had a quick birthday drink with Steve before hitting the sumptuous soft bed. The first bed for 7 nights. Heavenly.

Friday 25 November *Marseilles*

Woke suddenly at 12.00 to find a maid spinning around on her heels at the end of my bed, making a hasty exit. I'd forgot the 'Do Not Disturb' sign, once again. It hardly matters – they tend to ignore them anyway. Seemed like a good time to be getting up so I rose, showered and wandered down the corridor in search of coffee. This is a nice hotel. Luxurious rooms, the most comfortable bed I have slept in since the fabulous Halcyon Hotel in Holland Park, and Morrocan paintings displayed in and around the walkways and lobbies, complete with waterfall on a natural cliff face. It's an upside-down hotel too. The rooms are below reception. So I went up to reception where I was knocked-out by the most amazing panoramic view of the sea. The hotel appears to have its own harbour, swimming pool and terrace literally adjoining the Mediterranean. It must be lovely in the summer. Went down to the bar and ordered coffee. Bertrand Pourcheron was later to inform me that there are a number of footballers from Marseilles FC living here in the hotel, including Fabien Barthez, the maverick goalkeeper who used to play for Manchester United and France. I kept an eye out for him, but he wasn't around. I spent the better part of the day-off in the restaurant having a slow lunch (ham and cheese omelette and fries) whilst tapping at the laptop. When they closed the restaurant, I moved to the bar and spent a peaceful afternoon watching the sea crashing up against the rocks in between working on the diary and the *Oil* song.

It's Steve R's birthday so I arranged a band & crew dinner this evening. Bertrand showed up to take Pete T into town in search of new specs (he'd lost his in Barcelona, along with his cell-phone) so I asked him if he could book somewhere nice. He decided on a restaurant close to his home, on a small fishing harbour – a kind of fishing village within Marseille. Tonight, the bus will leave at midnight for Luxembourg, so everyone had left their bags in the day room, which was also Ian Mosley's. It was room 195 – the furthest room away from reception in the entire hotel. At 8pm we assembled and Bertrand arrived to show us the way to the restaurant. We arrived at a secluded little fishing harbour within Marseilles. It was like being somewhere else entirely. In the little harbour a kind of glass conservatory was perched overlooking the water and we seemed to have it to ourselves. It belonged to a nice little restaurant over the road and the staff came and went, taking our orders and feeding us delicious food all night. It was a good birthday night out for Steve R. I'd hoped to make it a band and crew dinner, but Ian stayed in bed, and Mark stayed in and played computer games. Marillion *esprit de corps* strikes again... I had oysters and a fish called loupe. Very nice and, of course, very fresh. All washed down with a good red wine. We discovered a circular hole in the window glass (where perhaps an extractor fan was supposed to be) and much mirth ensued when Yenz threw a bread roll through it which bounced right next to couple of tourists at the water's edge below. By their reaction, I think they thought it had fallen from space! It's the little things...

Afterwards we returned to the hotel and grabbed our bags, trundling them along the sea-front to where the bus was parked. Climbed aboard for the overnight journey to Luxembourg.

Saturday 26 / Sunday 27 November *Breakdown*

Was awoken by a strange 'skittering' noise. It sounded like we were skidding on ice. Not what you really want a 20-ton bus full of people to be doing really. I braced myself and waited for the outcome... a bang! Mercifully, not a big enough bang for a 20-ton bus hitting a wall, but as if we'd hit something... a dull bang. I wondered if maybe we'd hit a deer. Rolled out of bed and up to the front of the bus, but all I could see was a dry open road still rolling peacefully beneath us. I went downstairs for a pee and then returned to bed. As I reached the top of the stairs to the upper deck, the bus suddenly began rapidly decelerating and I was accelerated forward along the gangway. The bus ground to a halt. Out of the front window I could see that we were on the hard-shoulder of a French motorway. High snow-drifts were in evidence beyond the hard-shoulder, although the road was clear of snow and ice. My heart sank as I realized that, whatever all this was about, it wasn't normal and was going to cause us considerable delay. Sue's already in a room in the Holiday Inn in Paris waiting for me. I'm due there in the morning around breakfast time and we had planned to meet for breakfast before a day together in Paris. I couldn't believe it. I'm beginning to think we're cursed. Things haven't been going too well between us for a while now and the marriage has continued to hover in the balance for some years. Days when we can relax alone together have become very precious.

With a heavy heart I returned to bed with the distinct feeling that I might not be in Paris for lunch, let alone breakfast. I lay in the dark waiting for the next development. I drifted into sleep and then back into consciousness as I could hear and feel a banging noise coming from the front of the bus. Got up once again to see the flashing revolving yellow lights of a tow truck in front of us. Great.

Went back to bed and heard more banging and general muffled commotion as attempts were made to attach a tow bar to the bus. Later I felt the juddering motion of the bus being towed from the motorway. Looked at my watch. It was 6.30am. Cat-napped til 9.00 then texted Sue with the bad news. Text said: "Bus broken down somewhere in France. Gearbox. Towed off motorway. I'll get to you as soon as I can. It won't be soon. Sorry. More news when I have it. Sigh. X x x"

She was understandably disappointed, but seemed to take it well. She might not have said it, but I genuinely wondered how much more she could take of me and my music. The last straw is hovering above us.

Sunday 27 November *A tow-truck depot somewhere in France*

I slept 'til 9.00 and then woke Quinner, the tour manager, to ask what was happening as I really would like very much to go to Paris soon. He had no knowledge of the breakdown, having slept through the whole thing. You'd have thought that the driver might have felt it would be a good idea to let the tour manager know. He hadn't. Terrific...

Outside it was a cold and damp day, there were a few remnants of thawing snow around, and we were parked in some kind of tow-truck depot complete with mean-looking wolf-like dog in a cage. Beyond that, no signs of life.

Quinner went to speak to Eddie, the driver, and returned to say we were geographically "in the middle of nowhere". It's Sunday (of COURSE) so everything is closed. We seem to be in a very small village - literally a dozen or so houses - in the middle of open countryside. No town. No taxi. No-one to call for one. No train station. No nothing. Eddie had called the Scania offices and was told that a mechanical engineer was on the way. He arrived, as promised, at 10am and began ferreting around inside, outside and underneath the bus. He spoke no English. He was to continue ferreting around for the next four hours achieving little more than to shear-off a few bolts. Obviously not Scania's best mechanic – but I guess they call him in on Sundays in the middle of nowhere, France. I didn't envy him.

There really was nothing to do except wait. So we waited. Someone had the bright idea of putting on a DVD of the **Spaced** TV series. I'd never seen it before and it might have been very funny in other circumstances. After 5 or 6 episodes in rapid succession, though, I needed to escape so I went back outside where I'd spotted a Peugeot van. Inside was a young guy and I asked him, in my best broken French, if he knew where I could get a taxi to take me to a station where

I might catch a train to Paris. He spoke a little English and said that it was his father who ran the tow-truck garage where we were situated, and that he would ask his father to call for a taxi. The father appeared and bluntly and charmlessly went about calling a cab for me, which, he said, would be coming 30km to pick me up. Thank the lord! Rumour quickly spread of my impending departure and the rest of the band decided to join me.

30 minutes later - around 2pm - we were heading for the station in a place called Chalons En Champagne. Well, we're in Champagne country but I wasn't feeling much like cracking a bottle open. Eventually Steve R and I arrived outside the station in a taxi with Mark and Pete behind us in another. Ian had declined and decided to stay with the bus and the crew. Dunno why. We bought tickets to Paris for 22Euros (not bad), noted that the next train to Paris was at 16.16, and then retired to a little café across the road where I ordered steak frites and bière Noel (Christmas beer). Things were looking up (slightly). We ate and I then called Q to see what the latest news was from the bus. He said the remainder of our party has ordered taxis and would be arriving in ten minutes. Shortly after, the crew and Ian arrived at the café. So we were back together again. I moved to a table on my own so I could write all this down while it's still fresh in my memory. As I write, I'm on a train, it is 5pm on Sunday Nov 27, Sue's spent the day alone, visiting the museums in Paris. This is what passes for a "romantic day-off" on the road.

Arrived at Paris La Gare L'est and for the umpteenth time dragged my anvil-heavy suitcase containing all my tour-belongings (not knowing when/if we'd see the tour-bus again, we'd had to pack and take everything!), along a load of cobbles 'til we found the taxi line. Waited impatiently in the queue whereupon the band nicked the first available 2 taxis (all heart) and after another age (which was probably 10 minutes) the crew, who'd got there first, waved me in front of them. Thanks chaps. Finally got to the hotel – the Holiday Inn, Place de la Republique - and tried to contact Diz by phone to find out what room we're in. Couldn't get hold of her so waited to talk to a receptionist who, in his very best Parisian "don't give a fuck", denied all knowledge of her, and of me, until I wrote my name on a piece of paper whereupon he found me on the computer and gave me two keys for room 167. I said Sue had already checked in yesterday. He said *her* key wouldn't work now so she would need the new one. I didn't try to reason with him. I long-since learned there is no point. I took the lift to the first floor, thoroughly weary and looking forward to seeing Dizzy. I couldn't find the room. It didn't seem to exist. I ran into a member of staff and asked where is room 167? He said he'd find out, and went off down a corridor, never to return. I went back down to Reception and was busy arguing with the receptionist about the existence of a room 167 when Sue appeared behind me. She showed me to our room. I'm an idiot. It did, indeed exist but was lost within the bizarre corridor room-signage which was listed upwards along one corridor (1-147) and downwards along the other (201-164). To a stressed-out, knackered Englishman, with a logical mind, 167 was absent, but if you think upside down, there it is!

The room was a smoking room. It stank like an ashtray. I would have changed it immediately but Sue had already stayed there last night and today, so I couldn't really suggest it, to her or to the hotel management. Oh well. I'd get used to it. Here in France, us non-smokers are the weirdo-minority. Sue went down to the bar and ordered Kirs while I freshened up and showered after the long, frustrating day.

Made my way to the bar and we were soon joined by Q and Ian, who stayed for 5 minutes before departing to eat. Sue and I decided to go out and find a nice restaurant and make the best of what little remained of the day.

We never got there. We had an argument instead. I won't go public with the details but the fact is that it sprung up out of almost nothing. I guess it had been a difficult day for both of us. She'd been hanging around for me all day and I'd arrived exhausted and stressed out. During the argument she stormed off out into the street, vanished and didn't come back. The last straw began to fall for us both.

I went to bed in the ashtray of room 167. It was only 8pm but I'd only had 2 hours sleep last night worrying about her, listening to the events following the breakdown of the bus and knowing I wasn't going to make it to Paris for our day off together.

So the night-off from hell followed the day-off from hell following the night from hell. The bed was as hard as a table and the bottom sheet on which I lay was coarse like a deck-chair. This is an expensive hotel too. I have added it to my "never again" list, along with several other hotels of the world and all the American airlines.

Lay awake most of the night, (again!) and at some point, something inside me gave up. All I want out of life is to live happily with my wife and my children but I have long-since broken that particular dream. We've been trying to fix it for around ten years now and tonight, for the first time, I realise it's over. I'm too tired to do it anymore.

Monday 28 November *Paris*

"Woke" from not being asleep, for the second night in a row, to the sound of car-horns. There's yet another demonstration going on outside. I later found out it was restaurateurs protesting about VAT! Sue had returned at some point in the night and was sleeping. I got up and went into the bathroom. When I emerged from the shower another tense exchange passed between us and as I couldn't see further discussion helping, I thought I should just go out.

I walked out into the street, found a hairdresser and had my roots coloured, then took the Metro to the Bastille in search of my 'pet' sock shop. I needed something to occupy my frazzled mind and I couldn't face returning to the hotel and the argument which would inevitably continue. Finally, in "the most romantic city in the world" I accepted that we couldn't be fixed. I had lost my oldest friend. I was grief-stricken.

Got hopelessly lost on the Metro. Too upset to navigate. Took an hour to do a ten-minute journey. Bought socks in a daze. During this process Sue texted to ask if I could get her on Rufus Wainright's Paris guest-list tonight! She says it hurts her too much now to listen to my songs and would rather not come to the Marillion gig. Fair enough. I txted Mr Q (who knows everyone) and he sorted it out for her.

When I returned to the hotel, she had gone out so I packed everything I had into the pink suitcase and dragged it downstairs to where Ian and Mark were waiting to leave for soundcheck. Having moved our entire tour-possessions from our broken tour-bus and having somehow crammed my two other bags into the suitcase, it had assumed the weight of a small car!

Plan A was to grab a cab to the Elyceé. Looking outside however, the Place de la Republique was jammed solid and stationary because of the "l'Escargot protest" (the restaurateurs had decided to drive around the city at 5 mph and jam the whole place). After much thought, we decided our best bet, in the absence of helicopters, was to take the Metro, so we left the hotel and made our way to the gig on public transport and on foot.

Well, they don't have many escalators on the Paris Metro so we dragged our cases up and down a great many flights of stairs, changing trains and platforms on our way to La Pigalle. My case was like lead; my head was too. I was on the verge of tears at the permanent realization of the death of our 25-year marriage and, of course, I had a show to do tonight. By the time I emerged onto the street I was tired, heartbroken, sweating, pissed off, and - if I had been a band, I would have split up with *myself*.

I didn't want the embarrassment of arriving outside the gig wheeling my suitcase (there are always a bunch of fans huddled outside our shows waiting patiently for the night, and I really couldn't face anyone) so I went the long way round the block instead, with the intention of using the back door. This involved the delicate negotiation of the dog-dirty, fag-end-strewn, unevenly-paved sidewalks, lugging everything up Montmartre's steep hills, whilst trying to keep dog-shit off the wheels of the suitcase. This - were it to happen - might well have unhinged me. I would have been found in a shop doorway foaming at the mouth, rocking and screaming.

When I arrived at the back door to the Elyceé I found a locked metal gate, which never used to be there. It had been built since we were last here. I called Q and asked him if he could let me in. He duly arrived and opened the gate. In the meantime, as I stood dishevelled and desperate on the busy Montmartre side-street with my unobtrusive (ha ha) pink suitcase, a tall Englishman who'd clocked me in the street sidled up to me and said,

"Hello Steve."

I said, "Not now, mate - I'm having a bad day," and he said,

"Aw, don't be heavy with me man, I just want to give you my demo."

I felt my eyes widen and the adrenaline run with the onset of immediate violence and said,

"Why don't you just fuck off and leave me alone? I don't know you." I'm not a violent soul at all and never have been, but in that moment, I could have cheerfully strangled him.

He got the message and said, "Ugh, alright. Have a good gig anyway", which was sweet of him, considering.

I said, "Thanks." I should have said sorry too, but I didn't.

Quinner appeared and took me into the dressing room. I lay on the sofa, trying to believe that, perhaps - just perhaps - there was a chance of peace for the next hour or so. There was. It was blissful after the disappointment, physical stress, mania and insomnia of the last 36-hours. I lay foetal on the sofa and went to sleep, despite the constant comings and goings of band and crew. They were trying to be quiet – all giving me a bit of space, bless 'em.

By showtime the gig was rammed to all 4 walls. The Elyceé is sold out. Don't understand the mechanics of it all, but we're selling more concert tickets on this tour (per gig) than on the **Marbles** tour proper. Who knows? I don't understand the music business. Experience seems to be worthless in predicting what's next.

Sue texted to say perhaps we could meet up later – perhaps after sound-check or after the show. I replied that maybe it would be better after the show. She said fine.

Soundcheck went without incident. Everything's in place now and soundchecks have become a formality really. I decided against venturing out. After the last two days it was better not to "get out of the boat". Someone somewhere would probably go on strike, close Montmartre, have me arrested, or whatever else would stop me getting back to the gig. Unfortunately there's only one dressing-room at the Elyceé and no backstage area. There's nowhere to go to be alone and the dressing room, understandably, ends up full of band, band's partners/family/guests etc. and I just had to sit there among them all like a zombie. Normally, I'd have escaped to sleep on the tour-bus, but it's broken in the middle of nowhere, France – a bit like me.

There was no natural way on earth of getting my head and body together for a show. I had got hold of some 'e's' last week in Middlesbrough. Took half a one. I don't take a lot of drugs, but this was an emergency and without it, I wouldn't have been much use tonight.

Fortunately for me, and for Marillion, it was Paris! Ironically, the show was to be fabulous. An ovation early-on lifted us all. The crowd were great as they always are here. I really don't know what I would have done without them. Et encore une fois, Merci beaucoup, mes amis.

Afterwards, I signed stuff in the hall. Sue never showed up. She txted to say she couldn't find the gig. I was beyond asking why. At least she's safe in a hotel and not wandering the streets.

To everyone's relief, Phoenix had finally found us a replacement bus. It was Simply Red's. We have to give it back in a couple of days, but it'll get us to Lille for tomorrow's show. I went upstairs and found a bunk labelled Mick H. That's close enough then. There were stars on the ceiling.

I wonder if Mick's life is as fucked as mine?

PS And so it was, that shortly after my return from this tour, on the 9th December, I moved out of my marital home. The split with Sue had been a long time coming for both of us and we had both worked hard to hold our marriage together, but in the end, my work, my lifestyle, my stupidity, and perhaps, fate, finished it.

Mosley and Lucy took me in for a while, then I lived at Mark and Angie's empty house over Christmas, then at Erik and Rachel's in Oxford over the New Year while they were away in America. At times like this, you find out who your friends are.

2006

Early 2006

I guess I didn't feel much like keeping the diary for a while, so I'll sketch in a few details. In January I rented a house "next door to myself" back in Charlton so I could be close to the kids. I put my piano by the bed, along with some recording equipment, so I could work at any time of night or day. Sofi and Nial could pop in and see me any time they chose so I didn't have to abandon them, which would have been torture for all three of us. It's weird to live next door to your ex-partner, but if you've got children, I would recommend it. It's not about you, it's about the kids.

Although I had dreaded it, I found, to my surprise, that it was a relief to be living on my own. Not exactly a walk in the park, of course, but a relief nonetheless. I used to shout, "Honey, I'm home!" when I came home from the studio in the evening. It was an ironic reference to what I had lost, but it was also strangely comforting – a way of making the house less empty. I never made it to the "Tom Hanks – drawing a face on a football" stage though.

One morning in January (just after my car had been stolen, but that never made it into the diary either) I received a wedding invitation from my Norwegian chum, Jon-Arne Vilbo (guitarist, Gazpacho) who was to marry his girl, Lisa in the summer. I called him to thank him and say that I would be there but would be coming alone. When he heard of my separation from Sue he said, "That's awful. You should come to Oslo as soon as possible and get drunk with us!"

It was a most appealing proposition so I booked a flight. Probably the same week, and conscious of the trauma of splitting up, followed by an appalling Christmas, and having just about arrived at some kind of inner-peace, I looked at myself in the shaving-mirror and said out-loud:

"What you need now, is to live like this for at least a year. Quietly. Alone. Write some songs. Try and find yourself."

So a fortnight after that, I went to Oslo and fell in love with Linette.

Pronounced Linn-ett-a, Danish, stunningly beautiful, full of light and laughter, and possessed of a wicked sense of humour, she was a friend of Line (pronounced Lee-na), the lovely partner of Gazpacho's lovely (and barmy) Thomas Andersen. She was in Oslo for the weekend and at some point we were introduced. That was it. Just talking to her made me feel completely happy for the first time in many years. I was immediately smitten. Her own long-term relationship had recently ended and she was living alone in an apartment belonging to Copenhagen General Hospital where she worked. I figured she wouldn't be single for long, so I bit the bullet and asked her if she'd mind showing me Copenhagen some time... She said she'd be delighted. It's a wonderful city and they do say it's the happiest city on earth.

We met up a handful of times in Copenhagen and London during the spring and spent hours on the phone as 2006 progressed towards summer. I took her DVD's of Morecambe&Wise and Tommy Cooper. She had trouble following what Tommy said.

Saturday 28 May *Home – Lisbon*

Went to Lisbon to make an appearance on a TV show. Left home around 9.00 for Heathrow along the M40, occasionally glancing across at the other carriageway, which was jammed with traffic and thinking "I'm glad I'm not going the other direction!"

Half way to Heathrow, as I approached High Wycombe, I realized I'd left my passport on the dressing table. Turned round and joined the traffic jam I had been admiring.

Crawled back home (my rented "house next door") at 5mph and retrieved said passport, before heading, once again, to Heathrow. When I arrived, I was so late for the flight that my only option was to park the car in the Short-Stay car-park and run for it across the bridge into the terminal. It wasn't going to be cheap, but at least it's only for one day...

Sunday 29 May *Lisbon – Home*

I'm sitting on the cold granite floor of a holding-area in Lisbon airport. Right now it's 4.15 in the afternoon and we should have departed to Heathrow at 2.45. Around 2.30 we boarded the bus to the aircraft. It's hot here in Portugal today and the afternoon sun is beating down. The bus remained parked at the gate in the 30-degree heat long after it was packed with passengers. The sweltering heat shimmered up from the tarmac into the claustrophobic bus. Just as old ladies were beginning to expire, the thing finally assumed motion and took us to a TAP Portugal airlines aircraft where we sat down – already behind schedule. As I took my seat, I became immediately conscious (as I can't help but do) of the music playing in the cabin. "Easy-listening" muzak with bad synthesizers backing a pan-pipe playing the lead-vocal melody. *Hey Jude* was the chosen victim. It went round and round on a loop. After two minutes I was twitching.

Nothing happened for 15-minutes and then the pilot told us that there was a problem with one of the doors and that they were trying to fix it. 20 minutes after that, he told us that they couldn't, and that we must change planes. It took a further 45 (!) minutes of sitting on the plane (still enduring the worst pan-pipe music I have ever heard… In the end I asked for it to be turned off and the air steward seemed most grateful for the request. There was a patter of applause and several passengers actually thanked me!) before TAP managed to arrange a bus to transport us back to the terminal. When we got here they told us to go upstairs back to terminal 19 where we had been 2 and a half hours ago. Upon trying to follow this instruction it became apparent that we were no longer "air side" even though we'd just got off a plane, and we must all put our belongings and ourselves through the security scanners all over again! So I'm sitting here on the floor while an entire plane load of people get partially undressed ALL OVER AGAIN and undergo all the security screening bollocks we've come to enjoy so much in the modern world, for a second time, and for no logical reason at all.

Later...

I'm now at gate 19 and it's approaching 5pm. There's still no sign of us being asked to board anything back to Heathrow. I flew from there yesterday and, having almost missed the flight (after the forgotten passport and the long queue on the M40) I had, of course, left my car in the incredibly expensive "short stay" car park. This means that this delay is probably costing about £20.00 an hour in car parking alone.

Later...

It gets worse. While I was trying to negotiate security a second time, it turns out that half of the people from my flight were invited to board again. They left the terminal and got on a bus to another plane. After half of them had left, there was a snag and everyone else was kept waiting in the terminal - including yours truly. Some time later they all came back up the stairs again and one of them told me that the replacement aircraft has the same problem with the doors because the weather is "too hot"! Dunno if this is worth any thought or discussion because it's patently a fib anyway. My guess is that they tried to board them back onto the *same* plane, which perhaps, they thought they'd fixed. I would guess that it's still about 30 degrees outside – hot, but completely normal for Portugal in the summer – so it's totally daft to suggest that the aeroplane doors can't handle such an ambient temperature. I wouldn't be surprised if I'm still in this airport at midnight. Nick B has invited me to the Dave Gilmour gig tonight at the Albert Hall. I was quite looking forward to seeing Nick, and the show. Can't imagine I'll be back in England 'til late... if at all.

It's now ten past five and we've been invited to board the aircraft again. For some people, this will be the third time they've tried. I will hang on and see what develops before I bother. At least I can get to the bar from here...

Went to the bar and was amazed when I was sold a beer in a glass bottle which I was then allowed to take to the gate. Having been cut to ribbons by a maniac wielding a broken glass at one point in my distant past, I'm more than a little aware of the destructive power of a glass bottle – deadlier in my opinion than a knife – and so the whole charade of repeated security scans became even more frustrating and demonstrably pointless. I sit at the gate eating an ice-cream and drinking beer whilst writing all this down.

Later...

Well, around 5.45 we were invited to board a new plane. When I handed my passport to the official at the gate along with the laminated yellow pass we'd all been given when we came back the first time (the people who'd come back twice now had little green ones...) I was told that the boarding pass was for Copenhagen and that I couldn't get on the plane. "Where is the boarding pass for Heathrow please?" I said I don't know and could she please have me arrested because a prison cell is probably preferable to any more of this nonsense. She said she couldn't arrest me because she's not a policeman. I said well go and get one then, and she then flicked through my passport some more and found the right boarding pass in there and so I was allowed back onto the bus and back to a plane where I assumed the same seat as before and exchanged knowing weary glances with all those around me, while my finger hovered over the cabin-attendant call-button in readiness for pan-pipe music.

The plane took off around 6pm and the flight to Heathrow was uneventful. Hoorah. However, we landed around 8.35 and then the aircraft stood still on the runway for about 15-minutes – much to everyone's further frustration. By this time it really WAS "the flight that would not end".

We were eventually allocated a parking spot and we made our way from the plane while the TAP staff said bye and thanks somewhat apologetically. The passport-control hall was absolutely packed and we queued for a further 15 minutes snaking our way back and forth as we progressed towards England. By the time I got into the baggage hall, my pink suitcase was going round on the carousel. Well, that's something – last time I flew from Lisbon my bag didn't show up for three weeks!

I made my way to the short-stay car park and was relieved of a large amount of money before climbing into the car around 9.30pm. The Albert Hall was no longer an option. By the time I got to London it would be well-past 10pm and I'd probably not be let in.

As I drove along the M4, Nick B called to say "What happened to you, then?" I briefly outlined the afternoon's developments.

"That's shame…" said Nick, "David Bowie's just got up to sing an impromptu encore!"

Oh well. As long as I haven't missed much…

June

At the beginning of June I moved out of the house "next door to myself" and rented a house in Islip, near Oxford. Linette quit her job in Copenhagen and moved in with me in England at the end of the month. It was a sunny day and we walked through the country lanes of Islip with champagne glasses, sipping and laughing. A dream-like and treasured memory which began a new life for us both.

Saturday 29 July   *Praia-di-Mira   M.S. Club   h Natural*

Slept fitfully worrying about Sofi. I had the feeling she wasn't alright after the strange txt from late last night. We got up around 12.00 and ordered coffee and orange juice on room service. I called Lucy to ask her to have a word with Edgar about lunch today. Last night Edgar had suddenly announced that lunch has been arranged in my honour today with God-knows how many guests - 30 or so - including members of the Portuguese fanclub staff, a Marillion tribute band, and friends and family of Ze-Ze, the promoter and club-owner. I didn't really want to sit down to eat with 30 assorted fans and tribute-band members. All very nice people of course, but I need peace and space on gig days. I also need to rest my voice. Lucy said not to worry and she'd sort it all out.

Outside it was sunny and hot, so Linette and I sun-bathed on the huge terrace for a while. Txted Sofi a couple of times during the morning but heard nothing back from her. I hope she's alright… I decided to take the big orange suitcase to the gig so that I could take my clothes, headphones and bits of gear all in one bag like I had done in Majorca. Roderick showed up around 1.00 and joined us for coffee on the terrace.

We'd arranged to meet Edgar at 1.30 in reception so we made our way down there and hung around the pool-area until Edgar finally showed up at 2.15! He said they were having trouble at the gig getting the piano up the stairs. The legs had to be removed etc. Thankfully, this is not my problem. I remember, all too well, a time when it would have been…

Edgar drove us to the farm which Ze-Ze (club owner and promoter) uses as a weekend retreat. It's actually owned by Ze - his father - and this is the place where the expansive lunch – the one I cancelled – had been arranged. When we got there and swung into the drive through the big double gates. There were expensive cars parked in the courtyard and a couple of guys lounging around outside in dark glasses. The grounds were very well kept and there were fig trees, fruit trees, a vineyard and palm trees in plenty. To be honest, it looked like the home of a drug baron from some Hollywood movie. There was a slight delay while they decided where Edgar should put his car and eventually an electric garage-door hummed open and we drove inside to an area full of inflatable holiday paraphernalia, and a couple more sports cars - an Audi TT and a Merc SLK.

We were led inside to the dining room/kitchen. The large rustic kitchen area was at one end of a huge dining room where a long table was already set for about 30 people. When I say "set" I mean immaculately so – fine glassware, cotton napkins and silver cutlery gleaming away into the distance. I suddenly felt especially guilty at having earlier cancelled the party – they'd obviously gone to a lot of trouble. Masses of food had been prepared. There were now only 4 of us, plus half-a-dozen members of Ze-Ze's family and friends, to consume nothing-short-of a banquet. When I cancelled it all, I didn't really understand quite what I was cancelling. What a fucking diva they must think I am!

Oh well. We were invited to inspect the oven - a small cave built into the brickwork - all full of upturned roof tiles. In each tile lay a sardine grilling above charcoal. Beyond those were potatoes - small ones, still with the skin on. It all looked very traditional, and very appetizing. I was introduced to various family members and tried desperately to remember the names. One chap runs a vineyard and his own sparkling wine was being opened along with a couple of his white wines. I declined all in favour of beer. I have to sing today so I'll leave the wine alone. We sat down at the long table and course-after-course of seafood arrived washed down with beer and wine. I was introduced to Ze-Ze's father Ze. (which led me to wonder if Ze-ze's son would be called Ze-ze-ze?.) Ze owns this lot and is therefore something of the "Godfather" around here but you'd never have guessed from his demeanour. He's modest, friendly and relaxed with a warm twinkle in his eye. I was later to learn that Ze is in the jewellery business. He seems to be completely loaded and he is that rare person - a rich man with innate generosity and generosity of spirit. Everyone here seemed to genuinely love him and was totally relaxed around him. I too, quickly grew to admire him immensely. There were uniformed-staff on hand to serve the lunch but everyone in the family - including the old man and his wife, Clarice - seemed to lend a hand and take pride in the act of preparing and serving up the food. It was actually quite difficult to stop them from feeding me until I couldn't move and they would have been perfectly content to give us drinks until we couldn't stand up either. No one seemed remotely aware that I have a show tonight, despite the fact that they're promoting it!

When lunch was finally drawing to a close (with me, by this stage, constantly nervously checking my watch) it was suggested that we make a quick guided-tour of the farm. We walked down through gardens of flowers, fruit and vegetables and watched young goats being fed milk from a bottle. Ze proudly showed us the cockerels which had been castrated in order for them to grow fat and round. Then through the pig-house to a stable where a large Friesian bull stood, and back out into the Portuguese sunshine to walk past a white horse, then past an immaculate swimming pool where children were playing. An actual paradise, in every detail. Then on to Clarice's "museum" - a little barn which has been done out like a farmhouse from the last century. Old cooking implements and hand tools, a table set with old crockery and cutlery, and lastly a working still where she distills her own moonshine. What a place! We watched while Ricardo (Ze ze's brother) and his mother hand-turned a machine which removes the corn from maize husks.

By this time I was visibly twitching with the need to get to the venue and soundcheck and, more importantly, rehearse for tonight's show. I hadn't really managed any rehearsal for this one so far and was relying heavily on the songs having been retained since Majorca (2 weeks ago) in my unreliable memory.

I thanked everyone profusely for lunch and the tour of the farm, and we then drove out of the farm and to the gig, but not without making a detour to a little music shop to borrow a piano stool. Edgar had forgot to hire one. I sat in the back of Ze-Ze's Merc and twitched my way impatiently to the gig - the "MS Club". When we arrived there, a phone-call was made to the police to ensure Ze-Ze could park his car on the pavement (he knows the police... they come to his club when they're not working) and everyone disappeared into the gig while I called Diz to see if Sofi was okay. She told me that Sofi had everything stolen last night - her mobile phone and purse containing her driver's licence, and all her money - whilst at WOMAD festival. Oh well. Teenagers. I've already replaced her driving licence once after she said she'd lost it. She's a chip off the old block, so can't really moan.

I was relieved to know she's okay. Very relieved. Now I can get on with the gig...

Went inside the club to find a team of guys debating which way to position the piano. They've been doing this now for 4 hours. I climbed on stage and hauled the thing round myself into position and began rehearsing while much more debate continued as to whether another stage was required. I said no thanks it was absolutely fine, so Ze-Ze ordered another one immediately. When it arrived in a van with another load of chaps to set it up, I had to refuse it about 6 times before they all sheepishly went away again. Linette wisely went for a walk around Praia while I rehearsed for the rest of the afternoon and evening. It all sounded pretty good in the headphones until Roderick turned the PA on then the spill from the back of the bass cabinets annihilated my can-sound and made the piano sound not-so-much like someone *playing* the piano, but more like someone *building* a piano. Damn. It was all going so well. Roderick fought with the equipment for a few hours but to little avail. We just had to cross our fingers and hope it would sound better with people in the room.

At 8.30 I was STILL rehearsing and was pretty weary and quite stressed. I'd been quietly worrying about Sofi all day long and now the relief of knowing she was alright was somehow exhausting, along with the stress of the approaching show and worries over the sound. I couldn't seem to get any of the chords right.

I was shown into a "dressing room" which was a small w.c and shower behind the bar. (Well, you can't expect disco's to have a dressing room). I sat on the floor trying to calm down and relax for half an hour before the show. Linette returned and took me outside to walk along the sea. I hadn't really noticed the ocean yet and it was good to have a complete change of scenery. This is the Atlantic coast and the sea is so much wilder than a couple of weeks ago when we were in Mediterranean Majorca. We watched, and listened to, the waves crashing onto the wide and long sandy beach at Praia di Mira. There was a slight sea-mist which gave a spookiness to the scene too. Quite lovely. We found a bar and had a beer wheruopn Linette said we must wait for "a surprise". Oh God, I don't like surprises... After a while Edgar showed-up with a glint in his eye and then a police car drew up outside the bar. It seemed to be escorting a horse and carriage. We were beckoned forward to the carriage and Edgar said "You like goofy stuff - don't you? Get inside and wave to the people!" So we climbed up, and the carriage drove around the town behind the police car with the lights going round while I waved my best "Queen-wave" to the passers-by. I was amazed by how many people smiled and waved back despite not having a clue who we were. In England they'd have thrown stuff at me - quite deservedly too - but here, people seem to give you the benefit of the doubt. It was a dumb and silly thing to have arranged but it was brilliant and, strangely, put me in exactly the right frame of mind for the show.

By the time I walked on stage, I was quietly in-love with the good people of Praia di Mira. The club was now busy and the reception was very warm from the people. My sound was still a bit difficult to work with but it didn't seem to matter. The vibe was fantastic. I had decided not to read too much from the diary (mindful of the language barrier – my Portuguese aint great) but at the half-way point of the show the crowd began shouting for a day from the diary so I read the fateful "London to Mexico via Bangor, Washington, Chicago and Cat Stevens" 40 hour marathon journey from 2004. It took AGES to read out and I kept offering to stop, but the people seemed happy to hear it all. I must've talked for the best part of half-an-hour before resuming the music. I was really enjoying myself by now. The most memorable moment was *3 Minute Boy* when the crowd sang louder than any crowd I've heard on this tour. This one was right up there with Liverpool - my previous favourite.

After the show I decompressed in my loo-dressing room and Linette came by to give me a congratulatory hug. We waited a little while before I ventured outside. The bar-staff were great, sorting me out with a Caipirinha and a couple of FANTASTIC tuna sandwiches, which were very welcome - I hadn't eaten since lunch-on-the-farm and it was now 1.30 am. I signed a LOT of autographs and live **Spirit/Body** albums. Some guy bought 5 copies. Ze-Ze invited us upstairs where he opened a bottle of vintage Port and shared it out to all assembled. It was very good. The Portuguese seem to set great store by their hospitality and we were invited back to Ze's farm for lunch tomorrow. I now realized that Ze and his entire family were at the gig and they all seemed to have enjoyed it immensely. The old man came and shook my hand and as he explained in

Portuguese how much he enjoyed the show, his eyes filled up with tears. What an incredible and beautiful old man. I think we finally got out of there around 3.30. An amazing day.

Sunday 30 July *Praia di Mira*

Enjoyed a much-needed lie in and didn't really stir until 12.00. I called room-service and asked for omelette and coffee. I was told that the kitchen was closed now, but that they would "see what they could do". Omelette duly arrived 10 minutes later. I think I seem to have gained a bit of "clout" round here. Perhaps someone's had a word...

We had arranged to meet Edgar downstairs at 3.45 to go to the farm for late-lunch. When I got to reception, the receptionist told me she'd been to my show and enjoyed it very much. Maybe SHE made the omelette...

We hung around for Edgar who arrived half an hour late looking flustered and muttering about how the process of removing the piano from the club had become quite "complicated". I didn't ask...

Edgar drove us back to Ze's farm/paradise where we had, again, been invited for lunch. We sat down in the huge kitchen/dining room once again while Ze and his wife plied us with masses of sea-food (the cockles fried in olive oil were just *stellar*), followed by, well, masses more food and washed down with unlimited gallons of wine and beer. I slowly cottoned on to the fact that the only way to stop Ze replenishing my glass was to leave it full. This took me until about 5pm, though. Not having a show to contemplate today meant I could relax and enjoy the entire meal so much more than yesterday. The relief I felt at having got the solo show out of the way was such a wonderful contrast from the uncertainty and nervousness of its anticipation, that I had almost entered a state-of-grace!

Ze seems to have made his mind up about me since the gig last night and it would seem that he's decided I am family. When I first confirmed the show, Linette and I had planned to stay on for a few days afterwards and have a little holiday in Portugal. Ze has insisted that Linette and I check out of our hotel tomorrow and move into another of his houses in Praia-di-Mira. He seems to have a few... He has instructed his staff to go down there and stock the fridge, prepare the beds etc. so that all will be ready tomorrow when we go over there. Unbelievable. He then asked us, via his son Ze-Ze acting as interpreter, whether we had arranged a car. I explained that we would hire one tomorrow. He would have none of it. He took us to the garage and waved a hand towards the Merc and the Audi and said "Take your pick!". He insisted that we decide which one we'd like to borrow, assured us that this was all legal in Portugal (where the insurance laws are different) and, when we decided on the Audi TT, duly gave us the keys.

Later, Ze had to go out to work. He's a jeweller – I guess he must own quite a substantial business to be so wealthy. It was hard to quite get a grip on the exact nature of his work as we don't speak the language and everything had to be translated via Ze-Ze or Edgar. Before he left to "go to the office" he enquired as to Linette's ring-size. He was away for a few hours and, when he returned in the evening, he laid out half a dozen gold rings in various designs and smilingly asked her to choose one. She chose one with a dolphin winding around it and he duly told her it was hers. He would accept no payment. He has never asked or expected anything in return for all this generosity. I have the impression that the pleasure he feels in giving, is reward enough.

Monday 31 July *Praia di Mira*

Up at 11.40 to pack hurriedly for the 12.00 check-out. Nearly forgot my silver necklace with the little Mayan girl on it but Linette found it on the floor. I would definitely have lost it if I'd been on my own. That would have been a pisser.

Checked out and paid for Roderick's rooms as well as ours. 660 euros. There goes the profits! Loaded the bags and the rice pudding (which Ze's wife insisted on us taking yesterday) into the Audi TT and drove into Praia di Mira. Stopped at the first restaurant and managed to order coffees and omelette. Admired the waitresses jugs (no, really) which were of a plain local design - creamy coloured earthenware with fine blue stripes. We both thought it would be nice to take one home (a jug, not a waitress). Edgar texted to say he would pay for the first two nights in the hotel for Roderick and I. That's great news. I'm back in profit then. Walked round to the beach then decided to go back and move the car. Bought a towel. Parked the car and bought Bacardi and Coke to get change for the parking. Sat in the Salix beach-bar for a couple of hours watching the sea and drinking slow B&C's. This is the life. Had a walk round the shops. Nearly all selling beach and tourist crap. Tried to find a shop selling the kind of jugs we'd seen earlier but nothing doing. There was <u>one</u> ceramics shop which was just packed full of religious stuff. Luminous Madonnas and pot Jusus's. Even if I was religious I'd find this stuff pretty tacky.

Walked back through the town, onto the beach and along the water's edge. This aint the Mediterranean, it's the Atlantic and you surely can tell. It's much wilder - 6ft breakers roll in at unpredictable intervals. Occasionally two or three waves combine and break over each other and the surf comes further up the beach, drenching the unprepared. I was unprepared. Removed my shoes, which were now full of seawater, and walked barefoot heading south along the beach. We picked up a few shells to take home. Returned up the beach. Easier said than done. The sand is very fine and you sink in as you walk. It pushes your toes apart which is quite painful. There must be a knack to it. We experimented with different walking techniques. I settled on the "heel first" method which I found was less stressful on the toes but makes you look like a complete lunatic.

Settled down in another beach bar and ordered up lemon tea. Edgar was supposed to have called to arrange for us to pick up the keys to Ze's house but we'd heard nothing. Texted and called him several times between 5.30 and 7.00

to no avail. By 7.00 we were really in need of a place to call "home". I called Alexis Crossland (Rob and Alexis are staying at Edgar's house at the moment) and managed to get hold of her. They didn't know where Edgar had gone either. We decided to drive back to Edgar's house and meet up with Rob and Alexis there. We could always chill out at his place. Unfortunately we couldn't remember exactly where it is... Oh well, we'll see...

Climbed back into the car around 7.15 and took a wrong turn which meant we had to go back through the one-way system round the town. As we turned back into town my phone rang and, when I answered it, there was no-one there. Perhaps Edgar was finally calling. It rang again as we turned another corner up a narrow street. I pressed the phone to my ear. We were moving very slowly - certainly no more than 20 mph - so I had plenty of time to see a policeman waving at me from a bicycle he was riding along the street. He was gesturing me to park the car. Oh dear. He asked me to get out and he then asked me for the papers for the car and my driving license and i.d. By some miracle I had everything he wanted but most of it was in the big orange suitcase in the boot of the Audi so I had to get it out onto the street and start emptying it. I asked him what I had done wrong and he said it was because I was using the phone whilst driving. I tried to explain that I wasn't even talking to anyone but he was one of those guys who was on a mission to do it all by the book. He said I must pay a fine of 120 Euros. He took my passport and drivers licence and told me to follow him back to the police station. Back at the police station he went inside the building while I parked the car. As I walked into the station I called Alexis to tell her I had now been "arrested" and was being fined at the Police station so if she could get hold of Edgar, well, that would be great. Inside, the policeman was busy filling in a form while Linette did her best to reason with him and to explain that I actually hadn't answered the phone and spoken to anyone. It was pointless trying. He just kept repeating that using the phone in Portugal is considered to be a very serious offence and that there are more deaths because of this than because of drink-driving. Oh well. I saw no point in pissing him off. We must have looked to him like a rich couple in an Audi TT who wouldn't find a 120 euro fine too much of an inconvenience. He was doing his job and he clearly wasn't in the mood to let us off with a caution. Personally, I think he was a bit of a twat under the circumstances but I wasn't going to share that with him. Edgar suddenly arrived looking flustered and tried to mitigate also. The cop finished filling in the form, I paid the fine and he gave me my paperwork back and told me we were free to go.

I finally managed to get the keys to the house from Edgar and we returned to the house and showered. I suggested that we went to dinner with Rob and Alexis and Edgar so we all went over to the restaurant above the "Ego" bar. Dinner was great. After that we went over to the MS Club where Ze-Ze was hell-bent on showing me some photographs of my gig which had been taken by "a professional photographer". I thought they were all pretty average, but I felt we certainly owed Ze-Ze the courtesy of having a look. Said hello again to the staff of the MS Club who were all very nice people especially the barman who made us Caipirinhas and even managed to find Linette's lost cardigan from Saturday. Was introduced to a young nephew of Ze-Ze's who looked like Jack Osborne (now quite famous just for being Ozzy's son since the reality show "The Osbornes"). It was his 21st birthday so we all went upstairs to watch while he cut the cake and his mates all sang him the Portuguese version of "Happy Birthday to You". Talked to a couple of boys who were musicians and seemed excited to be talking to me - one a guitarist and the other, a bassoonist - before leaving the club. Popped round the corner for a last Caipirinha in the Irish Bar. After that, we followed Edgar over to "our" new house - a 5 bedroomed luxury home - in the TT, Linette at the wheel. I was too pissed.

The house was on three floors and only down the road from the beach. We decided on a bedroom and marvelled at the contents of the fridge – now stuffed with ham, cheese, milk, beers, bread and everything we'd need for tomorrow's breakfast. It occurred to me that we were driving this man's car, and living in his house without him seeing any form of identification or even having our phone numbers. We could have driven his TT back to England, or anywhere else for all he knew. And all this from a man who only met us 2 days ago. What a shame the whole world can't function on such levels of trust. Thank you Ze. If there's ever anything I can do for you, sir...

Monday 31 July *Praia di Mira*

Up at 12.30 after the late night.

Couldn't turn the oven on. No Kettle. Decided to go out for coffee. Washed my shoes in the bidet and put em out to dry on one of the 3 balconies (!) in the sun.

Decided to go exploring in the Audi. Drove back through Mira (keeping a wary eye out for coppers), and North through huge groves of maize and along a wide canal. The weather was strange. Cloud at ground level. And the canal-water seemed to be steaming like the Florida Everglades. There were no alligators in evidence though.

Passed girls in bikinis sunbathing on the mud next to the canal.

Arrived at a place called Costa Nova where the buildings were painted in coloured and white stripes. We mooched round the market stalls. There was a fish market displaying live crabs and eels, octopus, prawns and various fish. We found a shop where we could buy a kettle but decided against it. There's a coffee machine at the house so we bought ground coffee. And nuts. There was a store selling all kinds of Portuguese ceramics so we bought two jugs (like the waitresses ones I mentioned yesterday) in the typical local design. Walked along the street and found a café where we could sit outside. Linette put her jugs on the floor and I put my nuts on the table. How we laughed. Laughed more as we watched little old dear with bad leg trying to open a stall opposite. I'm sorry. She was clearly too old to be working. She was running a little beach-kiosk selling - well - crap (inflatable moose, postcards, Portuguese flags and the kind of plastic stuff that rarely lasts more than 1 day). She had a stick with a hook on it and she was trying to hang her goods up high on other little hooks. It was going to take her all morning. I was reminded of Julie Walters' classic old waitress sketch. It took her several minutes to hang one corner of a Portuguese flag on a hook, which promptly fell off as she turned round. This sounds cruel, doesn't it? I'm sorry. You had to be there. If she'd been my own Gran, it would still have been funny.

We ate omelette and drank coffee before going over the road to buy something from aforementioned amusing old-dear. Bought postcards and fabulous marbles. She garbled at us madly in Portuguese and I gave her too much money. While we walked away she fumbled around trying to get her purse open whilst making funny high-pitched squeaking noises. If we'd have wanted change, it would have taken the rest of the day. Bless.

Took some photographs of the stripy buildings and walked between them to the sea. There was a terrible smell of sewage, providing significant evidence to consider broadening my theory about the link between the Spanish language and the smell of sewage. I may have to add Portuguese, but it's too early to conclude.

Had a look at the sea and decided to return to the car and move on in search of Aveiro ("the Venice of Portugal"). Found it and had a walk around poking our nose into a church - all faced with Portuguese tiles inside and out. Beautiful. Walked through the shops and found a Bodyshop. Jeez - these are everywhere now. Dabbed myself with Sandalwood and Patchouli which hung around in the car for the rest of the day.

Walked along the canal and took photographs of the "gondolas" which were painted brightly with the kind of slightly unsound images which sailors tend to paint. One was of a man looking up a girl's dress as he held a ladder for her so that she could reach a bird's nest in the branch of a tree. I guess that sums up the sexes.

Returned to the car and decided to drive south to try to find the Palace Hotel at Bucaco. We'd heard about this yesterday from Rob and Alexis. It's an old monastery half way up a mountain, which has been converted into a 5 star-hotel. Stopped for gas and couldn't open the filler-cap. It needs a key and we didn't have it. Much head-scratching ensued as attendants came out one-by-one to have a look and then walk away shrugging. One of the windscreen wiper-blades had also torn itself in half (must be the sea air) so I bought a new one. Couldn't fit it and fiddled around for half an hour trying and failing to do it. Eventually I realized that the clips for the new wipers didn't fit the wiper arms of the Audi. The old clips that DID fit the wiper arms wouldn't fit the new wiper blades, which were slightly different. Doh. Still had enough gas to get back home so decided to return.

Found another gas station where an old Portuguese woman spoke not-only a little English but was also smarter than me and managed to get the filler cap open. It wasn't locked, just stiff. Double-Doh!. But Hooray! Gassed up and returned to Plan A and set off for Bucaco "straight across 5 roundabouts then right" said the brilliant gas-station attendant. And she was right. If everyone in the world was like her it would be a different planet entirely - no world poverty or famine, the trains would all run on time. It's a terrible shame she's not running TAP airlines.

Arrived at Bucaco and drove through a narrow gateway where a friendly chap relieved us of a few Euros before driving up the winding road lined by HUGE redwood trees for ten minutes, until we arrived at what is now The Palace Hotel. (Check out the website and read the guidebooks. It's amazing.)

I took photographs. We walked right round the place trying to gain access. Finally found a door which was closed but unlocked and it led us into the huge tiled and panelled foyer. Had dinner on the terrace. Amazing. Having been a monastery the place is built in ornate stonework, like one of those Indian intricately-carved ivory artworks on a grand scale – a cross between a gothic church and some kind of wizard's dream. Our table overlooked the gardens laid out in box-hedged squares - a style reminiscent of Elizabethan English gardens. Left to return to Mira around 10.00pm and managed to find our way back.

When we got to Mira we couldn't find the house so drove around for another 30-minutes until Linette spotted it.

A pleasant touristy day.

(PS I guess 2006 turned out to be Portuguese as far as the diary is concerned.)

2007

Friday 5 October *Home – Cervia*

Drove to Stansted. Made pretty good time. Met up with Roderick. Comedian Hugh Dennis was in the queue at check in. Comedian David Baddiel was also on the plane. Maybe they're doing something together. The Ryannair plane to Bologna was a shocker. The seats don't recline and are finished in yellow plastic. The visual onslaught continues overhead where gaudy adverts have been attached to the overhead locker doors. It was like being on a tube-train. Ryannair certainly know their market and treat their passengers accordingly...

There was a long, slow-moving queue at passport control in Bologna. After about 15 minutes the officials decided to move things along and didn't even look at mine. Bags were going round on the carousel when we finally made it there. We were met by Dave and Giorgio. Drove to Cervia to Hotel Rudy, which belongs to Anna and Giorgio. They're all pretty hard-core Marillion fans and very lovely people. We had a light dinner – Becks and red wine. Giorgio and Anna have offered us a few nights at the hotel for free, which is very sweet and generous of them. L seems to have ricked her neck!

Saturday 6 October *Cervia   h Natural show*

Woke up to discover L not well. In and out of bathroom with bad tummy. Oh no. We had breakfast and walked through the pines to the gig with Roderick and

Stephanie. The gig's a bit like a school hall! It will probably look alright in the dark. L was still feeling unwell so she returned to the hotel and went back to bed for the day. Soundcheck at 5pm. All fine apart from a dodgy mic lead (this is something of a triumph in Italy!). Went back to the hotel to spend an hour with L who is still laid out. She's unable to manage the gig so I left her watching crap Italian TV.

The gig was absolutely great. A brilliant audience – especially after the relatively half-hearted Dutch show the week before. "Passion" and "Italy" are synonymous words really. After the show I wanted to get back to Linette, but I was virtually mobbed as I tried to leave, and did autographs and photographs for 40-minutes. Came back clutching bottles of wine, jewellery, demo CD's, photographs and little notes.

Sunday 7 October *Cervia*

Got up around 11.00 and went down to breakfast where Stephanie Ringuet was waiting to give me my watch. Roderick was already on the plane home. Had a slow breakfast and showed everyone excerpts from the new *Somewhere in London* movie. Anna said we could borrow her car! Went over the road to the club Fantini and reclined on outdoor sofas in the sun by the sea all day. Steph returned and we stayed on. There was a dog-show today so there were dogs everywhere and a singing karaoke artist by the sea who looked like Lech Walesa in glam Gigolo clothes. He sang a song with a chorus which sounded like "HIV"... Reminded me of coonte facci from the old days – a story told to me by my old tour-manager/sound man Paul Owen (last seen doing monitors for Metallica). Can't remember the band - probably Slade - but they all checked into a hotel in Italy and one of the road crew, being tired and travel-weary, wasn't in the mood for form filling – he just wanted to get into a room and sleep. When the check-in papers were forced upon him, against the name field he wrote "Cunt Face". No one seemed to notice or comment, until an hour later when the local police arrived and assembled the entourage in reception demanding to speak to Signora Coonte Facci as his passport had not matched his name...

Walked by the sea. Drank another beer. L was feeling better, but delicate. In the evening we had dinner with Giorgio, Anna, their children Lorenzo and Bianca, and Anna's brother and mother. Little Bianca asked if I was bringing Pink Floyd with me. Drank the wine I'd been given which turned out to be "the best and most expensive wine in Tuscany". It was very nice. LOVELY seafood. L was trying to go easy with the food, and drink is now more or less out of bounds (we just found out she's pregnant! We're keeping it quiet for now). I redoubled my efforts in order to help.

Monday 8 October   *Cervia – San Germignano*

Woke to an empty hotel. G & A had gone home to get the kids to school. The children live with their grandmother during the season because G&A must work every day and night at the hotel! I guess the winters are sacred then, and they probably dread the spring coming.

Giorgio had arranged a car from local Hertz office. Sadly no convertibles available so ended up with VW Touran people-carrier thing. OK though. The Hertz car-rental man looked like John Belushi. Loaded up and drove to Tuscany heading for San Gimignano the slow way over the mountains. Got a bit lost to start with and had near death experience when I didn't see a white van coming at a road junction. Still getting to grips with the driving-on-the-right thing. Fortunately the driver of the white van had good control in a skid. Said sorry to him but he was in too much shock to absorb the apology.

Lovely drive. Stopped at the top of the mountain-road for a toastie and almonds and coffee. L feeling a little better. Drove back down the other side of the mountains and onwards in search of San Gimignano – a strange ancient village on a hill with old stone rectangular towers which, when viewed from afar, are reminiscent of a medieval Manhattan. We arrived at SG around 8.30 and found rooms advertised in a bakery. The lady at the bakery was called Barbara. Barbara drove us to a nearby villa. She said it's lovely – there's a swimming pool, satellite TV, a "wonderful view of San Germignano and a beautiful ambience!" But it was dark. Barbara said it was "Paradise!" We looked forward to the morning…

Drove back to SG and walked up the hill. I thought San Germignano was almost too well-kept. A hint of Disneyland about it. Had dinner in a hotel restaurant. Bright lighting, apple pudding and spicy cream. Back to b&b to discover breakfast finishes at 9.30 so, just 'b' then.

The satellite TV was bust and there was a man snoring like a water-buffalo in the next room. The walls were thick stone but I don't think they were joined to the ceilings because it was like he was in the room with us. L was up most of the night being sick. Poor thing. Happy hols, my darling…

Tuesday 9 October   *San Germignano – Tuscany*

In the morning a woman in the next room spoke loudly into the phone for half the morning before putting the water buffalo on who said, "Yadda yadda mama yadda yadda mama, mamma" for another half hour!

We were suddenly told to check out at 10 am so there was no time to enjoy the view or the pool (which was being cleaned) or the "ambience" as there was a digger digging a big hole next door.

I was still half asleep as I loaded the car. Hit L squarely on the head closing the tailgate. Last straw. I have hardly ever known her cry. I felt dreadful. So much for Paradise…

Back again to SG and had long slow salad at a café with a view of the Tuscan landscape. Amazing. People passing. Americans, Japanese. The whole world probably passes here in ten years. Bought a little framed photograph of Tuscan countryside. L bought a handbag while I queued for a loo, which, after waiting ages and paying the concierge 50 cents, turned out to be a hole in the ground. Took my business elsewhere... in fact, to the ice cream shop.

Drove to Siena and went shopping. Bought a G-star navy-blue winter jacket/coat.

Spoke to Lucy about whether or not to cancel festival gigs in June... Checked due date on internet pregnancy site. Apparently we're due on 12 June!

Drove to Livorno eating take-away pizza... Got lost. Reversed out of the Peage in Prato and also tried to enter at the exit. This is quite dangerous...

Finally found Livorno and checked into AC hotel. Comfier bed than "Paradise" in S Gimignano and nobody snoring.

L woke up feeling much better. Hooray! Drove around for ages trying to find a 5-star hotel by the sea. Couldn't. Ended up at a very nice beach bar just south of Livorno called Castiglioncello. You had to go down a load of steps to it, which seemed to belong to a hotel that was closed. The weather at this point was glorious and to find a private little beach bar with its own secluded beach was a Godsend. There were a handful of people in swimwear hanging around the bar and they wasted no time in making conversation. One particular chap called Rolf, was most eager to chat and shared with me his extensive (he thought) knowledge of contemporary music. He proudly declared that he didn't know much about any pop music since the end of the 70's. He then went on to ask me about my music. I hate it when this happens. It's hard enough trying to explain ANY art-form to someone so plainly ignorant of it, but I don't even want to mention the word Marillion for fear that I'll end up upset or violent or both. I kept saying I was on holiday but he wasn't deterred. He then told me all about England and then Belgium. To make matters much worse, he continued to stand between the sun and me until we were both forced to move away just to escape his perspectives on things-he-knew-nothing-of, and to catch some sunshine. However, the German lady who was also very 'sticky' called over an Italian lady who ran a 5-star b&b. She gave us a card and it did look lovely, but she was fully booked. Shame. However, she knew of another place and wrote the name down for us. Villa Le Luci at Castagneto Carducci. When the sun went down, we drove there and found Villa Le Luci almost straight away. Very beautiful and exquisitely decorated. Ran by a couple of gay guys. Giovanni showed us round and we checked in. Ate at a restaurant called (something) Magano in the strange deserted ghost-village of Borghi (also at the suggestion of the 'sticky' Germans). Very nice.

Wednesday 10 October

Woke up to a beautiful day and had breakfast in the beautiful kitchen of the Villa Le Luci. Don't mean to be sexist, but gay guys always seem to outclass straight folks when it comes to style, taste and attention to detail. The room was a haven, (even relatively so here in Italy where everything is already beautiful), the breakfast was cooked to perfection, the toast was lovely, the marmalade and jams were home-made and fab. And Rufus Wainright was singing *Under The Peach Trees* from the hi-fi.

the *invisible* man

2008 JUNE

Wednesday 11

2008

Wednesday 11 June

Linette gave birth to Emil at the Horton Hospital, Banbury. We nicknamed him Vibes because he often used to hiccup while she was pregnant and we'd watch her tummy pulsating. After he was born he often got the hiccups. He still does.

Friday 25 July

Got up with Vibes at 6.40. Had already given him a bottle of milk, but he'd decided he'd get up and there was no settling him. Snorting and grumbling like ET. Downstairs, changed his nappy and sat on the sofa with him for long enough to make a coffee at which point he nodded off again so put him back in his cot and went back to bed. He didn't sleep long. L got up with him around 8.00 and I slept 'til 9.30.

Saturday 26 July *Lisbon*

Didn't sleep very well. Despite the obvious luxury of the large bed and new bed linen I couldn't get on with the pillows. They felt expensive, but they felt wrong. One of the tricky things about travel is the pillow situation. The only solution is to bring your own, but there's something a bit embarrassing about travelling with a pillow under your arm –makes you feel like a four-year-old... or a vagrant.

Definitely not cool. Took every advantage of the lie-in – not an option anymore at home since the arrival of little Vibes. Called room service and asked for a couple of cappuccinos and a bowl of muesli and called L while I was waiting for them to arrive. She says it's a beautiful day in England and that Vibes is behaving "reasonably". Nial is still in bed.

I popped up to the 8th floor to use Frenchie's computer to send an email to Carl (our graphic designer) with a missing lyric *Trap the Spark*. I'd also promised Richard Barbieri a recent picture of Emil. I can't email from my room without paying Swisscom's rip-off tariff of 22 Euros for an internet connection. There's a little hi-fi in my room next to the telly. I loaded up the CDR of the latest mixes and had a listen. I think we're pretty close now. The tracks are sounding great and I only have a few minor details to ask Mike (Hunter – producer) to address. I was still listening to the mixes and making notes when L called back, to wish me a good gig. It was 1.15 and we're leaving at 1.30. Woof! I'd better shower and get dressed…

Climbed into a minibus for the 30-minute drive to the venue – The Atlantic Auditorium. The Count got deja vu on the way down the backstage ramp. After a little thought we decided it was reminiscent of the Auditorio Nacional in Mexico City. Inside, we entered the auditorium – a large 8,000-ish capacity hall with a beautiful wooden roof. There was a lot of noise coming out of the PA bouncing round the cavernous empty space, so we headed for catering where we helped ourselves to buffet lunch. Sadly there was no milk for the coffee, but there WERE cherries(!). Nodded a hello to Jean-Jacques Burnell, bass player of the Stranglers. He stared blankly back. Dunno if it registered or if he was just too cool to be pleasant to strangers. The Stranglers manager, Sil Wilcox popped in to say hi. We've known Sil for a few years now. We spent a week living and working at the studio on his farm in the West Country when writing **Marbles**. He was the one who introduced us to the convention idea and was instrumental in setting up the first one at Pontins holiday camp back in 2002. Nice chap. Good laugh.

Soundcheck was protracted whilst the local production crew tried to locate the source of massive radio interference on the guitar amplifiers, but it was eventually sorted out. Gabriel Perez and chum, Paco, arrived from Barcelona during soundcheck, so I sorted them both out with passes and beer. Mark's main keyboard computer had been dropped in transit and had to be partially rebuilt. Rothers Trio guitar amplifier had met a similar fate, but it was opened up and circuit boards fastened back in place. By some miracle everything then worked. Hoorah.

Gabriel wanted to speak to me about details regarding my solo performance on the opening night of his gig-within-a-gig at the Palau St Jordi in Barcelona so we went back stage and he talked to me at length while I tried - mostly in vain - to follow him. I'm sure it'll be fine… Edgar Diaz showed up with his girlfriend Diane, so I chatted with *him* at length about upcoming solo shows in Portugal too. We were still in the middle of this when Rich pointed out that it was 6.30

and we're on at 7pm! I'd forgotten we were on so early. We decided to go on 5-mins earlier to be sure not to over-run, so we hit the stage at 6.55.

"Are they going to turn the house-lights off?" I enquired.

"They're off! - that's daylight coming in through the ceiling," said Rich. Fair enough....

The gig went well. All the technology worked (at last!) and the band played well. I had a good sound – care of Phil Brown (who always works wonders) and I felt comfortable in the big space, pacing around the stage and along the top of the PA, which suddenly appeared before me like a cat-walk as I got to the wings. We'd gone for a pop set upon the advice of Edgar who reminded us of the songs which had had the airplay here, so *No One Can*, *Beautiful* and *Cover my Eyes* were wheeled out to good effect, I could see the crowd being won over as the set progressed – the hands in the air slowly spreading towards the back of the hall from the hardcore fans at the front. That's a good feeling.

We closed the show with *Neverland* and that was that. All five of us were pleased with it. That's a rare thing. I realized I'd forgotten to mention the website from the stage and I was quite pissed off at myself. Oh well. Maybe they wouldn't have known what I was on about anyway...

Had a long chat on the phone with L who seemed a little upset that I hadn't been in touch all afternoon. Sometimes, it's hard to find a moment. But I can also imagine how hard it is when you're at home with your imagination and insecurities, and your other half is out "in the world" and out of touch. Must try harder.

Went out front with Edgar and Gabriel to watch the Stranglers set. I thought they were great. I hung around for the B52's too. I thought they were good but this seemed like the wrong space for them somehow. I bet they're brilliant in a New York club, but the big auditorium just seemed not to fit them. Great players, great singers too - just not quite the right environment for them. Waited to hear *Love Shack* (well, you must) and then went back downstairs to the dressing rooms with Edgar and his girlfriend Diane for more beer. Had a bizarre Meatloaf incident. He appeared in the corridor - seemingly from nowhere - and marched towards me:

"I know you!" he said. "We've met! Now where was it?"

"We haven't met." I said, "But I know YOU."

"I'm sure we've met! Was it L.A?"

"No – we've never met."

"New York! ...or was it London?"

"We've never met."

"Who ARE you?"

"I'm the singer from Marillion."

"Oh man, I'm so sorry. I was getting my stuff together for the show and I missed your set. I'm really sorry."

"That's fine," I said "I know exactly how that is."

"The boys in my crew are raving about you guys – they said you're one kick-ass singer. I really wish I'd seen it."

"Well thanks."

"Let's hug!"

So we hugged, and then he disappeared back into his dressing room.

Sunday 27 July   *Lisbon – Home*

Woke up around 9.30 and texted L to see if she had time to call me. She was feeding Vibes so she called a little later. We chatted for a while. She says the weather is still sunny and warm in England. What a shame I'm missing it! Doesn't happen very often and we've had an awful summer so far. She suggested I catch a cab downtown and have breakfast in the sunshine myself. I decided that would be a great idea so I showered and took a cab into a square with a fountain and breakfasted at the café Nicole. Lovely. Had coffees, orange juice and omelette while being slightly irked by flies, people trying to sell me sunglasses (when I already had a pair on my face!) and having to keep fishing around in my pocket for euros to give to a steady stream of beggars. I think the word was getting around.

After breakfast I walked up the hill to where I remembered the fine old Brazilian Café is located. It's one of the oldest and most beautiful interiors in Lisbon and there's always a good atmosphere. When the old waitress asked me what I would like, I said, "Caipirinha!" This brought a smile to her face as she returned to the bar. Perhaps it was a little early to be hitting the cocktails but, hey, it's not every day you're in the Brazilian Café Lisbon.

Re-emerged feeling suitably Caipirinha'd and, in a rush of enthusiasm, decided to walk back to the hotel. It was MUCH further than I remembered from the cab-ride into town and ALL UPHILL. The afternoon was pretty hot and humid and I arrived back at the hotel 35 minutes later like a grease spot! Another Caipirinha was ordered at the hotel-bar while I read the newspaper and killed time to check out.

Checked out and was relieved of 70 euros for the 3 Caipirinhas and last night's omelette. Holy cow. It's a good job we've only got a few of these festivals. I'm not sure I could afford many more.

2009

Friday 23 January *Home – Oslo*

Woke for the third time at 7.30am to the sound of little Em's restless noises. I have a cold, which has blocked up my nose, throat and head, so Linette volunteered to do last night's feeds. Em still wakes up at around midnight and then again around 5am for night-feeds. I was grateful not to have to get up as I went to bed feeling truly awful. Didn't feel quite so bad at 7.30 despite a headache. The headache was probably down to last night's second helping of "medicinal" cognac, though.

We had to leave at 9.30 today to begin the journey to Oslo, so there was much to do. L and Em are coming too so there's much preparation involved – clothes, bottles, milk, soothers, nappies, baby-wipes, skin-creams, more clothes... and more clothes, and then there's Linette's stuff... and then there's my stuff. Most of my stage clothes (princely Indian robes and undertakers suit for *The Invisible Man*) were packed at the studio last night, but I'd brought a couple of shirts home for rapid-laundry and they were hanging above various radiators around the house. I packed the usual paraphernalia – laptop, power supplies, phone charger, headphones, leads and the all-important passports, along with all-important socks in between lowering the loft-ladder repeatedly to gain access to printers and my old boots. The word from Oslo is that it's rainy, snowy, slushy and to bring Wellington boots. I have some fabulous German fighter-pilot's boots given to me a few years ago by - you guessed - a German fighter pilot, and they provide a perfect barrier to the bad weather so I donned those before leaving. It took several journeys to load the car with suitcase, computer case, and the usual baby bags, hardware and transport. People take less gear up the Himalayas.

The journey to Heathrow was uneventful, thank heavens. I have recently been forced to miss a flight to Warsaw after getting stuck on the M40 in an enormous traffic-accident tailback, so I'm always a little nervous now until I get to the airport. We were travelling from Terminal 5 for the first time and Frenchie (our tour manager) had pre-booked our parking at the business car park nearby. We were lucky to find a bus already waiting at the stop so we bundled little vibes onto the bus along with the bags and pushchair. At the Terminal there was mild amusement at check-in as it seems that he has been added to Jon Cameron's ticket - not mine - as a travelling infant. We managed to sort this out eventually after the check-in girl phoned the Gate just in case there was any confusion. I was frisked twice at security (maybe he was enjoying himself) and we went and had a spot of breakfast in the Giraffe café. The burger wasn't up to much but the coffee was the best I'd had in months. Vibes had to be repeatedly stopped from eating the colouring-in crayons. L took him for a change of nappy while I killed time. I gave Dave Meegan a call to see how he's doing. His wife, Jayne is currently battling a leukaemia. Awful. He sounded well and told me that she's doing okay after a bone-marrow transplant in December.

The plane was 20-minutes late taking off - normal for Heathrow - and I spent the flight writing this diary. Vibes was reasonably well-behaved although he eventually got a bit bored with the confined space and began complaining. I walked him up and down the aisle for a while which gave him plenty of opportunity to flirt with the other passengers. Well, he's a single boy!

Upon landing we could see that Norway was under snow and the snow was still falling outside the window. Proper winter. Although we'd managed to leave the pushchair at the door of the plane before take-off, we weren't so lucky on landing and I had to carry Vibes along the 4-km long (but beautifully wooden-floored) corridor from the plane to the baggage hall. The baggage system at Oslo airport is fully automated. In other words, it doesn't work, and so we had to wait for almost an hour before the last of the cases and equipment came through. Finally got out into the snowy street and boarded a very nice coach which took us the 40-minute journey to Oslo.

There were a number of signs at the side of the motorway about Pigdaggs. Now, in English farming circles, 'daggs' would describe the small bits of shit which end up stuck to the wool around a sheep's bottom, so I couldn't help but chuckle. Linette, understanding the lingo, informed me that this did in fact refer to winter tyres being necessary.

Arrived at the hotel Opera and checked in whilst texting Jon-Arne Vilbo of the band Gazpacho to see if he was likely to have time for a quick half in the bar. They have a show tonight and he was about to soundcheck so he said it was unlikely, and that he'd see us later at the gig. As the evening passed, however, my cold began to take its toll and I decided I would have to go to bed once we'd got little Vibes off to sleep. L later changed her mind too and decided to stay "home". We decided to meet up with the Norwegians for lunch tomorrow instead.

Went to bed at 9.00 and slept pretty well. Not very rock n'roll! Vibes only woke up once around 5am for a feed and Linette took care of that. At 7 he woke again but we managed to get him back off to sleep for another hour around half seven. So all in all I had something resembling a much-needed good night's sleep. Or as near as I get to one these days…

Saturday 24 January *Oslo Rockefeller*

Woke around 8.45 and L got up and changed Vibes bum while I pretended to snooze. The cold hasn't really improved or worsened – fortunately it hasn't gone to my voice although my nose will be pretty blocked for tonight's show. She offered me another half-hour in bed while she took Vibes down to breakfast. I couldn't sleep so I got up and joined her. Most of the boys appeared in the breakfast room. Mark arrived with a book under his arm. **London – a Biography**. So far, mostly about open sewers, crime and the constant possibility of being arrested and hanged for just about anything whether guilty or not. Hanging being the only form of entertainment in - I'm guessing - the 16th century. And we worry about the credit crunch!

We returned to the room and I watched the snow going past the window. It was going sideways and upwards simultaneously. That's not something you see every day. Back down to reception to say hi to Stephanie Ringuet who had flown in from Paris to see the show and had brought Vibes a little present. We opened it. A bib with his name on it and a cuddly sheep. Upon close inspection I can report no daggs.

I was feeling crappy again so had a quick shower before meeting up in reception with Jon and Lisa. Jon is famously generous (Gazpacho are "amateurs" – this means he has a proper job in Norway and always seems to have masses of disposable income. He's either pathologically generous or loaded… definitely the former) and my main mission of the (early part of) the day is to try and stop him paying for everything. He's already lending me his guitars and backline for the show, so *I* should be buying the drinks.

Well, I failed. I managed to buy the first round, which turned out to be a coffee for Jon and a diet coke for Lisa. Jon then took over with the buying of drinks and we got onto the hard stuff. I never bought a drink for the rest of the afternoon. I was back on the medicinal cognacs and, as I write this, I'm feeling much better. Thomas and his girlfriend, Lina arrived with their 16 month-old little girl, Leah. They arrived in hotel reception from the street looking wet and very cold. It's about zero degrees outside and it hasn't stopped snowing all day. There's a bitter and damp wind blowing too. No wonder Jon thought our best option was to remain inside the hotel. Thomas is among the funniest men I have ever met and he wasted no time in launching into bizarre and surreal observations about life. His somewhat manic intensity is balanced perfectly by Jon's warmth, they really make a great double-act. They've been friends since they were young boys and it's heart-warming to be around and to witness such a lifelong friendship between two people. They usually have me in fits and today was no exception. The girls caught up, exchanged "baby-world experiences" and giggled while I passed my reading glasses around and everyone tried them on in turn. Thomas told us what we looked like. Jon was declared to be someone who would complain a lot in restaurants, while I was a "metal-detector guy". He put them on himself and he looked like such a freak, no-one could decide who he might be... possibly a deranged philosopher or shrink.

I asked Frenchie (tour manager) to call me when the band feel they are half-an-hour away from needing a singer. It's now 5.30 and there hasn't been a call yet so I reckon I'll wander up there and acquaint myself with the full horror of soundcheck with hired equipment. They're probably still busy building their own guitars and keyboards...

The afternoon social with Jon, Thomas and the girls turned out to be the high point of the day. There were even more technical problems at the gig than I could have predicted at my most pessimistic. Frenchie texted me to say not to hurry and that 6.30 was a more realistic arrival time for me. Then 7pm. Linette wanted to come over to the venue with little Vibes, so we left the hotel around 6pm and walked into town with Stephanie R where we found a café near to the Rockafeller (venue) and I ordered a steak for £20.00. (Actually, not bad for Oslo where you can pay £10 for a burger in McDonalds!)

We eventually gained entry to the club around 7.00. The band were on stage looking somewhat weary and frazzled. The guitar amplifier had already blown fuses, the keyboard-rig wasn't working and the monitors had yet to be set. I did my best to set levels of the few things that were working. The guitars that Jon had lent me were fine and I soon had them sounding good in my "in-ears". A further two hours passed before the doors to the club were opened at 9pm, by which time Mark seemed to have the keyboards functioning. Just as well because time was up. Once again Marillion – the band that rehearses for 2 months for a 1 month tour, and soundchecks for 5 hours for a 2 hour show, were still not ready!

There was just enough time to have a quick chat with Smick Hardgrave, our old personal assistant, and his Swedish wife, Helen, who had made the journey across from Stockholm, before it was time to get into my stage clothes.

We went on stage at 10pm and everything immediately went wrong. Steve R started *Real Tears for Sale* and all seemed fine until Ian came in on drums at a much slower tempo. The band slowed down to his tempo while I wondered what was going on in Ian's monitors. Clearly not right. We're running click tracks on this tour and we have backing vocals on 'tape'. A wall of vocals thundered in, in completely the wrong place during the verse. This has happened once before in Inverness and it means Ian hasn't got the click track so from now on, all the backing vocals would be in the wrong place. *Real Tears* is a pretty long and complicated piece of music so I could see nothing but disaster ahead... This was no way to start a show so I found myself, for the first time in my career, waving at the audience and walking off stage! Pete soon followed me – I think he'd come to the same decision. The rest of the band played on for some time until they realized I wasn't coming back. I was quite relaxed about it. I just sat down on a chair backstage and waited for the band to show up. My feeling was that, in this instant, it was better if we simply returned to the stage when the problem has been fixed and start the show again properly. Phil Brown, our monitor engineer appeared looking about as tense as I've ever seen him (not very) and assured Ian that it was a problem with the reverb level going sky-high for no particular reason and that it would now be okay. Are you sure? Yes I'm sure.

We returned to the stage. "Don't worry," I said, "I'll make a speech". When I got to the mic I explained to the crowd that I had realized I was wearing the wrong underwear and had returned to the dressing room to remedy the situation. Well, it seemed as good an excuse as any...

The show progressed quite well from here, although the keyboard sounds that I was supposed to be playing from my remote keyboard at the front never really happened. I got around this by using whatever I could access from the keyboard direct. These were approximations, but it was still music. Mark's sounds were often a bit muted, digitally glitching, or plain absent throughout the set. Over the years we've got used to this and I comfort myself in the knowledge that Roderick, our sound engineer, is probably compensating for most of it in the auditorium and that 95% of the audience won't even notice it. As long as we (particularly me) are putting out a good vibe, the crowd have a good gig. Well, I was enjoying myself throughout the show and all the technical problems were amusing me rather than depressing me. I became more than a little worried, however, when my voice began to get increasingly hoarse. Looks like my cold was taking its toll on my vocal chords... Managed to scrape through to the end of the show and left the crowd singing *Happiness is the Road* at the very end. They sang well, and appeared to be in great spirits. Phew!

I'd consumed quite a lot of tequila and Red Bull during the show and by the end I think I was pretty well-pickled. I lay on the dressing room floor for half an hour talking to the people who came and went. Can't remember who exactly, but Jon Arne popped in and said that the sound had been "interesting". Indeed. Talked a bit more to Smick and Helen. Helen sounded sloshed. Jon's wife, Lisa, wandered I, also hammered! I decided against socializing any further (no more drink!) and returned to the hotel.

When I got back, Linette was sleeping. I showered and cleaned my teeth before getting into bed. "How did it go?" she said... I rattled on for about an hour about the gig, life, the Universe and everything - occasionally getting the giggles, occasionally bursting into tears, and - at one point - suggesting we should change our surname to "Clearmountain".

Wednesday 28 January *Brighton*

The bus left for Brighton last night from the studio. I was offered a lift by Monika, Jim's girlfriend, who's in the process of emigrating to Denmark! L dropped me off at the motorway services on the M1. I'm going to be away for 3 weeks this time. It's hard to think of not seeing the little one for so long. He's changing so fast now that I can see new things in him every day; new awareness, new sounds, he's getting better at eating and at reaching out and picking up things. He'll be so different when I get back and I'll miss all the little victories he has in the meantime. I'll miss Linette too. We'll talk on the phone and maybe manage a few video-chats so hopefully Vibes won't forget who I am. I know L finds it hard when we're parted and that weighs upon me too. I guess I've had so many years on the road that I cope better. It's all still new to her. But I hope she never gets used to it, because in getting used to it, you have to change the way you feel somehow.

The journey to Brighton was problem-free. There was quite a lot of patchy fog – a depressing winter's day. I tried to keep Monika light-hearted as she drove - I know she doesn't really want to leave the UK.

We arrived in Brighton around half-past four. The gig is right on the sea-front by the beach. As I climbed out of the car I could already hear the band playing inside. It was sounding good. The tour-bus - my home for the next 3 weeks - was parked outside and I could see the huge frame of Charlie, our bus driver, at the wheel. We've worked with Charlie a couple of tours back and he's a lovable character. He was on the phone so we exchanged a wave. I put my last few things on the bus – my blue toilet bag, laptop bag and the all-important pillow from home. You have to have your own pillow if you want to sleep well on the bus.

Tonight's gig was booked as a warm-up for the 2nd leg of the **HITR** tour. The manager of the club is a fan and has been hustling Lucy for a while to see if we would play there. It's a little club – about 350 capacity and we were a pretty tight fit on the stage. I climbed up there and had a listen to my in-ear monitors. Phil Brown, our monitor engineer, had already done a great job and there was little for me to do except ask for a few little adjustments. The band joined me and we ran through *Asylum Satellite #1* and *Happiness Is the Road*. It sounded great so we left the stage.

Tour manager Frenchie wanted me to meet Russell, the gig manager. He wanted me to record an answering-machine message, but no one knew how the technology worked so we didn't bother. Russell took me on one side, shook me by the hand, looked me in the eye and I could see this was an important moment for him. "This is an unreal moment for me" he said, "I've had a lot of artists through here over the years as you can imagine. Some big names, but I can tell you that having you here means more than any of 'em. You've helped me a lot over the years and I want to thank you for that."

I never know what to say. "Er... You're welcome!" certainly doesn't seem enough.

I returned to the bus and was hoping to lie down and relax. I still have this cold hanging around and I needed to rest, so it was great to have a bed I could use. The bad news was that I had to sew the hole I'd ripped in my stage trousers, so I spent half an hour doing that (it's all glamour) before climbing into my bunk. I didn't sleep but it was good to lie down in the dark and be quiet for half an hour. I usually go to bed for an hour between sound check and gig if I possibly can. On tour, I'm permanently tired and often completely exhausted. It's physically very demanding to sing for 2 hours – sometimes longer...

Soon I returned inside the club and got ready. Lucy was floating around asking about stage shirts for the Convention. I'd mentioned that I want a shirt embroidering with the **Season's End** snowflake logo like the ones I wore on the first tour. I'd just had a couple of new shirts arrive through the post this morning so I asked Frenchie to give her one to take away as I was getting changed for the show.

We took to the stage at 8.30 and the band played really well. Everything sounded so much better than our dodgy gig with hired equipment in Oslo so we were all lifted by that. To my relief, my voice held out well despite the cold and I felt like I was singing really well, technically and soulfully. The little club was sold out and packed to the back wall with people. My chum Nick Eede (singer, Cutting Crew) had come over for the show and I was trying to locate him in the darkness but I didn't manage to pick him out anywhere. The response from the crowd was enthusiastic and I got the impression they were all really listening. I hope they were getting as much soul from it as I was feeling. It's hard to know sometimes with all that big noise happening. It's like trying to marry tenderness with a whirlwind. A great combination if you can pull it off.

After the show we had promised to go behind the bar and pull a few pints for the punters. Russell said the Foo Fighters had done it so we thought we'd better agree! In the end it turned out to be more of an autograph session than a bar-job but I did get some great feedback from people about the show. I managed to exchange a few hurried words with Nick Eede but sadly, never managed a relaxed conversation as he'd gone by the time the mayhem died down. I met a girl who is a dentist in Kingston-on-Thames who offered to fix my teeth for free! I didn't know whether to be grateful or offended! They seemed alright when I put 'em in this morning...

Eventually staggered back onto the bus and had a beer with the crew before returning to my bunk for the long drive to Bordeaux. I slept well, not even noticing the channel crossing. Apparently we were on a train through the tunnel.

Thursday 29 January *Bordeaux:* **Day Off**

We arrived in Bordeaux to a sunny afternoon and the bus groaned and swayed its way down the narrow streets to our hotel, the Ibis. Not luxurious but perfectly serviceable. I checked in and bought some wi-fi access so that I could make on-line video-chat with L and Vibes. It works quite well if the broadband is reasonably fast and it's better than phone-calls. At least little Vibes won't forget what I look like. Unfortunately, he can't really understand what I'm doing on the computer screen and he keeps reaching out and closing the lid to see if I'm behind there! We chatted for a while and then I took a walk into the city centre for a spot of late lunch.

Had a quick walk around inside the cathedral and then crossed the square and sat down outside at a table amongst many Bordeauxans. When the waiter came he told me that food is finished and I could only order drinks. Sigh. I've missed the food again. I walked up the street in search of a place which would serve me food, but was refused again. Eventually found an Irish pub who were prepared to make me Welsh rarebit! Nuts. I'm in Bordeaux and I have to have Welsh rarebit for dinner in an Irish pub! I sat outside in the street and ordered Irish Coffee and, when the Welsh rarebit arrived it was very good but HUGE. I slowly worked my way through stacks of sliced ham covered in melted cheese and horseradish but had to give up about half way through.

I wandered back to the hotel through the back streets, marvelling at shops selling herbs and oils, antiques, unusual jewellery and stopping by a music store where I eyed up a Rickenbacker 360 and a Fender Dobro-style guitar. The same street seemed to be devoted mainly to interior decoration – shops selling curtain materials and upholstery fabrics. I mused, once again, at the fact that we no longer see such a variance of shops in England thanks to the "Property Boom". Shop-rents are so high in Brackley that the only companies who can pay them are Estate Agents (now struggling and closing), lawyers, dentists (seemingly busier than ever), hairdressers (likewise) and the big chains like Boots. We have a lovely little market square surrounded by empty shops - all run out of town by a combination of high-rents and the killer-vaccuuming of business by Tesco down the road. At least we've got a new Waitrose, but one wonders how long it will last. It's a shame the independents can't make a living. There's a lot of people living in Brackley now on the new estates, but God only knows where they all go to buy their clothes and food. You sure never see 'em on the street! Back at the hotel I hunkered down in my room and watched TV. Can't remember what was on. I was tired and too full of rarebit to feel the need for more food so went to bed early.

Saturday 31 January *Toulouse – Bikini*

We arrived overnight at the new Bikini. The old Bikini was destroyed during a huge explosion, which happened in the AZF ammonium-nitrate factory in Toulouse on September 21 2001. Three hundred tonnes of ammonium-nitrate was stored in a hangar and went kaboom, destroying the whole factory and a fair chunk of the city. Steel girders were found 3km away!

The old Bikini was a great little club with a swimming pool to the side where, on summer days, Hervé, the owner, would cook for the bands! I remember Le Bikini being one of the few clubs where we were ever treated as gentlemen.

Normally you're lucky if Rock clubs give you more than a room full of grubby sofas and walls decorated for farmyard animals, so Le Bikini stood out.

Well, the insurers must have got round to paying up, because Hervé has his new gig. It's not in the same place, it's all new. There are palm trees outside, again a swimming pool, and I bet it's very nice in the summer.

We made our way upstairs to catering where an open fire was burning. Hervé had cooked an English breakfast and we ate, listening to the good-natured French banter going on between the staff. I returned to the bus and spent the morning reading **Conversations with God** by Neale Donald Walsch.

Returned to the club for soundcheck. Nice gig. Almost like a TV studio. Acoustic treatment on the walls, big stage, projection screen – a purpose-built gig.

I'm writing this one up at a distance and, to be honest, I can't remember the show. Having said that, Toulouse is usually fantastic so it must have been! I do remember being on the bus afterwards, chatting to Andy Ball (our guitar tech) about ambient music. On the bus he's currently listening to Boards of Canada and Jamaican Dub Pink Floyd tribute Easi-Star All-stars **Dub Side Of The Moon**. I also remember leaving town in the early hours, sitting up the front of the bus with Charlie after Edgar's Dias's Caipirinhas but that could well have been a few nights later. Stopped by the police. Can't remember what happened. I was very drunk.

Thursday 4 June *Home – Sweden*

Set off around 11.30 for the drive to Heathrow. Not a bad day in England as I set off waving to Linette and Vibes on the doorstep. Vibes is too young to know I'm going away and so isn't at all concerned. Linette seemed her usual incandescent self. I'm back in a couple of days.

The drive to Heathrow was great. Hardly any traffic on the M40 (for a change) and a nice clear open sunlit road. I had parked the car and made my way to the Departure lounge by 12.15. Frenchie and Jon were there and quickly checked me in. I was traveling with hand baggage only - my stage clothes are in the truck - so I went straight through to Security where the first chaos of the day presented itself. Terminal 5 opened a year or so ago in a blaze of anticipation followed by embarrassment as it became evident that the computerized baggage handling system didn't work. On day 1 just about every bag was lost and, in the chaos, most of the flights were either delayed or cancelled. 2 years on, the terminal still doesn't really function properly. When we got back from Montreal here a month ago we waited over an hour for our bags to travel the short distance from the plane to the baggage hall. Apologies were occasionally broadcast over the PA system offering no reason for the delay. The time before that, when we flew into here we couldn't find the bus-stop for the long term car park as no-one had put up any signs in the Terminal.

The security hall today was absolutely packed with people queuing for too few machines. A couple of English blokes in suits pushed past me in the queue as though I wasn't there. A family of Germans also found themselves walking past me as we were herded into yet another post-office-type queue, but the man quickly noticed and apologized. I insisted his wife and kids should go ahead of me also. I know what it's like travelling with a family. Nice chap.

It must have taken 30-40-minutes to get to the security machine (shoes off, belt off, computer out of bag, have you any liquids, jacket off, beep, come over here, body search, nothing found, go over there, belt on, shoes on, repack bag, jacket on), but I had plenty of time to spare. Went to the Giraffe café and ordered salmon and scrambled eggs and a smoothie fruit yoghurt thing. All very nice and, thankfully, very relaxed.

We fly at 2.25, so around 1.40 I went for a wander around the shops. Didn't see anything I needed. Bumped into Ian and Rothers staring up at the screen and stared with them until a gate was announced whereupon we made our way over there to find the rest of the band and crew. Frenchie (our tour manager) apparently made some kind of mistake with the booking resulting in the band flying economy while the crew flies business! He had realized the error and press-ganged them into swapping boarding passes with us, so we boarded and settled down in business class. I haven't flown business class for ages. It's more or less the same as economy except that you get offered a hot-towel (which remains hot for 4 seconds), a hot meal (which I didn't want anyway) and the stewardesses seem a little more relaxed. I'm a fan of British Airways and would prefer to fly with them over any other airline whether in business or economy. Having said that, we had a truly weird take-off. Down the runway at full throttle and into the air as normal but then the pilot seemed to throttle back and I heard the engines revving down and up and down as we seemed to turn hard to the left and, out of the windows on the other side of the plane, I could see the rows of houses on the ground and feel that we weren't gaining height. As the engines whirred and then cut back and whirred up and cut back I became increasingly nervous. Normally, planes are up through the clouds and into blue sky long before the engines cut back. Most of the passengers seemed oblivious to this and carried on reading, but a lady on my left had a puzzled expression too. I turned to look at Rothers who was looking up quizzically also – "Strange eh?" From my seat I could see the stewardesses sitting up front with their backs to the flight deck, both chatting away carelessly. Oh well, the time to worry is when the cabin crew look concerned! Eventually, the pilot must have been given permission to get on with it because the engines resumed power and we climbed through a bit of turbulent cloud into the blue cruise. I declined the food and ordered a Bacardi and coke. I only drink Bacardi/Coke on planes and beaches. They make me feel like I'm on holiday. After a while the stewardess said, "I recognize some of you... which band is it?"

"Marillion," I said.

"Oh, is Fish on the plane?"

"No, he left in 1988."

"Oh, I saw the band back then... now where was it?"

"You don't look old enough."

"Oh, bless you."

I've been in this band now for 20 years and I still seem to have conversations like this on an almost-daily basis. Most people don't know Fish quit and those who do think the band split after that. Only the hardcore have heard of me. Oh well, better a cult hero than a household name. You get left alone when you want to be alone, and there's a lot to be said for that.

We landed at Copenhagen without incident. Without incident as far as we were concerned anyway... I was in this airport only 2 weeks ago. We'd been to Denmark for L's mum's birthday. I made my way through the self-same passport control booth, down into the baggage hall and out into the arrivals area half-expecting there to be someone waiting to greet me. There was! Our lighting designer Yenz Nyholm who now lives in Copenhagen with his girlfriend. I said hello and then went to Starbucks to get a Chai tea. I like those. We were originally going to get the train from Copenhagen airport and I was quite looking forward to a train journey over the water and through Sweden, but the plans had changed – we would ride in minibuses instead for the two and a half hour journey to Kristianstad where we will stay. I dispatched Frenchie to the shop for beer to get us through the journey. I was in a van with Phil Brown, Jon Cameron and Count Mosley. Even Ian had a beer. Truly shocking. The van driver Corrinne told us that there had been a bomb found in a suitcase in Copenhagen airport earlier in the day and that they had only just reopened the airport! Well, you never would have guessed, I saw nothing unusual at all anywhere. Maybe that's why we were doing all the strange stuff at take-off from Heathrow. Maybe they were trying to decide whether to turn us around and land us again... Who knows?

Chatted to Phil all the way to Kristianstad who told me about some of the other gigs he's been doing in London. Tales of interesting musical instruments and interesting musicians, Goldie and gangsters, and someone getting stabbed outside Cargo in East London last week. Blimey.

We arrived at the hotel around 8.30 and I checked into my room. Not posh, not bad. I plugged my computer in and tried to get on line. Lots of email currently flying around about my forthcoming h Natural Polish dates and a general lack of ticket sales etc. Well, if they WILL put me on in Krakow the same night as a FREE open-air Lenny Kravitz concert, what do they expect? I'll go on early and go and see Lenny!

I called home and chatted to L for a while whilst chomping on a room-service club-sandwich. All's well there and Vibes has gone to sleep. I decided to do the same. I feel dog-tired and well up for an early night. Got into bed, put the telly on and found BBC World. They're reporting the bomb in Copenhagen airport too! I was later to discover that it wasn't a bomb at all - just some spare parts for a plane. Ah, security, security.

Friday 5 June

After a night of wrestling with an alien pillow (my own fault for leaving my own at home), I had a lie-in till half ten then got up, ordered cappucinnos (the staff are very nice here), showered and got myself together for today's gig. We leave the hotel at 12.15 for our appearance on the rock stage of Sweden Rock at 3.00. Climbed into the minibus with Mark, Ian and Frenchie for the half-hour drive to the festival site. Pete and Steve R are already there. Pete's doing a number with Neal Morse and Mike Portnoy earlier in the day. Apparently it went well. The first part of the afternoon was spent hanging around in Portakabin dressing rooms while the weather rained and fined up then rained again which was to be the pattern for the whole day. An hour before we were due on stage it rained really hard and I went over to the stage for an investigation. Guys were mopping a lot of water from the stage and Phil told me that if it's okay, perhaps they should pull the backline a bit deeper within the stage so that the worst of the rain will stay off if it rains again later. There was a band playing across the field on the opposite stage. They were called something about Pain and they were living up to their name on a number of levels. I asked one of the local crew,

"Who is that over there?" and he replied,

"It's a very angry man." Fair comment.

Everywhere, the throngs of guys and gals in black - pierced and tattooed - were braving the rain. In my experience, although rockers tend to look like axe-murderers to a man, they're usually quite lovely when you get to know 'em. I still couldn't help feeling very out of place here though, both musically and in terms of my general outlook. I guess I'll go on stage, do my thing and see what happens...

Well, it stopped raining, 3 o'clock came and we did our thing. There were a few faces I recognized down the front but not many. The crowd seemed to warm to us during the set and I think - oddly enough - *Cover my Eyes* seemed to be a turning point. We segued into *Slainte* - one of the oldies - and that really seemed to do the trick. *Neverland* closed the show and went down well. I got out to the front edge of stage whenever I could and tried to connect with the crowd. We encored, somewhat riskily, with *Happiness is the Road* and to the surprise of us all, had the crowd singing along and managed to leave them singing at the end of the show. You just can't argue with that much love. Everyone in the band seemed happy with the set and the reaction to it. Even Pete seemed pleased with it (a rare thing – he usually comes off stage cursing about something).

We made our way back to the "dressing room" and hung around a while for an MTV interview with some guy from Finland. He seemed alright.

At 6.00 there was a signing session so we went over to the merch shop area and stood in a stockroom for a while before being called over to a long trestle-table where we all sat on stools while people filed past. I said hello to Freddy Bilqvist, the photographer who was mercifully wearing a pink hat. He was unique for several square miles in this respect and a source of hope as far as I was concerned. There seemed to be a lot of people waiting in line and it took a while for them all to go by. Everyone seemed to have really enjoyed our set. I nicked a baby-sized Ramones t-shirt on the way out (by way of payment) for little Vibes and we went over to the backstage restaurant where we were provided with dinner. The restaurant seemed groovy. Black (of course) with chandeliers hanging above the tables. We ordered tapas and steak. Before the starters came, Mark received some awful and somewhat bizarre news. The family have just taken delivery of a new puppy which had been accidentally crushed when the new babysitter who was playing with the children, slipped from one of the kids tricycles. The poor little thing was pronounced dead shortly afterwards. Well, that put a bit of a downer on the dinner, and Mark seemed visibly upset. Frenchie made preparations to try and get him home ASAP and managed to get him onto the first flight out of Copenhagen in the morning. The steak took forever to arrive and when it did it looked great, but it was cold. Shame. Never mind. We managed to get our hands on Creme Bruleé a bit quicker and then left to take the van back to the hotel.

Got back to my room 404 around 9pm and phoned home. Once again, I couldn't really contemplate much except getting into bed and passing out. I remember passing Ronnie James Dio in the hotel lobby. Sadly, he was dead within the year.

Friday 12 June *Home – Sofia*

The alarm was set for 5am. I didn't need it. It's high summer and the dawn usually wakes me. So I lay in bed from 4.30 wondering if it was worth trying to get back to sleep. Decided against it at 4.45 and slid out of bed as silently as I could so as not to wake Linette. She stirred and asked me to come up and say bye-bye before I left. Went downstairs, made some coffee, showered and finished packing. Like last weekend, I'm only taking hand baggage so I packed my computer bag making sure I had the essentials – passport, wallet, keys, computer and charger and reading glasses (crucial these days – everything is a blur without them!). Crept upstairs and said bye and left the house at 5.40 for the drive to Heathrow Terminal 5.

The drive was pleasant. A nice clear morning without too much traffic apart from a white van that kept overtaking me at 100mph. Must have been a bunch of builders late for work. Currently working on becoming a bunch of late builders.

Found a parking space easily in the short-stay at T5 and took the lift to Departures where Frenchie and Jon were already at a desk checking in. No sign of the rest of the party yet, but I was probably a bit early. Hung around for a while trying to get through security which doesn't seem easy in T5 at any time of day. Shoes off, computer out of bag, jacket off, empty pockets, belt off etc... Practically naked through the electronic arch which STILL BEEPS ANYWAY and then they search you. Sigh. All pointless theatre (as previous rants herein explain).

Out of habit I made my way to the Giraffe café, past the suited smoothies who tried to sell me a raffle ticket to win the Lamborghini slowly spinning round on its turntable. What on earth would I do with a Lamborghini?! I don't think it would last long on the street in Brackley...

It was still a bit too early to contemplate solid food, so I ordered a fruit smoothie and a cappuccino and settled down to watch the airport go by and listen to the world music playing in the Giraffe café. Went for a wander round the shops and then bumped into Steve R so we walked across the hall to gate A11. By now it was 7.45 and I was almost awake. Said hello to the crew who were sitting around. Roderick had got up at 3.30 to get here. Hem had a gig on the Isle of White last night and had come to Heathrow straight from it, so he hadn't slept at all!

At around 8.10 the plane was boarding so I thought I'd call home and say bye to Linette. As I reached down into my pocket to pick up my iPhone, I could feel it vibrating so I answered it. It was L wondering why I hadn't called. We chatted as I boarded the plane. When I got to my seat I discovered I was in the emergency-exit row so my seat-back wouldn't recline. Just what you want after getting up at half 4...

Managed to move seats before the plane took off. Pete graciously offered to swap with me (bless him), but I managed to find a window-seat further down the plane, so all was well. A young (twenty-something, so young compared to me!) girl in the aisle seat stood up to let me sit down, apologising, seemingly embarrassed to be in my way. I explained that it wasn't really my seat and that it was I who should thank her for letting me sit down.

The Bulgarians on the plane all seemed smiley and friendly and that made for a pleasant atmosphere during the flight. I got up later on for the loo and got talking to a chap who was also very sociable and friendly. He told me that he divides his time between Sofia, London and Los Angeles. He used to own a chain of supermarkets, which he had sold and now he's in real estate. He said all this without even the slightest sense of showing-off or pride. He wasn't particularly dressed in a way which would imply wealth, just jeans and an ordinary jacket. I asked him whereabouts he was living in London. "Oh, in Chelsea. ...overlooking the river. It's a very nice view." Not skint then...

We landed on time in Sofia and were met at the airport by a few fans who seemed to own EVERYTHING we had ever released, which I dutifully signed for about 10-minutes. You can tell you're in the developing world when there are adverts in the airport for pole-dancing clubs.

A minibus took us into the city centre – a 30 minute ride. Sofia appears to be settled in a valley surrounded by mountains. The feeling of the place is hard to describe. At first, looking a bit like Greece without the olive trees, but as we hit the built up areas of town the advertising hoardings, all bearing huge slogans in Cyrillic letters, gave a distinctively Russian flavour to the place. There doesn't seem to be much here that's old. Even the old stuff seems to only go back to the early 20th century. At one point we passed a sprawling building site and through the gaps where the perimeter was boarded up I caught a glimpse of the demolition within. An acre or so of rubble and building foundations with completely intact huge bronze Russian monuments depicting the working man and the struggle of war, towering over the site. Someone had decided to leave them where they stand and work round them. I also saw something else I haven't encountered before. At the road junctions there are little control towers – a bit like the ones you see at airports for the air-traffic controllers to work in. These are much smaller and only really big enough to house one person sitting up in the air behind tinted glass windows. I think they're for the police to sit in, or maybe for controlling the trams - or maybe someone just sits up there with a machine gun in case anyone jumps a red light…

We soon arrived at the Grand Hotel Sofia and checked in. I was given room 504, a suite overlooking the street in front of the hotel with the mountains in the background. Lovely. I texted Linette the hotel phone number and she called for a chat. We have a press conference at the hotel at 5pm so I killed the two hours having a late lunch, writing the diary and trying to have a nap and catch up on sleep following the dawn departure this morning.

The press conference was a little slow. There were 15 people sitting staring at us but only a couple of them asked questions. Everyone seemed pleasant though, and one of the people there made a present to me of a Bulgarian Monopoly. It's amazing that they know I collect them!

Returned to my room clutching said board-game to my chest and then made my way to the lobby to leave for a radio interview with Mark and interpreter Elena (who looked like a 50 year old Debby Harry). The traffic was slow across town during rush-hour but we eventually arrived to find a few fans hanging around on the street asking for autographs and photographs. We made our way inside and were on-air for half-an-hour talking about our impressions of Sofia and the concert ahead. The rest of the radio staff hung around in the studio doorway smiling and handing round beer, vodka and whisky. They seem to have a good time working here. Elena and the DJ were on the whisky. Mark and I stuck to the beer although I think I caved in at one point and had a shot of vodka just to show some solidarity with the locals. When we left, all the radio staff seemed to want their picture taking with us so it took a while to leave. Lovely bunch.

Back to the hotel where there wasn't much time before band and crew were off to dinner. Alex, the promoter (who looks like Eurythmics' Dave Stewart) had invited us out, so at 8.00, we all ambled along the narrow dusty streets until we arrived at a place where people were sitting outside on the pavement having dinner. This is apparently, where we're eating. As we passed the street corner I noticed a policeman lining up a row of restaurant chairs into a makeshift barrier. He was doing this quite casually and with an air of tired resignation, almost boredom. Nothing out of the ordinary really until I noticed the body at his feet, wrapped in black plastic bin-liner with a waxy white human hand, clearly in view, and clearly dead, sticking out from the plastic! It's the first corpse I've ever seen and I confess it made me feel a little peculiar. What was truly surreal, however, was the presence of the diners sitting at tables in very close proximity to the dead body, seemingly oblivious to it…

"More wine, dear? What a lovely evening!" (in Bulgarian, of course)
`We went inside the restaurant and upstairs while I tried to convey to the rest of our party what I'd just seen! Mark shot up out of his chair and rushed to an open window so that he could take a photograph… No comment.

It took a while before my appetite returned. We were served a salad, a kind of flat salty bread (which I liked) and then large platters of grilled assorted meats, which were delicious.

During the evening I was introduced to a couple of pro-footballers (friends of Alex), one of which was wearing a long black jacket, which stretched to the floor. I asked if I could try it on and so we swapped jackets. Everyone agreed it looked good on me. Turns out it's the jacket he got married in. I asked if I could wear it on stage tomorrow and he said sure. Nothing seems to be much of a problem for the Bulgarians.

3 travelling musicians arrived and began playing frantic Balkan music on guitar, violin and accordion. I was reminded of **The Addams Family** and could imagine Gomez and Fester kicking their heels whilst throwing large knives across the room in time to the music. By 11.00 I decided I should return to the hotel, so I said goodnight and a few of the boys accompanied me back along the warm streets. As we left the restaurant I passed our drum technician, Andy, standing on a chair playing a row of large cowbells with an empty beer bottle. One of the promoter's chums asked if we would like a set of large cowbells and I gratefully accepted although I wasn't sure what we would do with them… Hang 'em up in the studio and bung 'em on the next album, I guess. Back on the street, the corpse had gone and I was now proudly sporting a Bulgarian footballer's wedding-coat.

Saturday 13 June

Slept patchily. Pillow trouble as usual and the room was too hot. I staggered around in the dark trying to find a thermostat to tweak or a radiator to turn off. Couldn't find either, so opened the window. This too was tricky as it involved pulling out some kind of a plastic safety device in order to turn the handle. Managed it in the end and sleepwalked back to bed. For a 5-star hotel, someone had really goofed with the curtains which weren't wide enough to close over the window without leaving a strip of window on the left, right, or centre. Woke up with the dawn, cursing said curtain condition then woke up later, then later, then later. Luxury. Finally got up around 11.00am Bulgarian-time (GMT+2) and chatted to L for a while before venturing out to have a look round the city.

I was searching for the church of St. Sofia which I'm sure was quite close. Couldn't find it but wandered around trying to get a flavour of the town. I'd promised my daughter, who I named after this place, an email with a couple of photographs of the sights. In the end, I decided to send a photograph of the little

Russian church and a poster of a military band, which seemed amusingly Eastern Bloc. I found it hard to find much to photograph. Nothing looked particularly impressive with my dodgy iPhone camera and without the ability to set exposure manually, everything was very dark and underexposed against the bright sunny sky.

Having (finally) learned not to wear myself out on gig days, I returned to the hotel and chilled for a couple of hours before leaving the hotel at 3pm. Once on our way in the minibus I realized I'd left my phone in the room, so I apologized to all and we returned to the hotel to get it. When we left the hotel for the second time I noticed a text from Jon saying he was having trouble starting up the Kurzweil. I have spent the last few weeks programming my laptop with an alternative rig for the live shows. Unfortunately it was at the hotel, so we returned a second time so I could go and get it. Left the hotel for a third time and managed to drive to the venue, some 30-minutes away. The venue neighbourhood looks surprisingly-but-distinctly Mexican to me – lots of makeshift market stalls and high-rise concrete slums. We got inside to discover that the gig is an ice-hockey stadium with the acoustical properties of a cave. It was going to sound er... lively! Jon seemed to have fixed the Kurzweil so that was one less thing to worry about. Sat down in the dressing room to discover a long line of rusty cowbells laid out on the floor. Last night's promised gift. They range from just a few centimetres across to great big things almost as big as a cows head! They sound good in a mad clunky metallic sort of way. I'm sure Mike Hunter will love 'em (if he can find anywhere to put em!).

There was quite a long wait before we could get up on stage and actually soundcheck so we hung around in the dressing room. I'd left my shaver at home (there's always something) so I borrowed Pete's, which I somehow managed to drop on the shower room floor. It emptied its cutters and heads all over the place with one sensational shattering tinkling sound. Oh shit. Me and Ian crawled around the big ice-hockey player's shower floor trying to find the shaver-components quickly before Pete came back. We managed to reassemble it and put it back inside his toilet bag just in time. I still haven't told him. I think it was working alright. He probably won't lend me it again.

Soundcheck worked out okay in the end and I actually had a good sound in my in-ears. Phil Brown's a genius. I think he had visibly aged 5 years since this afternoon. But it could have been a hangover.

We noticed that there wasn't a line outside... Normally a queue forms round the building as door-opening-time approaches, but in Bulgaria the people seem to wander in, in a steady flow of ones and twos. The hall was filling up but it was hard to tell exactly how! We were supposed to be on stage at 8.00 but at 7.45 the room was looking distinctly empty. We decided to wait 'til 8.15 in the hope that more people would show up. We all mentally prepared ourselves for a half-empty show and decided to make the best of it. However, when we hit the stage at 8.15, the hall looked pretty busy – not packed, but pretty respectably filled.

The crowd were to turn out to be great. By the third song I felt really connected to them. The band played really well and all the technology worked just fine. It turned out to be a terrific gig and a fitting end to the *Happiness is the Road* tour.

We all went back to the hotel in the mood for an end-of-tour celebration. In typical Marillion tradition, it never happened. Two of the band went to bed whilst three of us went out to the Rock Bar, which was so far beyond awful I can't even bother to describe it. Smoking's still legal in public in Bulgaria so I lasted about a minute before bailing out of there with Hem. We walked the streets for a while trying to find ice-cream which Hem seemed to need desperately. Everything was closed so we gave up. Went back to the hotel and ordered the second Club sandwich of the day. While I sat in Reception waiting for it, I watched a blonde hooker arrive, who was promptly escorted upstairs by the concierge. She reappeared less than 5 minutes later. Now THAT was a quickie.

Ate the Club sandwich and went to bed. It can't be good for you.

Sweden
The Uninvited Guest
*Whatever Is Wrong With You** Guitar on during v1 of *Whatever*
Between You and Me
Quartz
King
Hooks
Afraid of Sunlight
Cover My Eyes Wait for click
Slange
Neverland

Happiness is the Road

Sofia
Splintering Heart
The Uninvited Guest
Kayleigh
Sugar Mice
Man of a Thousand Faces
This Town / The Rakes Progress/100 Nights
Afraid of Sunlight
Fantastic Place
The Man from the Planet Marzipan
Between You and Me
Out of this World
The Great Escape

Neverland

Easter
The Space

Happiness is the Road

Thursday 5 November *Home – Helsinki*

Got up at 6.30, finished packing and tidied up just in case we have to sell the house while we're away. More of that later...

Left home drove to Heathrow T3 where L dropped me off. She's parking the car at T5 and flying to Copenhagen with little Vibes. She gets back in 10 days or so, just before me.

Checked in and through security with Frenchie. Bought a bag in Dixons for the audio interface (laptop to stage – I won't bore you) and bumped into Erik Nielsen, our old Web designer, who was on his way to Halifax, Nova Scotia, to a conference. He's now working for Elton John no less...

At the Gate I said hi to the boys – all in good form. The band has agreed to lend me £100 grand for a couple of months while I sell my house. The house L and I have had our eye on has come up for sale. It's a wreck, but it's in a perfect location on a village Green and has massive potential. There's been enormous interest in it and sealed bids are invited by midday today. We emailed one before we left the house, but I'm not hopeful...

The flight to Helsinki passed without incident until the landing when we pitched and rolled in the side-wind and landed on a snow-covered runway. The plane slewed sideways somewhat and, despite not being a nervous flyer, I must admit that lately I'm becoming a nervous lander and taker-offer!

We made our way through the airport to the baggage carousels and I went down a couple of staircases into the basement in search of a loo. As I stood at the urinal my phone rang. It said Bob Builder on the screen, so I assumed it was our builder, Bob, calling to give me his bank details so that I could pay him for some recent work. On the third attempt to answer the phone (I was peeing at the time) I said, "Hello Bob!" It wasn't him. "Er... hello... this is Roger from McIntyres. Is that Mr Hogarth? I'm about to make your day. Your bid on the house was successful!"

Bloody hell. I thanked him, said I'd be in touch and turned my attention to finishing peeing and leaving the urinal... When I emerged into the baggage hall, the bags were up and loaded and the band were already climbing into two minibuses standing outside in the snow. The mobi wasn't working too well, but I managed to get hold of Linette and give her the good news. Phew! Looks like we're buying a house! ...buying a wreck, actually. It should be an interesting few months ahead.

We drove into Helsinki and checked into the Hotel il Presidente. I invited band and crew to join me in the bar to celebrate my/our good/ill fortune and at 6pm we had a beer and contemplated colossal debt and building work.

Later I went out with the crew and Ian to a burger-place where I had a sort of pork thing, which wasn't bad. And wasn't good either. I also ordered a Mojito, which fitted the same description. This being a night off, we thought we'd go and check out tomorrow night's venue - the club Tavastia. It's a rock club. Quite goth and black inside – not ideally suited to what we're doing on this tour which has been, for the most part, more of a theatre gig. Didn't stay long and returned to the hotel - only a 10 minute walk. Watched a bit of TV and went to bed. It's been a long and eventful day...

Friday 6 November   *Helsinki – Tavastia Club*

Woken around 7am (that's 5am in England) by hammer-drilling and hammering coming through my bedroom wall. Lovely. I've stayed in hotels in many, many cities around the world over the years, and there has been dawn-building-work going on in about half of 'em. I really could have done with a lie in. It's tough to get a good night's sleep with a 16-month old baby and I've been looking forward to the chance. Nope.

I drifted in and out of sleep in between the buzzing and the banging until 9 when I gave up and went down to breakfast. I poured myself a bowl of muesli and some coffee and chatted to Phil Brown for a while (Phil always seems to be in the breakfast room) before returning to my room to begin looking for a surveyor who can examine the house we've almost bought. I spent the morning on-line tracking down window manufacturers (it needs new windows) builders, loan-arrangers etc, and then changed rooms to one higher up and on another side of the hotel, in the hope of escaping tomorrow's dawn-hammer-drills.

At 2pm we had arranged to meet up in Reception to make a short Merry Christmas video announcement. There was a big bronze moose opposite the hotel, so we trudged across the road and got into position. Unfortunately there was too much traffic noise, so we postponed the idea until tomorrow when we'll try again on the ferry to Tallinn.

Mid-afternoon, I went over to the gig to plug the laptop into the PA through the new audio-interface. At the gig, chaos prevailed – we're using a lot of hired equipment and 'house' equipment (this means stuff that the venue owns and supplies. Unfortunately, unless you're lucky, the 'house' gear is poorly maintained and, more often than not, fairly knackered and the crew and band have to work out which bits work and which bits don't through a process of trial and error. This is very time-consuming for all concerned and so these gigs take ages to come together and (as I've said before) it's not uncommon for the soundchecks to be longer than the shows.

The show was clunky, but had a really good spirit (piano trouble – the hired Yamaha P300 isn't responding properly to touch and it goes from quiet to silly-loud if I'm remotely expressive... murder to play!).

Spoke briefly afterwards to a few people hanging about. They all seemed really happy. Walked back to the hotel and got lost. Wheeling my computer bag behind me in the slush, I eventually found someone who gave me directions and made it back. I was only a block out. Stayed up too late watching TV and slept fitfully in between anxiety about house-buying...

Saturday 7 November *Helsinki – Tallinn*

Woke up at a much more civilized time than yesterday (9.45 no less) and went to breakfast to discover about 300 people in the breakfast room. Busy hotel this... Had a bowl of muesli with Rothers and returned to my room where I seriously considered going back to bed, but was embroiled once again in email to estate agents etc...

We checked out of the hotel at 1pm and were taken by cab to the docks, where we boarded the ferry to Tallinn. Crossing the Baltic by ferry I couldn't help but think of my chance encounter with Paul Barney – the only British survivor of the Estonia ferry disaster on Sept 20 1994. Let's hope this one stays afloat! Rothers had given me a sea-sick pill in case the Baltic was rough. It made my mouth very dry and made me feel a bit sleepy and even more peculiar than usual.

I made the trip from Helsinki to Tallinn without leaving the first-class lounge. A decent buffet was available so I had a spot of salmon and meat-balls, and cheese and biscuits, and a beer. All very civilized. Once we were under way we all popped out onto the deck to have another attempt at the Christmas message. The sea was flat calm – I needn't have taken the sea-sick pill and I wish I hadn't bothered. Went back inside and lay down on a sofa for a while and slept a little.

Soon, we docked at Tallinn and took a mini bus into town and checked into what turned out to be a really nice hotel with a fire burning in a high-tech fireplace in reception. Andreas, the promoter, had arranged a larger room for me as I wanted to take the electric piano up to my room to try and fix the main piano-sound which hadn't been at all right during the Helsinki show. The touch response has been basically screwed by whoever had it last. Robert and Pete set it up for me in room 447 while I enthused about the view of old snow-covered Tallinn from my window. After they'd gone I found a way to "factory-reset" it, which returned it to something resembling the piano that I thought I'd hired!

I lay down on the modern four-poster bed and watched BBC World news for a while before going downstairs to do an interview with an interesting chap who seemed to just want to chat about life and the world-in-general rather than asking any specific questions... Interesting, and refreshing...

Decided to go out with Pete and Rothers for a spot of dinner in the old town. Old Tallinn is truly medieval (or truly tourist-repro-medieval ...a bit of both) and we found a restaurant called The Peppersack where we were shown down to the cellar. I ordered up a cup of cocoa, which was lovely, so I had another (makes a welcome change from tequila and Red Bull) and some pork fillet. Ian and the crew later arrived and so everyone except Mark had come out for dinner.

After a while, a girl came into the room and began belly-dancing about the place. Well, I wasn't expecting that. I think she was a professional, she wasn't just an over-exuberant diner. She seemed to avoid our table – perhaps she imagined potential trouble... Robert told me he'd seen us playing on a big video screen across town. Great. Hell freezes over and Marillion get a little high profile exposure! It doesn't happen much anymore. Walked back to the hotel - just a 5 minute walk - but it was well below freezing and the cold was biting my legs through my jeans. Not a night for wandering around town. Watched a bit more BBC World on the big flat-screen at the end of the four-poster and settled down to sleep in the comfiest bed of the tour so far. Very nice. I'm enjoying Tallinn.

Sunday 8 November   *Tallinn – Nokia Concert Hall*

The next morning I thought I'd better go and have a look at the gig. There's a grand piano at the venue and I'd love to play it but I don't know if there'll be room on the stage for the band! Needn't have worried – the Nokia concert hall in Tallinn is a fabulous and new concert hall. The stage is huge and I actually had trouble locating the grand piano in the vastness of the wings. The manager of the venue disappeared and came back with the grand piano, a full concert-grand made by Estonia. I played one of these many years ago in the Riga Bay Hotel (where the Russians used to send the cosmonauts for R&R when they came back from space) and it was one of the finest pianos I have ever played (a close-second to the fabulous Bösendorfer which used to be in Sarm East studios in Shoreditch). I showed the chaps where to position the piano and couldn't resist enjoying the instrument for a while during the set-up of the equipment. I'm a man of simple tastes. All I've ever wanted was a concert-grand... and a yacht big enough to accommodate one. And staff to sail the boat and mix the cocktails. Is it so very much to ask?

I spent so much time fiddling around with the piano that I forgot all about our 2pm rendezvous back at the hotel to have yet-another go at the Christmas message! When I got back to the hotel, the band were all sitting by the fire, so we thought it might be cool to say Happy Christmas there, then again in the old town, then again in the snow, and edit them all together. Lovely. After that, we headed off to a bookstore in the shopping mall adjoining the theatre where we were to do a bit of autographing and I think I answered a few questions for Estonian TV.

We then made our way into the theatre for soundcheck. This was quite a protracted affair owing to the addition of the grand piano position. By the time we'd finished soundcheck there was only an hour to showtime. I fancied another walk in the old town so I walked across the park and found a restaurant where I ordered a hot chocolate and was invited to choose a table. I sat in the window. When the waiter came with the hot chocolate he said "Congratulations! You are our one millionth customer – you get free cake!" And he set down a plate with a slice of chocolate cake on it. Nice people these Estonians – good humoured and friendly. Everyone at the hotel had been really friendly too and nothing seemed to be a problem. I sipped my hot-chocolate and watched people - wrapped up against the cold evening-air, exhaling visible breaths - passing the restaurant, before returning across the park to the gig. Outside the shopping mall I (vainly) stopped to take a photograph of myself on the video screen. Well, it doesn't happen every day.

I had been warned (by yesterday's journalist) that the Estonian audiences are very restrained and, sure enough, polite applause was to be the order of the day. The people seemed unusually well-dressed for our show and I couldn't help wondering how many of this lot were fans and how many were just casual theatre-goers on The Nokia concert-hall mailing-list, up for a night out. Nonetheless, we seemed to go down well – they listened and responded politely. It was all very Japanese. During the second set I made a short speech about how I came to write *Estonia* - the chance meeting with Paul Barney - and what the song represents to me. I said we'd waited a long time to play the song here and I found it hard to introduce the song without my voice cracking with emotion. This was the song played at my own father's funeral and, as the song started, I quietly hoped that the people would understand what a big moment this represented to me. I concentrated solely on singing and playing the song as best I could. I think I got it all right and, to my relief, Mark made a beautiful job of the solo. At the end of the song the crowd didn't particularly go wild, they simply stood up as one - like they might for the National Anthem - and clapped respectfully. It was a beautiful reaction. They seemed not to be applauding, but giving thanks with due reverence to the 852 souls who were lost that night in 1994. I'll never forget it.

By the end of the second set, the restraint had given way to loud enthusiasm and two encores were vociferously demanded.

What a great night, in a great auditorium, in what's fast-becoming a special city in my heart. Thank you Tallinn. xx

Monday 9 November *Tallinn*

Managed a lie-in 'til 10.00 and caught the last few seconds of breakfast before the staff started locking up the cereals. The bags were being collected at 12.00 so I showered and packed and dropped my suitcase in the hall. I thought I'd go for one last wander round old Tallinn before we left at 2.00.

Walked up into the square and took a few photographs. Found a gallery selling ceramics and glass and had a mooch round. Bought a couple of little shot-glasses for a souvenir. L and I will share a Christmas toast in them (if I don't lose or break them before I get home). Returned to the hotel, stopping to take the occasional snapshot as I walked.

We left the hotel at 2.00 and bundled into a van which took us to the airport for the flight to Vilnius. All the Baltic flights were to be in those Fokker propeller planes – not much room in them and they do tend to blow around in the sky somewhat. Anyway the flight was fine and I slept a little so the time passed quickly. We de-planed (as the Americans say) and were bussed into the airport, which looks more like a branch of Barclays bank. Another van took us to the hotel in Vilnius - a far less appealing high-rise than the lovely hotel in Tallinn - but hey, you only sleep there. My room was on the 13th floor by the lift.

Made a date with Rothers to go out for dinner, but when I got upstairs I couldn't face a trip out in the cold mist and rain of Vilnius so I ordered a Club-sandwich on room-service, stuck BBC News 24 on the telly, and spent an hour or so looking at email. The news of the day was the 20-year anniversary celebration ceremony of the taking-down of the Berlin wall. The European leaders were all there making speeches. Sarkozy made a particularly unimpressive speech about the importance of France and Germany as leaders of Europe. That wouldn't have endeared him much to the Brits. Gordon Brown followed him and made what I thought was the best speech I've heard him make – full of compassion and a pro-active optimistic vision for the future of Europe and the world. I'm naturally sceptical of politicians, but it actually brought a lump to my throat. He's riding the whirlwind at the moment and he'll almost certainly get voted out at next year's general election by the (IMHO) self-seeking Etonian in middle-class clothing, David Cameron, but I suspect Brown does actually have the vision-thing in a Quaker-humanistic way that Blair never had. I'm reminded of the Russians booting out the great Mikhail Gorbachev in favour of the opportunistic (when sober!) Boris Yeltsin. Or kicking out Ken Livingstone for Boris Johnson. We all make the same mistakes. Anyway I digress... Hilary Clinton was next up. She made a good speech too, but Brown was a tough act to follow and her acknowledgement of the role the Pope and the Roman Catholic church had played in the fall of the wall, had, to my ears, a faint whiff of electioneering back home. Barack Obama sent a message by video. Then, last but not least, was Angela Merkel, the German Chancellor. Looking like she'd just got up - bad hairdo, no make-up - she told us how she was one of those people in East Germany who were trapped in the Eastern Bloc like so many others until that fateful day in November 1989, and the amazing feeling that freedom at last had come to her country. Incredible that she's now Chancellor of a united and peaceful - some would say pacifist - Germany. She, like Gordon Brown (only more-so) seems to me to exude a sense that her work and her position are far too important for her to be bothered by the fripperies of image. She praised Poland for its part in the process that would send communism tumbling – the strike by the shipyard workers union Solidarnoszc. She praised Hungary, Czechoslovakia and she said Poland would never again need to fear its neighbour. I like her. Lech Walesa was there and pushed the first domino, just as he had in real life.

Later there were fireworks to which TV can never begin to do justice. You have to be there, and I really wish I had been.

I went to bed and continued watching the rolling coverage whilst talking to Linette on Skype. She's at her mum and dads at the moment in Denmark. She sounded well if a little tired. Kids, innit?

Tuesday 10 November *Vilnius – Congress Concert Hall*

Got up and went down to the breakfast-room where I had a bowl of muesli with Pete T and Pete guitar tech. Back upstairs for more emailing about mortgages and borrowing, which I won't bore you with. Still don't know if the house-rebuild project is a goer, but I really hope we can pull it together. I decided to go out and find old Vilnius so I wrapped up warm to brave the cold, damp, air and went out, crossing the river and following my nose until I came across a hair-salon where I bought some odd hair-gel and asked directions. Walked for another 20-minutes and if I found the old-town it wasn't all that old, but a bit like Bond Street and quite posh. I wasn't seeing Vilnius at its best as the rain drizzled down so I gave up and walked back to the hotel, bumping once again into Pete T who walked back with me. He couldn't find the old town either.

Returned to my room for 10-minutes to look at more email about mortgages and house-buying/selling before going down to reception to climb into the van and to the gig.

The hall was a 700 capacity-ish wood panelled concert hall, more used by classical artists than rock n'rollers; in fact, the crew had had to wait to set-up while an orchestra finished rehearsing. There was a very nice Steinway grand piano at the side of stage. Unfortunately, it had been tuned to A442 that morning for the orchestra. Unlike the West where we use the A440 standard, the East tunes 2 Hertz sharper. We could only use the grand by having it tuned down to A440 or it wouldn't be in tune with our instruments. This would take an hour or more and we didn't really have the time. Shame.

Soundcheck passed without much incident and we returned to the dressing room. Along the corridor an orchestral brass section were rehearsing so we all went up the corridor to have a listen. The venue manager mistook our curiosity for irritation and went into the room to tell them to shut up while we tried to communicate to her that we were actually just trying to listen.

It's an early show in Vilnius so there wasn't much time between sound check and show.

The show wasn't very well attended – I think there were about 350 people in, but they seemed to be listening and enjoying the show. I thought we played well and it turned out to be a slow-burner. The crowd gradually warmed up throughout the evening. Like the Baltic shows, they're more reserved than our fans in Western Europe, but at the end of the show they rose to their feet as one, and demanded two encores in no uncertain fashion.

We were bussed back to the hotel and I realized I hadn't eaten at all today so it was arranged for us to have dinner in the hotel restaurant. Unfortunately it was getting late and I didn't get an order in until almost 11pm. By 11.20, nothing had arrived so I abandoned the idea and went to bed. Really must eat tomorrow.

Wednesday 11 November *Riga – Congress Centre*

Up early for an 8.15 am departure (that's 6.15 in England!). Checked out and climbed into a van which took us to Vilnius airport for the flight to Riga. We were on another Air Baltic Fokker – prop-powered and mightily cosy inside... I never managed to get my Animal snow-boarding jacket off before passing out. Slept for the whole flight and didn't notice take-off from Vilnius any more than I noticed landing in Riga.

We were bussed to the Maritim hotel, a conference hotel on the outskirts of the city. My room was quite nice and spacious. There was a view across the city and I could see a distant ship in the docks. There's also a strange 3-legged metal structure, which disappeared into the low cloud. I never saw the top of it the whole time we were there. Andrea (the promoter) had arranged club-sandwiches and soup for band and crew at 12.30, so I went back downstairs for what was a very welcome (and free) lunch. Nice touch. I like this promoter; he's not making a great deal of money from these shows but he's doing all he can to make us comfortable.

I went back upstairs and emailed for a while. Tried to sleep for an hour, but I didn't quite manage it. Frenchie texted to say there was food at the gig arranged for 5.30 before soundcheck. I really fancied a look round old Riga. We've been to Riga once before, many years ago in 1993, and I never had chance to see the old town back then. I called Frenchie to see if there was any way the promoter could be persuaded to organize me a car into the old town. He called back to say it was "sorted" and that Max, the local promoter (who I also liked immediately), would pick me up at 4.00. Sure enough, he was waiting for me downstairs and we travelled into town in his Mercedes Jeep – one of those old square Russian-looking ones. I had always wanted one of these and never had a ride in one so I enjoyed rattling along into town chatting to Max about rock n'roll and touring in Russia - something we have yet to experience. Max dropped me in Riga old town around 4.30. It was already dark. He said he'd pick me up at the same spot at 5.30, so I walked into a large square and then along the medieval-looking streets, past the churches, taking photographs as I wandered. Old Riga is lovely and thoroughly worth another visit when I'm not working. It would be very pleasant to come back with Linette and stay in one of the hotels here in the old town. Beautiful buildings competed for my attention in every direction as I made my way along the cobbled streets. Everywhere, there were little restaurants, bars, shops selling amber and local crafts, but I also passed art galleries and through one window, what looked like a small library where a business meeting was taking place. Riga seems to be a really vibrant place. I wouldn't mind living here. I found a bar called The Victory, a sort of Latvian idea of an English pub and made my way inside to escape the chilly weather. I sat at the bar and drank an Irish coffee while a curious eclectic mix of music came out of the speakers behind the bar. I remember Blur and AC/DC. At 5.30 I jumped back into Max's waiting Merc Jeep and returned to the gig for soundcheck.

Sunday 15 November *Rome*

Landed in Rome. The weather was a little cloudier than the perfect blue we'd left behind in Barcelona. We knew we were in Italy when the baggage carousel broke down… No one seemed to care and nothing was done to fix it – even after I pressed the emergency stop button which began a loud and piercing alarm. I moved over to the other side of the baggage hall to sit down and get away from the noise. 15-minutes later(!) the alarm stopped and the carousel started up again, so we picked up our bags and made our way outside where the promoters rep, was waiting with a couple of vans. He couldn't seem to get the side door to close, so we drove to Rome with it rattling. Nothing quite works perfectly in Italy, but the whole country seems to bear that in mind and work with it without getting unduly flustered. Everything seems to happen more or less as it needs to happen …eventually. We arrived at the hotel - a Melia park thing on the outskirts of Rome - and checking in took a long time but, eventually, it happened. My room's nothing special but it's fine, if a little warm… I opened the window to feel a light, cool breeze. I later discovered that there's a switch at the side of the bed to turn on the air conditioning but that it only blows warm air because "yesterday we switched off the air conditioning for the winter"

"Can it be turned back on?"

"No."

"What should we do then?"

"Open the window."

"Err okay. Do you have a code for the internet please?"

"Yes. 10 euros for 45-minutes or 25 for 24 hours."

I decided against an internet connection for the time being. It's Sunday so there won't be anything urgent to attend to. I returned to my room and watched BBC News 24. There was a report containing the usual dire warnings about our planet. First the glacier in the Andes which feeds the river which in turn provides Peru's capital, Lima, with its drinking water. This glacier is over 12,000 years old and has reduced in size by 30% in the last ten years! Scientists working up in the mountains and taking ice cores from the glacier predict that it will have ceased to exist at some point in the next 20 years. Meanwhile, on the other side of the world in Australia, the people of Adelaide are facing water rationing as their own river begins to dry up. Without a 50% reduction in the world's carbon emissions in the next 10 years, it's predicted that ALL the glaciers on earth will have thawed. The next news item was to say that the Copenhagen summit on climate-change is likely to end in a few days with no agreement from the world's leaders to legislate for a drastic cut in carbon emissions. It looks like the world will prevaricate and squabble until it is too late to stop a rise in sea-levels and a loss of fresh water supplies across the globe which will have unthinkable economic consequences. We, like every generation before us, will have much to apologise for, to our children. Sigh…

There's a "courtesy" bus that runs into Rome centre at various erratic times which are printed on a sheet in your room, so I went down to get the 6.45. Rich,

Phil and Ian were waiting also, so I joined them on the ride into town. A 50-seater coach had been provided to take the four of us into town. The bus driver had an annoying friend who seemed to be high on something, and they animatedly chatted to each other for the entire journey – the driver looking mostly sideways at his hyperactive chum, and only taking fleeting glimpses through the windscreen in between hand gestures and intense conversation. At one point we narrowly avoided hitting a high kerb in the central reservation of the road. The most scared I've ever been in a vehicle was a taxi-ride here in Rome some years ago when I made the mistake of climbing into a cab and saying, "Cavalieri Hilton please – as fast as you can!" I remember barrelling down alleyways at 70mph whilst nuns and children scattered into doorways to avoid immediate death while I did the Steve-Martin-thing where it took some time to pull my fingernails back out of my own thighs upon our arrival. Anyway, this journey was a close second – a similar carefree driving-style, weaving in and out of lanes, ignoring pedestrian crossings and bearing scant regard for traffic signals. I thought I was back in that cab until I remembered this was a 50-seater coach capable of demolishing a building.

To our immense relief and gratitude to the fates, the four of us were dropped off in Rome centre and I called my Roman mate (and photographic genius) Luigi, to see if he could find us. He said he was close and we would see him in a few minutes. For one disconcerting moment we passed one of those mime-people - all painted silver - and it waved at me and I wondered if it was Luigi providing a bizarre welcome to his city. It wasn't. He soon caught up with us. His hair's long now, but his unmistakeable good humoured and perceptive spirit is no less diminished. We walked down to St Peter's square, which I think is more beautiful by night than by day. Luigi used to work there doing security to pay his way through his photographic degree and he told us that only 5% of St Peter and the Vatican is open to the public. Blimey! We walked back up the street and found a little café. It was still warm enough to eat out, so the four of us had a light dinner and a beer at a table out in the street. I called L and said a quick hello so she could say hi to Luigi. He's one of those special people and so is she, so it made sense to pass the phone to him. She told me that little Vibes seems unsettled by everything that's going on: the travel, the strange bed, the kids, being hauled around. She thinks it's not good for him. I personally don't think it does anyone any harm to get used to changes, but then, I'm not there to see how he's responding. She says she thinks it's good that they're returning home tomorrow. We finished the meal with a lemoncello (well, you must) and asked for the bill. I guess that's the last time I'll be eating al-fresco this year! It's late November now.

We were running out of time to get the last bus back to the hotel so we walked back and climbed onto the bus. We opted for the back seat for the return journey - we thought it might be safer.

Back at the hotel my room had cooled down and was feeling a little chilly, so I closed the window and went to bed. L called me to wish me goodnight. She sounds tired. I woke in the middle of the night, hot and gasping for breath, and got up and opened the window again.

Monday 16 November *Rome*

Managed to sleep till 8.30 and then snooze till 9.30, listening to the sound of Italians and to diesel engines. I got up to see half a dozen workmen erecting a huge Christmas tree in a pot so big that they were barely visible standing up in it. Went down to the breakfast room and had a couple of coffees and a bowl of muesli whilst talking to Pete.

Went back up to my room and decided to go to Rome to get my roots done so I went down to catch the 11.45 courtesy bus. Amazingly, it came on time. After 3 attempts by the driver to get the door open, I climbed aboard the 50-seater coach and it pulled away for the journey into Rome. I was the only passenger. In these environmentally-conscious times I couldn't help but ponder upon the carbon footprint of a diesel-driven coach of this size, edging it's way along the gridlocked streets of Rome, just to deposit one singer in a downtown salon. Oh well...

I walked around the block trying to find a hairdresser amongst the restaurants, cafés and shops. I finally found one in a back street, the Vatican walls towering above us, and went inside. Behind the counter sat a formidable 60-something old dear - obviously the boss - bespectacled and dressed in the Mediterranean widow's outfit of black, black and more black. Next to her, a 40-something woman admitted to speaking English so I asked if they could possibly do my roots black. She rattled to the black widow in Italian and the response was a shake of the head and another burst of impenetrable Italian. "I'm sorry – we don't do men," she said. I guess we're just too close to the heart of the holy Roman Catholic Church for women to be allowed to touch the scalps of men! Strange indeed. Or perhaps she'd had Silvio Berlusconi in for a tint and vowed never to let another man anywhere near the shop-girls... I asked if they knew of any other places that might be prepared to touch my head and after more exchanges the woman translated that they would in fact colour my roots, "just this once!" Crackers. I was ushered into the salon and over the course of 90-minutes, a very talented woman painted my roots probably as well as they have ever been painted. I was charged a hefty €75 euros for the pleasure, and I emerged into the sunshine. Bought an ice cream - black cherry, very nice - and sat in a square for a while, watching the people go by and trying to keep the thing under control as it melted in the 23 degree heat. Frenchie texted me to say that there was no screaming hurry to get back as the departure for soundcheck had been postponed until 5pm, so I found a little café, drank cappuccino, ordered pizza and wrote this diary.

the *invisible* man

2010 NOVEMBER

Monday 15

DAY off !!!

2010

Wednesday 3 March *Home – Istanbul*

Spent the beginning of the morning trying to get the wi-fi working. It suddenly stopped. It's funny how equipment seems to know when I'm going away and fails just as I'm going out the door. L needs to be on-line a lot at the moment – she's busy sourcing stuff for the new house. I mean where DO you get the best price on aircrete breeze-blocks? Spent the rest of the morning clearing the shelves in the outbuilding. We're moving house in phases... Phase 1: pack everything down and store as much of it as possible in the outbuildings of the "new" (actually a relic of a cottage!) house. David Smith's coming on Saturday with a van. Unfortunately, I'm going to Istanbul at lunchtime today and won't be back 'til Friday afternoon. Phase 2: live in our house - now mostly empty - for a week, and then move to a rented holiday cottage next Saturday with a few essentials whilst putting our remaining possessions in storage. Subject to planning permission having been approved, a team of chaps – builder, plumber, electrician, sandblasters and labourers will commence work on the "new" cottage on the Monday. Unfortunately I leave the day after we move, and the day before the builders start, to go to Portugal with the band for 2 weeks for more jamming and writing. The trick is to try and avoid Linette having to move house in my absence – hence the phased system!

Spent the rest of the morning making trips in the car to the "new" house to put stuff in the empty outbuildings. Showered at 1.00 and left at 1.30 for the drive to Heathrow. Terminal 5 is now showing signs (nearly 2 years in) of working. Checked-in and cleared security in less than half an hour. Amazing. Sat in the Giraffe restaurant for a bit eating nachos and absorbing the Latin-American music until checking in at gate A20. The flight to Istanbul was uneventful. I spent it listening to the possible options for an **h Natural** live CD which I'm going to release in the spring.

We arrived in Istanbul airport to be greeted by the promoter who has been a little less than in a hurry to give us any money. Despite the terms of the contract he hasn't paid the advance fees that we insist on when working with new people in "new" countries. More money was promised in cash when we arrived at the airport and - surprise, surprise - he came without it. We have done a few gigs in recent times for which we were either paid nothing or only some of the fee, so we're cagey. All our bargaining power will be lost as soon as we have played the show and then the chances of getting money out of a man in Istanbul when you're on the phone from England are basically, zero. This is a dilemma when we know that there are fans flying into Turkey from around the world just to see us. To cancel now is to betray them.

Climbed into a van and was transported to an area of Istanbul which was like a Turkish version of a cross between Soho and Magaluf. Neon and pumping disco music along narrow lanes of restaurants and bars and, in the middle of all the noise and light, our hotel, the Interroyal, and about as royal as me. After being given a smoking room, and then another smoking room, I finally checked into room 510, a non-smoking room. Pretty basic. The bed-linen smelled of dust and the little 12" TV was something you wouldn't be able to shift on eBay, but at least there was BBC News 24 as an option on channel 3. I managed to speak to L before turning in. Steve and Mark were going out for a beer but I thought I'd rest so I didn't bother. I turned off the light and drifted into sleep to the sound of several pumping disco rhythms in the street below. The receptionist said the music is turned off at midnight. I later found out that it stopped at 5, but I had slept through it. I did hear the Muezzin though - probably just after the disco stopped - calling the faithful to dawn prayers. Dunno if it was a real person or a dodgy automatic recording. It was coming through speakers in the street somewhere and was suitably lo-tech and distorted. I gave the prayers a miss. Perhaps I'll pray now and give thanks for my life. You never know ...and I do have a very good life.

Thursday 4 March *Istanbul*

Got up around 11.00 (9.00 UK time) and tried to catch a quick hello with little Vibes on his way to nursery. I had just missed him. Never mind. I'm only away for a couple of days but I find myself missing him almost as soon as we're parted now. Texted Linette. All's fine so I got dressed and went out for a wander in search of coffee. Walked uphill along narrow lanes full of restaurants, fishmongers, and stalls selling hubble-bubble pipes and scarves. It's pretty chilly here - about 9 degrees - so I kept my coat buttoned up to the neck. Ended up sitting at a table where I was served by the man running the fish stall. "Do you have English coffee, please?"

"Nescafé" said the waiter in a surly growl.

"Fine" I said.

When it came in a little cup I asked "Do you have any sugar?"

"Taste it." he said with another growl.

I tasted it and there must have been at least 2 sugars in it. A good job I took sugar...

Went walking and taking in the atmosphere. Found a beautiful indoor alley full of shops selling textiles and jewellery. Found a shop selling fezzes. Bought another coffee and then a scarf from a market stall, before wandering back to the hotel. Bumped into Mark who took pics of me in various outlandish hats. Passed a fishmongers and marvelled at a fish thrown on the floor without a head. It was as big as a goat! Back at the hotel the crew were still sitting in reception with the equipment. The promoter STILL hadn't come up with the money so we weren't taking anything to the venue. Hmm... Back in my hotel room I can hear the sound of a budgie squawking in the next room. There's also the occasional barking of a dog. Perhaps people live in this hotel all the time. Pete says to keep my windows closed as the balconies are all inhabited by cats (to which I am violently allergic). Spent an hour or so writing this diary. Will go back out and try to find something to eat which won't put me in hospital. You've got to be careful in foreign climes...

PS Never wrote any more.. I should point out that we later DID get paid though.

Friday 25 June   *"Home" – Venice – Treviso*

Drove to Gatwick from our temporary home in Kings Sutton

Nice day. Nice drive. Missed the exit to the M23 talking about lime-mortar.

Checked in uneventfully and managed to drop Rothers spare strat at oversized baggage.

Had a Caesar salad at Café Rouge. Very nice. Walked over the bridge over the runway to Gate 104. It's uplifting to watch passenger jets taxi beneath my feet. The flight was full but okay. Flew over Venice when we landed. I hadn't realized (stupidly) that it is so close to the open sea. Derr!. Why else would it have been so rich? I was greeted in Venice airport by Dave and Giorgio who drove me to the edge of the island where we parked the car before going on foot over the new bridge and walking through the narrow Venetian streets and over the many little bridges. Had a beer by a canal before walking further into this amazing place. The weather was perfect – sunny and blue, but by early evening not too hot, just pleasantly warm. Bought a little Venetian glass goblet and a glass bracelet for L. Stopped at a little bar for home-made beer watching the tourists go by and discussing Italy's early departure from the world cup. Portugal and Brazil drew nil-nil today. We reckon it's been quietly fiddled... so they both go through to the knockout stage.

Found a table in a restaurant beneath old cloisters by a small side-canal and ate spaghetti vongole and drank an excellent red-wine while watching gondolas drift by, rocked by the wakes of occasional passing power-boats. Fabulous.

After dinner we walked back along the cobbled streets past the many shops - some selling carnival masks - and market stalls of fruit and vegetables. Drove to Treviso where the band are staying in a castle. The band took a later flight, not being bothered about seeing Venice... Madness. When we arrived at the castle a woman greeted us. She looked like a character from a Berlin cabaret. She prepared my room and gave me a beer as I said bye to Dave and Giorgio. The band were out somewhere having dinner (I later discovered they had been at a pizza place next to a garage!) so I went to bed.

Saturday 26 June *Treviso*

Woken at 5.30 by loud machine noise. Got up to investigate. It was a road sweeper. The loudest road sweeper I have ever heard – sounded like someone had attached an engine to my bedroom wall. Back to sleep til 7.00 when church bells began chiming from the tower opposite my room. They chimed every 30 minutes for the rest of the morning and I slept in-between them.

Got up and had breakfast with Steve and Pete and was later joined by the Baron who is somewhat eccentric. He thought Marillion was a beautiful name for a wine and asked permission to use the name for his next vintage. We said sure, in the certain knowledge that he will have forgotten all about it by teatime. I had a walk around the central square of the castle which has two 250 year-old magnolia trees - the largest magnolias I have ever seen - and two gigantic cedars of a similar age and monumental size. The estate staff were busy preparing for a wedding party. Trestle tables were stacked with glasses, cutlery and champagne-on-ice while chefs worked busily in the back rooms. Went for a walk into Treviso. It's a very small town - not much more than a village, really. A few restaurants, jewellery shops, photographic studios. Everyone seems to be constantly getting married here so I think there's a good living to be had for wedding photographers. Bought an adaptor in an electrical shop. Italian mains is unique in the world... Came back to the castle and wrote this.

Went out with Pete and Ian for a cappuccino before returning to leave for soundcheck.

For whatever reason, the diary stops here so I'm recalling the show through a haze... I remember the gig being open-air and set up in a 15th century town square. The weather was super-hot in the afternoon and my Yamaha P250 piano got so hot in the direct sunshine that it began to malfunction and we had to put cardboard over it to cool it down. As for the gig, we got changed in a building nearby that looked like some kind of civic office or library. My knee dislocated at one point during *Cover My Eyes* and I had to fall to the stage and try and put it back while singing. Managed eventually. The other memorable moment was at the opening verses of *Happiness is the Road* when one of Rother's FX-pedals

(Adrenalinn – I believe) suddenly turned into a drum-machine and began generating an inane cartoon rhythm. It still does this occasionally and Steve doesn't seem to know how to stop it or what causes it...

Thursday 11 November *Home – Haarlem*

Looked in on Vibes who was sleeping peacefully. He won't let me put him to bed and he won't let me go and kiss him goodnight once he's in bed. It's as though it messes with his need for it to be all about mummy at this stage of the day. He has me filed in another box - I'm to do with entertainment and not for last thing at night. I kiss him goodnight and L reads him a story, sings him a song and I have to leave! So I must wait til he's asleep for a last look in on him. Said bye to L - who seemed okay but understandably, like me, a little subdued - and drove to Charlton to pick up Nial who was ready when I arrived. To the Rose & Crown for a quick half with Sofi and Chris. "Blimey!" said landlord - "Twice in a week!" Said hello to one or two of the locals on my way out. Drove to the studio with Nial where the black tour bus was already waiting. Loaded our stuff and were soon on our way. Drank a Becks talking to Mark and Hemashu and shared a bottle of bitter with Nial before making my way to bed. Phoned L and said goodnight. The weather was stormy. Luckily we hadn't booked a ferry crossing – we were going onto the train and through the channel tunnel. I later found out that all ferries were cancelled owing to the treacherous sea-conditions. I climbed onto my shelf and began the process of getting accustomed to sleeping on the road again. It felt good and I slept pretty well although slightly conscious, at various points in the night, of bumps and high winds.

Friday 12 November *Haarlem*

Woke up in Holland around 8.00am and went downstairs to discover Nial already up. Rothers was up and complaining about his night's sleep - he only managed half an hour. Had coffee and called home. The phone wasn't answered so I txted to discover that there was a power cut in the village. It's always been the same - I go on tour and everything malfunctions! L's going to Banbury this morning and was getting Vibes ready. He came on the phone to tell me he was fine and, to my delight, said, "I love you, daddy". Made my day. I went wandering in Haarlem and I thoroughly recommend the place. A beautiful Dutch town. I forget just how much I like Holland until I'm there. As a society it seems to function so much better than England. More art, more (and better) cafés, better shops, prettier buildings and an atmosphere of relaxed social humanity. Public transport seems to work, everywhere there are people on bicycles and the people simply seem happier than their British counterparts. I found a café and had coffee before finding an Apple shop to buy a new battery for this laptop. The chap offered to put the machine on charge for me if I popped in later and so I went wandering and found a hair salon where I could get my hair sorted out for the tour ahead. Now I'm in a very traditional café called Café Brinkmann, all dark wood and stained glass and buzzing with the good people of Haarlem relaxing and having lunch. I confess I'm drinking Hoegaarden at only 1.30pm and I further confess I'm thoroughly enjoying it and I'm more than tempted to order another... Tonight's show is for the 25th anniversary of the Web Holland and so we can certainly expect a fabulous atmosphere from the crowd. I'm so lucky to be part of this 'thing' that is Marillion – no longer just a band, but a family, a way of looking at the world, perhaps, and a kind of groovy church. Am I describing The Grateful Dead? I never got their music, but I understand the vibe.

I have just ordered (by copying!) a glass of peppermint tea. Moderation prevailing (as it so often does these days – perhaps I have grown up... perhaps I am bearing-in-mind my "tour goal #1" of trying to stay out of hospital). It's a glass of hot water full of leaves - more of a salad than a drink really - and is accompanied by a small biscuit, a sachet of honey, and a sachet of sugar. I have just tasted it and it works very well without the honey and sugar, so I think I'll have it "in the buff" (although I am curious to see where the honey would take it... As with all honey, there's no going back without starting again, so perhaps I'll just imagine. Oh dear, these metaphors are writing themselves... Right! – back to the pond water and watching the world go by. More later.

Walked back to the gig and stopped in a flower-shop in search of tulip bulbs. They didn't have any but I bought two Eskimo candles instead (err... that's candles shaped like Eskimos...Christmas decs.). Back at the gig, soundcheck seemed to last about a week but was, in fact, only two and a half hours!!

After the unending soundcheck we said hi to a chap called Theo who had been invited in. He's gravely ill and his dream was for us to play *Fantastic Place* for him so someone at The Web Holland (our Dutch fanclub) has made it happen for him. It's a shame we hadn't rehearsed it... but he seemed very grateful. Back on the bus for a power-nap before showtime. The gig was typically first-night-clunky, but I enjoyed it. The occasion, as I said earlier, was a celebration of the Web Holland's 25-year anniversary so you might expect a rapturous response but, oddly, the crowd were a little slow to get into it. I felt very "connected" to the people throughout, though, and the ice eventually melted. I felt I gave a good account of myself. Nial, my son, did well looking after me. It's great to have him with us. Tomorrow will be a much tougher call. We'll play to Deep Purple's crowd in much larger halls from now on. I have mixed feelings about what to expect. There's the poignant fact that I first decided to be a "rockn'roll" musician whilst experiencing Deep Purple in the 70's and so to be playing alongside them all these years later is a curious feeling. We'll see...

Saturday 13 November   *Trier – Germany*

Slept late, rising at 11.00. Much better sleep last night, helped in no small part by the bus being parked for most of it. Rose and had coffee with Nial before going in to the big exhibition hall where we will open for Deep Purple tonight. It looks like it would hold 7000 or so. There won't be much for us to do for a while so I went and found catering and had a cup of coffee before meeting up with Phil Brown in the dressing room where we had a contact-lens tutorial. He's lent me a couple of his lenses and showed me how to put them in. I have a +2.5 in my right eye for reading, and a +1 in my left eye which has blurred my distance vision but brought middle-distance into sharp focus. It's a curious feeling... I'm typing into this laptop without the use of spectacles for the first time in a few years. It'll be interesting trying to get the bloody things out again later... When I get home I'll go and try getting a proper prescription pair of lenses fitted. It should change my life for the better!.

Soundcheck was slightly fraught after Ian M discovered his in-ear monitors were broken on one side... In the end he decided to do the show wearing headphones... I had a good stage sound so was feeling guardedly optimistic about the show. We're expecting to be playing to half-empty halls as we're on so early. We've put *Kayleigh* in the set to try to pull the people in from the bar... Had a spot of dinner in catering and then back on the bus for a power-nap. We went on stage at 8.00 to discover the hall more-or-less full. Fantastic! I quickly adjusted to the situation, trying to throw big shapes and perform to the back wall. (Freddy Mercury at the back of my mind... "What would Freddy do?"). To my surprise, the crowd seemed pretty open to our music and responded well to *The Invisible Man*. Who would have thought? We were going down well until *Gazpacho* which they didn't seem to "get" (note to self...). They rallied however later on and we received warm applause at the end of *Neverland*. This all bodes well for the rest of the tour and we came offstage with our spirits up. I looked at the clock on the dressing room wall and noticed ruefully that it was only 8pm in England! This is the way to tour! One-hour shows and all finished by early evening. I chilled in the dressing room for a while before going out into the hall to have a quick look at Deep Purple. Don Airey was playing a fantastic solo and the band were, of course, going down a storm. Everyone in the crowd I encountered seemed to smile and quite a few shook my hand and told me they enjoyed our show. Marvellous. Tomorrow Freiburg...

Sunday 14 November *Freiburg, Germany*

Woke to a beautiful morning and went downstairs to grab coffee. Outside it's actually warm and sunny, like a summer's morning in the middle of November. I arranged a cab into town as I wanted to show Nial Freiburg. I have been once before and it's quite beautiful. The taxi arrived - German taxi-yellow-Merc with a blonde woman driving - reminded me of my old How We Live song *Working Girl* which was inspired by a German taxi-driver all those years ago. Nial and I wandered up the main street. It's Sunday and all the shops are closed. A mixed blessing really – I could have spent a fortune on Christmas tree decorations, light fittings, jewellery, art. I even saw a wrought iron garden gate which I quite fancied!... We found a little Italian café and ordered cappuccinos and sandwiches before walking under the medieval arch and over the river. The back streets of Freiburg contain streams of rapidly running water - probably coming down from the heavily wooded mountains which surround the town. The air has a refreshing unpolluted taste about it which feels tremendously uplifting. Nial and I had a great time just walking around. It would have been wise to have stayed here for tomorrow's day-off. Now why didn't I think of that?! Oh well. I can't imagine Mannheim to offer the same delights...

We returned to the gig and I was drawn to the perimeter fence by the sounds of Arabic music drifting across the air. There's a couple of apartment blocks which appear to be fenced off from the outside world and the place is some kind of gypsy or refugee enclave. Children were out playing and there was a big Turkish looking guy fixing a motorbike wheel whilst substantial women wearing Romany-style clothes seemed to be hanging washing and going about their business. Frantic Balkan and Arabic music constantly blared from the place which created a joyous bustling atmosphere despite the bits of supermarket trollies and other litter strewn about the place. Scott - our truck-driver - later discovered that it's social-housing for travellers.

Soundcheck was much more relaxed than yesterday in Trier and everyone seemed to have a good sound. Ian's in-ears are working again so all is well. Tonight we're on at 7pm so I didn't bother with dinner and went for pre-show power-nap. I was surprised again to find the gig more or less full by the time we went on stage. This is better than we imagined, and these audiences seem to be genuinely keen to hear our music. My sound was great until the third or fourth song when I kicked out on one of the big rhythm accents only to hear my monitors die and see my radio pack go skittering across the stage away from me. I ended up singing the next 3 or 4 songs with no monitors whilst discovering that the clip had come off the pack, then that the pack was dead, then that I couldn't get to the side of stage for a replacement pack, then that I couldn't find my ear-pieces to put em back in my ears. I sang to the best of my ability, monitoring off the hall as best I could, until I finally got myself sorted out by the penultimate song *Kayleigh* at which point Steve's guitar rig died! Pete and I rolled out the emergency 'bass and voice' version of *The Bell in the Sea* until the rig was fixed (quite quickly as it turned out!) and we played the last 2 songs with everything back on! None of this seemed to bother the crowd unduly and they seemed to stay with us throughout. Another triumph. That's 2 in a row! Mannheim next, after tomorrow's day off.

Went out and had another look at Deep Purple. Don Airey is, for me, the star of the show. What a player! Ian Gillan seems almost unfeasibly relaxed but I suppose after all those years on the road, it's unsurprising. Didn't seem to get recognized by anyone in the crowd tonight. Went back to the dressing room and chilled out with a tequila and red-bull in one hand and a Becks in the other, before returning to the bus where we all watched Lee Mack doing a two hour stand-up routine ("I remember my dear old Nan's last words: Hello Lee, why are you coming towards me with that hammer?" etc.) bloody funny. He also did the best impression of Eric Morecambe I have ever seen...

Went to bed, briefly upsetting a grumpy Mark Kelly who had been trying to get to sleep amidst guffaws from downstairs. I didn't realize anyone was trying to sleep - I'm usually the first to bed and all the curtains seemed to be open. Apart from that, it had been a perfectly brilliant day in every way.

Monday 15 November   *Mannheim:* Day Off

What can you say about Mannheim in the pissing down rain? It rained all day without pause. Spent most of it chilling in my room. Went out late-afternoon for a walk with Nial. Had a beer in the Café Flo which is a potentially groovy place spoiled only by the attitude of the staff. Is it any coincidence that Kurt is a christian name here in Germany? Discuss... Walked back to the hotel, hoods up, head down, and passed Fish coming the other way! Didn't realize it was him until he'd gone past and I don't think he noticed us at all. Didn't want to shout him back in this weather...

In the evening I went out with Nial, Rod, Pete (not Trewavas – the guitar tech, Pete Harwood), Markus and Yens, who was in fine form, proposing to waitresses, etc, and we had a very pleasant dinner washed down with white-beer. I was so full by the end of it, I could barely walk and vowed not to eat all day tomorrow.

Tuesday 16 November   *Mannheim*

Spent all night trying to get happy with the pillows. I don't want much - just not-too-high/not-too-low/not warm - but you'd be surprised how difficult that is to achieve even in the best hotels. Didn't manage breakfast but rolled out of bed around 11.00. Met up with Nial and went over the street for a quick cappuccino before he had to go to the gig. Went wandering and did a little bit of Xmas shopping for Vibes and L. I noticed that the Christmas Market is being constructed in Mannheim, so we should see a few open in Germany before the end of the tour... At least it wasn't raining today in Mannheim, but it was grey and overcast and noticeably much chillier than our excellent day in Freiburg. At 3.00 the bus arrived at the hotel to take us to the Arena. Soundcheck went well - we're putting *Sugar Mice* in tonight, so we'll see how that one goes down... Said a hello to Ian Paice who had turned up onstage to do something. He seemed pleasant and relaxed. Later said hello to Don Airey who complimented us on "that last song" which, he said "is a Tour-de-Force... it's nice to hear some applause outside from our dressing room". Nice chaps. Broke yesterday's vow by having dinner, which was nice (fish). Came back to the bus and had the customary power-nap before returning to the dressing room for a TV interview at 7.15. They never showed - apparently their car broke down - so I concentrated on getting strapped into the radio system which had parted company with me during last night's show. We decided to tape it all together and then to tape it to me so I bent over while Phil and Frenchie fiddled about round my backside for some minutes. Hem came into the dressing room to tell Mark that the keyboard rig had crashed and Mark told him to restart it then. He didn't seem worried - certainly not as phased as me anyway. Quite a few of our shows have been compromised in the past by keyboard rig failures (understatement) so I was understandably a little ill-at-ease as we mounted the stage. We really don't want to screw any of these shows up. As it turned out, everything worked during the show but I couldn't quite "get my mojo working" tonight. I did what was required but I couldn't quite get inside the songs. The gig was bigger at about 11k capacity and the crowd seemed a little disinterested. This reaction was more in keeping with the one I was expecting from the whole tour, so I guess it's an indication of how well the first two shows went. When we came off stage Roger Glover was waiting for us at the door into the backstage area – just come to say hi and that he hoped we were enjoying it. Nice of him.

Once DP were on stage Nial and I went out to have a listen. Their sound was good tonight out-front and, to my surprise, I noticed that the crowd were still, on the whole, not the most responsive crowd on the planet even in front of the main attraction, so maybe their reaction to us was understandable. Perhaps there's something in the water in Mannheim...

Wednesday 17 November *Memmingen, Germany*

Woke up at 8.00 and spent a few minutes sitting at the front of the bus writing the diary. We're parked up in a car park somewhere on the edge of Memmingen (I assume - it's where we're going) and everyone sounds like they're still asleep. It's pretty cold up here. I'll go downstairs and make a coffee. More later.

It turns out we were in a car park next to a skating rink. When Yens found out, he went skating. I just went and had a look at him zipping about like Uncle Fester on ice - his baggy jammy-bottoms fluttering in the air amidst German housewives and their young children.

Checked into the Hotel Engelkeller around 12.00 and made my way to room 207 for a much-needed shower. Went out later with Nial and Hem for a wander and had lunch in Hampton's café on the square along with Roderick who we ran into. Much confusion ensued over the order and I ended up eating half of another chap's lunch before the waitress turned up with what I'd actually ordered! Said chap's girlfriend got quite arsy about it, adding much quiet mirth to the occasion... We're down near Munich and Memmingen has plenty of Bavarian charm. The centre is pedestrianized so we walked around the shops amidst old stuccoed walls and the occasional onion-shaped church tower. Tried on some jumpers in C&A (it's all glamour!) but didn't buy anything. Found a bar and had a beer with a couple of DP's catering chefs who were already installed there. The catering girls appeared, fresh from shopping, and Lorraine showed us the tree decs she'd bought. Nial and I came back to the hotel and left Hem in there having a bite to eat. Hem later called to say that Don Airey had shown up and invited us over to his hotel for dinner. He'd said where but not when. Mark, Steve, Hem and myself went over around 8pm to discover Don and his pals already on the dessert course. They offered me the strange dessert which looked like an explosion in a Mr Whippy van and I had one spoonful before deciding against it. Don seemed very relaxed and content to let his pals lead the conversation – apparently they're members of his village out somewhere near Cambridge, and a thoroughly entertaining bunch. In my experience, you can usually judge a man by the quality of his friends. We stayed for half an hour before leaving 'em in peace. Rothers said he was past wanting to eat, so I took Mark back to the bar from this afternoon and we had a spot of dinner before returning to the hotel.

Thursday 18 November *Memmingen*

Didn't make it downstairs 'til 12.00 and said a quick hello to the crew who were getting on the bus for the load-in. The band are going over at 3.00. Nial seems relaxed but doesn't look too healthy. I think it's his age... I hope he doesn't immerse himself too fully in the rock n'roll. I wouldn't want to be responsible for him going to hospital (that's *my* job). I went back into town alone and bought some gloves - needless to say I have left mine at home...

I bumped back into Don's village pals and wished them good morning before going and having a spot of light lunch in Hamptons again. Ordered Chai Latte and the waitress brought coffee. Oh well. It's Germany. Outside in the square the fire-brigade were back working on the Christmas tree (no doubt a small cottage still blazes on the outskirts of town) and the lights were on. Took a couple of pics with my crappy iPhone camera. I had left the good camera at home. Doh! I'll ask L to bring it with her to Berlin on Saturday. Perhaps she could bring a sweatshirt for his Nial too – he's come on tour with summer clothes. Went back to the hotel to pack and had a chat with Linette on the phone. All's well at home although Vibes has taken to putting a chair on top of the table and sitting on it. He's very proud of himself and obviously feels the need to be elevated, but if he falls off, L's concerned that he might break his head! He came to the phone and said, "I love you daddy - bye!" which is great. It's obviously lovely to be told he loves me, but it's equally lovely to know that, although he hasn't forgotten me, my absence doesn't appear to upset him at all.

We climbed aboard the bus for soundcheck and were taken back to the ice-rink where Yens was skating yesterday morning. It has now been transformed into a gig although there were still a few tell-tale exposed sections of ice-floor backstage yet to be boarded over. As you might imagine, it was pretty cold in there. We were shown to our dressing room - the bar, an American-style sports-bar complete with neons on the wood-panelled wall - and soon made our way to the chilly stage where we'd decided to knock through a song called *The Damage*. Unfortunately this involved me playing guitar and therefore having to take my jacket off. Shivered through the song whilst delighting in my guitar sound which is fabulous. Couldn't hear much else though. Ice-rink acoustics leave something to be desired... In the end we decided against *The Damage* tonight, agreeing to run it again at tomorrow's soundcheck. I'll believe it when I hear it...

Went to catering and had duck in orange sauce. Very civilized, considering the somewhat basic surroundings. Catering lady Lorraine said they had been plagued by "power struggles in every sense of the phrase".

Went back to the bus for a nap and emerged around 7.00 to see the place filling up. Returned to the sports bar for a tequila and red-bull to get into the zone before getting dressed and strapped into the radio system.

The gig went very well tonight. Good reaction from the crowd. All the gear worked and we returned to the dressing room in celebratory mood. Probably consumed a bit too much across the sports-bar and went to bed feeling distinctly sloshed.

Friday 19 November *Munich*

Munich. Awoke to discover the distinctive BMW building (like an upside down rocket... or 4 towers of cans depending on your p.o.v) across the ring-road on a rainy grey day. We are parked outside tonight's gig, the Munich Olympiahalle. Made my way inside. It's a fabulous hall – probably holds 10,000 people or more. Had coffee and washed. Asked Frenchie if there's any chance of someone running me into town and, after a few delays and false starts (we couldn't find each other... this place is BIG) I climbed into a mini-bus with Karl, the runner, who was very talkative in a good way. He told me that everyone he has met over the years were, without exception, very nice people. "That 50 Cent! He is such a nice guy! I tell you honestly, I would take him home to meet my mother! Alice Cooper, also a very nice man!" etc. Karl drove me round Munich showing me the sights and giving me insights into its history –"Here is the law courts, built by the Nazi's. Everything here is deliberately built on a large scale to make you feel small when you go inside – the doors, the ceilings... even the sinks in the washrooms and the taps are huge to intimidate you. Today this town is the fucking capital of the cops. If you lose your laptop, you would probably get it back same day. My best and dearest friend is my lawyer. A wonderful man! In this town, believe me, you need a good lawyer."

We arrived in the centre of town and Karl dropped me next to a small market where I wandered around and bought traditional Christmas decorations. This Christmas will be our first in our cottage on the village green and I'm looking forward to seeing the place trimmed up with decs from all over Europe which I have collected touring across the years. Yeah.

I took a cab back to the Olympiahalle. It was driven by an Indian guy who enthused about Deep Purple all the way there. "Ah the 70's! Now that was a time for music. Deep Purple. Fantastic! Not like today, all this clockwork stuff. No expression in anything anymore..."

Back inside the gig I was interviewed by a journalism student called Robert who gave me quite a thorough grilling about what it's like to get old in a rock n'roll band. He kept asking why we haven't split up and I kept trying to give him an adequate answer. I said that the best thing to do is to die young really. Unfortunately, for me, that is no longer an option. These journalists think that stars owe the world a legend at any price. The fact is, we all have families, mothers, fathers, partners, children and a mind, body and soul to try to look after as well as our music. We ignore these facts at our peril and, more often than not, at our self-destruction. There was a time when I wanted to be a "star". I walk out on these big stages and I feel I could hold my own up-against the best of them, but we simply never had the hits and so it hasn't happened to me. I have a good life and I don't get bugged by idiots on the streets, I don't feel the need for a limo to get me to the shops, or a private jet to get me from show to show (or home every night like U2). We make the music we want to make, WHEN we want to make it and I'm free. It could be worse... We also have the best fans of any band, many of whom I would be happy to relax and have a drink with. Anyway, I digress...

Soundcheck sounded bloody fantastic. This hall has a perfect acoustic for rockn'roll and I could tell from the stage that the sound out-front would be great. I went and had my customary hour on the shelf before returning to the Olympiahalle and our dressing room. Said hi to Lucy who has flown in today and also to Mark's partner, Angie. As we were getting ready, Roger Glover appeared in our dressing room to wish us luck. He looked me straight in the eye and said, "You can sing, man!" Thanks Roger. He also told us two jokes. "A rock n'roll manager is buried up to his chin in sand in the desert. What is wrong? ....Not enough sand," and "How do you know when an Agent is lying? He walks into the room and says hello." Frenchie later told us that DP had asked if we'd be up for a photograph with them before they go on stage tonight. We're slowly getting to know everyone in band and crew.

Showtime! It was a cracker. My sound was terrific and the band played really well on that line where control meets edge. During the later part of *Cover My Eyes* all the PA died! I simultaneously thought, "Oh no," and "Alleluya!" Accidents like this can often lift a crowd, depending on how the band reacts to it, and how long the power stays off. I raised a glass to the crowd, shrugged my shoulders and grinned. The PA was soon restored and from then on they were on our side. We left the stage at the end to widespread cheering across this huge hall. Lovely. I was wet with sweat once again. It's good to sweat again. I changed my shirt for the photograph with DP. Finally met Ian Gillan who made a beeline to shake my hand, and Steve Morse, who I have never met either. His guitar-tech tells me he fixes jet-engines in his spare time! Apparently he's restoring a MIG fighter at home... There are certainly some characters in rock n'roll. I feel somewhat unimpressive by comparison. Perhaps I should start work on a suspension bridge or build a rocket on the village green...

Went out to the mixing desk to watch DP's show. The sound was great tonight and they were going down phenomenally with the crowd. Caught most of the show before being pulled away. I would have liked to have had a beer with Joerg Baeker but it wasn't to be.

Saturday 20 November *Nurnberg*

Woke and looked out of the front window to see what I thought looked like the set for a movie about Hitler's Nuremberg Rallies. In fact, it was the real thing! Went to catering and had a bit of bacon and a fried egg with a few baked beans and then went for a walk with Nial into the neighbouring "Zeppelin field" where Hitler was presented to his troops on rallies and other ceremonial occasions. We walked around the arena and stood on the very spot from which he would make his impassioned, insane declarations to adoring masses. Wow...

We bumped into Roderick, our out-front sound engineer and one-time studio manager/assistant/engineer and walked back together. I split up with them so they could concern themselves with the load-in and spent a while on the bus writing this diary before going walk-about in search of the museum which would put all of this in context. I took a long walk past what used to be a lake - now drained - and along the Grosse Strasse a wide road consisting of granite blocks 30m wide by 1500m long which leads to the 'information centre', a huge semi-circular arched structure like the Colliseum in Rome. I walked up to the massive structure and along its interior walkway beneath the arches. There didn't seem to be a way into the enormous edifice and I spent some time walking around its circular perimeter before happening across a parked police car. I was given directions further along to a modern entrance-way where I walked along a corridor of steel and glass into the museum. I should have bought a book but, to be honest, I'm not sure if I WANT a book called **Fascination and Terror** on my bookshelves at home. I have my own fascinations and they are much more about beauty and peace than the perverted obsessions and theories of those old nut-jobs from 30's Germany. Now I'm here, I feel compelled to know more about what surrounds me - hence the walk - but I don't want any of this coming home with me. I would rather clean it from my shoes first. In the final analysis it all comes across as so much folly. We are on this planet for 90 years if we're lucky. Why don't we enjoy it while we're here? What is it that compels an entire country to embark upon forcing its will on a world which is already perfect and ultimately will shrug off their edifices, monuments and new societies. Time passes... and today the eerie and monstrous cheering which echoes around this place is simply that of the football supporters getting into their stride for the home match between Nurnberg and Kaiserslautern FC this afternoon in the neighbouring stadium (also commenced in 1936 but now looking more like Old Trafford). I bought my tour guide machine in English and held it to my ear as I walked round the museum, learning about the rise of Hitler's National Socialism, how he managed somehow to change German law and dismantle democracy unchallenged by any of the systems of government and law which simply seemed to roll over at the force of his legal sleight-of-hand

and cult of personality. It was one long barrel of laughs - **Mein Kampf**, the concentration camps, the conquest of France etc, although the ultimate horrors and disaster of the Russian campaign seemed not to be mentioned much. My tour was suddenly cut short by a txt from Frenchie saying, "Fancy a soundcheck?" I looked at my phone to see that the time was 3.18... As I stared at the screen I realized that my iPhone had, once again, reset the time to UK time (don't know!) which meant that it was in fact 4.18 and I should have been on stage since 4.00.

I hurried back along Albert Speers big granite road, along the banks of the lake and back to the show to find the band all but finished with sound check. Apologising profusely I checked my gear and sounds and all seemed fine. As I left the stage Frenchie ambled up and said, "D'you want to go to the football match across the road?" ...seemed like a good idea. We'd missed most of it, but I wasn't doing much and we could still catch the last half-hour. Went over with Ian and Pete and was met by a very nice chap called Gerhardt who seemed to be running the stadium! He took us to the VIP stand and we had excellent view of the match. Nurnburg were losing 3-0 to Kaiserslautern. Footballers have suddenly started to look like young boys to me! Jeez, now I must be REALLY old... We saw a goal to Nurnburg (3-1) and then a penalty awarded in the 80th minute which would have put the game at 3-2. Unfortunately he hit the crossbar and so the game ended in a 3-1 defeat. I enjoyed the experience though. I can never get over the intensity of colour at football matches – the green of the turf under floodlighting and the colours of the strip on the players seems almost trippily-rich. If you have ever been to a game live, you'll know what I mean.

After the game Gerhardt took us to a huge VIP bar/restaurant (like a shopping mall - they have a lot of VIP's...) and bought us a beer (I say "us" I guess it's the "royal we" – Ian and Pete had coffee). There was an enormous food bar/buffet running as well which he invited us to help ourselves from. We declined the food although it looked great. After the beer, he showed us downstairs and back out of the stadium. As an afterthought he said, "Would you like to see the pitch?". We would like to see the pitch. And so he led us back in and onto the turf where we stood in the centre of the pitch the players had only just vacated. I have never stood on a professional football pitch before (and I'm certainly never likely to play on one!). The grass was in amazing condition. Almost like a bowling green. It was inconceivable that 22 blokes had been tearing up the thing in studded boots for 90 minutes. I could do with some of that in the garden... Ian observed that it looked a lot smaller standing on it than sitting in the stand. It felt about half the size down there. It's still impressive though, how seemingly-effortlessly the players kick a ball from one end almost to the other in one volley. We posed for a photograph and left the stadium walking back across the narrow roadway into the gig.

Had a spot of dinner (coq-au-vin) and back to the bus for a lie down. That would have been enough of a day for most people, but I still had a show to go to! Received a txt from L. She's already in the hotel in Berlin having arrived safely with little Vibes who has been a very good boy all week, bless him.

On the night the gig seemed busy for our set. I could tell the room wasn't sounding as good as the Olympiahalle in Munich, but as I said before, that's a fabulous hall. All in all, the gig went well and, once again, the band came offstage with the feeling that this tour has the potential to revive our fortunes in Germany and claw back some of the fans who deserted us when they heard, and couldn't cope with **Brave**. Maybe with the passing of time, they'll see this show and reconsider. They might be ready for **Brave** now - especially if they check out **Marbles** and **AOS** on the way to it.

Sunday 21 November *Berlin:* Day Off

Slept fitfully, trying not to watch the clock as the night progressed and the bus rumbled along beneath me where I lay on my shelf. Bus driver Paul is going to drop me off at the Berlin hotel when we make Berlin (e.t.a. 9am-ish) so I was keen not to oversleep. I had set an alarm, but I've never been good at relaxing when I have an alarm set. I just wait for it all night.

At 8.30 I got up and sat downstairs with the driver as we entered this extraordinary city. It was foggy and everything appeared silver while the empty winter trees presented themselves as black skeletons either side of the road. We turned right on to Bismarck Strasse, a wide and Roman-straight boulevard which disappeared into the distance and into the morning mist, and straight on we went until, after 20 minutes or so, we made a short detour around the Brandenburg Gate to rejoin it on the old East Side. Paul pointed out the two lines of cobbles along the road, now the only clue to where the Berlin wall used to be.

We eventually pulled up outside the Radisson Hotel next to the Ferris wheel and alongside the canal. There's an enormous glass tube in the centre of the hotel which rises to its full height and contains a mega-aquarium full of tropical fish. Pretty surreal. Fish in the sky...

Unaccompanied by tour-manager Frenchie (who was still sleeping – the main party won't check in until 12.00) I underwent the traditional "never heard of you" ceremony which one must undergo when checking into hotels without tour-managers (group-bookings – try Marillion, try Jordache, try Lee, Mosley, Trinifold travel? No Hogarth, try Hoggarth, no, I don't have my passport. My girlfriend is already checked into the hotel with my son, room 3123 – well how else would I know? Yes, I know she's called Petersen and not Hogarth, that's because she's my girlfriend, I couldn't find a girlfriend with the same surname. I just want a room key so that I don't have to disturb her. I see, it's against the rules. Okay, I have my own room also. Hogarth. Yes, I know it doesn't say Steve on my credit card. It's not Neil, it's Nial, he's my son. No, the other one. Can I just go and see my family please!!!) Eventually she took pity on the sleepy, dishevelled, patiently sighing creature before her and said she would allow me into the lift to the third floor (which won't go to any floor you don't have a key for...) but I would have to knock when I arrived. I made my way to room 3123 where I found L and vibes already up and on their way to breakfast. It was great to be together again. L looked fantastic and Little Vibes seems to have matured a little and is behaving well and charming everyone he meets – especially the girls. He gave me big hugs and I carried him down to breakfast.

After breakfast we got ourselves together and went out for a walk. Amused to find Frenchie stuck behind the glass doors of the lift with all his bags as it refused to go up or down. We eventually managed to join him and to get the lift back down to the ground where he said he had already been 3 times. We went out and eventually settled on the idea of going on a tourist boat which was moored alongside the hotel. This turned out to be a good call. Vibes was thrilled to be on a boat and kept saying "more boat" just in case we got off. The boat took us along past beautiful Parthenon-like classical buildings, museums, art galleries and, eventually past the Reichstag (old and now new centre of German government) with its new Norman-Parkinson-designed glass dome glistening in the sunlight. Old postcards on the street show aerial photographs of Berlin just after the war and it gives us all hope to witness that so much can be done to bring cities back from the dead after the insanity of war subsides. Wars aren't won. They are declared by some kind of collective madness which overtakes foolhardy governments, and they are ended when the madness subsides - possibly out of mutual exhaustion. In between, a lot of people die, or have their lives forever ruined, and their cities annihilated. Then, with time, it all gets rebuilt by future generations who may remember the historical timeline of the wars but never quite remember exactly why it all came to pass. East Berlin now looks markedly more beautiful than West Berlin to my eyes. Who'da thought? The first time I came here in the early 80's, the wall was up and the Reichstag looked like a big black scarred and bullet-peppered edifice that someone had shot with a shotgun the size of a street. Over the wall was a space which killed you, and beyond that, East Berlin, dark, drab, miserable and sad.

To our delight, a waitress on the boat served hot chocolate, so we sat on the open upper deck in the sunshine and watched the monuments slide by. Vibes later discovered the wake in the water behind the boat and delighted in watching the water boiling and bubbling. I couldn't help but contemplate what I'd do if he fell in (truly unthinkable – but you can't help it) so, to his annoyance I kept an arm round him or a fistful of his coat from behind. The boat returned to the quayside by the hotel and we met up with Nial outside the hotel. L tried on Russian hats (which I think suit her very much and she thinks are too big) while Vibes delighted in running into his brother for a while before conking out and going to sleep in his pushchair.

We went to a steakhouse nearby to have a spot of lunch together. I had steak and a baked potato and couldn't swallow it! I occasionally get this thing where I can't swallow. It's very peculiar. Will have to go to the docs when I get home and see if they can find out why it happens. Eventually got over the non-swallowing thing and managed eating and drinking no problem. Vibes woke up just as we were paying the bill, so we took him back to the hotel room and ordered a spaghetti-bolognese on room service for him. Around 5 we went down to the hotel bar and had a cocktail whilst Vibes busied himself among the pebbles he'd found by the lifts. Chatted to Lucy, George and members of the crew as they passed on their way out and into the hotel.

Ate Sushi at the hotel restaurant (I can thoroughly recommend the Californian rolls at the Raddisson) before returning to the room to put his lordship to bed. It was a struggle – he seems to sense when we have a particular desire to be alone together! Patience, Mr h...

Monday 22 November   *Berlin*

L treated me to another hour in bed (thankyou, thankyou!) and took Vibes down to the breakfast room. I was still dozing when they returned and they were both patient while I got myself together. There was still time to get downstairs before breakfast finished so we all went downstairs and I ordered a fresh ham and cheese omelette from the chap at the bar. Lovely. Ate it in between taking Vibes on little excursions round the buffet to see what was going on.

The weather outside was raining quite hard which was a shame as it was our last chance to groove around in Berlin and we're reliably informed that the Christmas market will open today. We killed time for a while until the weather improved slightly, then wrapped up and braved rainy Berlin, borrowing two umbrellas from the hotel concierge. The Christmas market was a short walk away. It's open but many of the stalls are still readying themselves. Vibes rode a little carousel with me while L shivered patiently in the rain. We wandered around the market and bought a few tree decorations before returning to the hotel with a sleeping little boy in the pushchair. Had fantastic (and fantastically expensive!) hot chocolates at the hotel bar as the amazing tropical fish glided leisurely above us, along with a scuba-diver who was also in the tank doing a bit of cleaning. L said she was jealous – she yearns to dive again.

Soon it was time for soundcheck so I packed my things (I'm going overnight) and checked out of the room I never used. "There should be no extras – I never went through the door!"

"You never slept!" said the receptionist, full of admiration – this is Berlin after all. The fact is that I'd booked a room just in case Vibes wouldn't sleep then I'd have somewhere to escape to. Hadn't needed it. Decadent or what?!

We climbed aboard the tour-bus which had come to take us to the gig, much to the delight of little Vibes who LOVES busses. We went upstairs so we could watch our progress from the upper deck and I showed L and V where I sleep. We drove through rainy East Berlin to the gig and went straight downstairs to soundcheck. Linette and his lordship found a seat out on the left-wing and Vibes nodded along in time to the drums. He's already a rocker. All sounded well on stage so soundcheck was brief.

Took L and V up onstage to have a look at the gig from my mic-position and then went to our dressing room until a cab could be arranged to take them back to the hotel. They'll come back for the show and - with a bit of luck - they can watch from the mixing desk. On the way to the cab I ran into John (Richard B's former keyboard tech who had toured with us in the h Band days). He's now living in Berlin and was helping out on the local crew. I never met a human being who so resembles - spiritually and physically - John Lydon; the same fiercely-playful intelligently-dangerous intensity. Good natured always (unlike Lydon!) but you get the feeling you wouldn't want to cross him!

After my darlings left in the cab, I went to the bus and slept for an hour, as usual, before the show. My body goes into another mode for tours and I find I need sleep between 6 and 7pm. I can fall quite quickly into sleep at this time, and I awake fairly promptly around 7.00pm feeling ready (or as ready as I ever am – a mixture of anticipation and responsible-dread) for the show ahead. I have entered a new phase of the tour now where I seem unable to quite live-up to my own expectations in terms of performance, sincerity, or vocal dexterity. Perhaps I'm getting worse, or perhaps I expect more of myself, perhaps the sense of adventure has faded, but I still remain acutely aware of how much there is to gain from this situation, and every nuance missed, lyric not "lived" but merely sung, seems like a failure of duty. That's not very rock n'roll is it? I think that, out of the cliche of sex, drugs and rock n'roll, I have a new set of parameters which are more to do with drink, neurosis, sexual frustration and something which is neither hard-rock, rock n'roll, prog, folk, soul, in fact I have no idea what label I would place on our output. We have developed a need to excel beyond anything we have created in the past together. I have absolutely no idea where it goes from here. We must do something radical or risk a cul-de-sac. I also don't know whether anyone else in the band feels this. Nurse! The screens!

Well, the gig was a bit weird for me... I said hello after *King* in the usual way. Guten Abend Berlin! (vague cheery response). Vi gehets? (boos). Dunno why they booed that and it phased me somewhat. No one so far has managed to explain it! I felt that I couldn't get into the place where I exist as a performer after that, and I kinda limped along. Even before *Kayleigh* when I had the golden opportunity to mention that this - the band's biggest ever hit - was recorded in Berlin, I faltered and said something vaccuous instead. Oh well. You can only do yer best. And I do. It hasn't been good enough lately.

When we came offstage, I was to discover that L hadn't seen too much of the show. It had been a bit too much for Vibes from *King* onwards so she'd had to take him backstage. Another cab was arranged and vibes ran around in the dressing room in good spirits to the general entertainment of all. He did really well as it was hours past his bedtime. I saw the family off, sharing a cab with Lucy and went out front to have a look at DP. They are steadily improving across these gigs (just as I seem to be steadily declining!) sounding tighter and sonically improving too. It couldn't happen to a nicer bunch of guys. I wish them well.

Tuesday 23 November *Rostock*

Not pretty here. Out of the front of the bus I see typical Eastern-European drab ugly tower-blocks amidst grey cold skies. What's the opposite of the Maldives? Rostock! Had a coffee on the bus before braving the rain and the cold across the car-park, past the 3 buses and 5 trucks and through a big metal side door into what could have been a warehouse, steelworks, or slaughterhouse, into the gig. Down a couple of corridors to catering for a cup of coffee. Can't remember much about today, apart from the two heavily wrapped characters who seemed to huddle in the rain by the big steel door – autograph collectors I assume, all day long in the rain. This might represent a high-point in their lives... Do I know how lucky I am? Occasionally, but only momentarily...

I started to feel pains in my stomach and spent most of the rest of the day in and out of the toilet. After soundcheck I felt distinctly unwell and retired to the bus to sleep. Lying in the dark with my stomach aching and my body feeling strangely opaque and without energy, I tried not to worry, but the thought of having to roar around in front of several thousand people in a couple of hours was more than a little daunting. If I had a proper job, I'd have taken the day off and stayed in bed. I downed a few doses of Pepto Bismol and hoped for the best. By showtime I was optimistic from experience that I'd be fine once I got up there. I have gone up there feeling MUCH worse than this and still got away with it.

Back to the dressing room for Tequila & Red Bull (tastes horrible, does a job), into the stage clothes, and onto the stage for *The Invisible Man*. I gave it everything I'd got and the reaction overall was good by the end of the show. Afterwards I showered and said hello to Jim and Sweets who had driven down from Sweden, before making excuses and getting back onto the bus to bed. I later learned that DP had invited us to their dressing room for drinks. The rest of the band went. Typical of me to miss that one...

Wednesday 24 November *Braunschweig*

Woken by Nial around 10.00. We had agreed to get up and not miss breakfast in catering. I normally appear as they're clearing it away. We went over to the gig - a big grey circular thing which resembles a gun emplacement on a destroyer. The surroundings are immediately more attractive than yesterdays; I could see a single gothic bell-tower standing in a park, not seemingly connected to anything – looks like one of Carl Glover's album covers. I'm feeling much better today.

Had a bit of breakfast and then decided to take a walk into town with Nial and see what's going on. We walked past the tower which looks as though it was once joined to a nearby church with a bit missing – either the RAF or some other form of demolition. We walked past another big church into a wide square where there were trams parked and a huge Parthenon-like building (all these towns have a Rathouse (town hall) at their centre – maybe this was it...). Couldn't resist a quick look into a double-fronted shop called Afghan World – mostly rough-woven clothes including a pair of "genie" trousers which had my name all over them, but they'd have probably looked daft on me so I resisted. No evidence of Afghan coats, Afghan dogs, or opium, so we moved on. We entered a pedestrianized area of boutiques, department stores, the usual stuff found in every European town centre now and Nial decided to return to the venue for the load-in.

I decided I'd stay in town and have a wander. Found a newsagent and bought a copy of **The Independent** - a shadow of its former self - I remember when it was worth buying **The Independent** on the strength of its amazing photography (and the quality of the printing) alone. The headline is of the attack by North Korea upon a civilian populated island in South Korea. That Kim Jong Ill isn't just ill by name. He probably feels the need for one last paragraph in the history books before he pegs out. But the bastards always live forever. What is it about the obvious historically-proven futility of war as a means to ANY end (that I can see, at least) that these dictators fail to grasp? It doesn't matter whether you look back 5 years, 50, or 150, it just doesn't achieve anything.

Went to Starbucks and had a Chai latte with the intention of reading the paper, but bumped into Jens sitting in the window and chatted to him about this very subject (he reckons it's all about money and the need to keep stimulating the arms business by replacing weapons – it's a convincing motive in the absence of anything more moral) for a while until he left to get on with the show.

I walked around Braunschweig, taking a few photographs until driven back by the cold air to the gig. I had agreed to proof-read the new forthcoming *Web Fanclub Magazine* which took most of the afternoon. That Jim Sanders, sure generates a lot of words! It looked great as usual. There can't be many fan club publications so well put together as ours. It must take him AGES!

Soundcheck was fine. I hung around to help replace a switch in the midi-cricket bat afterwards. It's been a while since I did any soldering so I quite fancied doing it myself, much to the irritation of Nial who would rather have fixed it himself for me. While we were fiddling about I said hello to Don Airey and his tech/son Mike. Lovely people. Mike wanted a listen to the cricket bat so I passed him the headphones. He was amused and impressed. We're gradually getting to know DP's crew now. Chatted to the monitor engineer Rob (who's also a good bloke with a great face), equally fascinated by the cricket bat device. We went to catering for dinner and I had fish-curry (kill or cure) which was very nice. These caterers are awfully good. Finished proof-reading the mag and emailed my few comments before hitting the shelf!

Gig wasn't great for me. Went on-stage without my "in-ears" in my ears and had to fish around for them around the back of my head. Later lost 'em altogether and didn't get it sorted out for a song or two. Didn't help with the "getting-going of the mojo" and I didn't think I sang too well tonight. My voice is starting to feel strained and isn't going where I'm sending it without a struggle.

Pitching seemed difficult tonight, and the crowd seemed reserved. Naturally I'll always blame myself for a low crowd response, just as I feel inclined to privately take the credit for a good one. It's not quite that simple of course. During DP's set I said a quick hello side-of-stage to Steve Morse who said he thought it was a tough crowd for them tonight too. He briefly took me on one side and said, "You've got a great voice, man," before returning to the stage. Cheers Mr Morse. He looks nothing like John Thaw...

Back on the bus, watched some old **Mock the Week** episodes on Dave (TV Channel). Jeez, that Frankie Boyle takes freedom of speech to the acid limit: "The Queen is now so old that her pussy is haunted!" She should put him in the tower and stretch HIM a little. Funny though... It wasn't long after that he strangely disappeared from our screens. Apparently he'd said Olympic gold-medallist swimmer Rebecca Adlington had a face that looked like it was reflected in the back of a spoon, and that did it! My guess is that there was a quiet word from the Palace to find a pretext for his exile.

Still feeling a little under-par I thought I'd get to bed (shelf) sooner than later.

Thursday 25 November   *Oldenburg:* Day Off

Fell out of the bus into the cold air of Oldenburg. The slightest few flakes of snow were falling. Don't remember this place at first glance. Was not to remember it at second glance either.

Checked into a curious hotel - the Altera - a boutique hotel in the centre of town. Room 509. Nice. Has a place next to the bed to charge your iPhone or play your iPod through a little speaker. I stuck my iPhone on it and put the music on random shuffle. Spookily, first up was Frank Sinatra singing *Let It Snow*. Showered and waited in for L to call me. She's in Banbury shopping with the boy. Spoke to her. 5 inches of snow in Yorkshire, apparently, and snow forecast in the village later in the week. She's bought him a red sledge. Let's hope they get enough to give it a whirl.

I went into town and bumped into Rothers in the Christmas Market. He directed me to where Nial, Pete and Markus were having a Glühwein at a little stand, so I joined them for a while before going for a look round. Bought a little light-up house for Vibes (yes, another one) at a stall. The lady serving was from South Korea. We had a brief chat. She said she was very worried about the situation there. I'm not surprised. It must be awful to have your country on the brink of war with a regime run by a lunatic. No God of course, or these fuckers would choke to death suddenly on their own caviar. It never seems to happen. I told her I sincerely hope the situation blows over without further bloodshed. I could see how worried she is and I had to choke back a tear myself as I said it. What a world.

I found a café and spent the entire afternoon writing this diary, which has slipped somewhat since Berlin. Around 6.00 I walked back and saw a long-sleeved black t-shirt that I liked the look of so I went inside the shop and bought two before returning to the room. This took a while because I tried 'em on and kept getting distracted – there was some interesting stuff in the shop but, y'know, blokes get worn out with clothes shopping pretty quickly. I might go back tomorrow...

Well, we were all due in the hotel lobby at 7.20 to go to the Irish pub and celebrate Steve Rothery's birthday, so I managed a quick call home to Linette before I had to run. All seems fine. Sofi's popping in later. I was hoping to catch her on the phone but time is against me. The heating is working (just as well...). Vibes sounds happy, although he doesn't want to speak to me on the phone today. Kids are great – they don't do ANYTHING out of consideration for other people's feelings. You know where you've got 'em!

Met up with everyone (band and crew) and went round the corner to the Irish Pub and occupied one corner of the upstairs room. Paul and Scott - our bus-driver and truck driver respectively - had already been drinking for a good part of the day and were in rowdy good spirits, much to the amusement of all. Paul is a revelation – he's been very quiet so far into this tour and I have had difficulty sussing him out. Some people are two people – the sober one, and the one with a drink inside them. I tend to prefer the person with the drink inside them, although I can think of a few examples where this isn't true. Some people should never have a drink. Some people need a drink to show themselves. This seems a shame. I'm not sure if it changes me much these days... I just get a bit more amorous (which rarely seems to help – I'm probably amorous enough sober) and a bit more honest (likewise!). Well, we toasted Steve's birthday and had a spot of dinner – I had beef and Guinness pie and it was very nice. I finished Ian M's chips for him and they were also yummy – like school chips. I then finished Steve's apple crumble for him. Scavenger singer... At one point I thought it was going to get out of hand with the drivers, but the food seemed to calm 'em down a bit. Nial seemed quiet... he said he was tired. So was I, so we walked back to the hotel around 10.00 and to our respective rooms.

BBC World News 24 seemed to have inexplicably disappeared from TV channel 55 which left me with no choice but to watch CNN if I wanted English. CNN irritates the living daylights out of me – it's like some kind of pretentiously highbrow presentation of "news" (not news, but endless over-simplified and obviously-biased presentation of showbiz dressed up as fact and an obsession with global finance without ever shedding any real light on anything. Let's face it, those bankers don't go public with the bottom-line until it's been safely capitalized upon by themselves and exhausted of any potential profit at which point it's deemed fit for consumption by the proles. That's when we - the public - hear about what's going down. It's more or less the same with the news. Sort it out under the table and then let the public have the filtered dregs in the Press Release. The chattering classes (I include myself) form their/our opinions from the news and we debate it in homes and in pubs, but I believe (especially since Iraq) we have no more chance of knowing what's going on than a peasant in a field in China. Paranoid? As John Helmer once said, "Maybe a paranoid's just someone in full possession of the facts." These days I tend to agree.

L never called, so I dropped a txt or two. Turns out Sofi's still there and they're into girlie-chat-quiet-time. That's good. It also ruled out any chance of talking to L before half-twelve by which time I was selfishly grumpy and tired. Slept well, though.

Friday 26 November *Oldenburg*

Woke up with a sore throat and back-ache at 11.00 and chatted to L for a while before checking out. The boys all piled onto the bus to the venue at 12.30. I couldn't see the point so I'm sitting in the hotel café drinking cappuccino. I'll pay up and go and have another look at Oldenburg. As Mosley said yesterday, "You could spend a lot of money here..." He's right – I'd better be restrained. Ha...

Well, I have been. Went and had a look at some boots for L for Christmas. Turns out they were 350 euros. That's a lot if she doesn't like 'em. And a long way back to swap 'em. Went back to the clothes shop and tried on sweatshirts. They looked great 'til I put them on. Gave up. Came to a hair salon to do the roots. Time better spent... Just sat down in the chair and the girl was about to mix the goo to slap on my head when I received a txt from Frenchie reminding me it's ten past three! Time flies! I have to be at the gig for soundcheck at 4.00m so I made profound apologies and leapt back out of the salon.

Took a cab to the gig but, as so often happens with taxis, they only know where the front door is. I was dropped outside the gig (another huge conference hall) but couldn't see any evidence of buses, trucks, or rock n'roll. There was, however, a hotel called The City Club hotel next to the venue, so I dived in there to escape the cold and txted Frenchie who came over to point me at the right door.

Inside, in catering, I managed to find a bit of old roast pork left over from lunch which was absolutely yummy. Apologies to vegetarian readers out there... The caterers on this tour are called Gig-a-Bite and, although we haven't taken out caterers on our own tours for a few years now, they're better than any I remember us having back then. If we should ever need on-road cooks, we'll be on the phone!

Soundcheck went well after a slightly dodgy sound yesterday. My sound today is really exciting while very well defined. Phil Brown, our monitor engineer, doesn't rest on his laurels but continues to work on everyone's stage mix each day. I can hear mine constantly improving, despite not having asked. Cheers Phil (AND I owe him money). Back to the bus for a quick half-hour "on charge" before returning for a radio interview with Radio Oldenburg and then on to stage.

Now THIS was to be a good show. I felt much better tonight and much more at ease with myself than I have been for the last couple of gigs. The crowd seemed up for it, astonishingly clapping along to the first verse of *King* (only the second song in the set!). I think I would have remained in the zone anyway, but a good crowd always helps. Fantastic show all-round.

Cheers Oldenburg - I look forward to coming back.

Saturday 27 November *Hamburg*

Rolled out of bed and into the gig to grab a bit of breakfast around 10.30. Asked Frenchie to call me a cab into town. I love Hamburg and I was keen to go and have a wander round.

I was dropped at one corner of the lake by the Rathaus (town-hall) and saw a big sign saying 'Oakley' outside a shopping mall. Sadly, I have lost my Oakley sun-specs somewhere, I suspect, in Memmingen, so I went inside the mall and eventually found the Oakley shop and bought another pair. Ouch. You don't want to lose too many pairs of Oakleys...

Popped into Starbucks and grabbed a Chai latte to take out, walking through to the Rathaus square where there was a Christmas Market in full swing, packed with Saturday shoppers and tourists. There were many stalls selling food – cheese, meat, cooked delicacies, freshly baked breads and cakes, and drink – glüwien, egg-punch, beer, hot chocolate, along with little stalls selling tree decorations, wood carvings, knitted woolens, candles and, of course, bottle-brushes. I never understood the origin of so many bottle-brush specialists here in Germany. There seems to be a stall on every market selling every imaginable type of them. This is obviously a country which cannot bear the sight of a merely RINSED bottle, but must thoroughly scour the inside before reusing or disposing. Commendable, I say. Let's bring bottle-brush culture to the UK soon!

From the Rathaus I remembered my way back to the Marriott Hotel where we have stayed on previous tours, when playing the nearby Markthalle. There's a little shopping arcade beneath the Marriott which contains a train-set shop. Went and had a look at the miniature trains. At two and a half, little Vibes is probably a bit young for a train set this Christmas. They're not cheap and he'll probably bury it in the garden. Perhaps next year...

I went and tried the hair salon called Fon in the arcade. Kristina, the manageress, remembered me from a year ago. Nice. Got a worrying txt from L saying she's feeling dizzy and nauseous. Oh shit. Let's hope it's not the beginning of another illness. After Portugal I know only too well how hard it will be for her to be totally alone with a two year old while unwell. And how hard it is for me to be living away with that knowledge.

Finally got the roots done and returned to the lake where there was a Winter Market also set up - full of bars and shops selling cooked candied almonds ("Mandeln"), which have an unmistakable spicy warm festive smell. The Germans sure know how to do Christmas.

Took a cab back to the Sporthalle in time for soundcheck. The usual routine of soundcheck, dinner and nap, then pre-show tipple (in Oldenburg, I tried a tequila and Becks mix. Really horrible, but it did put me in a good place...) and up on to stage. Again we had a good show – although I wonder if I'm looking a little too desperate to please. I guess that's just because it's not our crowd and I can't just throttle back and feel the love. I sensed a lot of Marillion fans in the crowd tonight and again, we were listened to by the many thousands there who were clearly unfamiliar with our music. At the end of *Neverland* a roar of appreciation went up throughout the hall. Great.

Back at our dressing room, Roger Glover was waiting to shake hands and say well done. I showered and then sat in our dressing room regaining my strength for a while. Called Linette who tells me she's feeling better this evening, so hopefully this afternoon's nausea was just a passing thing. Klaus, the tour-promoter and mastermind of the DP/Marillion idea, came backstage to say that we had been offered a festival next summer on July 16th by the guy he had brought along to see us play in Nurnberg. He asked us to think of any appropriate band with whom we might do a tour like this again next year. Hmm... Serious answers on a postcard please...

I could hear the beginnings of Don's keyboard solo growling up the stairs so I went down and stood in the wings to listen to it. It's a "scripted" solo but it's different each night – he usually throws a tune in which has significance to the town we're in and tonight it was an oom pah waltz (about the Reperbahn) which had 'em all swaying in their seats and drew huge applause afterwards. I watched the band 'til the end tonight and Ian Gillan slid over and said hello at one point during one of the solos. At the first encore, an additional guitarist mounted the stage with Steve Morse. I didn't recognize him but he sure seemed to know his way around his white strat for *Smoke on the Water*. As he played, his facial expressions became strangely familiar. I went over to the monitor desk and watched more closely. Turns out it was none other than Jurgen Blackmore, son of Ritchie! He looked like Ritchie, but older. That sounds ludicrous until you remember that the last time I saw Ritchie Blackmore he will have been ten years younger than his son is now. The same thing happened the day we ran into Julian Lennon and I remember wondering who this bloke is? Like John Lennon only older...

As Jurgen left the stage he shook my hand and said he'd enjoyed our show. Steve Morse popped into the wings at one point and said "Hey! The man with the golden tubes! Why don't you come up and sing a song, man?" Well, that would indeed be a memory, but I'm not about to burst on there and sing *Smoke on the Water* without approval from Ian Gillan who, strangely, had neither introduced Jurgen Blackmore to the stage or acknowledged him when he left. "There's a lot of bad blood between Ian and Ritchie," said his assistant, Sally. What a shame...

Sunday 28 November *Essen*

Spent the day catching up on the diary and on-line paying a few bills. Didn't go into town. Cold here again – not really getting above freezing.

Soundcheck was uneventful (which is good!). Had my picture taken with Don

Airey. Early show tonight 7.00 pm. Teatime in England. The band played well. No technical problems at all, and I sang well, felt good. Didn't get quite the same reaction as last night, but don't know why. You just never know... Afterwards, I watched nearly all of DP's show from the wings by the monitor desk. They were really on form tonight.

Monday 29 November *Stuttgart:* Day Off

Took all morning to check into the Hilton. Didn't get a room 'til 1.30. Spent time waiting in the American-type sports-bar next door – Palm Beach or something like that. Had something resembling breakfast - grilled turkey and salad - while looking outside at the snow. Chatted to DP's monitor engineer, Rob, who was good company. He said he thought that our crew were "such a bunch of nice people".
    Finally, I was given my room and had a much-needed shower. Had a chat on the phone with L before hooking up with Rothers and Pete and we shared a cab into town to the Christmas Market – actually the most Christmassy of them all. Stuttgart thoroughly recommended, and made all the more atmospheric by the steady fall of snow and the snow-covered stalls and surrounding medieval buildings. Really quite something. Took a few photographs and consumed a bit of glühwein with the crew. Walked round the stalls with Nial. It's a big Christmas Market and stretches into the city centre. We bought a few things. Once again I marvelled at the ubiquitous bottle-brush stall. I decided it was high time to make a brush purchase. There were some particularly long stripy brushes which I couldn't help but admire. The lady running the stall was a bit of a character and, with a slightly manic gleam in her eye said, "D'you know vatt zey are for?!" I took a stab at radiator cleaning brushes, and it turns out I was "Kvite right!" She told me to have a feel... They were indeed very soft. "GOATS HAIR!" she shouted. "Is very static and zer dust sticks to it very good! Venn you haff finished, you lay it down unt zer static fades avay zen you can empty it!" Well, I was impressed and immediately made a purchase. Our house is now full of old-style column radiators and this could well be a boon! She showed me another equally stripy goats-hair brush of the sweeping brush type and said that this was particularly good for wood floors, what with the static effect n'all. "Vill last for twenty-sirty years!" she said. I had to have that as well.
    By 6.00 the cold was beginning to bite and Nial was clearly not dressed for it and shivering, so we found a Starbucks and warmed up with coffees and cake. We wandered back to where the cab had originally dropped me at the edge of the Christmas Market and waited five very long minutes at the taxi stand next to an ice rink where kids were busy skimming around. One little tot had a penguin shaped thing with handles on it and skates on the bottom like a kiddie-ice-zimmer-frame to hold onto and remain upright. Brilliant idea – haven't seen those in England either (mind you, I don't spend a lot of time hanging round ice rinks). The cab was mercifully snug and warm and soon we were back at the

Hilton. Wished Nial a good evening and said I'd probably just chill in my room. Spent the evening relaxing and watching Eddie Izzard's hilarious **Dress to Kill** video of his stand-up in San Francisco.

Had a long chat on the phone with L who's feeling much better after her strange dizzy-nauseous thing the other day. Maybe it was something dodgy in the curry...

Tuesday 30 November *Stuttgart*

Spent most of the day quietly on the bus, writing the diary and relaxing. I want to be my best for tonight's "last" performance with DP. The Porsche Arena is a fantastic hall but the backstage maze of corridors is much the same as the other gigs – featureless fluorescent-lit white-painted functional-not-decorative like a military establishment. The glamour usually ends behind the stage...

Soundcheck was a little fraught as Mark's main music-computer "the receptor" - which always reminds me of some terrible flesh-tearing dinosaur (I know, that's a raptor, but I can't seem to disconnect them in my psyche) - inexplicably ceased to function. We took a break whilst heads were scratched... and it transpires that he had a spare one which, fortunately worked. Hooray!

Had dinner for the last time in catering. The food has really been outstanding on this tour and it has involved super-human efforts of self-control on my part not to put on weight. No pudding. Although I did cave in one night when it was treacle sponge and custard. You can only push a man so far... Said fond farewells to the catering boys and girls and thanked 'em profusely for super scran throughout.

It's Roger Glover's birthday so we wrote him a card which I'd bought yesterday in Stuttgart, and signed it from the band. The crew wrote him one too. He later popped his head in the dressing room to invite us to their dressing room after their gig for drinks.

Went back to the bus, but never actually managed to make it onto the shelf. I spent a little time catching up with this diary. It's bitterly cold outside today, although the snow seems to have stopped for now. Bus driver Paul had invited a couple of old folks onto the bus for a look round so I said hello and suggested they be very quiet upstairs – I think Pete T was sleeping. Back into the gig and into the suit for *The Invisible Man*.

The last gig went very well as – indeed all the shows have, really. Expectations have been exceeded nightly, in terms of the audience reaction. Once again, all hands were raised to the very back row of the back-wall by the end of *Neverland*. We must leave tonight no later than midnight, which will just about give us time for a quick soda with DP after their show. I wanted to watch their entire set tonight, so I cheekily planted myself behind their monitor desk among their own guests of wives, partners, and friends. The strangest thing happened during their encore of *Smoke on the Water*. At some point there's a short drum solo (or keyboard solo, I can't remember) and Steve Morse suddenly made eye contact with me and came running over, around the monitor desk, barging people out of the way and - guitar still round neck - threw an arm round me and shouted in my ear, "Man, you're a great singer! And a great front man. And you can do it live! Not a lot of people can do that man! You're that rare thing. We should do something together if we get a chance." And with that he ran back onto the stage and continued playing the song. Very flattering.

After the show we made our way to the DP dressing room and Roger Glover opened the Champagne. We wished him Happy Birthday and had a few photographs taken together. I managed to get a picture of Nial with Ian Paice and with Steve Morse before we had to run off. Soon we were back on the tour bus and on the road for the long journey back to England and home.

Wednesday 1 December   *Bus – Home*

Was woken around 8.00 to do passport-control at the UK border in France before the bus edged its way onto the train which would take us the 25-minute journey through the Channel Tunnel. Back in England the scene outside was one of thick snow and ice. Kent is under at least 6 inches of snow and the roads were passable, but only just and only slowly. I saw many trucks slewed awkwardly and parked on the hard shoulder of the M25. At one point we pulled into a "services" and nearly got stuck. A truck was stranded sideways across the exit lane. We managed to reverse back up the road and found an alternative way out but it cost us a good 20 minutes or so – not good when you're impatient to get home...

As we made our way clockwise around the M25 the snow seemed to die away and, by the time we reached the M40, there was no more than a sprinkling so progress was much faster. Arrived back at the studio around 1.00pm - more or less on time - and gradually transferred all my possessions and bags of Christmas Market acquisitions into the boot of the blue car which, to my relief, started when I turned the key. Drove home avoiding the snowy country lanes - the last thing we all need now is for me to end up in a ditch - and dropped Nial home in Charlton before traversing the long lane towards Brackley and into the village.

Linette was busy in the kitchen and little V was at nursery. We were alone with an hour to ourselves. It was good to be home.

the *invisible* man

2011   MARCH

Friday 4

2011

Friday 4 March *Montreal*

Got up at 8.00. I'd been awake on and off since 6.20 and it was time to give up trying to lie in for the sake of it. Little Vibes was still sleeping. He has been sleeping past eight all week, so I wasn't surprised, although I know he probably wouldn't be long. L smiled and kissed me as I left the room. I count my stars that I found her. She really was sent to me by the kindest of fates.

By the time I had gone downstairs and boiled the kettle I could hear the patter of impatient and hyperactive little feet so I made my way upstairs to find him standing at the top looking down. "Daddy!" he exclaimed as he saw me. "Ah help you make a coffee?"

I carried him down the stairs and sat him on the kitchen worktop so that he could help. Coffee ended up all over the place and much mopping up had to happen. By the time we'd made coffee and I had put CBBs on the TV for him, L appeared smiling serenely and sleepily. As the weeks pass I love her more and more. I have come to adore her. I won't go on...

We drank coffee and watched TV with little Em while he had a yoghurt. He's pretty good now at handling a spoon and makes almost no mess. He does, however, wipe his mouth and hands with the soft furnishings so we're glad we didn't go for white upholstery. I spent the first part of the morning playing with him back upstairs in our bed – playing hide and seek and trying to be vigilant each time he lunged in the direction of my genitals. If it's not a knee or foot in the balls it's the spirited head-butt in the face. L has already had a couple of fat blue lips in the past. I have often had the eye-watering kick in the groin but nothing too debilitating so far...

Mid-morning I decided to try and put the doorbell up in the kitchen. This is a traditional mechanical bell on a spring which is operated by a chord, which runs around a set of pulleys, through a hole in the front wall of the house. Fabulously low-tech and irresistible. I spent an hour or so drilling holes and screwing screws. It's amazing how warm the top few inches of a room becomes and whenever you're up there doing a bit of work – it's not long before you're a bit hot and bothered. I decided against screwing the exterior part of the bell-ringing apparatus on as I thought I'd return to this at a second visit when I'm back from Montreal. I had yet to pack and Sofi was coming over around noon with new boyfriend Dan, so I didn't want to stress everyone out (including myself) unnecessarily. Vacuumed up the mess and cleared up before going and finding the cases so I could begin to gather my things together for the week in Montreal. L laid out some cold food for lunch and we were eating when Sofi arrived. Around about this time a man came knocking to deliver the terracotta wine racking cells that I had ordered. We already have an impressive display of plonk in the kitchen fireplace but a bit more storage has become necessary, especially since the last convention weekend – people keep giving me bottles of wine. It's a curse... Nial arrived too so I was able to spend the morning with all three of my children, as well as my wonderful other-half. I had time to reflect on what a lucky and blessed chap I am and, as I write this diary somewhere over the Atlantic Ocean at 30,000 feet, I'm still reflecting upon it... At 3.00 I bundled my cases into the car and said my goodbyes. Nial was still with us although Sofi and Dan had departed. Little Vibes had successfully hustled Nial into allowing him to play in his car and they were on their way across the green to it as I left for Heathrow. It was an uneventful journey (good) down the M40 and round the M25 to Terminal 5. I parked the car and made my way into the Terminal to find Frenchie waiting for me and looking quite dreadful. He says he feels not too good and has been pretty exhausted since the gigs in Holland last week. I can concur. I checked the bags in and we made our way through security without too much trouble. I took the shuttle train to Gate B43 and sat at a bar for a while, having a beer and talking to a man called Paul who worked for Motorola and was on his way to Beijing. He said it's a great place and the people are really friendly and helpful. I would like to go...

After a while Frenchie reappeared looking much brighter and then Ian and Lucy came, shortly followed by Mark. All seemed in good spirits. Someone said that Steve R was already on the plane(!). Pete is already in Canada having flown over a few days ahead of us to do a bit of writing somewhere in America with Eric Blackwood.

So here I am in the air, bound for Montreal – I've just watched **The King's Speech** in the back of the seat in front of me and now I'm about to put the laptop away and perhaps have a little snooze before we land in a couple of hours.

All-in-all the 7-hour flight passed quite quickly. We arrived in a cold, damp

Montreal, about an hour late due to 170mph headwinds. (Now that would blow the lid off your dustbin). We were met at arrivals by Lucy's friend, Annik and 2 guys, Andy and Richard, who had procured people-carriers and we quickly made the journey into town. The journey from the airport wasn't pretty. Outside the view was bleak, a bit rundown and lots of black concrete road-systems everywhere. We were downtown before the surroundings became prettier. I guess the time of year isn't doing the vista any favours. Once again, we checked into the Embassy Suites hotel where the receptionist seemed well-prepared for our arrival, handing us envelopes containing our room-keys and welcome packs. They look after us here. I arrived in room 607 to discover that it was identical to the one I was in 2 years ago. A kitchen, lounge with TV, sofa and desk, a large (and very comfortable) bed and a bathroom with shower and jaccuzzi bath. More of an apartment than a hotel. I tried and failed to get the internet working before conking out and going to bed. Didn't call home – it's 4 am!

Tuesday 8 March

Woke a few times but not for long and woke up properly to see light coming through the crack in the curtains. This is a very good sign. It was 6.30, so not much later than I normally get up! Texted L to say I was up and about and she called me to say hello. All's well in England but, like here, grey and rainy. Looking out onto Montreal today, you wouldn't have felt much like going out.

I went down to breakfast and the omelette-man made me an omelette. Frenchie joined me for a while before sliding off (he's something of a slider...) back to his room. Lucy appeared a couple of times to pick up breakfast and coffee for Ian who was "grumpy upstairs". I returned to my room and looked up the luggage-repair shop. I'm trying to get a dodgy wheel fixed on my Samsonite carry-on bag. All turned into a wild goose chase. The man said he'd have to see it to know if he could fix it so I got dressed and took a cab to a place on the other side of town. It was a shop full of bags with a counter at the back where people stood waiting for luggage. There was a large cage containing a loud African-grey parrot which the man occasionally sprayed with a water-spray bottle to calm it down(?!). He looked at the bag and said he could get it fixed in 10 days. Not much use then. I returned in the same cab which was driven by an Algerian man called Creme, who was very nice. He switched off the meter while he had waited for me but, even so, I was looking at a 40 dollar round-trip. I thought I might as well make use of the outing so asked him to stop at a supermarket where I bought toothpaste, hair dye, Becks beer and a bottle of Chilean red.

Back at the hotel I spent the rest of the day just relaxing and messing around with another one of Richard Barbieri's ideas. I'm really enjoying working on his ideas although I don't know what the world will make of it all. In the evening I ordered a bit of salmon on room-service. Still damp and cold outside so I didn't fancy a trip out. Tried to watch TV but I find all these TV channels hard to cope with. Half of 'em are in French and the English ones are just awful American stuff, 80% of which seems to be adverts. CNN was one of the few channels I could understand, but even then the earnest delivery of the newsreaders gets on my nerves. It's like they want you to believe that they just personally flew directly from some war or other and dropped from a helicopter through the roof of the studio to bring you the news. The truth - that they are actually people who look good and can read from an auto-cue – is obviously something far from their self-image. I won't go on... Managed to stay up 'til 10.00pm.

Wednesday 9 March

A triumph! Slept 'til almost 8.00! A brighter light through the curtain-crack today. Edged it open to see wide-open blue sky. That's more like it. The people on the street were wearing heavy coats so I guessed it must still be colder than it appears out there through my seventeen layers of glass.

Went down to breakfast to be greeted by the friendly staff of the Embassy Suites once again. Corn flakes today and, although the coffee's from an urn in the corner, it's not at all bad. Returned to my room and spent the rest of the morning and much of the afternoon with the headphones on in Barbieri Land. It's getting more and more peculiar as I load it with vocal textures and muttering and whispering. Lord knows what he'll make of it! Went out around 4.00 for a walk in the general direction of the old town. Walked through the heated arcade round the corner behind the Intercontinental Hotel and saw a black jumper in a shop window, which I quite fancied. Went inside to find the shop was run by two old-time tailors. I'm guessing here – possibly Jewish, quite possibly brothers. The one who served me seemed a little camp, so possibly gay. He reminded me slightly of an English actor whose name I forget. I asked about the garment and with a heavy French accent he said, "It ees zer last hwon! Very beautiful. In your size! I will get eet out of zer window."

He did so. It was very nicely made. Black ribbed knotted cotton with large black buttons. Italian. And looked it too. "Do you know zer actor, George Clooney?"

"Yes, but not personally..." I said

"He has one of zeese. Very nice."

I'm not sure this had the desired effect.

"Err, how much is it?" I enquired

"I give you 50%!" he said as he lifted the neckline of the garment to examine the price. $595. Hmm, at half-price that's at least £200.00. It WAS a very nice jumper, but I resisted the temptation to try it on in case it fitted perfectly, and I didn't want the old boy getting all worked up in case I bought it out of sympathy (I have a history..,), so I politely said it was more than I could afford and left the shop. Shame...

Thursday 10 November *Munich Circus Krone (Touring with Saga)*

Climbed onto the bus around 2pm for the journey to Munich. Had a couple of beers and decided to go to bed and relax.

During the show there were repeated bouts of low-end feedback, which Phil didn't seem able to eradicate. This is a much more serious problem than monitor trouble as it affects the show for the crowd and I could feel us losing them in addition to the inevitable effect on the spirit of the band. We rallied with *Neverland* but I think we all felt we'd let this show slip.

After the show in Wurzburg we had a bit of a meeting and decided that perhaps we need to dumb the set down a bit. Too much art, not enough rockn'roll. What we always do at a time like this is put *Slainthe* back in the set. There was also much talk of *The Uninvited Guest*. These are not favourites of mine, but I can see that they would do a job dynamically. There's a lull in the middle of the set with the onset of *Somewhere Else, Fantastic Place* and *Asylum Satellite #1* where we seem to be losing the SAGA half of the crowd. We decided that for Munster, at least, we'd try the straighter stuff and return to the more adventurous songs when we're back in our heartland cities of Cologne and Hamburg. Stayed in the dressing room for a long time after the show talking to Ian and Frenchie. It's rare that we socialize so it was quite a treat to just hang out, goof around, and reminisce. By chucking-out-time we were still there so we wandered down to the bus signing autographs for a couple of chaps who had been waiting ages in the cold. Nutters - bless 'em. Didn't stay up very long after that.

Sunday 13 Novembeer *Munster*

Recognised the lake at Munster so I must have been here before, after all. Hung about all morning on the bus waiting for the hotel rooms to become free and eventually checked in to room 252 at the Stadthotel. Very white and comfortable. Had a much-needed shower and headed over the road for a spot of late breakfast (Strammer Max - ham, eggs and cheese on toast - originally recommended to me in 1989 by Mosley, and thoroughly recommended to you) at Ricks Café over the road. Full of students – this seems to be a college-town and there are college-kids everywhere, most of whom seem fairly wealthy, sporting Macbooks and not skimping on the drinks orders... Germany is one of the few countries in the world (along with Norway and China) which isn't currently in recession. Having said that, it looks like the rest of Europe is currently relying on the Fatherland to bail it out... Let's hope the German people stay chilled about that prospect, although I don't think us Brits would be too charitable if it were the other way round (imagine the headlines…). But I digress...

Had breakfast and a "half" in Rick's and texted Nial in case he wanted to join me, but I think he was sleeping-off the after-effects of a night partying on the bus. Returned to the room and wrote a bit of diary and did a bit of tinkering with the h/Barbieri project 'til around 8pm when I took a taxi to Enchilada, a Mexican restaurant, where Phil, Rich and Ian M were already being served. I realized during the cab ride what a beautiful town this is. Many churches and antique-buildings lovingly preserved and fronted by well-kept interesting shops. Reminded me a little of Utrecht in Holland. Apparently we're quite close to the Dutch border here, and you can sense that from the architecture. Had a chicken tortilla thing, which was okay, and drank flaming B52's through a straw, like you do. Again, the place was full of students. They definitely have a bit more disposable dosh than our students back in England.

Walked back past a high-end hi-fi shop full of speakers that looked like green tubas and cost fifty-thousand Euros!

Met up with Nial and the crew in Rick's café for a nightcap, and returned to bed.

Thursday 18 November *Stuttgart Hegelsaal*

Arrived at the Schlossgarten hotel and was given a key to room 311. Still haggling with Mr Evans (our possible-buyer) and communicating with Sue to try and arrive at a selling-price for Brisbane House (our marital home until December 2005, when I moved out – since then, Sue's lived there with Sofi and Nial), so spent some time writing an email to the estate agent. Ordered my first Club Sandwich of the tour and reeled at the €24.00 internet-connection fee. Skyped Linette and said hello to little Vibes. Skype wasn't really working – the internet connection may have been ludicrously expensive, but at least it was crap.

Apart from that though, the hotel was very nice. I had the foresight to bring my pillow from the bus. This can make you look a bit like a dosser when you're checking in, but is worth it when you get upstairs and encounter those lovely-looking fluffy German and Dutch pillows which actually collapse, fold round your head and meet over your face when you lie on them, then you're awake all night folding them and fiddling with the bloody things. Showered up in the very nice bathroom (a rose in a little vase really does make all the difference to limp-wristed artsy-fartsy singer-types) and eventually made it out of the door around 5pm for a walk round town.

The hotel's situated right round the corner from Stuttgart's main pedestrianized town-centre – no 'Pound Shops' round here… This is the home of Mercedes and Porsche and the people sure ain't broke. The girls seem prettier and the guys a little more self-assured. The shops are well presented and everything looks clean, tidy and er… German. I was making my way to the small pre-Christmas market, set up in the main square. The wonderful and "proper" Christmas market we visited last year when we were here with Deep Purple is, regrettably, not yet set up (Nov 21 – I checked), but there are still a few stalls selling glühwein and Nial and the crew were already there. Nial was waiting for me on the corner clutching 2 glass mugs of glühwein, one of which was handed to me. We drank the hot, spiced, wine and watched the wealthy world go by. There was an Arabic band busking in the square which all added to my inner dreams of the nativity. They could have done with a camel... On the corner of this lovely square, one of the strangenesses of Stuttgart is a shop on the main street – right among the ritzy department-stores and clothes shops. It sells knives and guns! What first caught my eye was a cabinet in the window, full of Swiss-Army penknives in various colours. I was reminded of the one I used to have - a gift from EMI Switzerland - which sat forgotten in the bottom of my toilet bag for years until being confiscated at Heathrow airport... As I looked in the window among the passing high street shoppers, my eye was drawn to the high-quality kitchen knives and then along to larger hunting-knives, and then to a kind of dagger which could really have no purpose except for stabbing other people! It was then that I saw the guns – an impressive collection of smooth, brushed-steel hand-guns, and above them two beautifully engineered slick, black machine guns. Holy shit – this would have been shocking down a back street round the corner from Hamburg's Reperbahn, but here in the main square of ritzy Stuttgart?! Last of all, my eye caught the telescopic sight and silencer of what could only really be an assassin's rifle! Yours for €400... Mad world... I suppose wealth and firearms tend to be more common bedfellows than one might imagine. Perhaps Harrods should open a Mortar and Grenade Department...

Monday 28 November *Amsterdam Paradiso*

Arrived around midday at the American Hotel. Rooms not ready, so went to the bar to discover I'm still on the wall amongst rock n'roll's "great and good". Club sandwich and cappuccinos. Richard B arrived and joined us. Eventually checked in and agreed to meet up later to go and have a wander round town with Luigi (Luigi Colosanti Antonelli – photographer-genius and beautiful soul – he'd flown in from Rome, Richard had flown in from London) who would take some photographs. Eventually bad light drove us back to the hotel and we agreed to meet up later to go to dinner.

Was dog-tired so snoozed for a bit and never really recovered. We went to the Hard Rock (Luigi can't eat spicy food or we'd have gone Indonesian). It wasn't exactly a rip-roaring boys' night out. Rich was knackered, I was knackered and Luigi is in constant back-pain from displaced discs. It was a huge relief to get back to my room and relax. I put **MOTD 2** on. Luxury. However, someone began moving furniture about beneath my room by dragging it across the floor. This carried on until 11.15 when I went to reception and marched most of the reception staff into my room so they could have a listen. Turns out that they're trimming up the big room below me for Christmas. I suggested they knock it on the head - being as it was approaching midnight - and all went quiet until 6.45 in the morning when it started up again. I phoned reception and growled, and that seemed to put a stop to it. After that I couldn't really get back to sleep though. Drifted in and out of consciousness 'til around 11.00am and then went downstairs to speak to the manager about it. Worked out quite well as he bought me a cappuccino and cancelled my room extras. Fair enough. Met up with Richard, Luigi and his assistant, Frederica, and we wandered some more round Amsterdam. Luigi doesn't DO photo sessions – he prefers to just take photographs so he doesn't want anything posed. We walked around and found a beautiful street full of antique shops and collector's emporia. Meanwhile Luigi photographed whatever we were doing – chatting, browsing, drinking coffee etc. This carried on 'til around 2.00 when we went to the café Luxembourg for a spot of lunch, then back to the Paradiso for sound-check.

After soundcheck I climbed back on the bus and hit the shelf. I was still tired after last-night's furniture-moving episode and slept fairly well. Showtime saw me struggling to wake up. Hit the stage to a packed-solid Paradiso and, although we were constantly barraged by technical problems - mostly radio related - we finished the show to the most rapturous response I can remember here in Amsterdam or anywhere else. A career-high as far as I'm concerned. Everyone was applauding and up on their feet all the way up to the packed top-balconies. The crowd couldn't have reacted any more enthusiastically without actually jumping from the balconies. Amazing!

After the show I sat with astronaut Andre Kuipers family. His wife, Helen and two daughters, Megan and Robin, had come to the show. Andre is to blast off from Russia on a Soyuz rocket to live for 6 months on the International Space Station and is currently preparing for the mission, in Kazhakstan. Apparently Andre has requested our music to be uploaded to the ISS already! I really hope they all sing *Asylum Satellite #1* together. La la-la la, La la-laaa…

2012

Tuesday 10 April *Home – Caracas*

Out at 3am!...

My plan to leave home without waking up didn't work out and I seemed strangely alert during the journey, chatting with the driver. I felt a bit guilty for getting him up at this time of night. The M40 was deserted and took on the appearance of a runway.

Arrived at 3.50 to discover no check-in 'til 5.00 so sat around in a semi-conscious state 'til the desks opened. Through security. Most of the shops were still closed, so I hung around 'til 5.30 in the hope of buying some new lenses for my Oakley "Gas cans" which are, once again, scratched. They finally pulled up the shutters at 5.30 to tell me that they don't do replacement lenses anymore, even though I'd bought the last ones here. By now it was getting tight for boarding so I legged it to the shuttle train. By the time I made the Gate the flight to Madrid was already boarding.

We took off - only a little late - and made it to Madrid by 9.00 local time. We now had 3 hours to kill before we'd even get a gate. Hung around in the café eating very nice ham and cheese rolls and coffee. No Oakley lenses in the Duty-Free here either.

Marvelled at the scrum at the gate for Iberia flight to Caracas. Evidently there's no queue-culture in Venzuela.

Long, long, long way to go for a gig. Watched **The Promise** – a TV series about 2 girls going to Israel to stay with a wealthy Israeli family, and getting drawn into the conflict with Palestinian Gazans. Pretty harrowing stuff.

Met off the plane by the MAN who took us all though passport control while everybody else queued. However...

The first carousel which was announced for our bags broke. Went across the hall to another and waited and waited and waited. Eventually bags came but no instruments or gear. Marcus announced that the remainder of the gear was at the other side of the hall. Went there. No sign of it. Waited another 15-minutes before the MAN produced a trolley from a side room. It had been there all along. Great let's go. No. The MAN told us to wait. Asked Frenchie and me how much is all the gear worth as we must pay tax on it.

Waited another half hour before being allowed out – money having changed hands. Venezuela is basically, dodgy. When we were at last allowed into Arrivals a TV camera and crew were ready to interview us for (I assume) the news. I was excitedly quizzed by a young kid with indecipherable English asking what do I think about the "gears" which turned out to mean "girls". Told him the gears were very nice, but that I was married so wouldn't be requiring any in my room... He looked disappointed.

Bundled into a Toyota Third World minibus like something from the Sixties and given much-needed beer. The journey into town took 90-minutes past swathes of fairy-lit shanties impossibly crammed onto steep hillsides. 'Looked like Port Talbot refinery. Into the heavy traffic of Caracas. 6.30pm but already dark. Arrived at the Gran Melia hotel. We had already been given room keys in the mini bus. The hotel was all marble and gold 5-star decayed splendour. Nice hotel-room but characterful - the AC was very loud and there was no way to quieten it without turning it off. Some problem in the cistern of my loo meant that it never stopped filling and constantly trickled water into the pan. I never worked out how to turn all the lights on. The TV burst into loud life at 4am the first 2 nights. Well, having checked in I went down to the lobby bar where a disinterested barman called Jesus charged us £5.00 for a beer and £25 for tempura of 6 prawns. Nice though. Had two lots for £50. Holy cow. Not cheap here then. Went to bed at 9.00 to the sound of the cistern re-filling.

Wednesday 11 April *Caracas*

Woke to the sound of the cistern filling and a txt from L saying she was going to Buckingham to have Vibes' feet measured. Went down to breakfast and ordered an omelette from the omelette man in the restaurant. Sat with Ian and Phil who claimed to have been there since 7.00 am. I was tempted to sit by the pool, but remembered the sun-burning incident in Brazil through heavy-cloud and decided to go back to my room. My mobi rang and it was L saying she'd had her handbag stolen in Buckingham! With it went her phone, purse, money, credit cards, house keys, car keys – there was even a prescription in the bag with her name and (crucially) address on it. Nightmare. We'll have to change the locks on the car AND the house. And, of course, I'm in Venezuela. 'Very frustrating not to be able to help her.

Today we are guests of honour at a Rock n'roll school across town. Took the goat-bus to the rock-school which is situated in the hills overlooking Caracas. It took well-over an hour to get there and brought back all the memories of time spent in the past in Brazil in goat-buses, nudging over pot-holes at dead of night, exhausted after gigs. We entered the rock-school via a service elevator from a car-park. Very **Man from UNCLE**. Hot rooms, lots of media presence and then off to join Mark K in keyboard masterclass in a little room full of students. He played a bit of *Neverland* and I sang... Very **X Factor**. I was asked lots of questions by the music-students and their teachers about singing-technique and concluded that I should warm-up but don't. We signed loads of autographs to pupils and teachers and had our pics taken with them all. A good experience all-round. Returned to the hotel for an hour, before meeting up with promoter Barry and assistants Colin (American tech) and Moses (Venezuelan interpreter/fixer). Went across town to a meat restaurant and ate meat and ordered rum and Coke. There was nowhere to put the Coke in the tall glass of rum which arrived, so worked my way down the rum adding Coke where possible. Left the restaurant somewhat cross-eyed and returned to bed. I suppose there would have been a time when we'd have been hustling to go out to a club or two, but nobody was really bothered least of all me. The cistern was beckoning...

Thursday 12 April *Caracas La Terraza del C.C.C.T*

Managed to Skype L about changing locks, but it all got complicated. It's hard to change a lock from the other side of the world. Nial was in London still trying to make the US work-permit people happy. He failed, so now I can't take him to America.

Left the hotel at 10.15am for soundcheck. Had a feeling it might be complicated and it turned out to be just that. The CP300 promised had become a Yamaha X8 yesterday which I have no idea how to use. I only want a USB output from it as I'm going to use my laptop to make the sounds via a program called Mainstage. Decided against freighting the Kurzweil as someone would be bound to drop it or lose it. Spent all morning waiting for the stage crew to provide mains power across the front of stage. When they did, some bright spark promptly plugged the hired X8 (from America therefore 110-volts) into 240-volts and blew the fuses. That was the end of that, but we eventually found another weighted keyboard and, after much head-scratching between key roadie Craig and Steve Rothery (who reads about these things – thank you Steve), they got the thing outputting USB and I got Mainstage working.

While they were trying to get all that together I went nature-watching. A small moth fluttered around at the rear of the stage and glinted iridescent blue as it did so. I followed it around as it flitted from flight-case to flight-case to black drapes and when it eventually settled I could see it had vivid red and black wings, which complimented its shining turquoise body perfectly. Ah, we don't get these in England...

Soundcheck slowly came together and we were all done by 4pm. 5-hours – not bad! Returned wearily to the hotel with the laptop. I didn't want to leave it on stage in my absence. Skyped home again. 'Turns out L's bag had been stolen by some old dear with a child. Who CAN you trust?

The opening act was really good. Venezuelan Celtic. Go figure... Gave Craig my laptop to plug back in and returned to the dressing room to get ready for a 9pm show. Snuck out front without the security men and said hi to a few of the people. Really nice bunch. Put me in the mood. However, just before showtime, the word came backstage that my laptop was gone! Craig had left it on the keyboard rig on stage and someone had helped themselves to it. The stage and backstage area are completely surrounded by security men with guns so, if I was a gambling man, I'd bet on one of them having taken it to subsidise his wages. Venezuela's dodgy. Oh well, there goes my lyrics, diaries, photographs, music, accounts, life etc... I hit the tequila to get my attitude together before hitting the stage. Frantic re-writing of the setlist occurred in order to compensate for me now having no keyboard-sounds.

I actually sang well (against the odds) and could hear that the out-front sound was great. The band sounded fantastic. Well done all. Barry G came back afterwards to say he'd loved the gig and not to worry, he'd replace the laptop. I warned him it wouldn't be cheap, but he didn't seem fazed.

Back at the hotel, reception was swarming with soldiers in red berets and comic red laces in their black boots (not that I laughed...). Apparently the president of Ecuador is staying at the hotel, but I have come to doubt all things official. Who knows? The truth these days represents a security-breach, so no one gets it. Apparently the soldiers had closed the bar, so a last drink wasn't an option. I was fried anyway, so went to bed and lay awake most of the night contemplating the implications of anyone uploading my lyrics, diaries, personal photographs etc, to the internet. I've just got to pray they reformat the drive and sell it on.

The following morning I went down to breakfast and put the word out to the promoter's people that I'd be happy to buy the laptop back. Despite the flight home leaving at 6pm tonight, we're supposed to leave the hotel at 12.30 as the traffic and check-in will combine to use up four hours! Spent my last free hour in Venezuela on a sun lounger under a canopy by the pool. Poolside was pretty much deserted and I wasn't in the sun - in fact it came on to rain quite heavily - but it was nice to have a bit of peace and space without the sound of the toilet cistern filling or crap-TV blaring away in Spanish.

Met up at 12.30. Frenchie paid my extras being as my credit cards were all now blocked – both Linette and I having suffered thefts on opposite sides of the world! We filed out under the watchful eyes of the soldiers with the red laces and back onto the "goat bus". They were right about the traffic. 40-minutes into the journey we passed the rear of the hotel – it had taken that long to get round the block. We drove along one side of what looked like either a huge drain or a river. I still don't know. Every now and then it was possible to see between the trees and bushes down into the drain/river which swirled in torrents and seemingly was flowing uphill.

At one point I saw two people having sex alongside the main drain in between the two carriageways of road. Missionary position, a naked bottom going up and down between two splayed legs. Well, it's natural – you just don't normally see it happening from the motorway.

Back towards the airport in the torrential rain surrounded by steep sugar-loaf shaped green hills of rainforest, occasionally clustered with tin shacks with barred windows – baby strollers and washing lines reminding me how lucky I am to live where I live, how I live and how easy my life is, despite the week of being burgled.

The long journey back to England was to be more luxurious than the journey out – the band had upgraded to Business Class. We boarded the plane and I made ready to recline my big seat to horizontal so that I could sleep. I was tired after last night's show and the sleepless night of worry that followed. True to form, my seat refused to recline and appeared to be broken. A maintenance man appeared and began ripping off the upholstery and yanking around at the mechanism pulling out crumpled sheets of paper, magazines and rubbish from the complex machinery inside. No use. It couldn't be fixed and 'Business' was full, so I didn't have the option of moving to another seat. I was beginning to allow myself a, "Why me?" moment. Sometimes you just enter a vortex for a while... There was only one thing to do. I pulled rank and swapped with tour manager Frenchie who, during the flight, managed to recline the thing anyway (maybe it IS me? Bad vortex...), so I didn't feel quite so bad. The 'Business Class' experience is a whole other level to economy and we basically were spoiled rotten by the cabin crew. We ate a fine dinner and I then stretched out and went to sleep. Woke for breakfast and hot towels and landed an hour late in Madrid which made the connection for London pretty tight. We'd left Caracas an hour late - probably due to seat maintenance - and had failed to make up the time. Hurried across Richard Rogers' amazing wavy-wooden-roofed airport to our London-bound flight which was already boarding. Soon we were back in Terminal 5 where I discovered I had lost my baggage tags. Normally I wouldn't have noticed but, of course, our bags never turned up on the carousel so, after an hour's wait, we headed to baggage services to report the loss. The reps there were really helpful and said not to worry, the tight connection had probably scuppered us and the bags would come on the next flight and be delivered to the studio. Oh well. Much to my relief, when we did eventually make it out into Arrivals, a driver was waiting to take me home. Spent the journey chatting to the Pakistani driver who was the son of the chap who had picked me up at 3am the other morning and listening to the FA Cup semi-final between Liverpool v Everton. Our producer, Mike Hunter, lives for Everton FC, so I felt for him when Liverpool stole the game.

Back home the sun was shining on the village green and I felt like I was back, a Universe-away from dodgy Venezuela and the tin-roofed shanties of Caracas. Lucky lucky lucky.

Friday 8 June *Washington*

Landed at Dulles. Nice flight. No trouble. BA staff always friendly and helpful. Spent most of it listening to, and assembling the lead vocal comp of *Invisible Ink*. We're all still recording our new album "Sounds That Can't Be Made" despite now being on tour. The woman next to me kept talking to me. Her husband seemed relieved that she was leaving him alone!

No trouble with immigration. Bought a Chai in Starbucks and was amazed to be asked for my autograph by a bloke who had gone to the trouble of hanging around there all day. Bundled into a black minibus that took us to the Embassy Suites in downtown Washington. Happy hour – free nachos and plonk! Then went to Legals for a seafood blob-out, including their fabulous chowder. Jet lag crashed me out at 9pm.

Saturday 9 June *Washington*

Woke at 7.00. Not bad. Starbucks opposite the hotel, so mighty handy for cappuccinos and Chais. We'd been offered a tour of the White House by one of the heads of security, Dave Keane (not his real name) who had shown me and Sue round, back in the days of Clinton. Post 9/11, everything's changed and there's about 4 levels of security to pass through now before you get anywhere near the place. We weren't allowed anywhere near the West Wing (last time I had actually poked my head into the Oval Office!) but had a look round the state rooms which I hadn't seen last time, so that kinda completed things for me. Dave took us down into the basement where the service staff do the laundry, the cooking etc, (and where Richard Nixon's one lane bowling alley can still be found and used by Obama himself) and showed us one of the stone windows stripped of the white paint to reveal the black scorch marks made when the English torched the entire building in 1812! Later went to the Smithsonian Museum of Air and Space and marvelled at the tininess of the X15 and the command module of Apollo 11. Both unbelievably small. I think Neil A is a good deal crazier than he ever made out! (I mentioned this to his son Rick who confessed to telling the old man, which, I'm told, made him chuckle).

Returned to the hotel and worked some more on the vocal comps. Nervous about my chest, which feels tight, and my voice, which seems to be affected.

Sunday 10 June *Washington 930 Club*

Gig day. Eric and Wendy took me to the gig soundcheck. Had a couple of hours to spare, so asked Eric if he was up for taking me to the other Museum of Air and Space out by Dulles Airport. Inside, there's the Discovery Space Shuttle. Totally amazing up close. Looks like it's all stuck together with gaffatape and polystyrene. Truly peculiar and amazing. It just doesn't look like it would fly in air, but those astronauts managed to seemingly, effortlessly, glide the thing down to earth. I am lost in admiration for their skill and guts. There's also a Blackbird there – the dark titanium stealth fighter which, I believe, had a top speed of over Mach 3, although much of its spec was classified; not to mention Enola Gay – the bomber which dropped the atom bomb on Hiroshima, and much smaller than I had expected. 'Hard to know what to feel when standing next to such a machine.'

The Washington show was very iffy vocally and my sound was much worse than I have been used to. We're slumming it - there's no monitor desk on this tour - and it was always going to be difficult. Overnight on the bus and in the morning I woke up half-blind with a burning in my eyes. Oh dear. Looks like I'd sweated hair product into my eyes last night at the boiling hot Washington gig.

Monday 11 June *New York:* Day Off

Checked into the hotel Marcel around 1pm and made my way in the slowest elevator in Manhattan to room 405. Frenchie got me into see a doctor mid-afternoon – a demurely charismatic chap called Dr Primas who bore a resemblance to Paul Simon, and he prescribed me more drugs than I have ever possessed in my life. Antibiotics, sinus clearing tablets, eye drops, steroid tablets, and more tablets (I never found out what they were for). He said if I wanted to return tomorrow for a steroid injection, he would bang one in my backside – "You'll feel much better after that!" During the day, my right eye hurt less but my left eye began to burn much worse. I couldn't sleep because I couldn't close my eyes. The pain got much worse. By 6.00 I called Dr Primas again who referred me to an eye specialist who could see me at 9pm. Paced up and down in severe discomfort 'til then. Around 8.30, when it was almost time to go, I had become nauseous and faint. Frenchie found me sitting on the bathroom floor, unable to stand. We tried to cancel the appointment but the eye doctor insisted he see me, so I was bundled into Eric's car, grey and in cold sweats feeling truly dreadful. The eye doctor's name was, appropriately, Dr Burns. Dr Burns was a small slightly shabby looking Jewish genius with a twinkle in his eye. He told me to lean back and, like a magician predicted what I would feel. "The pain will stop in seconds…" - it did - "and in 5 minutes you're going to feel much better". Sure enough, the nausea and general awfulness began to lift and I soon felt not at all bad. Wow. After 8 hours of burning pain it was almost inconceivable that I should feel fine in a moment. Dr Burns prescribed me yet more drops, drugs and creams to go in my eyes and I returned to the hotel able to sleep. Heaven!

Tuesday 12 June   *New York   Irving Plaza*

Gig day I decided to go shopping for a new gig jacket. I'd emailed Jason Hart – I figured that being a gay New Yorker he'd know exactly where I should go shopping for a cool jacket. Turns out he couldn't help: "Oh I have absolutely NO style at all" he replied. I asked him if he had a current number for Rufus Wainright and called Rufus who, after the initial shock of being cold-called by me after such a long time, suggested Barneys department store uptown, so that's where I went, eventually settling on a kind of wedding coat by Fendi (Italian).

Later in the afternoon I returned to Dr Primas, who duly banged a steroid shot in my bum. It worked – I felt terrific for the NY show.

The reception when we went on stage was incredible. Can't imagine anyone walks on to a stage in NYC to that kind of rapture and affection. The crowd lifted us and we in turn, turned it on, lifting them. A great gig. I txted home, "Darling, we just tore the arse out of New York City." What a great feeling. I returned to the Marcel and sat down in the shower, immensely relieved it was over. 24-hours ago it would have been inconceivable to walk on stage at all.

Wednesday 13 June   *New York   Irving Plaza*

NYC 2 was great too. I had the questionable idea of sitting on my piano during the encore and as I sang the opening line of *Kayleigh* it crashed to the floor with me on it. By some miracle, I wasn't even bruised and kinda bounced back up without missing a word. Needless to say, the whole thing is now on YouTube and very funny. Being as the piano was now on the floor, I thought I might as well stand on it... I later asked Nick and Frenchie to get rid of it and they duly removed it from the stage, just in time for Mark to point out that *3 Minute Boy* was next... I play piano all the way through it! I ended up playing Mark's piano while he spun round his other keyboards and played opposite me like we did on the **Season's End** tour all those years ago. We had a laugh and finished the show in great spirits. Overall, I felt the gig didn't have the amazing vibration of the first show, but then the set list was a little more sedate. People I later ran into in the street in Philly were unanimous that NY2 beat NY1, so what do I know?! Overnight to...

Thursday 14 June   *Philadelphia:* Day Off

Woke to a sunny morning in a truck stop and wandered over to look for breakfast. Found Mark K in the café and had a coffee with him. Mark and I have had our ups and downs, but we are getting along well again on this tour. I ordered a bit of wholemeal weird cereal as it was the only thing vaguely healthy on the menu and Mark paid for it, bless him.

Afterwards I had a wander round the shop. I bought a big torch for home and marvelled at the display of various types of Viagra at the check-out. One brand was called Rock All Night. I couldn't help feeling for these trucker's poor wives bracing themselves for their return after a few weeks on the road...

Around 1.00, the bus rolled into Philadelphia and we checked into the Hilton hotel next door to the wonderful Reading Terminal Market. Dropped bags and went walkabout. Walked through the fabulous market which blazes brightly coloured neons above the bustle of food stalls, meat, fish, cafés, craft stalls, second-hand books, cookies, huge vegetable stalls piled high with green leaves of every type. I ordered a Philly cheese-steak (which you HAVE to) and watched America go by for a while. I later found an excellent coffee stall and a café/bar which was showing the Euro 2012 footie first-round games, so ordered a beer and settled down for an hour before returning to the hotel for more vocal compiling.

I later watched a movie (something I never do) **The Curious Case of Benjamin Button.** Very moving, beautifully directed and wonderfully acted by Brad Pitt and the incredibly gifted Kate Blanchett. It somehow made me very homesick and I cried like a baby.

Friday 15 June *Philadelphia Theatre of Living Arts*

Next morning I needed my roots doing, so found a hair-dressers on the strip called Look At Me Now (underneath – 'Sylvia - the psychic reader and advisor'). I was the only white customer; in fact, the only customer with any hair to speak of, all the other customers were guys having their hair shaved to within a millimetre, the fashion being for the hair to literally look like it's painted on the head with a very sharply defined hair line round the edge. Emerged in an hour, suitably blackened and improved, went back to the market and spent a few hours chilling out, watching the footie and enjoying the atmosphere of this fantastic bustling corner of Philly. It's Ian Mosley's birthday tomorrow, so I bought him a book in the second-hand bookstore. **On The Road** by Jack Kerouac. Seemed fitting... I bought myself a picture book about America. A collection of photographs assembled and commented upon by one of my favourite writers, the sensitive and brilliant John Steinbeck.

Returned to the hotel to pack and drop bags before returning again to Reading Terminal Market to chill some more before soundcheck at the TLA. I could live in that market (and, as you can see, I kinda was!). The ever-helpful Eric Pastore had offered me a ride over to South Street for soundcheck, but it was a warm, sunny day so I decided to walk. It took half an hour or so but I felt I'd soaked up a little of Philly by the time I showed up outside the gig. Was gifted strawberry margarita by fans sitting on the street at tables, and chatted for a while, being photographed and signing people's records. Everyone says they're grateful we came back to the US. They're a very sweet bunch, our American fans. It would be quite an idyllic life being me, if not for the constant worry of whether or not I can deliver what these people expect and deserve.

Soundcheck was a bit strange – my Kurzweil levels seemed all wrong, but Nick and I eventually straightened everything out.

The gig is probably best forgotten... my Kurz went mad and played out of tune – something it has never done. We could only guess as to the cause: either iffy mains (low mains voltage), the heat, the dropping of the piano last night, or stray radio interference. I wasn't singing very well and the studio-dead acoustics that the TLA takes on when full of people, didn't help much with the situation. I later learnt that reviews of the show were excellent. We really do get away with murder...

After the show I showered and kept out of the way, returning to the bus and, as is usually the case, was in bed asleep before most of the band or any of the crew had appeared.

Saturday 16 June   *Boston Paradise Theatre*

A long day not feeling very well. Spent most of it in the dark dingy dressing room of the Paradise Theatre in-between trips to the Blue Café next door, where I was given complimentary cappuccinos – the guy behind the bar was a fan. Thanks mate.

After soundcheck (painful and depressing as my voice really isn't working too well) I asked Eric to take me into town to find Legals Restaurant. He managed to get us a table by the water (nothing short of a miracle – it was Saturday night and absolutely packed, but he blagged it and said I was a famous rock star from England (I later discovered that Eric comes from a well-known "Italian" family in NY, so that's probably where the leverage really comes from!). We ordered lobster and when it arrived it was the size of a puppy, and probably older than me! It was lovely though, and a real pleasure to get away from the (not very aptly named) Paradise and enjoy another environment with Eric and Wendy's cheery company.

We returned to the gig with Eric's brakes grinding away on the discs (a running joke, despite his obvious embarrassment) of his Jeep. He has recently had it into the garage for a full service and lord knows what they've done to his brakes! I was bursting for the loo and very nearly didn't make it. I now have diarrhoea to add to my list of ailments, so spent the last half hour before showtime running back and forth to the loo. At least there IS a loo backstage here now – there never used to be. In the old days you had to go out front with the punters who would be passing things under the walls of the cubicle for you to sign – "Could you dedicate it to my mom, Tabitha?"...

The Boston show was fairly raucous and out-of-control. Again the Kurzweil was doing random stuff. My gear doesn't like this country. The crowd, again, were fantastic and in full-on party mode singing Happy Birthday to Mosley every chance they got. Ian seemed genuinely touched.

Sunday 17 June   *Quebec:* Day Off

Woke up on the outskirts of town and disembarked into a baking hot afternoon in Quebec. Soon we were checking into the Best Western hotel. There were no rooms ready, so we sat around for a while until rooms became free. I was fortunate to be given the first one, so dropped my bags and Skyped home briefly before taking a cab to the old town where I found an Italian restaurant.

It's a glorious day and everyone was out walking in the old town. I ordered a thin base pizza (proper) and a gin & tonic and watched the Germany/Denmark game on the TV. Fabulous. Germany won, but Denmark gave them a good game and very nearly had 'em. Not bad for such a small nation. Needless to say I was cheering for the Danes. I have contemplated having the Danish flag tattooed on my backside but was advised against it on the grounds that I wouldn't be able to sit down for a month.

Came back across town and spent the rest of the day holed up in my room relaxing, working and watching TV. Was very grateful to discover a program late on the telly about the manufacture of Bentley cars. It was all shot at the factory in Crewe and detailed the predominantly handmade approach to creating a Bentley. Fabulous to see such accomplished craftsmen and craftswomen at work and talking with their broad northern accents – a welcome treat for a homesick Englishman after a couple of weeks of American and Canadian twang. After that, to my further delight, was a similar program about the Mini, with similar footage from the production line of the new (now BMW owned) Mini in Oxford – just down the road from my home in England. I went to bed and felt comforted, grounded and aware of one good reason to be proud to be British. It's comforting to realize that Margaret Thatcher didn't manage to completely wipe out every last vestige of British manufacturing expertise, even though it took foreign ownership to make it possible. Thank you Germany (kerr-ching...) and no offence, but nonetheless I wish the Danes had stuffed you in the footie.

Monday 18 June   *Quebec The Imperial*

Went down to the breakfast room and had a coffee with Phil and Nick before returning up to my room. Had a slow and pleasant lunch by the river in a very nice café with old chums Steeve (with two ee's) and lovely wife Kathleen, before returning to soundcheck.

Nice gig. Sound was good at soundcheck, so made my way outside onto the bus and hit the bunk for a little nap. The in-house engineer Mo, said the band was sounding great and that our engineer clearly knew what he was doing. Nice one Phil. The hall was packed for the show with one of my favourite audiences of the tour – you can't beat the heart and soul of the French Canadians. What a vibe!

Tuesday 19 June   *Montreal L'Olympia*

Woke to find the bus was parked at the rear of the L'Olympia theatre with which I am now fairly intimate having done two conventions there. Made my way backstage and dropped my stuff before wandering out in search of a Starbucks.

The whole area has been pedestrianized for the summer, so the roads are closed and tables and chairs are outside in the street giving the neighbourhood a holiday feeling, made even more festive (and very gay) by the million pink baubles strung between the lamp posts for as far as the eye can see. This IS the gay district of Montreal and everywhere on the street were guys who certainly looked a little more aware of their physical appearance than us straight guys who tend to be a bit more scruffy... I walked beneath the endless pink baubles until I came across a Starbucks, which beckoned me to the first much-needed megaccino of the day. I have taken to putting honey in 'em. I also tend to order a Chai latte for good measure, which I can work through once the coffee has kick-started my system.

Returned to the gig and spent the rest of the afternoon finishing the vocal comp for *The Sky above the Rain* so that we could upload it to Mike Hunter back in our studio in England. After that I'd agreed to do a TV interview with a French chef who runs a thing called The Rock n'Roll Cook or Heavy Metal Kitchen or something. He was a very charming man with a beard who looked like something from the Old Testament. He was accompanied by a very beautiful wife who operated the camera while he asked me 'what my first culinary emotion was?' I said **boredom** with my gran's egg and chips. He then asked if I could remember my first culinary rapture. I think I said the fish n'chips from Bamfords on the sea-front at Scarborough... I suspect he was hoping for more sophisticated answers. You can take the boy out of the North... He made us a present of wholemeal muffins made without something or other (gluten or wheat or gawd knows what) and some home-made almond-milk which I found to be quite delicious.

We have also been doing nightly meet-and-greets with a dozen or so competition winners. It was so hot backstage that I had to bail out of the room half-way through and drag everyone out into a bigger space. I'm still not feeling very well. At one point a very Bohemian looking lady who, I believe, was native Inuit, made a big speech about deserting the band after Fish left and then rediscovering us recently. She said she had brought me a present by way of an apology and gave me a shell-box which contains an exquisitely carved bone arrowhead – a beautiful object I will look after and treasure. I was running out of time as I had agreed to sing a bv with opening act Sundomingo and they were upstairs on-stage rapidly approaching the song. Walked out on stage to a roar of recognition and sang said backing vocal. Couldn't hear a thing I was doing. Poor sod's had hardly any monitoring. And WE complain...

The Montreal crowd was amazing as we expected and despite slight monitor woes we had a good one. I lost the plot a little during *The Invisible Man* when the follow-spot operator decided to point it at Pete T for the whole of the song. So there was I performing this incredibly intense piece of heartbreak-psycho-drama in the dark while, in my peripheral vision, Pete, bathed in white light, threw rock–God shapes and grinned at the crowd. I couldn't really blame him - it was a great crowd - but *The Invisible Man* deserves a bit more gravitas. As I paced angrily offstage at the end, I had forgotten about the presence of the keyboard-riser which was (ironically) invisible in the darkness. Walked straight into it with both shins and fell on my face. Again, I was lucky not to have sustained any real damage beyond cuts and bruises. I could have been unlucky and broken/fractured my legs, wrist or nose...

At the very end of the night I returned to the empty dressing room to raid the fridge for the last bottle of the rock n'roll cook's almond-milk before climbing onto the bus and onto my shelf. Fortunately the steroids I'm taking for my voice and chest seemed to stop my shins from swelling up and I was in surprisingly little pain, considering the general wounding and bruising clearly visible on my legs and arms. I'd split my jeans with my right knee when it hit the metal edge of the riser and yet I felt remarkably unscathed. Maybe I'm indestructible...

Thursday 21 June   *Chicago:* Day Off

Arrived in the sun-drenched street of Chicago and checked into the Embassy Suites in a part of town which felt quite arty/designy – like an American version of Bath. Opposite was a row of little stylish shops. On the corner was a Starbucks, always a welcome sight in the USA where, otherwise, the coffee can taste like engine-oil.

Checked into my room and set up my computer at the table before popping down for megaccino. Had a wander around a fascinating little shop full of interesting homey things - cut glasses, picture frames, quilts, cushions (L would love it) crockery, cutlery - all with an Edwardian sort of feeling. A painting of geraniums on the wall caught my eye. I ended up buying it. Ironically, it had come from Belgium all the way to Chicago so that an Englishman could take it all the way back to Europe...

Spent the rest of the evening working on the lead vocal for *Gaza* – one of the big songs on the next album which is currently keeping me awake for all sorts of reasons... They're going to call me an anti-Semite when they hear it and I'll be reviled for it in certain quarters, but sometimes one has to stand up for the oppressed and powerless and the Palestinians deserve greater public sympathy and awareness. Dunno if a song can ever change the world, but Lennon and Ure & Geldof had a stab. The band are with me all the way, so that helps a lot. I confined myself to headphones for the rest of the day and evening, and ventured out around 8pm where I discovered Ian and Phil in a steakhouse on the corner of the next block. It was some kind of micro-brewery too, so I ordered a honey beer which was very nice, and a steak, which also filled a corner... Went back to the hotel afterwards and to bed.

Friday 22 June   *Chicago   Park West*

The morning was spent having my roots done in the salon across the street and drinking slow megaccinos in Starbucks. We're absorbing another hour of jet-lag as we travel west and, although you wouldn't expect to feel just one hour, I guess it's all cumulative and I do feel quite odd. Went shopping to the gent's clothes shop across the street and bought a stack of coloured t-shirts with nothing written on them! Also bought a very nice retro pen made of blue and yellow striped lacquer – quite unusual and a very nice rollerball nib/refill thing. I will now have to conclude the shopping apart from trying to find something nice to take home for Linette. Perhaps in LA or in SF...

Around 3.30, the ever-generous Eric Pastore and ever-grinning girlfriend Wendy picked us up at the hotel to take us to soundcheck at the Park West and I arrived in the familiar dressing room to discover Rick Armstrong looking very relaxed. It's always nice to see Rick. Soundcheck was lengthy and I almost wandered off and lost interest altogether at one point while Mark disappeared into the mysteries of his complicated keyboard rig. It takes him all tour to get the bugs out of it and get it to work all night without crashing or crapping-out and then he always updates the software before each new tour and has to start all over again... I have come to drink beer during soundchecks – it's the only way I can cope with the process. I find it much more stressful than the gigs, especially when I'm having vocal problems and am therefore much more conscious of the time spent needlessly singing and needlessly shouting across the stage in an attempt to communicate. To quote Joe Walsh, "I can't complain but sometimes I still do."

Returned to the hotel and had an excellent light dinner in the hotel's Italian restaurant on the street watching the people go by. It's hot here in Chicago, so everyone's out in their summer gear. A universe away from the pleasant-but-rarely-glamorous view from my cottage window in England (unless Linette's going by, of course...). After that it was time to dive back into Eric's squeaky-braked Jeep, and back to the Park West for the now-routine meet-and-greet. I think Lucy decided we don't have enough to do on these gig-days...

The M&G was as usual very pleasant and good-natured and then it was time to get ready for the stage. We're opening with *The Invisible Man* – might as well hit them with a whopper (as Mike H calls them) for starters... my sound was kinda strange, but I'm used to it now. Part of the decision to make this tour involved a major compromise with the monitoring and we just have to accept that. The crowd were great and I left the stage happy but knackered. I'm giving 110% every night and I can really feel it.

Saturday 23 June   *Chicago   Park West*

Spent most of the morning in Starbucks with Rick Armstrong. He's having a hard time of it at home lately and – for what they're worth - I'm offering my own perspectives on marital breakdown (avoid the lawyers as much as you can, and stay close to the kids). I returned to my room to continue working on the *Gaza* lead vocal. That took up the rest of my "free" time before leaving for soundcheck.

Andy and Annik popped in to photograph the process. It's a mental way of making an album, but our life has become road-life and hotel-life. Technology now makes it possible to turn every hotel room (and broom cupboard) into a recording studio. All you need is a good laptop and a decent audio interface. Off to soundcheck again with Eric and Wendy.

"Why do you need to soundcheck again when it's the same venue and the equipment hasn't moved?" I hear you ask. A good question. We tend to change the set-list from night to night and this usually involves songs which we haven't played for days or weeks. Everyone feels better if such songs get a run-through before we're in front of people. That way, we can recall the chords and check that the technology works.

Just before the meet-and-greet tonight, my mobile rang and I stood in the dressing room to hear, "Hi Steve! This is Andre Kuipers calling from the International Space Station..." We had quite a long chat. I passed the phone round so the band could share the thrill. He wanted to thank us for the music. A phone-call from Space! Bloody hell. I hope he's paying for the call... That got the night off to a good start...

Sunday 24 June   *Los Angeles:* Day Off

Arrived in LAX and made our way to the baggage hall. Popped into Starbucks on the way and bought a Chai latte. It was refreshing not to have to "do immigration" and simply walk to the baggage hall and out into the street. I stood with Ian. The temperature was, thankfully, a little cooler than Chicago. I sat on the slatted seats in the baggage hall contemplating the fact that the backsides of Harrison Ford, Jack Nicholson, Johnny Depp, Liz Taylor, Richard Burton, Marlon Brando, Al Pacino, Robert de Niro and you-name-'em have probably graced this bench. We had no trouble picking up the bags and bundled into a cab with Phil and Pete. *Babylon Sisters* by Steely Dan has to be listened to whenever one arrives in Los Angeles, so I found it on my iPhone and put it on as we negotiated our way to the Sunset Marquis Hotel. It was just as I remembered it – possibly even more rock n'roll with pictures of Tommy Lee, Jeff Beck, Morrissey, Slash etc, on the walls. We were checked in by Frenchie and I made my way to room 226 which was very nice and spacious. Plugged in my technology and spent a little time working on the vocal comp of *Gaza* in-between ironing a couple of shirts. Didn't actually make it out of the door. Ordered dinner in my room which cost $80.00 (maybe I won't do that again... but it was very nice – scallops and brussell sprouts) and worked a little more until I went to bed.

Woke up in the night wheezing with the distinct feeling that maybe I was allergic to the bed... It's a pet-friendly hotel, so who knows what's been in here... Liz Taylor with a couple of tabby cats?... Y'never know.

Monday 25 June *Los Angeles:* Day Off

Woke up early absorbing another 2 hours of jet lag and wrote the diary for a while before meeting up with Frenchie and the band to take cabs to the other end of Sunset for an appointment with the Social Security office. We all need US social security cards as part of the process of minimizing US withholding tax on our gig income (not profit, income), so we went through the airport-like security machines and took our place in the queue. Each of us was given a ticket and had to wait until it was called. I was given ticket number A25. A19 was up on the screen. *Hey 19* by Steely Dan, another quintessential "Sound of LA", started up in my mind and I began singing it. No one got the joke. There was a moment of nervousness when Pete T was taken into a back room. Pete's one of those people who constantly looks like he's done something illegal and is harbouring a great secret. Anyone in authority usually takes a closer look at him... I was called to a window in the office and interviewed by a woman with an eastern European accent. She wanted to know where we wanted the SS cards posting. Not the UK – it's against the rules. Not New York – it's against the rules etc. Frenchie scrabbled around trying to find an address while I imagined Pete T in the back room panicking over the same question. Frenchie's mobile kept going off. It was Pete panicking. It was soon all resolved and we posed briefly outside the building for the ever-present Andy who had accompanied us to photograph the proceedings.

Initially I decided to walk back up to Sunset with Rothers to take a cab back to the hotel but, having got back up there, I decided I would walk back. It was a long way but it was Sunset Boulevard all-the-way and I wanted to soak up a few old memories and feel like I was really here. The first time I came here was with the Europeans in the 80's. Tony Childs picked us up from the airport in her old yellow Buick and showed us the town. Back then I went to our record company (A&M) offices which were on Charlie Chaplin's original studio lot, and met Herb Alpert and Jerry Moss (THE A & M). All the memories are confused and distant now, but the feeling is still there and I'm STILL trying to decide if I love this town or loathe it.

Stopped in at Sunset Sound studios and asked the manager if there was any chance of us popping in for an hour to listen to some rough mixes. Also wandered around Sam Ash's guitar shop and saw a b&w picture of Steven Tyler hanging out with Andy Warhol. Over the road in the Guitar Center I marvelled at Van Halen's 4-bass-drum (each pair joined together with a strange bellows system) black and white stripy drum kit. Totally over-the-top. Popped in and went upstairs to the percussion dept where I have bought skinned tambourines in the past, and bought a skinned tambourine.

Wednesday & Thursday 27 & 28 June *Los Angeles House of Blues*

Both LA shows were terrific. Keith Emerson appeared backstage after the first one and said the show was quite brilliant.

After the second show, I discreetly crossed Sunset and sat on a wall, just watching the world go by 'til 2am in the warm night-air. At one point a couple of quite-a-bit-younger-than-me guys sauntered past and one said to the other, "Are you around tomorrow?"

The other replied (totally relaxed and matter-of-fact), "No. I can't do tomorrow - I'm recording with Aretha Franklin."

"Uh-huh." Little or no reaction from his friend. Only here...

Monday 8 October   *Home – Sao Paolo*

Overnight flight. Fairly uncomfortable in "Economy" sitting next to two girls reading **50 Shades of Grey** (S&M girl-porn, currently all the rage). I spent the journey with Karl Pilkington, watching **An Idiot Abroad 2**. The BA staff were very nice as usual.

Finally touched down in S Paolo at 5.15 am local time (9.15 in England) and stood at the baggage conveyor with Rothers for over an hour waiting for bags. Ah, S America! Met in arrivals by Renaton – a muscular and very rock n'roll promoter's-assistant who generally sorted stuff out. Nice chap. A further 2-hour ride in a minibus to the hotel.

Skyped home and went to get my roots done down the road. They said they didn't do guys. I said I'm not like the others, and they let me in.

Walked back and there's a little parade of shops and restaurants. Poked my nose into a Chinese delicatessen and was offered complimentary mint tea by a smiling, bobbing Chinese old dear. Bought water, canned ice-coffee and some cashew nuts. Further down, there was a little coffee shop, so I stopped there for a cappuccino. Rothers was going out and invited me along with some fans. He seems to have a global dialogue via Facebook. I have learned to keep my head down. I just don't have the time for it. I declined his kind offer – thought I should stay in and chill. Agreed to meet him in the lobby at 10 am tomorrow – they're taking him to the beach. That could be nice...

Tuesday 9 October   *Sao Paolo*

Got up and had breakfast watching the crew arrive with the rest of the band (minus Mark, who had stayed home an extra day for Angie's birthday). Said hi. The buggers got upgraded to Business! Nonetheless Mosley looked like death – said he'd been sick...

In reception at 10.00 there were two girls waiting (Anna and Fabiola) who stuck us in a car and drove us to the beach! At the outskirts of S Paolo we picked up more fans. Paolo and his wife (who cried like a baby as we were introduced!) and Melissa, who later told us that her ex-husband was a big fan and would be taking us up in a helicopter once we got to the beach. Hope he knows what he's doing...

Stopped at Santos FC football stadium - home of Pelé, and the new mega-star

Neymar, who I'd previously never heard of - and had a look round the trophy room (they've won a few), before driving out to the helipad. Saw cops gassing up at a gas station – one holding the pump, whilst the rest stood on the forecourt with their hands on their holstered guns. Seemed a bit tense... Asked Paolo why and he said, "There is much violence here." I guess to be a cop in this country is to be a target...

The helicopter building looked like something straight out of a John Le Carre novel. The Terminal was being refurbished so was a bit of a building site. We picked our way across the shattered marble floor strewn with electric cables and into the hangar where stood a couple of shiny helicopters. Another was outside, fuelled-up and ready to go. Said hello to the pilot and climbed into the machine – Rothers in the front and me behind with Paolo and Melissa. She was sitting next to me. It was tight in the back but I didn't want to get too cosy with her in case the ex-husband (piloting the chopper) got the hump and pitched us all into oblivion! Up and away... I've been in choppers before and I'm always amazed by how LOUD they are. Everyone had big green headphones to talk – it's the only way you can. The doors had been removed, so I was open to the elements and the downdraft. Exciting stuff, although I tried not to think of the crash statistics. The last thing Linette said to me was, "Be careful!" and here I am, barely 36 hours later, in a door-less helicopter with a load of people I have never met, swooping over tower blocks and the ocean. Well, he never killed us or I wouldn't be writing this... It was a terrific start to the tour.

After that we all went to a restaurant on the beach and had a late lunch. A lovely experience. Anna and Fabiola drove me back to S Paolo while Rothers elected to stay on and meet Melissa's mother who had invited us over to their home. I was later to discover that he announced he was tired and went to bed upstairs! He certainly has his own uncompromising window on the world. Who else would sleep while everybody else holds a party in their honour? Anna and Fabiola (what a great name!) drove me back through the legendarily and permanently gridlocked streets of S Paolo ("I'm so sorry! Now we are really close..." Anna kept saying for the last half hour of the journey) and I eventually got back to the hotel around 7.00. Went to bed at 8.00.

Wednesday 10 October *Sao Paolo*

Went out with Nial in the hot sun. Walked to the shopping mall via a pharmacy to pick up mozzy spray and factor 30. Arrived at the big mall, sweating, and wandered around aimlessly. Lots of luxury goods – nothing I'd personally want. Found a nice American diner type of thing and we both had Caesar salads and later a couple of Caipirinhas. Chatted about life and work. A typical boys' conversation during which not much is really said. He's a lovely kid, my boy, and I'm very proud of his honest soul and resigned demeanour, but sometimes I wish he was as naturally articulate as his sister. It's like getting blood out of a stone! Always pleasant company though. We walked back and said we'd meet up later.

Paulo (the promoter) has offered to take band and crew out to dinner at 8.00. I think I Skyped home again and then had to leave the hotel at 4.30 to go to Kiss FM, the only Rock radio station in S Paolo. Went there with Rothers. More traffic, and then an hour hanging about before going on-air. Rothers was unusually talkative, and it went well.

At 8.00 we went over to a fabulous restaurant where we all ate copious amounts of meat, drank Caipirinhas and, enjoyed the excellent starter buffet of sushi and every kind of salad. I loaded my plate with palm hearts and artichoke hearts. Yum. The meat was as good as it gets and I was full in no time. I think we were back in the hotel by 10pm, but I'll remember it as an outstanding meal. I sat opposite Paulo, getting to know him. After all these years, I'm slow to judge music-business folk, but I like him. He's as Latin as it gets. So smooth that water runs off him, but with an easy and good-humoured temperament. He looks more like a rock star than all of us put together and he dresses well. He also says he's not doing this tour for the money but that he is a fan. His two production assistants, Renaton and Baffo, are both good chaps and the crew speak highly of them, so all in all, it bodes well for the tour.

Thursday 11 October *Gig HSBC Arena, S Paolo*

There was much to do if I was to have keyboards to play tonight. The keyboard I will have is a locally hired thing. The one I have specified will not be coming as it's not available. I am informed that its predecessor, the Yamaha P200, will be there. I'm not using my usual sound source, the Kurzweil K2500, but have reprogrammed all my sounds into my Mac laptop using a the Mainstage program. There is much that can go wrong in the conversion from midi to USB and also the merging of my keyboard output with the midi output from the radio-cricket-bat. I had rigged all this at home and got it working perfectly, but I decided to get to the show early (along with the rest of the band, each managing their own technical complications) so that I could check everything. Arrived at the hall and Nial, at my request, had set up the P200 in an upstairs dressing room, so spent the next hour or so working on sounds. The P200 was then moved downstairs so that we could plug up the cricket-bat-radio system which, to my surprise, worked perfectly. Soundcheck dragged on for more hours and at 7.30 we were STILL on stage. Even by our standards, 5-hours is extraordinary...

At 7.30 the doors were opened to the gig and we had to stop. I managed to get back to the hotel for 40-minutes to pick up my things and have a much-needed rest before returning to the gig for the 9pm meet and greet, which turned out to be mostly with the people I'd been at the beach with yesterday. Showtime at 10 pm...

The show went well. Really well. Everything seemed to work and my sound was good if a bit swimmy... The crowd response was wonderful. Just about everyone I had plain sight of in the front few rows were in a state of either rapture or tears. Brazilians are something else. So full of emotion and passion. Fabulous.

After the gig I showered and then went outside the dressing room to "do the photographs and autographs". There was a tray of Caipirhinas so I had a couple while repeatedly being told I was great by all around me. Nice work if you can get it... Bless 'em all. I'd been the last one out of the dressing room as the only one to shower, and the rest of the band had gone back to the hotel ahead of me. I was driven back alone in the mini bus through the slow traffic of S Paolo and when I got to the hotel there were fans in the lobby. God knows how they find out where we are. More photographs and autographs and then back up to my room on the 6th floor. Peace at last. I put on the TV and began trying to txt home but realised I wasn't feeling too well. Feeling worse and worse with the passing minutes. It was like I'd been poisoned. I didn't feel particularly drunk and the room wasn't spinning, but it became obvious I was going to be sick. I had hardly had anything to eat all day. Spent most of the night on the bathroom floor and eventually made it into bed at some point in the middle of the night.

Friday 12 October   *Travel S Paolo to Rio*

Woke at 7.00 for long enough to txt L and apologise for vanishing on her and then went back to sleep until check-out time at 11.00. Got up and realised that the lights weren't working and that my laptop was dead meat. Not starting up, not charging. Oh dear... Phoned down to reception to be told that today there would be a power cut all day long. No lights, no power, no elevators. Terrific. Took my bags along the dark corridors and down the 6 flights of stairs to the lobby. I had felt not too bad when I woke up, but as the day progressed I knew I was in trouble... By the time we got to the airport for the flight to Rio de Janeiro I felt truly awful. Faint and sweating I managed to check-in and through security to the Gate where I lay between 3 seats until a change of Gate was announced and had to make my way back downstairs. By the time they announced the flight I had worsened and really wasn't sure if I could get on the transit bus. Somehow I managed.

On board the flight I sat and suffered, waiting for it to be over. What a way to return to my beloved Rio! I had looked forward to taking a walk along Copacabana with Nial. It was raining hard as we exited the airport onto the minibus and it was obvious that the dream of having a beer with my boy in the sunshine was not to be an option. Pissing it down! ...and beer ever again was truly unthinkable. Rattled along the streets of Rio for 40-minutes or so and finally arrived at the Othon Palace hotel – slap in the middle of the beautiful wide curving bay which is Copacabana as the 3-metre waves curled and crashed on the beach. I slumped down onto a sofa until Frenchie pressed a room key into my hand. My mobile wouldn't work at all now. Up in my room I managed to secure an internet connection and Skype home briefly before going to bed at 5 pm. The promoter's boys had been out to buy me anti-hangover stuff. Little pills and a phial full of detestable yellow liquid which I drank down as per the instructions. Fingers crossed... Woke at 11pm feeling significantly better but not great and watched TV for half an hour before returning to bed until the morning.

Saturday 13 October *Rio de Janeiro*

Woke at 9 and opened the curtains to a rainy grey Rio. Cloud obscured the mountains from half-way up and mist obscured much of the view.

Went down to the breakfast room to see if there was anything I could stomach. The breakfast room at the Othon Palace has the most terrific view of the Atlantic and the beach. What a shame it was such a grey day. Last week was bright sunshine and 30-degrees. I found porridge and had a couple of bowls. That should help...

Back to my room. We didn't have to check leave until 3.30. Went back to bed 'til about 12.30 then made my way down and along Copacabana to Don Camillo the restaurant where L and I had dinner on New Years' Eve 2006/7 (BTW I'm writing this on a plane looking down (and across!) at the Andes) Ordered and ate (!) an excellent steak. Phew! Finally out of the other side of the poisoning. Those 2 Caipirinhas must have been pure spirit. I must have drank the best part of a bottle of Cachaça...

Soundcheck in the Vivo Rio was a more straightforward affair than S Paolo. We had the same gear, so there were no new problems once we'd got Mark's keyboards plugged in which took some time. Returned to the hotel and once again, went back to bed.

The Rio show was notable for two things: first, the amazing atmosphere in the crowd – these people are like no one on earth when it comes to heart and soul. Second, the complete loss of Mark's keyboards during *The Invisible Man*. I had to sing half of the song with guitar bass and drums. In the end Mark came to the front of stage and played my piano for a while – wrong sound, but at least it worked. Things like this take years off my life I'm sure. I really must learn to relax, but I'm a perfectionist and T.I.Man isn't the kind of song you can light-heartedly busk through.

Afterwards I spoke with Sabine from Germany who had travelled especially for this show. She said she thought it was great. You just never know. That cheered me up a lot. We didn't stay long... we were more than a little aware of our early start tomorrow. Felt guilty driving out through the security gates past fans who had hung around desperate to meet us, but I'm not tip-top and I need to get to bed. I think I made it into bed not too long after midnight. What a shame to come to Rio, hungover, in the rain with no time to enjoy this incredible city...

Sunday 14 October *Porto Alegre*

It was always going to be ugly. Getting up at 6.00 when you fell into bed at 1.00 is never good. Checked out and climbed into the minibus for the drive to Tom

Jobim airport. Queued up with all the equipment and crew at check in. We have a LOT of gear even though we haven't got drums or keyboards... Frenchie checked the band in first and gave us our boarding passes, so off we went through a very relaxed security system. "Do you want me to take my laptop out of my bag?" I asked. "Nah..." said the man at the machine. He never actually said, "This is Rio, man", but that's what he meant. When I got to the Gate, the girl at the top of the escalator looked at my boarding pass and said, "You're too late." I broke a sweat – we have a show tonight and the crew are still nowhere to be seen. It eventually transpired that she meant "early". I said I would come back earlier when the gate was open...

Bought a cappuccino from a little coffee stall and relaxed for a while. What I love about this airport is the recorded announcements. They have been the same since I first came here in 1990. It is a man's voice and, although slightly camp, the sexiest airport announcements I have ever heard. If you can imagine Bootsie Collins in star shades, pearls, lurex Speedos and gold stack-heeled thigh-boots relaxing on a bed of ostrich feathers with a cocktail in one hand and a mic in the other while two of Prince's backing singers rub oil into his exposed thighs – well, it kinda sounds like that. A seductive semi-whisper: "The next... flight.... to...Monte...videy oh... LEAVES... from... gate.... thirrrtyhh... at... NINE....fifteen..." I hope they never change it. He tells you all you'll ever need to know about Rio. In Brazil the national sport and passion is football. They call it futebol, pronounced foo-té-boll. But in Rio, they call it foo-chih-boll – more sensuous. That's Rio. If we ever have serious success here, I will try to get access to those announcement samples. I could have them periodically going off at home. "I'm LEAVING... for Tescohh... to go... shopping... at fourrhh... FIFTEEN!"

The flight down to Porto Alegre took two hours. I probably tried to sleep and I probably failed. Spent a bit of time with headphones on editing my live sounds in the laptop. Flying blind somewhat in that regard as I have no keyboard to trigger them. We arrived and got into a van into town, which didn't take long and we piled out and into a nice hotel. I bought Ian a coffee in the downstairs café as Frenchie checked us in and made my way up to room 310 – a suite of a room with a sofa, table and chairs, loads of space and windows overlooking the wide Guaiba river upon which Porto Alegre is built. Lovely view. I Skyped home and then had a little sleep before the 3.45 departure to soundcheck.

The gig was a modern theatre. Very nice. I wasn't expecting a lot of people. We didn't have many when we played here last time. Soundcheck was slow but sure. Mark's hired keyboards are all old and clunky – the buttons don't work and the pitch-wheels don't do much either. He's having to work around it... Can't remember this show too well. I have let the diary slip I'm afraid and I'm actually writing this from my hotel room in San Francisco de Motazal in Chile. The audience was small, but not as small as feared. They hustled us into playing *Easter* and that went down well – everyone singing along. I had planned a hot bath in my hotel room jacuzzi, but I needed to shower at the gig so the jacuzzi never happened. If I was a proper rocker there'd have been a couple of girls in there bubbling away offering to scrub my back! But I never was a proper rocker, more of an Eighties aspiring avant-garde post-punker forced into a rocker's skin. And anyway, all that glamour is for young men. When you reach a certain age - even if you're single - there's something a bit seedy about it.

Back to the hotel and to bed. Leaving at 11.00 tomorrow morning for the airport and the flight down to Buenos Aires.

Monday 15 October   *Buenos Aires*

Spent all day on a plane. Headphones on giggling away at Karl Pilkington with **An Idiot Abroad 2**. Made it into the hotel room 504 around 6.00 and decided I'd go and try to find a place to eat. In reception around 7.00 I bumped into Paulo who immediately took over and insisted on organising me a restaurant and a car to take me there. "When you get there, give the owner this!" he said, thrusting an envelope into my hand. "It's tickets for your show tomorrow." There could have been anything in it…

We haven't been lucky with the weather on this tour. It's pissing it down like a monsoon here in Buenos Aires. Ate steak and sausages alone and watched the rain out of the window. At one point I watched a guy going through the bins across the street. It looked like it was his job to rake around and pull out the plastics, probably for recycling. As he did so, his children goofed around in the pouring rain with a couple of broken umbrellas. They'd probably found those in a bin somewhere. It was a moving sight. Kids having to go to work with their dad at night when they really should have been sleeping. Running around in the pouring rain and going through the bins. Their mother is probably working too. Linette, young Vibes and I have a lucky life. Again I was humming Joe Walsh's "Life's been good to me so far…"

Returned to my hotel room with the other half of the excellent bottle of red I'd been given in the restaurant (see previous Joe Walsh quote) and watched the telly.

Tuesday 16 October   *Buenos Aires Gig*

For me this was to be the surprise of the tour. Last time we played here it was a sit down theatre. All I could see from the stage was rich people (who get to sit at the front in the expensive seats) checking each other out. I'll never forget this one guy who looked me straight in the eye half-way through the show and made an exaggerated yawn… He'd probably had the ticket given him by the promoter, or by some sponsoring bank or tobacco company. That was to be the only show in my life I ever said, "Thank you and goodnight!" before the end of the set. Understandably I wasn't looking forward to this one. Couldn't have been more wrong. The venue was a stand-upper - a rock club - so the hardcore were down the front. The audience were very excited and kept singing like football supporters in between songs. I told 'em I felt like Lionel Messi – that went down well...

Before the show Paulo came in the dressing room and made a heartfelt speech about how much the band's music means to him and what a pleasure it has been. He said that - even if we come back here someday with another promoter than him - we will always have a friend in him and he will be there to give advice if we need it. Very sweet of him. During the show he was in the pit dancing and grinning. I have never known this from a promoter. We played *No One Can* at his request and I dedicated it to him from the stage (a bit strange to dedicate that one to a bloke). The crowd sang the choruses with the same intensity as *Easter* and *Sugar Mice*. Lovely. Strange to look out from the stage and see all these hairy rockers lost in this romantic poppy love song... We're onto something in this continent... I hope we can take advantage of the way our music resonates with South Americans, get the records into the shops, a little promotion, and we could really build things up here. I'm a bit too jaded to imagine it will happen, though. The music business (like the TV business) seems to be sewn up by a handful people.

Wednesday 17 October   *Buenos Aries – Santiago Chile*

Went down to breakfast and mused with Phil Brown at the presence of a number of books of erotic photography in the breakfast room. We took one down, which appeared to be a history of erotica from around the world, and browsed. A bit early in the morning for all that... all I can say is that those Japanese need therapy. Dolls with bandages and octopus tentacles inserted into their orifices. The last time I saw anything like that, I had found it on the shelf while living in a house belonging to an anaesthetist in England. Somewhat worrying... Another memorable image was an old black and white photo of a really fat ugly Turkish-looking woman sat on a chair pulling her buttocks apart to reveal her anus. Serves me right for looking, I suppose. I decided against the scrambled eggs at that point and stuck to coffee.

We checked out and were driven the short distance back to the airport by the huge River Plate (which looks like the sea – so wide that the other bank isn't visible owing to the curvature of the Earth!). Hung around for an hour checking all our equipment in and then sat in a café with Phil and Ian for a while. Can't remember the flight so it must have been alright, or I was asleep. In fact I spent a lot of it writing this diary – hence the remark in the Rio paragraph (scribbling away looking down and across at the glacier-topped Andes).

When we landed we made our way to the baggage hall and I found myself signing autographs for the airport staff – we must be quite well-known here then. We picked up bags and they all had to be re-scanned. Suddenly, one of the contact lenses I was wearing in my right eye decided to bend itself double. Very uncomfortable. There didn't appear to be any toilets in this area of the airport, so I decided I'd go ahead into the Arrivals Hall and find a loo while everybody else waited for the scanners to finish their work. As I emerged through the sliding glass doors, a cheer went up and about a dozen fans were all waiting there wanting photographs and autographs. I tried to smile as my right eye winked desperately at the doubled-up contact lens contained beneath the lid. Eventually I was set free and rushed to the gents where I found a mirror and removed the offending lens. I unfolded it and put it back but it still felt strange. Taking it out again, I realised it had broken in half and half of it was still in my eye. I never managed to get it out and I'm convinced (as I sit here on the flight up to Caracas via Lima) that, four days later, bits of it are still in there somewhere.

We were taken then by van out of town and along the freeway for about an hour to San Francisco de Motazal. This is - as far as I can see - a place only notable for the huge hotel/casino complex where we will stay for the coming days. We'll actually play here in a room at the Casino on Friday night, but first, on Thursday. We'll play in Santiago whilst staying here. Paulo must have done a deal. It's a nice hotel so no one's complaining. I was given a key for room 119 and made my way down two floors – Reception's on the 3rd. The entire place is built surrounded by the foothills of the Andes and the view outside would be wonderful were it not for the Casino and car-parks. We were advised that there's free dinner in the restaurant at 8.30. It was 8.00, so there was half an hour to freshen up and plug the technology in. Back home its midnight, so I thought I'd leave L alone and Skype home in the morning.

Dinner turned out to be across the car park in the Casino. We entered through double wooden doors and along thick carpet, into a room full of one-armed bandits. Blackpool in Chile, basically. The place was an onslaught to the senses. Muzak coming from the ceiling, whirring bandits, bells ringing and, from another room, something that sounded like a TV gameshow. It WAS a TV game show! We entered a room where a kind of cabaret band played short snatches of well-known songs while a little guy in a suit babbled in Spanish for all he was worth. Every time he finished a sentence with a flourish, the band punctuated it with a chat-show-type snatch of music or a roll of the drums. Cigarette smoke filled the air as Werner (our local promoter's rep) led us to a table and asked for menus. That was enough for me. I only needed a couple of tabby cats on my knee for the vision of hell to be complete. I was gone in a flash. Managed to get a chicken burger in a no-smoking area next door and later returned to game show land to say goodnight to Nial who had only just arrived (the equipment truck got lost) to order food. Sat with the crew for 15-minutes watching the little guy babbling, the band doing their Jonathan Ross thing, and two palpably bored and disinterested girls in sparkly dresses shuffling from one foot to the other in time to the beat. It reminded me of **Sale of the Century** (if you're old enough to remember it – a TV game show from the Seventies compered by Nicolas Parsons ("Live from Norwich!") who is still alive as I write this, compering **Just a Minute** on Radio 4). I turned around and made eye-contact with a guy wearing a headset and staring at a laptop screen - possibly the TV program director or editor - and although he said nothing, the weary look said "I know!…it's rubbish, but it's a living". Returned to my room and watched Robert de Niro and Joe Pesci in one of those Las Vegas gangster **Goodfellas** type movies. Very very apt here...

Thursday 18 October *Santiago Chile*

Woke up and Skyped home (all well – it's 1.00 in the afternoon there and they're having lunch) before going down to breakfast. A big room, floor to ceiling glass walls, offering great views of the green hills outside. Getting milk which was neither skimmed nor hot proved complicated. Almost no one here speaks English and my Spanish is er... limited to muy bien and manhana. Had muesli and coffee which was not nice and returned to my room.

Left at 2.00 for Santiago. The drive took under an hour and it was a lovely sunny day with a wide-open blue sky. I gazed at the snow-covered Andes in the high distance as we travelled along the freeway. Pete T said this is the Pan-American Highway and that you can drive all the way to Canada. Dunno if he dreamt it.

The venue is a big old arena tucked away somewhere in the back streets of Santiago. The seats are laid out in an amphitheatre style, so despite its size the crowd will feel close to me tonight. Should be good if someone shows up! Soundcheck proceeded well after the obligatory 1-hour wait while Mark gets his hired keyboards working. It's a nice venue – quite funky, but with a good vibe and lots of history. We ate backstage in a brick-built room full of funky lamps and old photographs on the wall of shows from way back. Ladies in Billie Holliday dresses, bands in suits who look like The Shadows, circuses with trapeze in the high roof, Folie Bergére-style topless dancers and even dolphins leaping out of tanks. There was nowhere to go - no hotel, no tour bus, just a dressing room - tastefully decorated and with chaise-longes. Unfortunately only two chaises and Pete and Mark had bagged 'em. Rothers was sleeping like a drugged bear in the only other dressing room (I'm not going in there!). So I sat on the floor for some hours until 8pm when we were due downstairs for the meet n'greet, grip n'grin, shake n'fake, or whatever you choose to call them. I subscribe to the, "Nice to see ya, to see ya, nice" philosophy.

By showtime the place looked busy. Dunno if we're sold out, but I think there's 4000 in there. The show was amazing. I felt good and in a good place. I was feeling the love from the people and banging it back at them, magnified sevenfold. By the end of the show I could see each and every person in the room was on their feet arms raised. Wonderful. Went downstairs for the aftershow and was photographed a lot by fans and media folk before returning upstairs and into the van for the return journey to San Francisco de Motazal and the Casino hotel. Arrived at 2am and ran a bath and luxuriated in the bubbles with a cup of tea 'til 3.00.

Friday 19 October *San Francisco de Motazal Chile*

Woke up, put the kettle on and Skyped home again before going down to breakfast. Went through the same difficult ritual of getting milk, neither hot or skimmed while every variation arrived first, and ate muesli and drank dodgy coffee before returning to my room. Spent much of the rest of the morning and much of the afternoon composing a LONG email to a guy in LA who had criticized my knowledge of the Middle East and thought our song *Gaza* to be one-sided and factually suspect. He had emailed twice - both times in a courteous and fairly respectful way - and so I had been meaning to reply. It took a while to get the thing balanced and backed up with figures, but the more I looked at it, the more comfortable I was to send it. The statistics of the injured and dead *alone* put Israel on very dodgy ground morally. I ended by attaching the Israeli Foreign Ministry's stats and rested my case.

Soundcheck soon beckoned and we went back over the car-park to the Casino building where Frenchie showed us to a room which was the kind of room Pinochet would have had a birthday party in (maybe he even did!! Dunno if it's old enough) – like a state room in a palace. Huge thick carpet, obviously designed and bespoke for the room. At least twelve huge crystal chandeliers – spheres made up of hundreds of crystal drops. Pale cream walls with ornate mirrors. Very clean. Not very rock n'roll – in fact, not remotely. I'm told tickets for tonight's show START at $200 a pop. Blimey. Paulo must be bankrolling the tour with this one. Well, fair enough – it can't have been cheap to put this tour together...

Soundcheck was pretty straightforward. The cricket bat was double-triggering a lot, so Nial put the thing on a lead and it worked a lot better. We spent a bit of time getting *Cover my Eyes* and *This Strange Engine* together. My voice sounded a bit rough – I must've got carried away at the excellent Santiago gig last night...

It was great to be able to walk back over to the hotel and relax. I Skyped Linette again and said night-night. Spent another hour on my Palestine/Israel email and then chilled a bit before returning for the show. What a weird one! It was hard to really get myself "up for it". I feel uneasy doing gigs for people with loadsamoney or - worse - charging people who haven't loadsamoney LOADSAMONEY to see us play. The room felt so decadent. It wasn't quite so bad with the lights off, but you could tell that some of the people felt that they'd *bought* us. One guy came up to the stage and was thrusting an album at me to sign while I was actually singing. I couldn't be too indignant, I get the feeling that the Chileans are simply naive about this stuff. He thought I'd sign it. I kept waving him away. I could tell that the harder-core fans were at the back – mostly stage-left, celebrating in the shadows silhouetted beyond my view. What was interesting was that, as the show progressed, I watched the people at the front slowly lose themselves in it too. It was good to watch... We encored with *This Strange Engine* first and then *No One Can* which seems to go down really well here, followed by *Garden Party*. That did it. Everyone was up and we finished the night at a similar energy level (on a smaller scale) as Santiago. Phew! What a relief!! I did the photos and autographs and returned to my room for another bubble bath. Very nice...

Saturday 20 October   *San Francisco de Motazal:* Day Off

A real day off!! Not travelling, not doing interviews. An actual day off! Bliss. I had a lie-in until L txted to say she'd been waiting ages to speak to me, then rolled out of bed and Skyped home.

Went down to breakfast to do the cold milk-not skimmed thing again. They brought me it hot. Had muesli and coffee while people kept coming up asking to have their photograph taken with me. "Don't get up, it's okay, carry on eating your breakfast – I'll just crouch down here. Your show last night was amazing" etc...Anywhere else in the world, I might have got arsy about it, but the Chileans have this good humoured unpretentious naivety, a naturalness that it seems only natural to respond to... er... naturally. I finished my muesli and took my (now) cold milk to my room so I could put the kettle on and make a Nescafé. And then I thought I'd ask for an ironing board and an iron... Called reception and waited 5-minutes until they answered the phone. When they eventually did, I asked for an iron and an ironing board. I was met with a confused silence. Then they put me on hold, and then someone came on who spoke English. An iron and an ironing board – we'll send one right away...

Right now, the bell boy is checking out his spots carefully in my room mirror. I called to ask for another iron. The one they sent me doesn't get hot, so they sent him to see. I showed him that it was broken but, instead of leaving to get another one, he made a phone call to reception. It took them ages to answer again, and he had a conversation in Spanish. Then he said they will bring another. But he hasn't left. He appears to be waiting for something. I thought I might as well write this down as it's quite strange and therefore, quite interesting. Now he is standing quietly against the inner closed door to my room. I think he's reading his mobile phone. How odd. I have been trying to iron my shirt now for over an hour. At 4.00 I will go down to reception as it has been arranged for me to go round a vineyard. I particularly like Chilean Merlot, so maybe I can buy a nice bottle.

Well, the Chilean vineyard trip was most pleasant. A young chap called Hector made the tour and told us all about winemaking. Lots of details and stats which I can't retain. My enduring memory will be that they put egg-whites in the cement mixture when they built the cellars. Apparently this lends a slightly elastic quality to the brick-built cloisters which helps them to remain standing during earthquakes which are common in Chile. The other one was that they use a helicopter to dry the dew from the grapevines because the sun damages them if it hits them when they are wet. Now that's extravagant... Nial came too and took a couple of comedy shots of me trying to look tipsy among the barrels. At the end we had a bit of a tasting. I thought it was okay, but it was a Cabernet

Sauvignon and I prefer the Merlot, so I bought a bottle to take back. We were also made a gift of the wine glass which says Santa Rita on it – the name of the vineyard. Now how the hell am I going to get THAT home?

After the tour I sat out on a bench for a few minutes gazing at the landscape. It must be amazing here on a summer's evening relaxing in the evening air and gazing up at the hills. We returned in the van to the hotel and I met up with Mark in the bar. There's a nice roof terrace to sit out on, but he seemed to prefer being inside and it was getting a bit chilly (if you pardon the pun). We had a half and then a Pisco Sour (the local poison) before I returned to my room to write the diary. L called again at 10.00 – she was up late after having girlfriends round for the evening. Said they'd been dancing to a disco CD she'd found. I can't imagine her and her girlfriends dancing round our kitchen...

I said goodnight then went to bed myself feeling lonely. Cheered up when I found the Man United/Stoke game on the ESPN channel. It had a Spanish commentary with that bloke who shouts GOOOOOOAAAAAAAL!!!!!!! for twenty seconds every time someone scores. I'm glad they don't do that in England... We won 4-2.

Sunday 21 October   *Santiago – Lima – Caracas   Travel day*

Up at 10.00 and thought I'd make myself a nice cup of coffee before Skyping home. Big mistake. Couldn't get the sachet of Nescafé open and pulled a bit too hard with my teeth, breaking one of my front veneers clean in half. Not painful – just cosmetic... or anti-cosmetic. I gathered up the broken veneer and went off in search of the crew. I thought I could try and Superglue it in. Found Pete Harwood and Phil Brown in the breakfast room and Pete said he had some Superglue and went off to get it. What a star! I returned to my room and, on the second attempt, managed to glue it back on without ingesting too much cyanoacrylate... Skyped home then returned to the diary. I don't have to leave 'til 3.00 so I split the day between listening to my Danish language course(!) and emptying my suitcase and ironing everything and putting it back. Well I might as well use the iron after all the grief I had getting one. L Skyped around 2.30 for Vibes to say night-night. It's great that we can do this. When Sofi and Nial were small I simply used to vanish for weeks. Rotten. It's much easier these days. Still hard, but not as bad as in the Nineties when there were no mobiles to txt from, only insanely expensive hotel landlines. Sometimes things weren't better in the "old days". I ordered a seafood soup on room service which was lovely before finishing packing (4 bottles of red now in my suitcase... I hope none of 'em break...) and meeting up with everyone in the lobby.

Back once again into the van and off to the airport. Never had chance to say a proper goodbye to Baffo and Renaton. Didn't realise they weren't coming with us. Should have thought... It's a different promoter in Caracas. So I'm up to date! I'm writing this on the second flight. It took an AGE to check in in Santiago – they just seemed to have no system and no idea. Bought myself a t-shirt and

Vibes also with Chilean flags on. Finally boarded the A320 up to Lima and had to get back off the bus in Lima and back onto the plane to get the t-shirts I'd forgotten in the overhead locker. Tried on a fur hat made out of llama wool in the airport. It was for Sofie... but it buried me and it was 75 US dollars, so I declined. The onward flight to Caracas is a little thing (Embraer E190 jet – never heard of 'em) and I'm sitting here juddering along. The laptop battery is about to give up and I might as well have a little nap. Still two hours to go...

Landed at 2.00 am and managed to get through immigration at Caracas without too much fuss. The bags took a while to come through and then we had to endure the 1-hour wait while Customs haggled over what they might decide to charge the promoter in tax for us to enter the country. Venezuela may have again elected Hugo Chavez under the impression that he's their best bet, but I can't help thinking (with no political bias whatsoever... in fact with an instinctive socialist bias) that he is going to run this country into the ground. Everywhere there are people with jobs who do nothing and have no reason to care. I'm not saying capitalism is the solution either, but maybe some kind of Dutch capitalism (fairly high taxes, care for the poor, money spent on the arts, great public transport system, no Lamborghinis in evidence on the streets of the cities) is as good a society as anyone's going to come up with. We can learn little from the USA just as we can learn little from Russia, Cuba and Venezuela. England would perhaps be okay if we could banish private education and the class-system which relies on it, but, having travelled far and wide these past 30-years, I've learnt that if you want to create a good and fair society, you'd do well to imitate Holland.

We FINALLY were allowed to leave the airport around 4.00 (which I'd already told Linette would probably be the case) and we rattled into Caracas in an old bus which gave me asthma, arriving in the hotel around 5.30. Skyped home and went to bed around 6.30am.

Monday 22 October   *Caracas*

Woke around 11.45 and Skyped home. The internet here is mighty- clunky and it's hard to get a constant audio signal. Video signal is also poor, but turning it off doesn't seem to improve anything. Opened the curtains to a cloudy misty day. We really haven't had much luck with the weather on this tour. It's been sunnier (though cooler) in England! Went down to the lobby and was followed by smiling security man (dressed in brown) Carlos. Dunno who has hired him but he's following me around, either for my protection or my moderation – who knows?

Ordered coffee at the little bar in reception and was immediately accosted by four guys with records and posters who wanted photos and autographs. Nice chaps who respectfully went and sat down when I asked them to just give me 5-minutes. I called them back over after the first cappuccino had hit my system and they showed me the gig posters – not on paper but some kind of plastic material, about 5ft by 4ft. They said they'd nicked them from the airport. I managed to persuade them out of one of 'em and gave it to Nial as a birthday present – it has, of course, got his birthday October 23 emblazoned across it.

Spent the rest of the day trying to gain access to the hair dressers. I later discovered that they're closed on Mondays. I'll try again tomorrow. The staff here are pleasant but not bothered. Nothing really happens when you ask. It's not just the language barrier, they're just not arsed. Spent the afternoon by the pool trying to get a Club Sandwich – it took an hour. The sun made a half-hearted showing in the late afternoon but then clouded over again. In the end I was joined at poolside by Nial, Nick, Andrew and Mark K. We eventually managed to get 4 club sandwiches and four beers for £80.00 and that was after we'd haggled down from £120.00. Viva socialism!

I'm writing this still on a sun lounger and it's getting dark. Now the sun's gone down, the sky has cleared and, behind me, a mass of third world tower-blocks with a mountain of rainforest rising up into the sky and I can see the top of it for the first time today. I have the pool area to myself. I'll go and shower – it's the mosquito hour so I'm asking for trouble if I stay out her any longer...

Went out in the evening to the Hereford Steak House. We're a bloody long way from Hereford here... We all went because it was free – the promoter was paying. I wouldn't have gone, but it's my boy's 21st at midnight and I didn't want to abandon him on such an evening. We sat together and he witnessed - probably for the first time - the band talking good natured drunken nonsense. There was much debate about how fast spiders could run if they were the size of humans... I kept saying to Nial, "Imagine trying to write a song with 'em!"...

The food was good and the beers and wine plentiful. The restaurant itself is a bit of a dead spot, it would have been better to go to the Hard Rock or somewhere... Never mind.

After that we returned to the hotel and sat out on the terrace for a while. One by one everyone went to bed until there was only Nial, Phil and I left. We hung on 'til 12.00 so we could wish Nial a Happy 21st. Phil was fairly sloshed and I wasn't exactly sober. Phil was on his high horse about Caracas, saying he really doesn't like the place and can see no reason why we would ever want to come back. He's got a point. There's nothing in this country that really welcomes us apart from the fans. Getting in through the airport has involved parting with large amounts of cash, I have had my laptop stolen here already this year, and the promoter makes it difficult technically for the crew to put the show together.

Tuesday 23 October   *Caracas Show Day*

Woke to an email from L saying she'd gone out shopping so went straight down to breakfast. Had a small omelette and some coffee before returning to my room to grab Nial's birthday cards from Linette and Sofi. Made my way down to the gig and gave them to him. He was visibly moved when he read them and asked me if could hang onto them for now so they don't get lost. On stage things were fairly chaotic. It's Venezuela... The room was a sort of ballroom with tables. Jeez, we're turning into a cabaret band...

I made my way down the corridor to the hairdressers and asked if they could do my roots. The salon operated in the classic socialist way. About 10 staff doing nothing and two working. Nonetheless Cesar, who seemed to own the joint, asked me to come back in one hour as they were too busy right now. I did so and was shown to a seat where I waited for a further 15-minutes observing the "action". One of the staff sat in a corner bursting bubble wrap one bubble at a time (it's a living) while another chatted on her mobile. Interestingly ALL the customers (now about four, not including me) were men. Men of about 70 years of age wearing suits and shiny tasselled slip on shoes, looking every inch like South American politicians, were having their already short hair not cut, just sharpened round the edges. They looked very slick. Something interesting was going on in the back room... I could see a woman placing a stick up the nose of a guy and then frantically fanning him with a Spanish paper fan. The longer I watched, the more I understood what was going on. They dip sticks in hot wax which is wound round the stick like honey, but before it cools to a solid it is inserted into the nose whereupon the frantic fanning cools the wax further so that it solidifies. The stick is then yanked out removing all the inner nasal hair. Ouch. I was offered the service but declined. I would have sneezed for a week. Eventually Cesar beckoned a woman in my direction and she went off to prepare hair dye. She returned and began applying the stuff. It felt very concentrated burning into my scalp. I mused at the thought of all my hair falling out to reveal a red and blistered bald head in time for tonight's show. Fortunately, that never happened. While the dye was cooking Cesar offered me a manicure (they don't say that at Toni and Guy in Banbury). My Spanish is fairly non-existent, but there was something about bonita mentioned. Dunno if he was saying I would look good afterwards or whether the manicurist was particularly good-looking. My right hand is currently covered in red marks around the nails from bashing the strings of my guitar each night during *King*, so I could hardly see the point of a manicure – a bit like doing a paint job on the car before driving it into the wall. In the end, they did a good job on my hair. They wouldn't take Visa so I needed cash. I promised I would return with money and that seemed to be good enough. Went back to the ballroom looking for Frenchie and bumped into Pete T who gave me the money, bless him. Returned to the salon and paid up. He also told me that lunch was free in the restaurant, so I went back there and had an excellent bit of chicken and rice from the buffet. I was offered a drink and decided on iced tea. It was the best iced tea I have ever had.

Soundcheck was okay. The crew had worked hard to get everything working. My sound was similar to trucks crashing in a tunnel. The ballroom is very ambient and I'm getting a lot of slap of drums off the back wall. Oh well, as I've often said in the past, hopefully it will be better with the room full of people.

Returned to my room feeling tired and dozed for an hour before getting up and getting myself together. We had agreed to meet by the elevator on the third floor and did so. Some bloke was checking into his room and said, "What is the band playing downstairs?"

"Marillion," someone said

"Is it the original line-up with Fish?" he said

"No."

"Hmm..."

He vanished into his room. Well, it's only been 23 years, you can't expect people to notice.

Down in the dressing room I decided I was going to need help. I mixed a tequila and Red Bull - my first since the awful poisoning Sao Paolo - and it did the job. I suddenly felt really cuddly and up for it. Barry Garber appeared and we chatted for a while. There was an opening act on stage. Quite a decent rock band. They'd just finished, so I went up on stage and sat behind the drum riser watching the crew working. Today is Nial's 21st birthday and I wanted to be near him and to appreciate everyone's efforts. The room was rammed with people – I guess the tables helped it to look busy...

The gig was great for me, although I could see the boys struggling a bit with the sound. I spent most of the night pacing around in front of the mic line, no doubt over-singing as I monitored with my in-ears dangling, mostly off the room, but I worked the crowd for all I was worth and they went with it. It turned out to be the surprise good gig of the tour. Afterwards, stuck next to the elevators, I was mobbed for the best part of an hour while nervous security men kept offering to pull me out of there and I kept declining, saying the people are fine and I'll sign everything. It took a while. I was kissed on the cheeks a lot – mostly by men. After that, I had a quiet beer out on the terrace and a walk around the swimming pool looking up at the half moon which was lying on its back like a bowl. That doesn't happen in England

Wednesday 24 October *Caracas – Mexico Travel Day*

The phone rang at ten past four in the morning. It was my alarm call. "You've got twenty minutes..." said Frenchie in his usual deadpan style. I got up and showered, then quickly packed and made my way down to reception. I had no extras to pay, so that was that. We all piled into the goat-van and left for the airport. Unbelievably, there was a traffic jam on the freeway out of the city. At 5am!

We nudged along in stationary traffic for about an hour until we eventually made it to the airport. All the equipment was brought in just as dawn was breaking. Check-in took an age. There are security men everywhere. Half of 'em are ours and the rest were going through suitcases at random. Ian M got searched along with Nick Todd and Christian, the LD. When I eventually got to the desk, the man wanted his photograph taken with me! After check-in came more security of course. Shoes off, but no need to take laptops out of bags – it's different everywhere in the world. After security came border control – it's as hard to get OUT of Venezuela as it is to get in. Out of the dozen or so border desks, only one had anyone working. One guy to process a queue which must have consisted of a hundred people. It grew with every passing minute... I ended up standing in line with Ian, behind two girls – one of which was wearing a little bomber jacket covered in hand guns, each one in Warhol-esque bright colours. I said to Ian... "Guns! You wouldn't normally associate guns with the fairer sex..."

"No..." said Ian thoughtfully, "...Daggers!"

And so it was that, having got up at 4.00, we arrived at Gate 23 around 9.00 for a plane which was boarding at 7.00 and taking off at 8.30, to discover it hadn't even arrived yet. When it did arrive Frenchie was called to the desk and given a high-vis jacket. They were taking him onto the runway. They wanted to search every case of the equipment before loading it. After another hour or so, we boarded and all the carry-on bags were searched again at the door of the plane. They sure are careful here...

I can't remember when we took off, but not long after we were in the air the pilot came on the tannoy to say that we were in fact currently flying south to avoid tropical storm Sandy, and that there might be some turbulence... Great... As it turned out there was hardly any and, as I write, the descent has just been announced – landing in 20 minutes. "Please discontinue the use of electronic devices". Bye...

Getting into Mexico was also time-consuming. There was a long and slow-moving queue to immigration which must have taken well over half-an-hour. After that, a wait for bags and then join another queue to have everything scanned again. We'd landed around 2.00, but it was nearer 4.30 by the time we emerged. Having said that, there's such a noticeable difference between the disinterested and surly attitude of the Venezuelan officials and the good-natured and welcoming Mexicans. I have said for years that Mexican people have a lot of heart and unpretentious warmth and I found it to be so once again. I bought some Cadbury's milk chocolate in the duty free - a little bag of miniatures - and handed them round band and crew. I think everyone found a bit of chocolate to be a good thing after such an early morning and long day travelling. There was a policewoman eyeing up our equipment and generally watching over the baggage carousel. I offered her a chocolate, quite certain that she would decline, but no, she broke a big smile, thanked me and took one. As I left the baggage hall a customs man asked me if I have a certificate for all the equipment. "Frenchie! Help!" It turned out that we didn't have the piece of paper he was looking for. Again, after a short chat with his superior, he waved us through. No 40-minute wait, no bribe dressed up as "tax".

We exited the hotel into the 30-degree heat of the Mexican afternoon. I popped into Starbucks to grab a Chai. It took another hour to get into town to the hotel, which seemed very nice. Again, everyone here is so friendly and says hello whenever you pass them. Arrived in room 713 and set up my laptop so that I could Skype home in the morning. L will be in bed now. It's midnight in England. The minibar was locked and I was gagging for a beer. A lady came up to unlock it and mysteriously began pulling objects out of it like Mary Poppins. First came a full-sized umbrella, followed by a mirror, then a wooden terraced tray full of chocolate and crisps. There's a constant underlying force of the bizarre in Mexico – another thing I love about the place. I Skyped home and let Linette know I'm safely arrived.

Later went downstairs and met up with the crew and Ian M and we walked a little way across town to a little traditional restaurant and had a fine Mexican dinner and a few excellent margaritas. Returned to the hotel around 10pm and went to my room to lie on the bed. I didn't last long – it had been a long day...

Thursday 25 October *Mexico:* Day Off

In theory it's a day off... In practice we've agreed to devote most of the day to **Rolling Stone** magazine. We were picked up at 4pm to be taken in a van to **Rolling Stone**'s office which is in a beautiful old Spanish-style building in one of the wealthy parts of Mexico City, right around the corner from the Il Presidente Hotel we used to stay in. It was there that I saw David Hockney in the breakfast queue... The greeting at **Rolling Stone** was really warm and respectful. We sat at a big table for a while as one by one different members of the magazine's staff appeared and seemed genuinely delighted to have us there. I was offered Jack Daniels and Coke and given presents by the magazine. T-shirts and candy skulls with our name on. Next week it's the Day of the Dead (Nov 2) so there are skulls and skeletons much in evidence.

We were shown upstairs to a room which had been lit for TV – it has been arranged for the band to do a filmed on-line chat. People from around Mexico and around the world had submitted questions. It was fun. Everyone was relaxed and feeling at home. In front of us was a little table covered in candles, flowers and little gravestones with skeletons waving from beneath them. Quite voodoo-ish and very **Rolling Stone**sy. I was invited to take a grave with me and so I tried to pack it carefully into a box with newspaper in the hope that the delicate waving skeleton wasn't damaged in the journey home. We said bye and see you later and then got back into the bus (stopping for photographs with staff and even a passing traffic warden) to go to soundcheck for the one hour acoustic set we have agreed to play for **Rolling Stone** magazine tonight.

It turned out to be a restaurant. Soundcheck was chaotic and hellish. Phil Brown doesn't like digital desks and that's what he had. Apparently all the controls were on-screen, and the screen was broken. There was persistent 200Hz feedback which took ages to get rid of. We hadn't rehearsed and were frantically trying to make a plan and decide upon a set. In the end we decided to do the one-at-a-time thing where I start the show and am joined by the band one at a time. "Backstage" was a back room where a large table had been set for dinner. The crew had arrived to hang out and have fun and were working their way through Mezcal Tequila.

At 8.30 I went on and began the show with *The Hollow Man* from **Brave**.

People talked over verse 1, so I stopped and asked them to be quiet. That might be an understatement... I think my actual words were, "Just because we're playing a restaurant doesn't mean I'm a fucking cabaret singer, so if you don't want to listen to me, just let me know and I'll fuck off."

They quietened down a bit after that, but there was still a constant murmur so I abandoned the song and tried *Cover my Eyes* instead. That seemed to bore them less (or maybe it was just louder). Pete T then joined me and we played *The Bell in the Sea*, bass and voice. The Rothers joined us, and on it went until all 5 of us were on stage. In the end, the whole thing was very well received.

After the show we sat down to dinner... The food was excellent and we were really well looked after by the head waiter – a typically warm smiley chap who couldn't do enough for us. At one point in the evening we were introduced to the owner of the restaurant and his wife. I told him to give the head waiter a pay rise and said he was terrific. After the owner had gone, he punched the air in celebration. Great. I didn't stay late, although I was a little worried about Nial who was drinking Tequila copiously. After my poisoning in Sao Paolo I was keen for him not to go through what I'd been through. Tomorrow's a gig day and he'll have to work!

I returned first in the van with Pete T. I guess this is the new me. In the "old days" I would've hung out and partied, talked rubbish, got sloshed etc, but I seem to be losing the appetite for all of it and a quiet room with BBC World on the telly (even if I have seen it all before twice earlier) is an attractive prospect. Peace at last n'all that.

Thursday 26 October   *Mexico   Metropolitan*

A beautiful morning outside, apart from the building work going on outside my window. I thought I'd try my luck and see if I could change rooms, so I called and asked to speak to the manager. She was called Monica and was very nice, saying that if I give her a little time she will see what is available and perhaps move me to a suite on the other side. Nice...

I decided to walk down the avenue to Starbucks and buy a cappuccino. When I got back, Monica the manager was waiting for me and I was shown to suite 902 which is bigger than our house and has a balcony so I can sunbathe. Hooray! I Skyped home and then creamed up with the factor 30 I'd bought in Sao Paolo and sat out on the balcony for half an hour or so. Didn't leave it too long – it's midday and you've got to be careful. Spent the next couple of hours writing this diary and opening and closing doors, curtains, cupboards etc. I'm now in room 902 a suite with an excellent view of the golden angel, the high-rise buildings and the Mexican hills beyond.

At 4pm we had to be down in the lobby for the van-ride to the Metropolitan. We arrived round the back of the gig and I remembered the street – they should call it Electrical Street but they don't. There are a number of shops selling electric motors, compressors and washing machine spares. Mexico's great. Round the front of the building is where Fernando Aceves took the picture of me with the umbrella which appeared in **Rolling Stone** on the same page as Bono and Al Gore, and opposite Amy Winehouse, Keith Richards and Liv Tyler. Backstage out in the yard, a trestle table had been set up and a hot buffet was being served. I hadn't eaten yet at that point, so I tucked into chicken and rice. The Mexican lady smiled warmly as she served me and so did the guys. Everyone here treats everyone else with warmth and respect. The world should be like the people of Mexico City.

I was pretty hoarse at soundcheck. Oh well – it will either go one way or the other... Last time we played here I ended up sitting on the statue at stage right. I decided I should start where I left off last time. I could sing *Splintering Heart* from there, so I climbed up to see how best to do it... I decided I'd need a stepladder if I was to have any hope of getting up there unseen at the beginning of the show. I could climb from it onto the PA to the right of the curtains and with a bit of luck, most of the people wouldn't notice until the light hit me. Frenchie said he'd organise a stepladder...

Between the soundcheck and show I took a walk with Nial round to the church of St Judas (Rothers informs me that this is in fact St Jude - patron saint of lost causes - not Judas Iscariot. Either way, it seems an odd choice of saint). The church had been visible from the van on the way here and, being one of the few old buildings we'd passed I thought it might be worth a look. Inside was somewhat busier than English churches – it seems the Mexicans are into their catholic religion in a big way. The altar was highly decorated in the colourful Mexican way – quite festive really compared to the sombre classical churches of Europe. There wasn't really much to see so Nial and I made our way back to washing-machine street, stopping occasionally to be photographed and give autographs to passing fans. Everyone here is so humble and appreciative, so it never feels like a chore. I can really feel the altitude of Mexico City (7000-feet above sea level) making me noticeably out of breath while walking around, climbing stairs, etc. I kept feeling a little light-headed at random. The show was going to be hard work... I better be careful I don't fall off the narrow ledge getting to the statue.

"Are you SURE about this?" the boys kept saying... They needn't have worried – it all worked quite well. Not too many people saw me creep out and onto the PA then up onto the ledge and along to the statue where the light was to hit me for the beginning of the show. The boys agreed it looked great. The show itself went really well. It was physically more demanding than usual, owing to the altitude. I suddenly felt really unfit! Puffing and panting between each line of the songs. The crowd though (about 3000 of them - sold out) were in amazing form, singing along particularly with the old pre-me hits but no less loudly with *Easter* and *No One Can*. Getting off stage was a relief. Some night's I wonder if I'll live through it. This was one of those...

Friday 27 October *La Condesa Mexico*

Again, a tremendous atmosphere. Despite feeling knackered and struggling vocally the crowd lifted me - moment by moment - above the tiredness and the altitude which makes everything that bit more strenuous. Found myself weeping as they sang, "*No one can take you away from me now*".

The next day I walked along the wide avenue that is the Paseo de la Reforma. It reminds me a little bit of Las Ramblas in Barcelona. The wide road has a central strip of narrow parkland where people can walk. At the moment it's filled with bizarre papier-mâché sculptures of dragon-like creatures. Brightly painted in acrylic yellows, oranges and greens and covered in Mexican mythological mad creatures, skeletons, little aliens and every creature known and unknown to man. There is also a photographic exhibition of portraits of women in support of breast cancer awareness, and a Nescafé exhibition of sculptures and installations made entirely from mugs. It's obvious to me as I walk along that this city is trying really hard to express itself. Positivity and ideas are everywhere. The people seem smiley and happy irrespective of their backgrounds and an atmosphere of warmth and good nature fills the street.

I used to like Mexico City and the Mexicans. Now I love the place. It has a beating heart that puts most other cities to shame. Our two shows here were among the warmest reactions we've ever had anywhere. My enduring memory was of that aforementioned last encore at La Condesa. I'm standing at the edge of the stage - in-ear monitors dangling - leaning out over the crowd holding out the mic and just soaking up the sound of the crowd to find my own tears coming. Amazing people. Everywhere I can see people crying. So honest and unafraid to show themselves. They sing "*No One Can Take You Away From Me Now*" – tears rolling down their cheeks. It's not a song, it's a promise.

"*Are you strong enough to be beautiful?*" Yes you are, absolutely, Mexico City. A million thanks.

2 0 1 3

Wednesday 16 January *Paris*

Steve Rothery and I were to travel ahead of the band to Paris where a promo day including radio sessions had been arranged. We flew to Paris the night before to be "rested" and ready.

Arrived in Charles de Gaulle airport, Paris to discover the Christmas decs still up. Really beautiful. The French totally leave us Brits standing when it comes to decorative aesthetics. The airport looked lovely. Unfortunately, France isn't always the most efficient country on earth and when the workers aren't actually ON strike, they are often a rule to themselves. Tonight I wondered...

We walked miles from the aeroplane to the baggage hall (God knows HOW the bags make the journey to the carousels in less than a week!) to discover, unsurprisingly, that nothing happened for half an hour or so before a carousel was announced. Then more "nothing" happened for another fifteen minutes until an announcement was made (in only French, of course, leaving the non-French-speakers to have to ask around among the bi-lingual passengers for clues) to say that it would be the other carousel across the hall. Everyone crossed the hall to wait at the other carousel. After a further delay, another French announcement came from the tannoy and everyone returned across the hall to the original carousel. After a while the one across the hall juddered into life and bags began to arrive. Everyone crossed the hall again and began picking up their bags with occasional Gallic shrugs. I soon saw my suitcase appear and hauled it onto the floor. This was eventually followed by Steve's bag. Predictably, his guitar and pedal-board didn't arrive and it took a further half-hour to discover (in some kind of English) that we needed to be elsewhere for outsized luggage. I took a photograph of an advertising poster showing three girls wearing hats made out of newspapers. I thought it might come in handy as an image for *Paper Lies* during the **Brave** shows at the forthcoming conventions. With much relief we eventually located to find Steve's guitar still in one piece and made our way through disinterested (which is good) Customs into the Arrivals hall where we found a man holding up a piece of paper which simply said "Mr. h" on it. That turned out to be me and we followed him to the car park and he took us into town. The traffic wasn't too bad (Paris can be hellish) and we made pretty good time (under an hour) into the city-centre arriving at the hotel around 10.30pm.

The hotel seemed small and was undergoing building-work. A slightly grubby night-porter checked us in and I was given a key to a room on the fifth floor. This turned out be the roof! My room was accessed by taking a small elevator to the 4th floor (that was as far as it went) and then up a flight of stairs to the next floor where signs on the wall guided me out into the night air and across the roof to another door with my room number on it. I arrived huffing and puffing with my bags and opened the door to reveal a room, barely big enough for the double bed it contained. Around the bed were a few small items of furniture and all the light fittings had ill-fitting shades showing signs of heat-damage. I tried to straighten one of the lamp-shades and it wobbled around and fell off. It was then that I noticed the wallpaper which was designed from 18th century pornographic lithographs of gentlemen shagging half undressed ladies. This confirmed my suspicion that the room either was, or had been, a brothel. Rock n'roll, I suppose. I could have forgiven the wallpaper as some kind of French weird-chic if the room had been bigger and not quite so shabby. I phoned down to reception and no one answered. The phone didn't seem to work. That did it! I dialed my French chum Stephanie Ringuet and asked her if she could sort me out a room at Le Relais Montmartre. She called back and said, yes there's a room. I decided I'd scoot and the office could sort it all out in the morning. Dragged my bag back across the room, down the stairs and into the lift and asked the grubby man at reception to order me a cab. I was out of there.

Taxi'd across town to Le Relais on Rue Constance, just round the corner from Le Moulin Rouge where Christopher, the friendly night-receptionist from the Ivory Coast, showed me into Room 4 opposite the desk on the ground floor. No bag-hauling or staggering around on the roof necessary. This was the room I remember doing the promo in for **Not The Weapon But The Hand** with Richard Barbieri. I like it here.

Finally in bed at midnight.

Friday 25 January   *Toulouse Bikini*

We were back at the Bikini. Didn't write much about the gig. The legendary Hervé wasn't feeling sociable today. Shame. I hope nobody from our crew has upset him. There was a sign outside the backstage elevator saying, "No chewing gum. No guns."

Today was to be memorable for another tour-bus breakdown. All was well until we made ready to leave at 2.00 in the morning, at which point it became apparent that the bus wouldn't go into gear. I lay awake most of the night wondering if it would be fixed. It could be worse, and it has been. At least this time I don't have the added pressure of a marriage on a knife-edge and a wife in another city waiting for me to arrive for breakfast. Just a partner waiting for me to have lunch!

Saturday 26 January *Barcelona Bikini*

Up at 6.00 to find Frenchie lying downstairs in the lounge. He hadn't really slept having been trying to sort things out for most of the night. We were still in the car park at the Bikini. He said there are no direct flights to Barcelona and trains are also difficult.. Hmm.. We have a show in Barcelona tonight (also at a club called Bikini!) so we've got to figure out how to get the crew there for the load-in. In the end we just had to throw money at it, and so 5 cabs were ordered and arrived to take us to Barcelona at 10.00 am. I got in the back with Ian and snoozed my way to Spain. Rothers was in the front. To my great surprise we made great time and arrived in Barcelona around 1pm.

It took 30-minutes to check in as the receptionists were Basil Fawlty and Manuel combined. L and Vibes arrived shortly after me. There was a kiddies play area behind the hotel so we took little Vibes down to trampolines and gave 20 euros away to the play-area woman. There were lots of little kids bouncing around and going round on little rides. The place must have been a goldmine – no doubt owned by someone in a position to do a deal with the council for the spot. Enjoyed the best cup of coffee this year from Café Bou" by the trampolines

Soundcheck went well. Rothers and I had been invited to play a couple of acoustic songs at a radio station "Just across the road". (Not). We played *Everybody Hurts* and *Wrapped Up in Time* which Frenchie said he enjoyed – knock me down with a feather. Back to hotel I went to Frenchie's room to lie down for 30 minutes so that L and Vibes could relax in our room.

Tonight's gig was really good. The keyboards worked perfectly. I wandered backstage during *Ocean Cloud* to find Lucy, Fiona and Angie deep in conversation. Oh well. I guess songs about blokes rowing across the Atlantic are not every girl's cuppa tea.

Sunday 27 January *Barcelona Bikini*

Today could be best described as "When a breakdown of communication takes 10 years off your life."

My good friend and brother, Gabriel Perez, had arranged for me to sing a duet with Catalan rock star Pep Sala at the medal ceremony of the Men's Handball World Championship Final between Denmark and Spain to be held today at The Palau St Jordi Stadium across town, which Gabriel manages. The King of Spain is to attend, and the thing will go out live on TV. I had agreed to do this some weeks ago. It seemed like a good idea at the time – I'll be in Barcelona anyway with Marillion and, as the performance is to happen late afternoon, I can nip over there after Marillion's soundcheck and before our, somewhat smaller, show. A couple of weeks ago Gabriel emailed me to say that the thing would have to be done as a "playback" (mime) as there wouldn't be the facilities to sing live through the PA and no time to check sound or set it up. I asked Gabriel to send me the track so that I could get the lip-sync exacty right for TV. He had sent me the song and I must confess I hadn't given it too much attention ahead of today, so I spent much of the day listening to the track and trying to learn every last nuance of my vocal so that I could mime it flawlessly. I'm not someone who phrases words mechanically and I'm constantly pushing and hanging against the groove, so these things take a lot of learning. I would have much rather sung the thing live, but it wasn't an option.

Around 4pm we took a taxi to Palau St Jordi, where the Handball Final was sold-out to around 20,000 people attending. The taxi dropped us at the perimeter and we walked the rest of the way. I was wearing headphones and repeatedly playing the track – still not too sure of the phrasing. Inside, we were greeted by Gabriel who showed us to our seats. Linette was thrilled to be attending the final between Spain and her home country. It turns out the Crown Princess of Denmark was in the house too. As the game progressed, my heart rate redoubled at the prospect of playing to this huge crowd and to the attendant royals – especially as I was still trying to hear the track in my headphones against the roar of the crowd, and not really feeling like I was too sure of the phrasing.

From here, the day took a turn for the worse... Spain gave Denmark a humiliating thrashing as Denmark's spirit appeared somehow broken. Denmark was completely outclassed and one could only wonder how they had managed to progress to the final only to appear so inept today. I felt for Linette and our Danish lighting-designer, Yens, who had tagged along to watch. The Spanish home-crowd were going nuts as Spain scored yet more and more goals over a crushed Denmark. By the time the game was all-but-over Gabriel reappeared to escort us on the long walk through the corridors of the hall to the side of "stage" i.e. the central area where the Handball game was concluding with a 35-19 victory for Spain. I said hello to Pep and everything seemed to happen at once: "Hello my friend! I have placed a low frequency tone at the front of the playback so that you know the key of *Easter*."

"What?!?! I'm miming *Easter*? Which version?"

"The acoustic one we made last time in Barcelona! Didn't you get my email?"

"Yes, but Gabriel sent me the other track *Boig Per Tu*. The one with the band."

"The one with the band?! No, my friend, you will sing *Easter* and then we'll play the version of *Boig* for 2 pianos,"

Oh my God. The acoustic version of *Easter* is completely free, has no rhythm and is impossible to mime either vocally or instrumentally. As this fact hit me like a thunderbolt, a technician was strapping a radio pack to me and placing a pair of in-ear buds into my ears. At the same time, another assistant was holding up his fingers and counting down 5 – 4 – 3 – 2 – 1 to our time in front of this enormous crowd and the television cameras.

In a daze, I walked into the glare of lights and the crowd and sat down on one of the piano stools. As I did so, I trapped the wire beneath me and both the in-ear buds flew out of my ears just as I heard the first piano chord sound from the PA in the stadium. I was to make the entire "performance" monitoring "from the room" 150m away from the nearest PA speaker. On the bright side, even if I'd known the song backwards, there's no way in physics I could have mimed in time with it, as I was hearing the music probably about 1-second later than it would be coming out of people's TV's. Anyone watching, would have seen an idiot Englishman's mouth moving about a second after he sang, while his hands hit the piano in a similar fashion which had nothing to do with the music. The horror.

Sometimes you've just got to dig in and not have a nervous breakdown or soil yourself. This was one of those.

The second song *Boig Per Tu* - Pep's big hit - went by in a vague dream also, and at no point in either of the non-performances did I manage to get my ear monitors into my ears. Well, I certainly know how to fuck-up horribly when I most need to shine… At one point I heard boo-ing which I felt was well-deserved and all my own work, but I was later to discover that some of the crowd had taken exception to Pep introducing the song in Catalan, not Spanish. There's a move at the moment in Spain for Catalonian independence and, although we were in Barcelona – the capital of Catalonia (or Catalunia) Pep's use of Catalan was interpreted by some of the Spanish handball fans as a provocation.

As soon as the "performance" had ended we had to dash across town where Marillion were holding stagetime until my return. It had been arranged to have a car at the Palau S Jordi with the engine running waiting to whisk us back. That never happened either! The King of Spain's security weren't allowing anyone inside the perimeter fence so we had to run down the road. The fresh-air did me good…

Had a great gig with Marillion though.

"Never get out of the boat.."

Saturday 5 October *Home – Mexico City*

I heard Nial moving around first. It was only a matter of five or ten minutes before young Vibes heard him too and he was, himself out of bed. I expected him to appear, but I heard him descend the stairs looking for whoever was downstairs. Then he came back up and appeared. "Who's left all the lights on downstairs?"

It was 7.45. I waved to him, got up and went downstairs with him leaving L in bed for the last half-hour of peace until Monday – a promise made last night. Nial reappeared and we had coffee while Vibes and I wrote numbers on pink *Post-It* notes and stuck them on the front door. He's doing well now with his counting and I'm sure he'd have been able to number the notes to twenty, but he wanted me to write a few anyway. Strangely, the post came 2 hours early and I heard the letter drop through the letter box at 8.00. Vibes decided to take the post to his mum, so I made her a coffee and that was the end of her lie-in.

At 9.00 I decided I couldn't put it off much longer and began packing to leave for Mexico City. Steve Rothery and I are to play a charity show next Tuesday. It's sold out and, to quote the organisers, "The show has, in financial and media terms, far-exceeded our expectations." That's great, but we'd better live up to it then... The pressure is, as ever, on.

Experience has taught me to allow at least a couple of days to soak up transatlantic jet lag... It's a mistake to try and sing when it's 4.30am in your head – hence the Saturday departure for the Tuesday show. Around 10.30 I left for the airport. The on-line meet & greet car parking I had arranged requested a telephone call 30 minutes before arrival, so I called them from the motorway when I passed Oxford services. I dialled the number but it rang unanswered. Strange... Upon repeated attempts, it slowly became apparent that maybe I'd been scammed. Called home and Linette "Googled" a few reviews of said company – all saying that it was a scam and that the comparison website was a fraud. Off to a good start! I guess it could have been worse... I could have given them my car before I found out they were crooks! Oh well.

Made my way to the long-term car park, Terminal 5, kissing goodbye to the fifty quid I'd paid the fictitious meet-and-greeters, and took the bus to the Terminal, where I eventually found Phil (our sound man) and Rothers waiting for me. We checked-in and Rothers wandered off alone while Phil and I went to the Giraffe café for breakfast. Eventually the Gate was announced and Phil and I took the train to the Gate where flight BA243 was already boarding. I was recognised by the air steward at the door of the 747, who had seen the band several times. I hoped in vain that he'd bump us up to Business class. We do seem to be much better known in Mexico and from time to time throughout the flight I was asked for an autograph or chatted to by cabin staff who knew about the band. I settled into my window seat for the long journey and spent much of it trying to copy my old 1992 diary into the laptop. Unfortunately the economy seat didn't allow enough space to open the laptop AND be able to read the diary, so I had to read a couple of lines then close the diary to write them in the laptop. An insanely slow way of doing the job, made slower still by my addled brain's inability to remember what I'd just read. Stuck at it for a few hours but eventually gave up in favour of drinking beer and watching the Alan Partridge movie **Alpha Papa** in which, bizarrely, Marillion are mentioned several times. There were few laugh-out-loud moments but, overall, the movie was a good-if-inane watch. I'm not easily pleased. Must be my age...

Right now we're over Georgia. 33,000 feet over Georgia, but it's a clear day and the ground is constantly visible. It has been more or less clear for the entire journey and from my window I have looked down on the green fields and rugged south-west coast of Ireland, the blue white-wave-crested Atlantic and now, the dark dusty-looking expanse of America. Still two and a half hours to go... I'll have another beer...

The in-flight map tells me I'm looking down on Galveston – the coastline of Texas and the broad sweep of lagoons and sand-bars that make up the Gulf of Mexico. I remember listening to the song with my dad. Glen Campbell's beautiful cowboy tones singing the song that always brought a tear to me, and still does. All those years ago I never dreamt I'd ever look down on that beach.

I still have a vivid memory looking along the ungainly extended wing of the 747 as we banked hard over Mexico City to come into land. The wings broaden and extend backwards until you can see daylight through them and the inner guts of the wing, normally hidden from view – pneumatic rams and hydraulic tubes. I'm suddenly reminded that this is a machine made of thousands of inner components and, as I gaze up along the wing, now pointing up at the sky in a most un-wing-like fashion, and at a shocking angle to the horizontal, I feel the slightly empty shudder of fear as I realise how easily this thing could fall on the city below and that inevitable flash-back to the twin towers and mad Mohammed Atta. The damage, the damage.

I put the aircrew on the guest list.

Well, here we are, improbably intact with feet on Mexican soil (Mexican corridors, actually). No problems at all at immigration or with baggage. We were met in arrivals by Daniela, Leonardo's cousin. We continue to be strangely famous and were photographed and asked for autographs by ordinary members of the public in the Arrivals Hall. Jumped into a van and we were driven into (or further into – Mexico City airport seems to be well-within the city itself, maybe it wasn't always, perhaps the city just sprawled out, enveloped the airport and kept going) town to the Eurostars Suites at 78 Rio Amazonas. Not long into the journey we began to see flashes of lightning and then heavy, heavy rain. When we arrived at the hotel, we couldn't get out of the van. Hung around waiting for someone to show up with an umbrella but nobody got it together. I eventually lost patience and climbed out, getting pretty drenched in the short distance across the pavement. The roads were awash with water. When it rains here, it's monsoon-like!

The hotel doesn't have much of a reception, just a dingy marble desk and a few tubular chairs. A welcoming committee awaited us but we didn't really know what to do. There being no bar or café, everyone just stood awkwardly about. By this time we were all knackered and my thoughts were focussed solely on checking in and getting to bed. Leonardo and his wife Gabriella seem very nice. I felt for them, standing around in this dingy hotel on a Saturday night waiting for some grumpy and shattered Englishmen.

The bed was slightly softer than the floor, but there wasn't much in it. Couldn't get on with the pillows. I should have brought my own... Eventually rejected all three pillows in favour of a cushion.

Sunday 6 October *Mexico City*

Sleep was fitful and interrupted by time-lag. Awake at 4.00, and finally gave up and got up at 5.00. Went out at half-six looking for coffee and at 7.00 found a Starbucks across the street. The staff were already there and the metal shutters half-open. I pleaded but to no avail. It's Sunday and they don't serve anyone 'til 8.00.

Came back and began assembling some vocal files for Richard B. The internet and computer audio-recording combine to allow us to work and exchange files across the world as easily as being in the same room. This soaked up an hour or so and provided a diversion whilst waiting for the breakfast room to open downstairs at 8.00. Went down to find Phil and Steve already at a table. We've all slept terribly of course and we've all been up since 5.00 (that's 11.00am in England). Mexican food is very 'other'. They were serving sprouts for breakfast. I had quite a few. Leonardo appeared in reception with some money for us to cover our expenses and fees, and so Phil and I went across the street with him where we sat in the entrance to the big shopping mall drinking Starbucks coffees and talking to him about the Project and life-in-general. He's a nice chap. I like him.

Spent most of the rest of the day chilling out and working on music and copying out old diary entries from 'the days before laptops'. Had a look at my bank account and my credit card on-line account to discover that the car-park scam payments hadn't actually been taken! Good news – I'm a hundred quid better off! But... perhaps someone's just waiting to use my card details for a bigger withdrawal later! I couldn't remember which card I'd paid for the parking with, and there was no way of finding out as it wasn't mentioned on the email confirmation I'd been sent. I'm gonna need to phone the bank and the Visa company and fess-up.

At 7.00pm I had arranged to go out looking for dinner with Phil. We remembered the traditional restaurant we went to last year and figured it would be quite close to our hotel. Getting there involved running the gauntlet of a little gang of fans who had assembled outside the hotel (I wonder how they found out... Rothers!!!) and the street-guys who try to entice you into dodgy strip clubs as you walk down the street, and just as Phil and I decided we were lost, we found the little restaurant and ordered up dinner. I had chicken with chocolate "mollé" sauce. Strange, but it kind-of works. Phil took a photograph. Washed down with a couple of small Margarita's and followed by excellent home-made rice pudding.

Returned to the hotel and went to bed "early" – whatever that is...

Monday 7 October *Mexico City*

We were to be picked up today at 4.00 to be driven to the school where Projecto Antares does its work. No sign of the jet-lag diminishing. Awake at 4.15 and got up around 5.00 again. Phoned home and all's well. Little Vibes doesn't seem to be missing me much and is more concerned with the details of the present I have promised I'll bring him home. Linette's been busy looking into the possibility of starting up an internet-based shop selling kids clothes from Denmark, also selling on market stalls and through hosting parties. I spent the morning online and on the phone to my credit card people and bank, trying to warn them about the car-park scammers and pleading with them to look out for the payments without cancelling all my cards or I'll be in Mexico City without the means to pay for anything! Spent the rest of the day until 4.00, writing the diary and chilling out – trying to ride the waves of nausea which overtake me periodically. I seem to find it harder to cope with jet-lag as I get older. Maybe I just can't remember. Also, I think the altitude of MC makes us 'lowlanders' a bit strange and nauseous – a feeling which never really left me until we were on the plane home.

We were bussed on-time over to the school and spent a pleasant hour as guests, sitting in on a class. Today they were shaking percussion in order to improve motor-skills. I shook some bells and maracas to some Mike Oldfield recorder instrumental, and then the kids were asked to make a picture of what they felt when they were listening. I joined in and scribbled the usual flowers and sticks of dynamite. The kids were sweet and affectionate – they all had their picture taken with us by Fernando Aceves who had first contacted me about the whole idea. It was nice to see him.

After that we were taken over to Coyoacan, one of the oldest parts of MC where Leonardo had arranged dinner in a restaurant on the main square by the Jardin Cenetario. Steve and I both plumped for the Tuna with pistachio cream. It was lovely. Phil and I tasted the recommended Mezcal which is drunk with a brown salt with a very distinctive earthy complimentary flavour. I later discovered it was flavoured with worms... Ordered coconut flan for desert. This too was very nice but a bit too dense to manage. A good job we have a gig tomorrow... it could have got ugly with the Mezcals if the brakes had not been firmly applied.

Back to the hotel in the ever-present white people-carrier (or white-people carrier in this instance).

Tuesday 8 October *Mexico City Club Lunario*

Up at the crack of 6.00 again unable to sleep. Breakfasted at 7.00. The Skype has stopped working so I have discovered Facetime which kinda does the same thing but is a little more Mac friendly. Spoke to L who had been to Beaconsfield Services for a meeting with a Danish clothes-selling person. She said it went well. Vibes was home from school and seemed fine. No sign of Nial.

Went over to the gig at the enormous Auditorio Nacional. Sadly, we're not playing the big room (which is wonderful) but the club underneath (which, as it turned out is a bit of a bare-walled acoustic horror). The room came as a disappointment as we walked in. Having played the Auditorio Nacional in the past, I have found it to be one of the best spaces in the world, acoustically, visually and technically. I thought the Lunario might be its cousin. No such luck. It's just a bare basement with a stage and a PA. When Steve and I arrived around midday, Phil was well-stressed out, muttering to himself. The sound engineer hadn't yet shown up. Phil had, professionally, emailed ahead with his requirements for the out-front digital desk so that it might be set up ready for our show. Nothing had been done and no one in the building seemed to know how to operate the desk. The mains transformers for our 240V power supplies had not arrived and were still in a car somewhere across town. Phil had arrived at 10.00am as arranged to find almost nothing and no one ready for him. It quickly became apparent that Steve Rothery's hired amplifier wasn't working properly and so another selection of amps was hastily arranged to be sent over, but no one was certain how long this might take. Mexico City's traffic is legendary in its tendency to move slowly... At least the piano had arrived but I didn't really get on with it at any point in the day. It just didn't sound right or respond to me as I'm used to. This could have been the instrument or it could have been my monitoring. I tried everything, eventually rejecting my "Ultimate" in-ears for Shure in-ear-buds which sounded more natural. It took a couple of hours before Steve R had an amp and a sound he could work with. We rehearsed a while in front of some of the kids from Projecto Antares who we'd invited along to the soundcheck. They weren't allowed into the show as the club serves alcohol. Eventually we didn't feel we could do much more and decided to return to the hotel. By this time I was a nervous wreck and still very tired from three night's lack of good sleep.

We were driven back to the hotel by our ever-present and helpful driver Enrique and, although we would only have an hour there, it was a precious hour before the return to the club for meet-and-greets and the show. We were taken downstairs to have a look at a series of photographs inspired by my *Faith* lyric. These comprised a child's hand holding various objects as a metaphor for faith. I was flattered and moved. We went back up to meet those who had been selected to meet us (upon which criteria, I don't know) but all were fans and thrilled to be there. Fernando Aceves was there to take photographs. We also signed photographs and album covers for everyone.

I have mixed feelings about the gig itself. On the negative side, I couldn't get comfortable with my sound and played the piano appallingly as a consequence of not feeling the instrument responding to my touch. I sang fairly well although I often struggled to hear myself properly. Having rehearsed my own re-working of John Lennon's *Instant Karma* until I was blue in the face, I nonetheless made a complete mess of it. Kate Bush's *The Man with the Child in his Eyes* was similarly murdered. When I played *No One Can*, the audience sang the chorus affectionately. I was grateful to have Steve there to share the situation – it would have been a long old night if I'd had to play this room alone. On the positive side, however, the atmosphere in the room was very warm and enthusiastic. The Mexican audience once again lived up to our high expectations, and the show, for the most part, was really well received. I had to keep reminding myself that everyone was having a great night and, secondly, the gig had been a success both financially and in terms of exposure for the Project. This was all that really mattered. Our performance was, at this stage, a mere detail.

After the show I sat in the dressing room, physically and emotionally wrung out. The high-altitude of MC has a strange effect on me and I think I'd have to be here a long time to get used to it. Steve R crossed the room and gave me a hug; a rare show of affection from him – he must have enjoyed himself! It took a while before I was ready to do any more autographs but I eventually went back out and sat on the edge of the stage. I was mobbed, but respectfully so, and a couple of uniformed security people appeared almost immediately to keep an eye on things and keep the people moving. This prevents any one person 'settling down' and excluding the people who are patiently waiting. Firm but fair n'all that. A table was set up for us downstairs so that we could do yet more autographs and photographs. After that, we packed our things and returned to the hotel. I was surprised to find that I was sitting on the bed in my room before midnight! What a relief. Now I could enjoy just existing again, and drift into sleep, at peace.

Wednesday 9 October *Mexico City – Home*

We till unable to sleep past 7.00am so got up and spoke to L for a while on FaceTime. She's fine. She says Vibes has been a good boy in my absence. She played me a little video recording of his harvest assembly yesterday and all the kids singing a song. To my ear, on laptop speakers and even down a long internet line from England to Mexico, they sounded better than I did last night!

Went down to breakfast to find Phil already seated – he'd already been down there for an hour. Rothers soon appeared. We watched a little breakfast TV... Latin American media is a laugh. The female newsreaders look like porn stars who then talk reverentially over footage of the Pope blessing the assembled throngs in St Peter's Square, Rome. The male newsreader looked like a well-suited pimp. The male studio host looked like Ricky Martin and at one point everyone got up and started dancing, hand on stomach and hips swivelling. Brilliant. I guess in England, we're not too far away from this breakfast television - Susanna whatnot is doing **Strictly** and that Charlie Stayt - much as I like him - is almost pimp-smooth. I'm not sure he'd be up to a Macarena at 8.00 am though. I ate muesli while pondering all this and then bailed out, crossing the street to Starbucks for a proper cup of coffee. The kids in Starbucks all recognise me now and grin away and wish me good morning in English. Lovely race of people, the Mexicans. Beautiful too in a completely 'other' way. They have all the warmth of the Brazilians but coupled with a kind of soulful sincerity it's hard to deny. I find the Chileans to be the same.

Had a wander round the department store in the mall, marvelling at the latest Samsung flat-screen TV's which look amazingly sharp and real. Ewan

McGregor was covered in blood. You could have reached out and dabbed him.

Came back to the hotel and wrote this diary while slowly packing my things and hanging on the phone for BA Customer Services. I was exploring the possibility of upgrading to Business (and a bed!!) on the return journey. After much holding on I was quoted 25,000 Avios points and 250 quid. It's a good deal, but it would have punched too big a hole in the wages, so I declined. Checked into Economy and decided to opt for a window seat at the back. At 1.00, Leonardo and Gabriela were to pick us up and take us back to Coyoacan for lunch. Ex-**Rolling Stone** journalist Juan Carlos Villanueva was also tagging along. JC's a nice chap and I've been trying to find the time for a beer with him since I got here. Down in the street it was sunny and warm. JC told me he now writes for Mexican Airlines in-flight magazine and showed me an article he'd written about a new movie called **Gravity** starring George Clooney and Sandra Bullock. It was a profile of the movie's director. The article opens quoting my opening line from *The Space* and, after three pages, closes with my closing lines from the same song. I have never seen my words quoted in print before. It's only taken 25 years... At this rate, I might yet achieve some kind of minor notoriety... but I'll probably have to snuff it first.

Leonardo and Gabriela arrived 25-minutes late (not late at all in Latin America). There is a demonstration on the main avenue and it's causing chaos with the traffic. We debated whether or not to go to Coyoacan bearing in mind the traffic but decided to risk it. Gabriela is one of the therapists at Projecto Antares and proudly showed us an article in **The Reforma** - Mexico's national newspaper - which details our visit to the Project on Monday. There's a good sized picture of yours truly on my hands and knees drawing flowers and sticks of dynamite with the children. It's funny how something like this achieves more profile for Marillion than a full-sized tour show would. You can see why so many show biz types cynically 'do a lot of work for charity'.

The drive to Coyacan took almost an hour but it was worth it. We had lunch in another beautiful restaurant overlooking the gardens. Conrado and Adriana joined us. Conrado is an absolute ringer for Bono. I think he's a lawyer or something. He and Leonardo must have come straight from work as they were both suited up. Fernando Aceves later arrived and we enjoyed a Mezcal together and ate hibiscus flower enchiladas, which were sweet and lovely, followed by a kind of Huacan pizza. This was followed by a desert of corn pie - also delicious, but strange to me - and the best cappuccino I've had in years. The coffee however was blown off the map by a small measure of hot chocolate served in a small cup made from some kind of half-seed or gourd. They make hot chocolate here by grinding the roasted berries on the premises and then adding water, not milk. This must have been what Walter Raleigh tasted all those years ago. No wonder he brought it back to England. It was the best beverage I've ever had. Not sweet, not bitter, VERY chocolatey and strangely refreshing – more so than coffee. Essence! I found it really uplifting.

We were running out of time, so we paid up (Leonardo insisted it was on him despite my offers) and then dived into a shop next door where I was on a mission to buy a radio-controlled car for Vibes. His requirements had been very specific: "Red with a stripe on it. And a horse". In other words, a Ferrari. Managed to find one and, while I was paying for it, the little man in the shop thanked me for the music. Half of Mexico seems to know who we are.

Drove back to the hotel and checked out. I rode with Leonardo and Gabriela to the airport while Steve and Phil rode with Enrique, the driver. We arrived in good time and, despite a long and tedious check-in, we still found we had over three clear hours to kill before boarding. The airport is massive and the walk to the gate was the longest I can remember making anywhere. I felt for Rothers who was carrying an insanely heavy bag of foot pedals and wearing a guitar slung over his shoulder. We sat at the Gate for 3 hours chatting to Phil while an electric storm raged outside. Fortunately it had worn itself out by 8.30 when we commenced boarding. We'd half-hoped the air steward fans might have arranged an upgrade for us, but it wasn't to be. As I made my way to the back of Economy yet another air steward - this time English - said hi and said he'd seen us play in London. Take-off from MC was delayed by someone getting sick and having to get back off the plane. This means they have to remove their bags, which can take quite a while. We eventually departed about an hour late. The really good news was that my seat row remained empty throughout the flight so I could lie-down. I think I managed to get more comfortable than I had been in the hotel bed and, as I write, we're coming in to land and I'm feeling better than I have for days! I have been looking down on a calm Atlantic Ocean for the last hour but, with England, comes the clouds. Once below them we got a superb view of London on our approach from the east. Landing was smooth amidst the familiar sound of baby cries. The change in altitude must really hurt them. They always go quiet again once they're down. We landed 45-minutes late. It's good to breathe the air of England again. I suddenly feel physically much better. Only immigration, the bags and the bus to the car-park to endure now, and then I'm FREE and going home!

Friday 8 November *Manchester Academy*

Slept well. Went to the café and bought bacon rolls for the crew. Came back and distributed 'em. Adam and Mark appeared from Manchester United and took Pete and me to Old Trafford for lunch.

This was followed by a tour of the stadium. Great to stand by the pitch. We weren't allowed on. Somehow the place has almost as much atmosphere empty as it does full. We shuffled between various other parties of Chinese and Japanese doing the tour too. It's amazing what an icon Man U has become in the Far East! We were shown the changing rooms and I took a pic of Pete T standing in the corner where Ryan Giggs gets his gear on and off (insert your own joke here). We walked down the tunnel and as we did so, our tour guide, Arthur, pressed a button and set off a recorded sample of the crowd cheering as the team emerge from the tunnel. What a laugh! Corny as hell, but a good memory.

We returned to the Academy for soundcheck. The room's a bit of a cave and it came as a shock to hear the drum sound all boomy and indistinct. Apart from that, all seemed to go well. Had the pre-gig nap and lay in the dark on the bus feeling nervous. Nerves don't strike me often, and I've been playing shows long enough now to know that I'll be alright once I'm on stage. Still... they do strike - usually when I don't feel we're on top of our gig - and it ain't pleasant. I remained edgy all the way up to stage time, getting dressed for *The Invisible Man* (insert your own joke here too) which was to be the opener.

When I got up there the Manchester crowd were amazing, as usual, and the nerves gave way immediately to focus and one of the most focussed performances of the song I remember. The show was thoroughly enjoyable from start to end. Afterwards I hung out in the backstage bar for a while, chatting to Aziz Ibrahim and doing the pictures and autographs before returning to the bus and overnight to Aylesbury.

Saturday 9 November *Aylesbury Waterside Theatre*

Rumbled out of sleep in the middle of the night. The bus appeared to be traversing a cobbled stone road! I lay in the dark, listening to (and feeling) the judder of the wheels and trying to figure out how our bus-driver had managed to find a cobble-stone road between Manchester and Aylesbury. It felt like we were back in Poland. I was later to discover that this was, in fact, the A41! I guess it's just buggered. Woke in the morning to a view of The Waterside Theatre which, from round the back, looks like the USS Enterprise with a sprinkle of Cotswold dry-stone walling at its base. Inside, the dressing room was decorated with flowers – roses, lilies, freesias. Lovely. You can tell we're not promoting this one ourselves... We're too tight to spend £20.00 on something as "bloke-pointless" as flowers.

"I wonder what they're charging us for them?!" said Pete. (See what I mean?)

I went next door to the Friars production team and thanked them for the flowers – a nice touch.

Ran into David Stopps (long-time manager of Howard Jones) whose claim-to-fame in Aylesbury is/was Friars – a rock club with roots in the 1970's. Tonight's show is being promoted as part of the Friars legacy so there are flyers in the dressing room with notable artists who played the club back-in-the-day. You name 'em, Dave had 'em. There was a time in Aylesbury when you could have popped out and seen David Bowie twice in a month, Nick Drake opening for Genesis, XTC opening for Blondie and later in the 70's, The Police, The Clash, Ian Dury and the Blockheads... The Talking Heads, Madness... and on it went. I'd have moved here myself if I'd known. No wonder Rothers, Fish and chums settled here from their Edinburgh and Whitby hometowns and began hustling Dave for opening slots. I met David Stopps briefly in New York at some point in the 90's. He was hanging at one of our gigs with our managers, Tony Smith and John Arnison. Unfortunately I was in the throes of mid-tour-Montezuma's-revenge at the time and couldn't get out of the toilet for more than 5 minutes. Questionable American tour food has a habit of turning my intestines to liquid from time to time – always a dilemma when there's a 2-hour show to perform/endure. But I digress... the point is that this was my first chance to get to know Dave Stopps. I like him. He's got an essence of Bob Harris (BBC DJ and long-term presenter of **The Old Grey Whistle Test**) about him. They could be brothers. Good natured, intelligent old hippies with a seemingly encyclopaedic and undiminished love of music and the artists who make it. Back in the early eighties when I was rattling round London with the Europeans, Marillion were a regular opener at Friars while Fish hustled Dave into managing the band. "I'm not a manager – I'm a promoter," said Dave and so it went on until Dave eventually caved in and agreed to manage Marillion. Record company interest soon began to happen whereupon Fish began campaigning to get rid of him. This was the history as recounted to me by one of the band, and I recounted all this back to Dave whilst he smilingly nodded and said, "Yup, that's about right!" A few months later, after Dave had begun managing Howard Jones, his single entered the chart at No.2, just as Marillion's first single entered at 26. Dave said, "I bumped into Fish and he congratulated me, saying, "It's not a competition, y'know!"

"Oh yes it is!" I said.

Fair enough.

I wandered onto the stage to have a look. Been here before a couple of months back to play a short set for charity along with The Zombies and Argent. It's a beautiful state-of-the-art theatre and judging by the state of Buckinghamshire's roads, they must have blown the road-maintenance budget on building this place. Money well-spent, I'd say.

I spent a while working on this diary whilst Mark's daughter, the beautiful Freya, popped in to show the children their rock n'roll grandad! I typed away in the corner whilst catching glimpses of Mark playing the fool and entertaining the baby. Blimey – I now have a child the same age as Mark's grandchildren, and he's younger than me! What a life.

Soundcheck was a little nervous – Mark had decided to transfer the entire keyboard computer to a laptop which, only yesterday, he said was "blue-screening" on him and losing data. Ah, no gig would ever be complete without the ever present fairy fluttering at the back of my mind and whispering, "This is probably the song where the keyboards stop working – good luck!"

After soundcheck I hit my bus-bed and slept for an hour. Back in the gig I said hello to my lovely Sofi and enjoyed a pre gig-cuddle. Peter Brown gave me a copy of his first album. I'm on it somewhere... mumbling.

The theatre was sold out and the show was superb. The keyboards worked flawlessly and so did my voice. After all the problems last year, in and out of throat doctors, jamming cameras down my throat, steroid shots, antibiotics and wondering if I have reached an age where the old pipes start to degenerate (it's gonna happen at some point), it's a terrific feeling to know that it was all just a blip and I'm back stronger than ever. When we third-encored with *Garden Party* and *Market Square Heroe*s, the audience caught fire. Lovely.

After the show Dave Stopps presented each member of the band with a little glass plaque engraved with the dates they'd played Friars in the past. I just had the one date on mine, of course, whilst the rest of the boys had a list. Really sweet of him. What a bloody nice, thoughtful and classy bloke.

I went out into the aftershow bar and had a chat with John Mitchell (from It Bites). John has become a hot producer and is mixing stuff for all the young bands now. He was absolutely hammered and a much better comedy-drunk than Dudley Moore in **Arthur**. He kept kissing me on the lips and congratulating passing girls on their breasts in between enthusing about the gig and my singing. Marvellous, and proper rock n'roll. Well done, John.

Unfortunately Linette couldn't make it in the end. She has spent the last four days running her stall at the Christmas market in Waddesdon (selling Scandinavian kids clothes – a new venture). She's hardly seen little Vibes and he doesn't want her to go out. Fair enough.

Climbed back onto the bus and overnight to Rouen.

Sunday 10 November *Rouen – Paris*

Woke up by the river. It turned out to be the Seine. There were barges moored alongside us, cranes along the dock and across the wide expanse of water, the land rose up to green hills and church spires. Even the industrial bits of France remain somehow beautiful. You've either got natural aestheticism or you haven't.

Went inside and had a spot of coffee and croissants served to us by the effervescent, smiling Valerie and then took my laptop and diaries off in search of a café in town. It was a 20 minute walk along the river. The gig is currently in the middle of an enormous fun-fair which runs for a couple of miles (at least) along the river bank. The fair wasn't yet fully open – it being 10.00 in the morning. The town however was shut up like crab's arse in a tsunami. It's illegal to open a shop in France on a Sunday unless it sells food, and few of 'em do. I headed for the cathedral and found the seemingly-only-open café in Rouen – the Brasserie Paul. The Brasserie Paul goes back a long way – I have a leaflet expounding its impressive client list from over the years. Installed myself in there for much of the day. Had steak and chips, coffee, and wrote the diary. Sofi and Dan are looking after Vibes today while Linette works at Waddesdon, and they picture-messaged me photographs of him enjoying himself at the Limes Farm café. Great. They look like they're having a fine time of it. Isn't technology wonderful sometimes?

Returned along the river through the fun-fair which was now heaving with people. There's nothing else to do here on a Sunday so it was rammed. Back at the gig, soundcheck seemed fine. Had the customary nap and returned for the early show – it's 8.30 tonight. At 8.15 Linette called to say that she's in hospital with Vibes!! Apparently Sofi and Dan bought him some Rocky Road at Limes Farm Café. He's had it before but not from there. This one must have had peanuts in it and he's had a bad allergic reaction. His face has swollen up and he can't breathe through his nose. She's taken him to A&E – they've put a drip in his arm and they're giving him intravenous anti-histamine. She says not to worry – he's slowly getting better. Shit! Always when I'm away. I can't do anything about it so I say I'll call as soon as I'm off stage. I went on stage comforted by the fact that he's recovering steadily, and "put my other head on".

The gig was great. A slow-burner to a not-entirely hard-core crowd. We had 'em by the end. This always feels more rewarding. Conversion is a bigger achievement than confirmation. When I got off stage I called L's mobi to discover it's switched off! No one's answering the landline at home either. Called Sofi who had returned to the hospital and handed the phone to L. While I was on stage he went to the loo, started lolling and passed out. They hit him with adrenaline and he's now back with us. Oh my... After we'd finished the call I decided to go home. Tomorrow's a day-off in Amsterdam anyway. Stephanie Ringuet said she could give me a lift to Paris. She booked me a room in the Terminus Hotel opposite La Gare du Nord and Frenchie and Lucy arranged me a ticket for the Eurostar tomorrow morning at 8.00am. We figured it would get me home quicker than a flight to Heathrow. L kept in touch by txt as Steph and I drove back to Paris but by 2.00am when I checked into the hotel, my phone was going flat. I just had enough battery to txt L the hotel phone number – just in case he took a turn for the worse in the night.

Monday 11 November   *Paris – Home*

Slept fitfully and kept waking up wondering what time it was. There was no way of finding out – no watch, no clock in the room, no time display on the telly, and my phone was dead. I'd arranged an early morning call at 6.45, and so I got up, showered and went downstairs to the breakfast room. I was followed into the breakfast room by a black guy who mysteriously seemed to know that my friend had paid the hotel bill but not paid for breakfast. I was reminded how it must be to not have any money in this world. Suddenly, they have their eye on you... I told him that's fine, I'll pay cash. Dunno what they charged me for my coffee and orange juice – but I bet it wasn't cheap.

After four hours sleep herself, Steph had returned to the foyer, bless her, and brought me an iPhone charger. I could charge the phone on the train. She came over the road with me and I was once again indebted when I tried to pick up my ticket at the ticket office. They didn't want to give it to me as Lucy had paid for it on her credit card and I wasn't Lucy. What a pointless policy. There I am trying to pick up a ticket in my name, holding a passport in my name, and mentioning the name of Lucy Jordache who booked the bloody ticket, and it's still not enough! They wanted to know her home address. I said Tring but I couldn't remember the street address. THAT wasn't good enough either. Lucy and Ian's address is in my phone of course, but it was flat. Fortunately for all of us, Steph found the address in HER phone otherwise the woman in the ticket office would have been peeling my fingers from her throat and I'd have been arrested for assault. This jobsworth bullshit is bad enough when your little boy isn't in hospital...

The Eurostar left Paris on a beautiful morning and arrived in London to pouring rain and grey sky. I managed to charge my phone during the journey. Vibes had had a good night and, at one point, called me to say hello. I told him I was coming to see him. He sounded really pleased about that. So was I. Took the tube from St Pancras to Marylebone and the train to Bicester North where Lucy picked me up and took me to the Horton hospital in Banbury. Found my way through the maze of corridors to the children's ward and there they were. Little Vibes was still a bit swollen around the eyes and lips, he had the drip attachment in his arm, but he was his usual smiling self. We had a lot of cuddles and he wouldn't let me out of his sight. We hung around all day until they allowed us home around 5pm. He fell asleep as we got into the village and slept for an hour or so on the sofa. I kept running in and out to check he was alright, but he was sleeping peacefully. Phew, what a scare! We all went to bed early. L slept with him and I slept comfortably and with much relief in my own bed.

Tuesday 12 November *Home – Haarlem*

Around 8.00 I heard them get up. Vibes was obviously feeling fine. I could hear him rattling away and the thumping of his feet on the floor as he ran around like a dervish. I had a bit of lie-in and got up around 9.30. Had a decent cup of coffee (rare to get on the road) and he got dressed so we could go and kick his new football around on the village green. I had the presence of mind to bring home the Man Utd football strip I'd bought for him at Old Trafford. It fitted him, and he was very happy with it. We went out and spent the next hour playing footie until a car came to take me to Heathrow for the flight to Schipol.

"Only 6 sleeps, Vibesy," I said as I left...

I bought a new phone-charger in the airport...

Was picked up by Mark Kennedy at Schipol and driven according to the random directions of his Satnav to Haarlem. The 15-minute journey took 35, but soon I was back in the bosom of Frenchie and the tour bus. I had missed soundcheck, but I had a good sound for the show. I really enjoyed the gig until I went to the aftershow, where everyone seemed to complain about the sound, the set, the band etc...

I couldn't help pondering the psychology of people who follow an artist for years, buy all their albums, avidly buy their concert tickets and then find themselves one day in a position to talk to that artist only to choose to criticize them to their face…

"Hello Mr. Bowie. I have waited my whole life in the hope of maybe one day getting to meet you in person so that I can criticize your show, your work, your band and to tell you that you haven't really done anything since **Hunky Dory** worth shit. I preferred you with the orange hair. And what's that with the acting?! I mean, really! **Labyrinth**! Goodness, that was worse than Tin Machine – in my opinion, your worst mistake of all!"…

"Oh hello Mr Gabriel! I have waited my entire life in the hope that maybe someday, just for a moment I would have the good fortune and time in your presence to ask you why you made that sell-out poppy disappointment of an album, **So**. Surely you are better than that. What a shame you left Genesis after that fine piece of art **The Lamb Lies Down On Broadway**. I liked that very much – so much more than your solo efforts which, frankly have been disappointing. I'm sure you must be grateful that I have decided to remain honest in your presence and not simply lie and tell you that you are great. I'm glad I crossed the room and interrupted you to tell you all this. Have a nice evening."

Am I sounding a bit touchy? Well it had been a tricky couple of days…

Overnight to Paris and a day off in my beloved Le Relais Montmartre…

Wednesday 13 November   *Paris:* Day Off

Woke and went downstairs to the bus kitchen. Most of the band and crew were up. It was one of those perfect blue, crisp late autumn days. As usual in Paris, there was some kind of demonstration going on and the bus progressed slowly along the Boulevard Rochouart until we reached the Moulin Rouge, where we all piled out with our bags for the short walk up the hill and round the corner into Rue Constance, to the hotel – Le Relais Montmartre. It was around midday. We all piled into hotel reception which is very small but beautifully formed, and hung around while Frenchie checked us in. I've chosen room 004 on the ground floor near the door – it's my favourite. I had arranged to meet Stephanie Ringuet for lunch at 1.00, so spent the hour showering and recovering from the overnight drive.

Had lunch with Steph in Le Zebra brasserie on Rue des Abesse. Most pleasant. I'm afraid I ordered a couple of Irish coffees too. Very civilized. Suitably mellow now, I spent the afternoon chilling in my room and snoozing and writing my diary. Steph said she had a spare ticket for the Queens of the Stone Age at Le Zenith that night, so I texted Nial to offer him the experience. I know he's a big fan. He was delighted. He'd been to the Louvre with Nick Todd.

Before Nial departed for the gig around 6.00, we had a quick "half" in the Zebra round the corner. We don't get chance to enjoy these very often so it was nice to be with him. I never managed to have dinner – just spent the rest of the day chilling out in my room recovering reading and sleeping.

Thursday 14 November *Paris Bataclan*

Had a bit of a lie-in. Went down to breakfast around 11.00. I was more or less alone. Munched my way through French bread, a little bit of cheese, and a little bit of marmalade, and some coffee. Returned to my room and read a little more. I'm trying to finish **The Bonfire of the Vanities** by Tom Wolfe in time for the book-club meeting back in the village next week. It was my idea, so the least I can do is read the book. Popped out and walked along the Rue des Abesses in Montmartre looking for a pair of glasses for *The Invisible Man* (it's not every day you can say that...). We are opening the set with this song on this tour and at the last show in Rouen I managed to drop them and later stamp on them. A new pair will be required. I don't need anything expensive, just something that looks quite old-fashioned. Paris is a good city to go shopping for spectacles. There are many opticians selling really stylish and peculiar glasses. I tried on quite a few. Some were just the ticket, but of course very expensive at about €300. I didn't need anything so dear. Eventually found what I needed in a pharmacy on Rue des Abesses – only €16. That's more like it. I returned to Le Relais to find Pete, Steve and Mark waiting for a taxi. I quickly packed and joined them, but half way to the Bataclan I realised I'd left my phone-charger plugged in the wall back at the hotel. I dived out of the taxi and returned. Fortunately this meant I was able to buy some gloves in a shop around the corner. I had noticed the gloves earlier, but the shop was closed. It was now open so I popped in and bought them. Soft black leather gloves with little zips at the back. Quite rock 'n' roll and yet quite unusual (leave it...).

Arrived at the Bataclan, said hello to Laurent (who runs the fan club) and Lionel (who turns up every night and gives us wine!) and made my way to the dressing room. This, I remembered, is the dressing room where Mark had the marshmallows on his head. He could have done with them again today... The now legendary characterful and character-building keyboard rig was to throw today's curve – fortunately during soundcheck. Eventually Mark traced the problem to a faulty memory card on one of his master keyboards. Fortunately he had a spare one. Unfortunately it was out of date. This meant the current info had to be reconfigured from a computer. This took him about an hour while we hung around with fingers crossed. Eventually, all seemed well and we ran through *Montreal* and *Pour my Love*, the former being declared too clunky to perform and the latter declared airworthy and included in tonight's set in favour of *Beautiful*. I returned to the bus for pre-show nap.

The show itself was really enjoyable. The wonderful Parisienne crowd were once again living up to their reputation. The reception after *The Invisible Man* was rapturous and the atmosphere remained "electric in the heart" throughout. The keyboards behaved and the band played well. My voice is holding up well on this (albeit short) tour, but I seem to experience none of the problems which began last year in America. I'm singing as well as ever. I had really begun to think I was losing it... It's a huge relief.

Afterwards I chatted to our promoter Laurent who appeared with a bottle of

Ruinart Champagne. Not a big fan of "champers" (although I did taste one many years ago that was lovely – slightly cognac-y tasting; never found out what it was called. I was at a millionaires' house at the time, so it was probably something special and prohibitively pricey) but you have to join in with these rituals when generously extended. Returned downstairs and signed a few things. The Bataclan has its own café out on the street in front of the gig so I went and joined the Italians for an Irish coffee or two. Got on the bus and went to bed dangerously close to THAT line, but thankfully not quite.

Friday 15 November *Köln*

Woke up around 9.00 and went downstairs to have a look out of the bus window. Was greeted by the sight of an industrial wasteland. I hadn't seen anything quite this bleak since we played the shipyard in Gdansk, Poland. Outside there appeared to be an enormous hopper for storing minerals or grain. The weather wasn't helping – it was grey and oppressive. I exited the bus to see we were at the side of a river (that'll be the Rhine then). There was a huge bird-shaped crane in view and various old grey warehouses.

The gig itself (Essig Fabrik) must be some kind of converted old factory. I got back onto the bus and made myself a coffee with a sigh. Should we STILL be playing gigs like this after all these years? I suppose I should be grateful it's sold out, but I sometimes wonder if we shouldn't be setting our sights a little higher. We're not a punk rock band after all. I decided to get the hell out of there. I'm told there's a tram into town at the end of the street, so I grabbed my laptop and diaries and headed for the tram. Got on the first one I could and, upon enquiring, was told it was heading OUT of town. Got off, crossed the street and got the next one INTO town, using the river and the constant presence of the famous twin-spired Dom Cathedral to get my bearings. Had a slow brunch in the Hard Rock Café.

The food wasn't great - I think they franchised all these out a few years back now - I've eaten in the Hard Rock's in Amsterdam, Mexico City, London and Köln recently and the food's been pretty dreadful. It used to be great. Shame. Having said that, the staff in the HRC Koln couldn't have been more friendly and pleasant – especially the guy on the door who was from London and an absolute diamond. At one point as I was trying to pick through the contents of the Chicken Club sandwich, I was approached by a couple who had tickets for tonight's show. I dutifully made small talk, signed their ticket and smiled for their camera. My teeth were probably full of food debris. Classy.

Walked up through the pedestrianized area of shops to Media Markt and tried to buy electric toothbrushes for Linette and I. Ours are getting old and I think the batteries are going. It took a while to find electric toothbrushes but I eventually did. Unfortunately, the model on display, which I thought would be good, was "not in stock in zat colour", so I decided against it. Bought L a charger lead for her new iPhone instead and then installed myself in a hotel café by the

Roman museum to drink hot chocolate and write the diary.

Returned to the venue by tram around 4.00. They're just beginning to build the Christmas markets – one up against the Dom, and the other in the street to the south between Altermarkt and Heumarkt. I have been to these markets many times. I was once shamefully sick all over Joerg Baeker's bathroom floor after a particularly good night out here on the Egg Punch... Sadly, we're here a bit too early this year. I usually buy tree decorations. I have a solo show in Krakow coming up on Dec 2, so there'll be every opportunity to invest in a bauble...

Back at the gig soundcheck seemed to go smoothly. My sound was good, especially considering we're playing an old factory. Went to catering for a bit of dinner. Steak and chicken in sauce. Very yummy. Back on the shelf for pre-gig (and escape from the gig!) snooze and then into battle.

Tonight just might have been the best show of the tour. Hardcore fan Sabine certainly said so, and she's been to all of 'em. Someone shouted for *Montreal* at one point and as we'd ran it at the Paris sound check, and especially as native Montrealan Jordan Zivitz caught my eye in that moment, I thought WTF, let's give it a go. Mark K gave it the all-clear programming-wise and off we went. I think we played it better than we ever have, either live or in rehearsal. The rest of the night was terrific too. There has always been a great vibe for the band here. Köln never lets us down.

Afterwards I chatted briefly with old chums, Joerg and Alex before returning to the bus and my little cell to finish **The Bonfire of the Vanities**.

Saturday 16 November *Uden Markant*

I was hoping for a traditional cobbled Dutch town like Haarlem, a beautiful old square and a café to sit in. I looked out of the window of the bus at some kind of funky Milton-Keynesian car park in fairly dense fog. I asked around and the general consensus was that Uden didn't really have much going on at all.

I eventually clambered out of the bus and round the corner and found a small modern street with a handful of shops and a delicatessen with, bizarrely, a chicken rotisserie outside on the street, a solarium and a funny little café in which I eventually installed myself. The café was staffed by people with Downs Syndrome. This worked quite well once you were hip to it. One of the waitresses kept involuntarily bending double and crying out. I got used to it, although I found it set me asking questions of myself and my attitudes - never a bad thing - and I admire the town for giving it a go. I ordered hot chocolate which eventually went cold during the time I spent writing in the diary.

I returned across the street to the gig. This is a modern and recently built venue. We were later to meet the architect who was, surprisingly, female and looked more like a model. I guess I was expecting the stereotype middle-aged bloke in half-lens spectacles and a Paul Smith cravat.

Phil Brown says the room is one of the most acoustically dead he has ever encountered in his life. My stage sound at soundcheck wasn't bad though. We didn't spend any longer than we had to. Everything is just about set by now and our monitor man Nick Todd is well on top of his gig.

Had a spot of dinner in catering and returned to the bus to relax.

The show was, again, really good. The band played well and I sang well. I hadn't been happy with *Gaza* last night in Köln - I couldn't seem to get inside its skin - but it was much better tonight and I remained focused inside it. The crowd seemed quiet. I couldn't tell if it was the acoustic properties of the room making it hard for us to hear any crowd-noise, or whether they were just a bit half-hearted. At times like this, you have to forget about the crowd and focus on the music. If the music's right, it's right, and the crowd will feel that for what it is. Overall, I preferred the show at "my end" tonight, although I have to concede that last night in Köln was THE occasion.

Afterwards I chatted to the guests backstage in catering and also to the local promoter who remembered promoting The Europeans in Holland 30 years ago! Phew.

I was just getting settled down into a social when Frenchie announced we had to leave. We return to England tonight AND it's foggy so we have to be cautious if we're to make the channel tunnel reservation.

After the bus was underway, I sat for a while chatting to Nial and Markus, the drum tech. Markus wasn't looking forward to going home. I told him I have learned that life is too short to be unhappy and that he must free himself if he's to be of any use to anyone. Of course, it's all easier said than done. He filled my pockets full of chocolate mice as we talked...

Eventually I went to bed and was in a deep sleep when we had to all get up and show passports to the border inspectors. I followed Yens through. "I'd keep an eye on him if I were you..." he said. They let me in though, the fools.

Arrived back at the Racket Club around 9.00am and loaded all my stuff into the Mini while the bus driver surreptitiously attached furry dice to my rear-view mirror. Very nice. I'm not sure Linette's going to like 'em... Returned home in my Mini Cooper along the country lanes of middle England on a bright morning, furry dice bobbing away in the window.

the *invisible* man

2014   APRIL
Saturday 5

I am the invisible man.

2014

Friday 4 April *Home – Miami* British Airways BA209 Seat 19D

Woke at half seven and watched a bit of telly (news) in bed before getting up. No news really. They still seem no closer to finding any trace of that Malaysian airliner.

Had coffee and went to school to drop Vibes off with Linette. There's an assembly today where they give out "achievers certificates". Vibes got one for being considerate and caring. The only one awarded for that. Bless him. Good boy, Vibes. Assembly took longer than I thought so we bailed out at 10.00 and went home so I could pack for the 10.45 departure. I always forget something. This time it was socks.

The drive to the airport was uneventful. Checked in and went to the Club lounge at gate B (you have to take a train) where I had a beer and ate tuna sandwiches with Lucy. Spoke to Ian M on the phone. He sounded much better and really wishing he was coming with us. He had surgery on his stomach recently and we all decided it's better if he chills, so that he's fighting-fit for the South American tour in May. We're taking another drummer, Leon Parr, with us.

Boarded the 747 to Miami and Lucy went upstairs. I went downstairs. The flight was uneventful and the time passed quite quickly. I spent it reading Nile Rogers' autobiography *Le Freak*. What did I learn? That he REALLY knew how to party… and that record labels don't know a hit from a hole in the ground. Ate Caesar salad and then ruined my good intentions by having banoffee dessert and, later, a shedload of scones with jam and clotted cream.

Immigration was painless in Miami. Bought a Chai in Starbucks and Lucy and I got a cab to the Best Western on Miami Beach. Frenchie's booked me a sea view on the Penthouse floor, bless him. My only grouse is the lack of a bar here. I was really hoping to have a Mojito by the sea before turning in for the night. It's 8.00 pm (1.00am in England) so I'm too tired to venture out.

Watched crap US TV for a while and nodded off around 9.30.

Slept fitfully - what's new?

Saturday 5 April   *Miami Beach*

Got up at 6.00 and watched the dawn slowly break over the Atlantic.

FaceTimed L. She's had her hair cut. It looks great. Mind you, she'd look great anyway, with a mohican… wearing a bin-liner. Vibes was happy and kept telling me he loves me and blowing kisses.

Went down to breakfast and was reprimanded for forgetting the breakfast voucher-thing. You've gotta have a system. Went back to my room for it. Had bacon and scrambled eggs. Lucy appeared and refused coffee and orange juice (she only drinks water and Coke. Me - I drink EVERYTHING, except water). The waiter brought her coffee and orange juice anyway so I drank her orange juice. We talked a while about her mother's death, and the pros and cons of having kids. She's never wanted children.

I went off for a walk in search of a Starbucks - the only place in America I seem to be able to get a decent cup of coffee. It took ages, but was pleasant enough. Jees there's some money here – even modest hotels have a Lamborghini and a couple of Bentleys slung outside.

Returned sipping a cappuccino along the beach. Nice enough in a wide-flat sort of way. I wouldn't swap it for Cornwall though.

Stayed in my room reading and tweaking the diary and exchanging email with Robert Hammond who's publishing my diaries in June and November this year. He said it's raining in Surrey. I wrote, "Miami is sunny and blue. Infinitely preferable to rainy Surrey (until you get shot). As I get older, I have lost my desire to lie in the sun so I'm locked in my hotel room with the AC keeping me cool. I am someone who loves to be near the sea, the mountains, the desert, the English countryside, but would rather know it's close-by and occasionally look at it through the window, or an open door, than go trudging around in it, wearing myself out and having to clean up afterwards."

Outside my room above the sea, helicopters occasionally buzz by, speedboats bounce on the water, pleasure craft glide and there are a few serious ships at anchor in the distance, reminding me of what's ahead. A light plane just went by, towing an advertisement-banner with a large logo of a machine gun and writing saying, "SHOOT FULL AUTO MACHINE GUNS! LOCK AND LOAD SQUAD MIAMI," and then later… "CAMEO. MEMPHIS BLEEK HOSTS TONIGHT".

Went down to the pool-bar (there IS a bar! …but's it's outside and closed at night) and had a chicken Caesar salad and a couple of beers in the hot sunshine. Lucy joined me and we chatted some more. I was concerned that I wasn't really enjoying it and wondering if I was tired of life. I remember a time when I would have been so excited to be here. "What's WRONG with me?" I pondered… Lucy had caught too much sun and retired to her room while I hung on and read Orwell's **1984**. A strange tale to be filling ones head at Miami Beach.

Went upstairs and Skyped L again. Vibes was already in bed, it being 9.30 in England. She sounded much better after last week's cold.

Took a cab to South Beach. Miami's equivalent of Blackpool - somewhat brighter of course, and infused with the same stag-weekend vibration. A bit more of a gangster undercurrent though, and a sense of the potential for getting shot. I saw a black guy playing drums on the street with a load of paint-pots for tom-toms and an old cooking tray for hi-hat. He was truly brilliant and had that impossible-to-define/easy-to-feel tight swing/rock-solid groove about his playing that Andy Gangadeen has. A life's work. What on earth is he doing on the street? I found one of the many bars playing loud music (complete with DJ) and sipped a Mojito at a table while grooving to a remix of Shalamar's *Gonna Make This a Night to Remember* and reading about the Ministry of Truth (there was no Ministry of Sound in Orwell's 1984). Finished my Mojito and decided to walk back. It took almost an hour… Further away than I thought!

Dropped in and wandered around a Walgreens picking up mixed nuts, an iced coffee and some mouthwash, but abandoned them when I saw the length of the queue at checkout. Just as well – I still had another half-hour walk ahead. Back at the hotel I said hi to Annik who was sitting in the cafe with Lucy (who, by now, was looking well-sunburned) and returned to my room to watch crap American TV. I'd had every intention of going down to reception to greet the band and crew's arrival, but I was crashing and couldn't.

Sunday 6 April *Miami Beach*

Woke for the thirtieth time and decided to get up. It was 6.20. Decided to sit on the balcony and photograph the dawn breaking. Did so and over the next hour took periodic shots with the iPhone. They didn't really do the sunrise justice though. When the sun came up huge and red, it just looked like a dim dot in the picture.

Went downstairs and had breakfast. I had an omelette and coffee and orange juice. After quite a while, Phil Brown appeared and I heard how the bus hadn't arrived at the airport last night so they all had to wait 2 hours. A good job I didn't wait up for 'em. Came back up to the tenth floor and FaceTimed home. L seems tired. They'd been to the pub for Sunday roast. The weather was drizzly in England. Here it's blue and hot.

Went for a long walk to South Beach with Phil and Nick. We stopped in a beachside bar for a beer. Very nice and reminiscent of the Mediterranean. Kept going, past a gay bar full of straight people while a drag-queen with enormous hair beckoned and coaxed passers-by, until we arrived at South Beach. Fabulous art-deco buildings look like they're made of ice-cream. Admired the cars and motor bikes. Unfortunately the street drummer wasn't on the street. I'd hoped to get his picture, and for Phil and Nick to hear him play. Drank Mojitos at bar and watched the zoo go by.

Took a cab back to the hotel and went to the pool-bar for a beer and a sandwich. Called home to say night-night to Vibes who was tearful and missing me. Rick Armstrong had arrived in town so we met up at 7.00 and walked along the boardwalk to the Tiki bar next door, and had a couple of beers. A successful-looking guy with a beautiful South American wife came over and shook my hand – fans bound for the forthcoming Criuise To The Edge. He was from Chicago, she was from Sao Paulo. After a while the crew appeared along with Lucy so I ordered a Caipirinha to get into the new mood. However, Rick suddenly announced that he was going across town with Steve R to see John Wesley play. Much as I would normally have tagged along, I declined as I'm still not quite up to a late night. Made my excuses and returned to my room to chill.

Monday 7 April *Miami Beach – MSC Davina*

Up again at 6.00. The jet lag shows no sign of abating. I find it bites harder with each passing year. Opened the sliding doors to the balcony and went back to bed so I could watch the sunrise and listen to the sea, Truly, "I feel the wind blowin' through the palms of my mind" today. Remembered that I hadn't watched Dan Robinson's latest version of *The Invisible Man* - the movie we're intending to play behind the song on the next tour - so I opened the laptop and watched it. It's really close now. I maybe have just one last suggestion but I'll speak to Yens about it too and get his perspectives.

Went down to breakfast around 7.30 to discover I was alone in the breakfast room. Maybe everyone else had had a late night. The crew appeared in one's and two's, sunburned and hungover. Chatted with our drum technician, Marcus, 'til 8.30 then went to my room to FaceTime home. L and Vibes were having lunch and seemed fine. Packed and I *think* I managed not to leave anything behind, although my Bose headphones had gone missing – I realized I'd left them on the 747 from Heathrow. Sigh...

We boarded a bus to the port where we all piled into a building where we were "processed" and shown to a waiting room for the 'Yacht Club' i.e. the part of the ship reserved on this occasion for artists. There was half an hour of tension as I had already lost all the paperwork Frenchie (tour-manager) had given me. Found it later (where I had folded and carefully put it) after I no longer needed it. Said hello and chatted to Steve Hackett and his lovely wife Jo for a while until we were shown onto the ship, the MSC Davina. It's HUGE and as we walked through the corridors, the Arabic looking lounge, the casino, and into the marble reception area, I felt reality slipping away somewhat. We were shown into a little library where unformed staff gave us Champagne and then I was shown to my cabin by a butler(!). There's a balcony with a view of (for now) downtown Miami and the docks. Had a beer and took it all in for a while before going exploring. Went up to the Yacht Club "One" bar – past the sun loungers and hot tubs, and slowly became aware that I was listening to myself as *Alone Again in the Lap of Luxury* trilled from discretely concealed loudspeakers. Went to the bar and ordered a tonic water. I'll stay off the hard-stuff 'til later. Sat and relaxed in the sun while people wandered up and politely asked for autographs, photographs and declared undying love for the music. Lovely. When we're back at the Racket Club (Marillion's studio), breaking our heads trying to create the next album, I really must remember their words, and the sincerity with which they say them. There's a lot of deep faith out there.

Said hi again to Pete T and family who arrived in the bar just as I was leaving. Went downstairs looking for a shop that sells socks, and ran into a guy called Garth from Canada who is terrified of boats but has taken on his phobia to be here. He said we're worth it. He's a hockey player and towers over me. He showed me to the shop-deck where I got accosted at length in the casino by passing fans before discovering that the shops don't open until we set sail.

Returned to my cabin for a while and then ventured downstairs to the Topsail restaurant on the 15th deck where I had some finger-food and a cappuccino. Chris Squire was relaxing with his family at the table beside me. I have never met him and I didn't want to bother him. Said hello to John Wetton who I had met before, up in the Lake District when Pete and I did the charity gig with It Bites a few years back. Went back up to the artist and VIP "One" bar and said hello to Patrick Moraz, who was introduced to me by Geoff Downes. Joined Geoff D at a table with his partner Martine and Asia's manager Martin Darnell. Ended up getting embroiled and missed Steve Hackett's set. Damn. I'll catch his next performance later this week.

Later, ran into Nick Beggs who's playing bass with Steve Hackett. It was good to see him. We both went down to deck 6 as he offered to accompany me in my search for socks but no luck. We could have had a polo shirt or a handbag, no problem. Nick and I discovered a bar selling cakes and ordered strawberry tartlets and Guinness. Marvellous. Nick told me about a band called Lifesigns whose album he recorded, and they're about to play upstairs on the deck. We went upstairs to have a look at them and I noticed Frosty, the drummer from Cutting Crew (who we'd toured with in the 90's – Nick Eade's a good friend) was with them and played "out of his skin" during their set. Hooked back up with Rick Armstrong who sat with us for the Lifesigns set. I'm permanently blown away by the fact that, here I am, sitting under the stars in a brisk-but-warm tropical breeze watching a rock n'roll band doing their thing in a space the size of a market-square while the floor below my feet feels solid - there being almost no sense of movement - and we're in the middle of the fucking ocean!! I can't get over it. It's incredible.

Afterwards, Lucy introduced me to Simon Collins (who looks a lot, and sounds quite a lot like his dad, the legendary Phil) and Matt from Sound Of

Contact who were getting ready to play on the deck stage. By this time the jet lag was getting the better of me so I wished them well with their show and came back to my cabin to settle down with BBC World.

Peaches Geldof has been found dead today. How awful. She leaves behind two young children, a partner, and, no doubt, a desolate and devastated father. Poor Bob. As a father myself, I can't begin to imagine the pain. What a truly terrible thing to happen. It often seems to me that those who are at the centre of wonderful things and achieve fame and riches, often seem to pay dearly too. I'm reminded again not to envy ANYONE – you never know what they have to carry.

Went to bed and couldn't work out how to turn off the TV. I tried all the usual buttons on the remote but nothing would kill the screen. Woke after a while to see it still shining away. Got out of bed and pulled the mains out at the back.

Around 2.00 I was woken by a distinct smell of burning! My dad was a sailor and said that fire on board a ship is what all sailors fear most. There's nowhere to run. Shit. Got up and opened the sliding door to the balcony. The smell is more intense outside. We're in the open sea so it's got to be coming from the ship. Called the concierge and she said she could smell something too, down on deck 15. She said they would check it out and apologised for the disturbance. I poked my head outside my cabin door but all seemed fine outside in the corridor. Lay in bed somewhat nervously for a while trying to decide if it was getting worse, better, or if I was just getting used to it. Nodded off for a bit and when I woke again the smell had definitely cleared. Phew…

Tuesday 8 April *MSC Davina*

Woke for the umpteenth time and decided to "call it" and get up. It was 7.45. Hooray – that's almost normal getting-up-time (not for musicians of course, but for those of us with a school-run to do). The sense of triumph at having finally arrived in this time-zone was quashed by the realization that the clocks had to go back another hour last night so it's only 6.45 and I'm almost back where I have been all week. The good news is that I don't have to sing until Thursday so I still have two more days to adjust. I better had – we'll be on stage at 10.30 - that's 4.30 am in England - a hell of a time to be singing!

Ordered coffee from room service and wrote the diary 'til ten past eight. There's breakfast upstairs in the "One" bar (I wonder if that's a coincidence? "Going for the One" n'all that). There are a few Yessisms on the boat. You can buy a raffle ticket to win a Mini Starship Cooper which is parked up on the deck. If you win, you can drive it away! Bloody long drive to our house though from Miami.

So I went up to the "One" bar and had scrambled eggs and bacon and a cappuccino with Lucy. She had slept well and didn't smell any burning. Apparently our tour manager Frenchie and sound man Phil had had a party in one of the elevators last night – just going up and down the 15 floors inviting people in and giving them drinks. Sounds like fun. Maybe I'll join them if they have one tonight.

Went walkabout and spoke to a fair few fans. All very pleasant. Fans of many countries and fans of every gender (male, female, gay) too. The most moving and memorable moment was a hug from Oren, an Israeli chap, who had once been a soldier in Gaza. He didn't really explain why but, far from being offended by my words had chosen to acknowledge them with a hug. I couldn't help but shed tears. My emotional connection to this song is very raw. It has been an enormous pressure putting those words out there and, although I stand by them, I understand that they can easily be misunderstood and sound like an attack on Jewish people, which was never my intention. My words were an appeal to the world on behalf of a Palestinian child, Ahmad Saleh al-Nakhala, who grins up at me from my laptop screen. His father collected birds and was shot dead attempting to net songbirds, too close to the wall. We've all got to spare little Ahmad a thought and not forget him as Syria and Ukraine push the Palestinian refugee-issue out of the media once again and Obama seemingly forgets the pledges he made when he became President.

This cruise really is a fabulous thing. Everywhere people are having the best time here in the sunshine. Marillion don't play until Thursday so we continue to be gentlemen of leisure. Colin, a very nice man from Clacton who trains people to drive trains (a train driver trainer!) just bought me a rum and Cola and it's only 11.00 in the morning. Tricky staying off the food and drink all day. For me, it's all free so I could pig-out and get sloshed from morning 'til night. I'll hang on another couple of hours before I have any more… then I'll go looking for Jason Hart who's playing with Renaissance. I got to know Jason when he used to play with Rufus Wainright and he has since opened for us a few times. Maybe I can persuade him into a pink gin.

I decided I'd buy some wi-fi time and managed to FaceTime home. Incredibly, I found myself looking at Linette, wrapped in her coat, and Vibes out in the street in the village with the stone walls of our house behind them. Don't know how it connected – I guess L's iPhone must have still been sniffing out the home wi-fi. Here I am sitting on a ship in the middle of the ocean, talking face-to-face with my family out in the street in a small village in England.

Went down to the Topsail restaurant on deck 15 to discover the weather worsening considerably. Outside we seem to have run into a storm! Thick dark cloud above us, torrential rain lashing the windows and the sea becoming increasingly rough. I met Larry and Mike, the co-promoters of Cruise To The Edge. Mike said he's a big fan and it's a privilege to have us play here. Cheers Mike. I was introduced to Chris Squire and his wife Scotland (now *there's* a name – well, she's bonny…) and they surprised me by telling me they'd seen us play at the Forum in Kentish town a couple of years back. Chris said, "I enjoyed it. Really enjoyed it…" Steve Hackett joined us and paid me a compliment, "he's very good at that drama thing". (Well, I *think* it was a compliment…) I soon made excuses and left them to chat. I didn't want them to feel like I was hanging on.

These people were my heroes when I was seventeen. I get nervous that I'll say something dumb if I hang around.

All the time, the weather was worsening and eventually the organisers and captain took a decision to change course and head not for Honduras, but straight to Cozumel. I guess we DID cruise to the edge after all! But we didn't like the look of it and turned back. This is Cruise To The Edge NOT Cruise *Over* the Edge.

By 8.00 in the evening the weather was much calmer and the skies were mostly clear although the sea is still shaking me around a little as I write. I just got back from the restaurant where I had lobster for dinner. Nothing to pay. They're treating us very well here.

Dunno if it's the rolling of the ship or an inability to adjust to the time zone but I started to feel somewhat iffy so decided on an early night. In bed by 8.30. Still can't turn the telly off.

Wednesday 9 April   *MSC Davina – Cozumel*

Woke up for the thirtieth time at 7.00 and decided to get up. My mobile phone has burst into life and is tinging away so we must be back somewhere near a network. It was freezing. The AC in my room has malfunctioned and seems stuck on max. Called the concierge and asked for coffee and an engineer. They sent both and as the maintenance-man began unscrewing the ceiling I thought I'd better leave 'em to it.

Popped down to the front lounge and chatted to Pete T's son Callum, who had reacted to yesterday's bad weather much the same as me and had gone to bed early feeling strange. Said a quick hello to John Wetton who's here singing with UK and with Steve H (the other one). By this time we seem to have docked in Cozumel. It's not a particularly sunny day outside, but it's still only 9.00 am so I'll hang on and then maybe go and find a beach to look at. I couldn't get eggs in the downstairs lounge so I went back up to the "One" bar again and had a spot of breakfast with Lucy. We talked about rock n'roll wives (and ex-wives) for a while. Nothing I can repeat here.

Mark K joined us briefly. Apparently the whole of Steve Rothery's family were seasick all day yesterday. Oh dear. Steve seemed to have been okay though.

Right! I'm off to find a beach. We have to be back on board by 5pm and I think Marillion have a meet n'greet cocktail party at 6.00. Our first 'work' of the cruise so far. D'ya feel sorry for me yet?

Decided to take my computer bag with me so that I could FaceTime L if I found some wi-fi. At the end of the access jetty there's a line of shops – "Cozumels ONLY Mall" it proudly announces. Selling silver jewellery, tee shirts, bags and odds and sods for the tourists. Grabbed a cab and asked him to take me to the Wyndham Hotel. Sure he said, and promptly took me to somewhere which definitely wasn't. I never found out if it had *been* the Wyndham once, or not. Still – it was a very nice private hotel complex with a lovely little beach and adjoining beach-bar. Just the ticket! I bought a one-day guest-pass for $64.00 –

not cheap, but the wi-fi, the drinks, and the food all seemed to be free. FaceTimed home and had a chat with L and Vibes. They sounded well. She said she'd give me another shout when he was sleeping.

I spent the afternoon sitting under a coconut tree on the beach reading **1984** and sipping beer and, at one point - finally - fulfilled the dream of a Mojito by the sea. Really idyllic. I had to block-out occasional pumping-disco grooves from a bunch of girls working-out near the hotel reception, but y'can't have everything. Around 4.30 it was time for me to get myself together for the return trip. L had vanished. I figured - correctly - that she'd nodded off getting Vibes to sleep. She often does.

Returned back in a cab to the gargantuan sight of the MSC Davina, dwarfing the sea-front. Had a mooch through the silver shop but decided it was all too dear to be buying on a whim. Almost bought L an abalone and silver pendant, but it was $200 and I wasn't sure she'd like it. Returned to the ship and popped into the Pantheon theatre where UK were on-stage. John Wetton was singing well, and Eddie Jobson was in good form. Their sound was very clear, but perhaps a little loud... I must be getting old. Bumped back into Nick Beggs briefly and then ran off to get myself ready for the cocktail party meet n'greet. Met the chaps upstairs at the "One" bar to discover that Steve R has, "done his back in and can't move". Oh lord. Then there were three.

Rich walked those of us who *could* walk across the ship to the cocktail "do"…

It was truly intense and I was being photographed and autographing for well over an hour solid. Something of a feeding frenzy, but everyone was very nice. I arranged to have breakfast with Oren, the Isreali ex-soldier tomorrow so we can talk further about his experiences in Gaza. It's too late to change what I have written but it's never too late to hear new perspectives – they can change how you sing the song. Hooked up with Rick Armstrong on the way out and we went up on deck to watch Tangerine Dream, who I really enjoyed. They were making electronic ambient music 20 years before it was officially "invented" and are credited with having invented the sequencer too. Love 'em. I was constantly asked for photographs and autographs during TD's set which, although happy to do, was a bit distracting. Unfortunately the seated area was all full and Rick and I couldn't really hide anywhere. After their set we popped to the cabin where Rick said he could let me have a pair of earplugs in case Yes's set was too loud for me. As it turned out, I didn't need them. Bumped into Steve Hackett again coming out of the lift, and asked him if he fancied being our guitarist tomorrow if Rothers is still horizontal. I was joking, but he still said he could always busk it if we were desperate.

Rick and I hid in row D of the Pantheon theatre and watched Yes. I thought they were incredible. Jon Davison sang pretty perfectly all night, never heard him miss a note. The band were tight and, for the most part, the sound was good. Alan White played particularly well, but I couldn't fault anyone really. My head swam as I tried (not for the first time) to imagine how they ever WROTE this stuff. I wouldn't know where to start.

Thursday 10 April *MSC Davina*

Woke up around 8.00 and wrote this diary for a while before going up to the "One" bar where I had a long and enjoyable chat with Oren about his early life in Israel, Saddam's SCUD missile attacks, and his time in the army. He says he knows me from my songwriting and he knew I wouldn't take sides over Gaza. It was good to find an Israeli who understood what I had said. I really like Oren. Chatted to Alan White and his wife Zhi-Zhi and congratulated him on last night's show. I couldn't help but mention the fact that he had played with the Plastic Ono Band. He said he was only 20 years old when he played with John Lennon. That's him on Instant Karma and Imagine (which I often cite as the best song ever written). They're coming to see us play tonight. Goodness me. And all before breakfast…

Returned to my room to chill and practice my guitar-playing. It doesn't seem to be improving. Went back upstairs to the bar to have a bit of lunch and chatted to Leon - our drummer for the cruise - and spoke briefly to Ian Mosley at home in England on Lucy's iPad. He sounds much better. Steve R's family returned from an excursion ashore and I chatted to Jo about Steve's back-trouble. She says she thinks he'll be okay for the show. Phew!

Said hi to Geoff Downes and Martine before returning to the cabin to relax, keenly aware of tonight's approaching show… I'm reluctant to miss Steve Hackett, but I should really rest now. I hope he has a good one.

Well, soundcheck was chaotic. Nothing seemed to quite work and we only just had everything half-together when we ran out of time. I had a half-decent vocal sound though and could hear the band so figured I'd get through it. Straight after soundcheck the doors were open and we had 20 mins to stage time. Got dressed for *The Invisible Man* and hit the stage. Pleasantly surprised to find everything that needed to work, worked for the whole show. I set about pounding around the stage and doing my thing and I think we had a really good one. Leon never missed a cue all night. Afterwards I sat in the dressing room for half an hour with the crew. Phil Brown, our sound engineer, came back and said it sounded great and that we were the classiest act he'd seen on the boat (he's biased, mind you). Phew.

Back in my cabin by 2.00 am. STILL can't turn the telly off without getting out of bed. Kept drifting into consciousness in the middle of the night to hear Oscar Pistorius' clipped-accent in court discussing the finer details of having shot his girlfriend in the head – not the most soothing of lullabies… Strangely, the TV later switched off on its own somehow.

Friday 11 April *MSC Davina*

Woke up in the middle of the night wondering what time it was. It was 10.20! We're supposed to be on stage on deck at 11.00 for the "storytellers" set which is effectively a question/answer session with the public. Leapt out of bed and made my way to the upper deck with just enough time to grab 2 cappuccinos to drink on my way to the stage. The Q/A went well although it was so windy up there it was often hard to hear what we were being asked. I signed autographs and did photographs with the fans for almost an hour afterwards. Many people here from South America and Mexico. Came back to my cabin to chill out for a while and write the diary. Right. I'm off to lunch!

Managed to get to the restaurant at the other end of the boat and was only stopped once for a photograph! I think everyone's already got one… Returned to the cabin and had a little snooze. I'm a bit weary from last night's show. When I awoke I tried Jason Hart's room-phone and managed to find him in his cabin. We met up at a bar by the casino and, in between more photographs, had a beer (him) and pina-colada (me …and I'm the straight one!) before going to check out the Strawbs who were playing in a club on deck 6. I wanted to say hello to Chas Cronk, their bassist. The Strawbs had almost finished their set and sounded much rockier than I expected. Hearing the thunderous noise coming down the corridor and Dave Cousins' banshee voice, they sounded more like the sex-pistols than a folk group. Chas came over to say hello and introduced me to Dave Cousins. Chas's wife, Savina, was there too. She's a masseuse and used to massage my neck many years ago in Hampton (near Twickenham) after general tour-abuse usually left me somewhat ricked. Both Chas and Savina are among the loveliest people I've known and it was fantastic to catch up. I dragged them up to the "One" bar along with Jason and we enjoyed a soda together. Lucy took my photograph with Simon Collins who happened to be there. By now at was 7.30 and I was planning to go down and catch Tangerine Dream in the theatre, so Jason and I wandered down again to deck 6 but not before watching the crimson sun setting on the horizon. I put my arm around him.

"Jason – we're having a romantic moment…" I quipped.

"Indeed we are." he replied.

Down in the Pantheon theatre I found a good spot behind the mixing desk leant back, put my feet up and luxuriated in the lush landscapes of synthesizers fused with real percussion, flute, soprano sax and violin, as Tangerine Dream "did their thing" among tunnels of coloured lasers. I really like what they do and I would love to work with brilliant old Edgar Froese. Particularly liked their percussionist, Iris Camaa, who played tuned congas, electronic drums and cymbal-swells. She has a joyous and vibrant stage-presence. You've either got it or you haven't. It would have been worth the journey to see Tangerine Dream alone.

When their set was over, there was a frantic scramble to make ready for our show. Fortunately we'd been able to leave our drums and keyboards set in place from last night so that saved valuable time. We ran through tonight's opener *Gaza*, and then it was time to let in the crowd and get on with the show.

Once again, the show felt great. My voice was, if anything, a little wider-open than last night. After the positive comments I'd been getting all day about last night's sound and lights, I felt more relaxed too. Leon - our temporary drummer - played, once again, faultlessly and the band sounded great throughout. An impromptu audience-led reprise of *STCBM* added to the spirit still further. We encored with *Easter* which had been requested during the earlier Q&A session this morning. Yens left the house-lights up and the crowd sang it. A perfect end to a triumphant cruise. We gave a good account of ourselves and I'm now on nodding-terms with Prog-rock-royalty!

Frenchie walked me back to my cabin and after staggering around a bit I decided to have a bath. It was wonderful. Crawled out and into bed for a few hours sleep before waking up at 7.00 - conscious of the early departure.

Saturday 12 April   *MSC Davina – Miami – Home*

Made my way to the Topsail lounge and joined Steve and Jo Rothery for a coffee or two. Said hello again to Alan White's wife, Zhi-Zhi. She told me they used to live in Kirtlington (just down the road from me), but now live in Seattle.

We disembarked without much trouble and spilled out into the Miami dockside terminal where a bus was waiting to take us to the airport. Tangerine Dream band and crew were on the bus and were most complimentary about our show last night. I said hello to Edgar and offered my services if he ever should need some vocal textures. He seemed interested and his wife, Bianca, gave me their numbers. Chatted to Linda, the flautist/sax-ist about her native Austria. Her son sings in the Vienna Boys Choir and does more touring than her! All the "Tangs" seem like lovely people.

At the airport the BA staff checked us, and our bags, in - even though we don't fly for another 8 hours. That was civilized and classy. (Other airlines please note!) Ran into Rick Armstrong so, along with Leon, we went to a burger place and had a slow late-breakfast. Rick regaled us with tales of his father, Neil's near-death experiences - about six of 'em - mostly rocket-related, apart from me driving him round the M25…

I later returned to the BA desk and asked if, by any remote chance, they had found my Bose headphones on my inbound flight last Friday. A man went off to check and came back after 5-minutes to say yes! He said they were in storage and he'd bring them up to the executive lounge for me. Made my day! I seem to be in a good vortex at the moment. Hung around in the lounge for several hours chatting to Frenchie, Jack and Lucy til the flight was called. Another 747 – we were upstairs. John Wetton was up there too. Kept exchanging nods as he passed by, and eventually got talking. I like John Wetton. Very nice chap. We took a quick selfie in the half-light of the 747 cabin. We both look like criminals.

I guess I slept for 3 hours and then just lay around awake but relaxed.

Sunday 13 April   *Heathrow*

They put all the lights on at 6.00am and served breakfast. Landed just before 7.00am. Back at Heathrow in the passport queue I ran into Steve Hackett and Jo who were both enthusing at length about our Friday show. So, as you can imagine, I felt, and still do feel great. What a successful adventure on the high seas. Ahaaargh!

Wednesday 30 April *Home – Mexico City*

Up at 7.10 and helped get little Vibes ready for school. Took him to Charlton (the same school his big brother and sister went to – always a bit of a mindf***k to be back here 22 years later, but it's a nice school). Today he waved at me as usual from all three windows of his classroom (our ritual) showing, thankfully, no sign of sadness or distress.

Drove home and frantically prepared photographs for Robert Hammond, publisher of this diary, until 10.15 leaving 30-minutes to pack. Never really long enough, but I don't like packing – I'd rather concentrate on passport, keys, computer, money and risk the rest. I can always buy stuff when I get there.

Left at 10.50 to a lovely sunny day. Our little front garden is looking lush. We're going to have a lot of peonies and irises this year.

A new taxi driver, Thomas from the south of Poland, took me to Terminal 5. Read *The Outsider* by Albert Camus and glanced out periodically at spring fields full of sheep and new lambs. Glimpsed a hare.

At Heathrow Terminal 5 said hi to Ian in the street and then to the crew queueing up at check-in. Check-in and security were uneventful. Went to Huxleys for eggs Benedict – just what I fancied... but it wasn't great.

Got the little train to the Terminal B and gave Mark K the old photographs I'd found of him in Mexico while going through my old prints trying to find shots for the diary. Chatted with Phil, Frenchie and Ian. The TV on the wall silently announced the death of actor Bob Hoskins. I once stood next to him in a book shop in Hampstead.

Spoke to L on the phone and said bye for now and I'll text u when I land. Joined the wrong queue and very nearly boarded the plane to Phoenix, Arizona. That would have been interesting... Boarded the right plane and was waved upstairs on the 747. Flying Business again. Very nice. Took off an hour late due to someone not turning up on time. Lunch was nice. Caprese to start and steamed cod to follow. Read a bit more Camus. Not much more than 100 pages long. Took me a while to get used to Camus' short and succinct prose. Walked back a few seats to check Mosley's progress. He seems relaxed but is complaining that someone near him keeps farting with appalling olfactory consequences. Returned to my seat. I'm sitting next to Rothers who has nodded off and maintains his legendary status by snoring like a mythical beast. I'll put some in-ears in and watch a movie...

Watched **The Wolf of Wall Street**. Very entertaining although I found the decadence of 80's Wall St. Perfectly portrayed by Scorcese – somewhat depressing. This was the culture that brought down many western economies while the perpetrators, of course, grew unimaginably wealthy and, therefore, untouchable. Who pays for it all? Ordinary taxpayers who struggle every week to get by. Nothing ever changes. Nonetheless I did nearly wet myself laughing after the Quaaludes-overdose-drive-home scene. After the movie I reclined the seat and snoozed for a while until the cabin crew came round with sandwiches and scones an hour before landing. I'm a sucker for a clotted cream tea…

Managed to get through immigration without any fuss and pick up my bags. In the Arrivals hall a handful of fans waved eagerly and asked for autographs and photographs. If I can be forgiven for quoting myself, it's always "bizarre to come so far to an outstretched hand and easy conversation".

Made my way out onto the street and waited almost an hour for Frenchie and Phil who had been detained by customs. Not really what you want at 3 in the morning in your head. Arrived at the hotel and by then didn't feel tired so put the telly on. 30-odd channels in Spanish and only CNN really watchable (and then, barely). BBC World gets a bit tedious after a while, but I would have been grateful for it. Stayed up 'til 11.00 (5am in England) and then went to bed. Woke up at 3.00. Here we go again.

Thursday 1 May *Mexico City*

Applied all my energies to staying in bed until around 6.00 when I gave up and got up. Went down to reception to pay for wi-fi codes and discovered breakfast already being served, so made my way to the café for muesli and omelette. Jack appeared around 6.45 and so we drank coffee and chatted about brain surgery (Jack's current reading).

Went out and found a Starbucks 2 blocks away. V good. Decent morning-coffees are assured for the rest of my stay.

Returned to my room and FaceTimed home to L. She looks fantastic and sounds well. Pernilla (her chum from across the Green) was in the kitchen - she'd brought her boys round to play - so I said hello to her. She hardly ever stops laughing. Said a brief hi to Vibes who was understanably a bit distracted.

Came down to poolside and spent the morning proof-reading *The Invisible Diary* (as I now call it) *Volume 1*. Coming together nicely… but v. time-consuming. The sun was shining and the morning air not too humid and warm. Perfect for me. At 1.30 the laptop battery was flat so I returned to my room and Facetimed home again to say goodnight to Vibes. He seemed a little tired and unbothered. I think he still doesn't quite connect the "me" on the screen to the actual "me" and anyway, what use is a dad who can't play with you? Kids can be very brutal in their honesty. It takes a few years to acquire the mask we all wear in later life.

At 2.30 I was picked up by Leonardo and Gabriela Beltran who run the Projecto Andares charity which Rothers and I played the acoustic show for, last year. Leonardo had emailed so I had suggested lunch in the old Coyoacan district where we went last time. We returned to the restaurant we had been before - El Corazon del Maguey - which specializes in regional Mexican cuisine – all peculiar stuff but nonetheless tasty …and Mezcal! This is drank after biting down on slices of orange dipped in worm-salt (no kidding – some kind of dried, ground, worm mixed with salt into a powder which looks like paprika and tastes musky and dark). Strange to start with, but once you get into it… I ordered a Mezcal Caipirinha, a beer and, after Leonardo ordered straight Mezcal, well, it seemed rude not to join him. The food was great and the company was most pleasant. Gariela's son, Rafael, joined us after a while. Phil Brown had asked me to bring him back a bag of worm-salt so he could take it home to show his wife, so Leonardo asked the cafe owner who duly brought some as "a gift". Afterwards we walked around Coyoacan which was packed with Mexicans relaxing (it's a public holiday today) and the atmosphere was most festive. Street sellers abounded, selling brightly coloured arts and crafts – an old man was playing tunes with a leaf, another was playing an accordion and there was a band playing on a stage in the square. Everywhere, different musical melodies and styles mingled on the air. Mexico's amazing. Everywhere I glanced looked like a wonderful photograph or a movie. The light here, combined with the variety of the features of the people and the general-eccentricity of the culture, make for instant living-art. We went to "Mexico's oldest ice cream shop" where Leonardo bought strange ice-creams; for him, chamoyada – a dark coloured spicy ice-cream (I had a taste. Hmm…) and for me a lemon sorbet coated in worm-salt. He joked about "Montezuma's revenge" as he passed it to me. He had a point… I shouldn't tempt fate – I don't want to start this tour with screaming diarrhoea so I donated mine to Rafael who was happy to have it and, no doubt, is already equipped with whichever Mexican antibodies keep Montezuma at bay.

We returned to the hotel around 6.00 and I watched a bit more CNN. Lots of coverage of the unrest in Ukraine and the continued search for that missing Malaysian air-liner. The toxicology report on Peaches Geldof showed heroin as the likely cause of death. Same as her mum, then. I feel so sorry for the family. And for it to be so public must be hell.

At 8.00 I decided I couldn't stay up any longer and climbed into bed. Woke up slightly less often than last night.

Friday 2 May *Mexico City*

Up at 6.00. Blearily Facetimed home and said hi to L who seems okay. Went to Starbucks and returned with Cappucino, Chai and a croissant. Arranged a hairdresser for later in the day and then came down to the poolside to write this diary and continue proof-reading volume 1. It really is glorious here today. There was a note under my door this morning informing me that the mains power will be off "for Annual maintenance" from 7.30 until 11.30, so I can only work until the laptop battery craps out, which is any second now…

Returned to the room to discover still no power. This was evident when I climbed into the lift. The lifts were still working but the lights in them weren't so, as the doors slid shut I was plunged into pitch darkness, fingers crossed until I arrived at the fourth floor and they opened again to let in the daylight. With a flat laptop and no means of charging it I figured I'd go downstairs and wait for the departure to lunch. JC our chum and ex **Rolling Stone** journalist had invited us out to lunch and had sent a chap to pick us up. I joined Ian, Frenchie and Mark (who wasn't coming but then changed his mind) in reception and we set off for the restaurant in Luis's car. After half an hour in thick traffic I was regretting going out. A further 15-minutes saw us arrive at the restaurant, which turned out to be the venue where Rothers and Pete were giving their "masterclass"! This was a gig which Rothers had managed to crowbar into the schedule. I had hoped to avoid it – not because I wasn't interested, just because I want to rest and start this gruelling Latin-American tour in good shape. I probably came across as Mr. Big-Time Miseryguts but I didn't want thrusting into a fan feeding frenzy today and, after all, I thought we were nipping out for a quiet lunch, not a 45-minute drive to a gig. Managed to hide in a spare room until the fans had left and then we were taken outside onto the street where a table was set for about 20 people. Lunch was very nice but I bailed out after an hour to return to the hotel for my appointment with the hair-painters. Got back 10-minutes late and was dropped off at the salon where I was to spend 2 hours undergoing the paintress. The salon windows were wide open onto the sunny street. The faces of people in Mexico are so err... utterly Mexican. As I said before, everything and everyone looks, to my English eye, like part of a movie. Made my way back to the hotel, conscious of the laptop under my arm and the warnings that MC isn't as safe as it used to be.

I bumped into Paulo, our South American promoter, and arranged to have a drink with him in the bar at 6.30. Somehow I got it into my head that it was 7.30 and arrived an hour late. Sat alone in the bar over a Mojito for a while and then heard a voice shout, "h!". It was Dee McCloughlin – one of our past tour-managers. Dee's a prince and I haven't seen him in a few years – last time he slid L and I into the McCartney and Crowded House gig in Hyde Park. Turns out he's staying in our hotel too, tour-managing Franz Ferdinand. Went over and joined him and FF's manager, Cerne Canning. They were on their way out to dinner so we only talked for 15-minutes or so. Dee offered me a drink so I ordered another Mojito and Cerne paid for everything. Arranged to meet Dee tomorrow and they went off to dinner. After they'd gone I asked for my tab to discover Cerne had paid for my earlier Mojito too. Cheers, Cerne. Intentionally or unintentionally, very generous of you. Went back to my room – crashing once again, and was in bed by 9.00.

Saturday 3 May *Mexico City Pepsi Centre*

Woke at 5.00. Worked steadily at a lie-in until 8.00 before getting up and out to walk the 2 blocks to Starbucks. When I got there, they didn't take US dollars and I'd forgotten the credit cards. Came back and tried again, returning with cappuccino.

Spent the morning by the pool reading/correcting Vol 1 of *The Invisible Diary* and writing this one. Decided to have a "proper" lunch as it's a gig day so went to the cafe and had burger and fries. Burger undercooked and greasy. Fries really nice.

After lunch I went and found Dee in reception and we spent a pleasant hour chatting about his work with Crowded House who he tour-managed for many years. Fascinating stuff.

Returned to my room and got my stage clothes together for the show. We left at 3.00 and were bussed to the venue - The Pepsi Centre - about 3500 capacity. Looked good. There was an escalator backstage – you don't often get an escalator. Soundcheck was protracted. Rothers pointed out that the mains into his rig was metering at 200 volts and time ticked by while it was sorted out. I'm running my sounds from a laptop and working with a new tech, Tom Lee, but all was well. Mark K was wrestling with hired keyboards ("Not what I ordered!") and trying to get them to talk to his main computer… Hmm. Pete and Ian seemed to be relatively happy. It's always tricky with hired gear. I spent an hour working out what to wear. I'm a singer (mind you, we're not all divas - Joe Cocker wanders on in whatever he put on when he got out of bed).

By showtime the gig was just 300 short of the 3500 capacity and looked busy. I knew they'd be a great crowd and they were. Mexico's always a vibe. Most of the show was terrific from our point of view. The keyboards crapped out (as is their tendency) during the last song *Neverland*, which was a shame, but all in all, it was a good night. Surprised myself by getting through it without fainting – MC's famously high altitude makes physical exertion somewhat harder and I'm not someone who's constantly in and out of the gym. Nonetheless I seem to remain naturally fitter than I ever imagine I am. Just as well… Saw promoter Paulo afterwards who said, "That was a GREAT show man!" …Happy days.

Did a quick meet and greet after the show with aftershow guests. A lot of pretty women (Lord knows who invites them – maybe Paulo's put em on the rider) and then into the bus and back to my room for a much needed shower. No bath sadly – I could have done with one. Fell into bed around midnight (not bad!) and woke at 4.00! Bugger. Slept fitfully wondering how I could have lost my electric shaver – it had vanished yesterday and I had to go on stage last night looking like a dosser. Got up in the middle of the night and staggered around still trying to locate my missing shaver. Just about took the room apart before I finally discovered it under the fitted bathroom-sink. How on earth I had managed to drop it on the floor and then kick it under the sink unit without noticing, I'll never know.

Sunday 4 May *Mexico City Metropolitan*

Spent the morning by the pool writing this diary and reading through the first volume. Chatted by the pool with Paulo, who's still complimenting us on last night's show. He said the lights looked great. Well done Yens. Chatted for a while with Cerne, Franz Ferdinand's manager, and thanked him for paying for both my Mojito's the other night. He said I'm welcome. We talked about Marillion's famous "business model" how we'd invented crowd-funding etc, and I explained how it all happened. Cerne said bye-bye and I later chatted some more with Paulo. His father wrote books about anthropology. He remembered going to Egypt with his father when he was a kid and climbing into a limo. His father took him on one side and said, "Remember, son. This is not *your* limousine. This isn't even MY limousine. It's a moment, and that's all." Paulo said that had been a lesson to him. I noticed a tattoo of the Egyptian-God, Isis, under his arm. He later explained, but I already knew.

I was still talking to Paulo when I had to run back to my room to be ready to leave for the show at 2.00. Mini-bussed to the Metropolitan and soundchecked. The sound was strange. Well-defined but not really gelling. Most unusual. Metaphysical problems cannot be identified or defined, so you can't fix them. There was nothing I could ask Nick Todd for, as it was already there. It just wouldn't merge together into music. Never mind. We went upstairs to the dressing room and snoozed around 'til stage time. Early show 7pm.

Hit the stage for *Gaza* and on the downbeat Rothers had no sound. Walked straight off again and we started again. I felt like a twat but, hey, shit happens. Tried again and all was well. *No One Can* was met with an ecstatic response once again, like last time, and everyone sang the chorus as an act of faith. Incredible. Tonight we had added *Cover My Eyes* and *Hooks In You* which had the desired effect. I nearly expired singing 'em though. At one point I was wondering if I might pass out and missed out a line of *Hooks* just to recover. We were occasionally beset with technical problems but nothing that ruined the show really. At one point during *Man of a Thousand Faces* my radio mic and radio monitor pack failed simultaneously. Apparently the fuse had gone in the mains board. Nick Todd, to his credit, identified the problem and sorted it in enough time to have me up and running again in time for the complex harmonies at the end of the song. Encore 1 *Kayleigh, Lavender, Heart of Lothian* went down ecstatically and then came Encore 2 *Neverland*. One of those moments where I remained balanced on the head of that elusive pin. I never combined tuning, tone, and soul so well, for so long in my life. I have never sung better than that. The crowd went completely nuts as we staggered exhausted from the stage.

Afterwards we were invited up to meet Paulo's guests (he has his own dressing room! What a scream!) and as I entered the room everyone clapped. It was a wonderful moment. Signed stuff downstairs and then climbed aboard the mini bus back to room 4305. Amazing night.

Monday 5 May *Mexico City*

Slept 'til 5.00 am and stayed in bed 'til 8.00 before going down to breakfast. Joined Pete, Phil and Yens at a table and had some coffee and chickenny scrambled eggy thing. Very nice. Walked down to Starbucks and grabbed a cappuccino and some coconut water and returned to the hotel to spend a little time in the sun before my phoner to Clarins – an Argentinian magazine (I think) at 11.00 am. Seemed to go okay. Snoozed for much of the afternoon.

We were to meet at 7.00 to go to dinner. I got down to reception around 6.45 and had a beer in the bar with Conrado who was to take us to dinner on behalf of promoter OCESA. One by one, members of the band and crew began appearing and, around 7.15 we boarded minibuses for the short journey to *Bonita* – the restaurant where we were to have dinner. A table had been set upstairs for 20 people. I sat next to Conrado and Andrea - the young daughter of his friends Luis and Miroslava. Opposite me sat Juan Carlos Villanueva. Next door-but-one to me was my good friend, photographer Fernando Aceves. Spent the evening chatting to JC, Conrado and Fernando as umpteen courses of exquisite food kept steadily arriving. Asparagus and cheese. Tacos packed with steak, pizza slices – all fabulous and cooked to perfection. Conrado supplied the best tequila I have tasted (called 1800) along with beer and red wine, and later Mojitos. It was getting dangerous but I stayed the right side of the line. Down the table our crew were sloshed and jolly. Phil came over later, somewhat merry and affectionate. It was a really pleasant evening. Dessert arrived. I had pineapple in some kind of sweet sauce and a little ice cream and apple pie. Then it was time to go. We hugged each other and said thanks and bye-bye before returning to the hotel and as I climbed into the elevator to go to bed, Phil pointed out that it was only 11.30. It felt like 2.00 in the morning. "Is that it?!" said Phil, determined not to let the night end there. I imagine the crew carried on partying long after I was in bed. Went to sleep around midnight and woke again at 3.30. Just can't seem to get through the night.

Tuesday 6 May *Mexico City*

Spent all morning waiting for Brazilian phone interviews. They were supposed to start at 11.00, but the first one was late and that got in the way of the second one. Then the third and fourth did the same thing. Unfortunately that meant the fourth phoner - **Journal do Brasil** (I had once been on the cover) called while I was still talking to the third and they never got it together to call me again. Renaton, Paulo's rep, said they'll reschedule tomorrow. I hope so.

By the time I was finally set free to leave my room, it was 2pm. Went down to Starbucks and bought the regulation cappuccino and Chai latte. Yens was in there so I bought a sandwich and ate it while we chatted. He said he felt a little claustrophobic with so many people there last night. He's a more sensitive soul than he appears.

Returned to the hotel and packed for the 4 o'clock departure. Signed a couple more things on the way out of the door. There's always a couple of fans hanging around at the hotel in Mexico. Bussed back to the airport for the overnight flight to Sao Paulo. Boarded the plane without incident. 9 hours in Economy trying to sleep sitting up. Watched **American Hustle**. Enjoyed it although the unexpected twists and turns in the plot frayed my nerves somewhat. Good film. One of the stewardesses and the girl sitting a couple of rows in front wanted their pictures taking with me. We must be more famous in Brazil than I thought! The stewardess came by later and gave me a bracelet for good luck. This resulted in the girl across the aisle wanting to know who we were. She turned out to be a surgeon! Gawd, I'm getting old – she looked like she was barely out of college.

Wednesday 7 May *Sao Paulo Kiss FM session*

Landed in Sao Paulo feeling pretty wrung out and walked miles in the airport looking for Starbucks. Eventually found one and hung around outside with Ian waiting for Renaton to get the vans and buses organised.

Off we went, the now familiar drive to the Divino Blue hotel we stayed at last time (where I spent all night on the bathroom floor). The slow crawl through SP's legendary perma-gridlock.

Went to bed for a couple of hours then met up in the lobby for another long slow drive across town to Kiss FM. Paulo came too. "I could send you with Renaton or Baffo, but if I come too, then they know I'm serious about this one!" he said. We performed *Beautiful* and *Easter* as we'd rehearsed it in Mexico. Everyone seemed happy and the interview and music gave us over an hour on prime time rock-radio. Here you can reach millions of people. After that, Paulo took us all out to a Mexican restaurant where we ate fabulous tacos and I drank several pina-coladas, mindful not to end up on the bathroom floor again this time. A most pleasant evening.

Thursday 8 May *Sao Paulo – Rio de Janeiro Vivo Rio*

Woke at 7.30 by the alarm. A surreal dream-like-half-asleep journey to Rio but comforted by the knowledge that I felt infinitely better than the last time I made this journey. I had been poisoned and felt like death. I'll never know how I got on the plane back then. This time, I was only tired out.

Sat in the S.P. "Domestic-flights" airport listening to Paul Simon's *Hearts and Bones* feeling emotional and close to tears. Such an amazing song. I don't know how he sings of such heartfelt truth so dispassionately. Feeling and not feeling at the same time. But beautiful. So much contained in those seven words *"..the arc of a love-affair"*.

People kept coming over and asking for autographs and photographs. Arrived at the Othon Palace around half-two and went back to bed. Soundcheck at 4.30.

Soundcheck went well but was protracted due to technical issues. Returned to the hotel and walked down to the sea (across the road) to watch the wild Atlantic waves rolling endlessly towards this magic place - Copa Cobana - wondering if I'd get mugged. Didn't.

Returned to the show and we hit the stage at 10.00. Technical hell from the off. Mark reset everything and we lost half of the sounds for *Gaza*. The double-whammy was that my in-ear effects had gone down too so my sound was all wrong for the whole show. If anyone could have sorted it out, it was our own excellent Nick Todd. He did his best, but the effects had crapped out and weren't returning. It was one of those halls where you can't really hear the audience noise, so we all thought we weren't going down particularly well. Hard work all round.

Afterwards, Paulo, Phil and Yens appeared one-by-one and agreed it had been a fabulous show and Yens said the audience were so loud that he couldn't call the follow spots. Amazing. Paulo made a 30-minute speech afterwards about how he thinks it's all going in the right direction, we should make a DVD here, we should collaborate with some Latin American artists and make an acoustic thing etc. I remembered the message I had once received from Sergio Mendes which I still don't know was genuine or not. Now that would be something... and an education for both of us!

So I returned to my room in the Othon Palace where I had left the sliding window wide open onto my narrow balcony overlooking Copa-Cobana, and I gazed down at the floodlit boiling Atlantic Ocean on the beach. This is the best time of day to gaze at Copa-Cobana. From here I can see the genius of the mosaic-pavements stretching away below me. The post-modern mad monochrome designs of wavy lines to salute the sea, and stripes to tip their hats at Mondrian and a Banksy-esque extrapolation to the zebra crossings (although Rio beat him to it by several decades). I love this place so much – where a perfect laughing loving palm-tree-lined work of art affectionately kisses the untamed crashing sea. Once again, I have no one to share it with but you. But I'm finding it hard to close the glass and sleep. Why would you ever want to shut this out? The ambient temperature of the air - 25 floors up - is totally comfortable at 2.30 in the morning. I feel like I could sleep on the roof. Rio de Janeiro. My heart's birthday. You still shame the rest of the planet into mediocrity. Now THIS would be a place to die. CNN is invading my room quoting statistics of money and stocks. A billion here, invested. Profit loss, marketing. Yawn. I find it all tawdry, misguided and sad – especially in this enchanted place. Someone's got to explain to corporate America soon that it's not all about wealth and God. Lennon said it best: "Imagine there's no heaven..etc." Put it on and sing along.

Tuesday 13 May *Buenos Aires Gran Rex Theatre*

Woke up at 11.00 and had a Facetime chat with Linette. Managed to squeeze a quick hello out of Vibes but he's not interested in having a conversation. Ordered a couple of cappuccinos which arrived 25-minutes later and were undrinkable. Ordered some extra milk to try and calm 'em down a little.

"Hot or cold, signor?"
"Cold please."
"In a glass?"

"In a jug would be good."

"Perfect, signor."

After another 10-minutes a jug of hot milk arrived...

It was a nice day so I went out for a walk to see if I could find the button shop I'd found 20 years ago when I last stayed here at the Sheraton. Couldn't find it but passed a jewellers shop and a ring caught my eye in the window. Thought I might buy it for Linette so popped in and enquired as to the price. Txted her to try and find out her finger sizes. It happened to be exactly the right size! To cut a long story short, I eventually emerged with the ring – silver with a large 'watermelon tourmaline' stone, and a necklace of small beads of uncut sapphires, rubies and emeralds. I hope she likes it... I didn't have enough US dollars so popped back to the hotel to borrow cash from Ian and Mark. We'd earned an extra bit of money from the merch so what-the-hell. Came back and FT'd home again before it was time to go to the gig at 3.15.

Boarded the minibus for the journey to the Gran Rex theatre. Soundcheck passed without incident. We've decided, at Paulo's suggestion, to add *The Uninvited Guest* to the set tonight so ran it a couple of times. Returned to the Sheraton and dozed in bed for an hour or so before returning. When I hit the stage for the show it was obvious something had changed sound-wise since soundcheck and I was unable to fix it really for the whole show. Oh well. The sit-down crowd looked like more people than last time and I was later to find out that there were 300 more people. Great! It took a while to get under their skin but slowly they came to life. At the end of the show, before encore 1, Paulo was saying to me, "The security are not letting the people come forward but you must make it happen!" I went back on stage for the encore and asked the crowd to come forward, but I could see security men in the aisles sending people back to their seats. I was straight down off stage where I grabbed the back of the collar of the security man and - smiling - gently pulled him back to the stage as the crowd followed us both down to the front. Now the party had started... Before encore 2 Paulo appeared again and said, "Now we must go for a walk!" Flanked by him and Renaton I walked along the aisle - now full of people - singing *Sugar Mice* to the back of the theatre, stopping to shake hands and receive hugs from the crowd as I walked. This - although pure Latin American showbiz - really ignited the crowd and from there on we had them. Finished with *Neverland* and that was that. A terrific reaction and quite an achievement from everyone on stage considering the difficult sound.

At midnight everyone wished me a happy birthday and I raised a glass of Champagne with Paulo, who is beginning to resemble a South American manager rather than a promoter. After the show we returned to the hotel. There was a perfect full moon in the sky which looks nothing like the moon in the northern hemisphere. It appeared to be a different way up. Is that scientifically possible? I tried to photograph it but there's never much to be achieved without special equipment. This was the first hotel with a bath since we began this tour so I filled it up and relaxed for a while. When I pulled the plug at the end, the water came up through a drain in the bathroom floor and filled the room with water. I put a towel on the carpet and called reception. A maintenance man arrived and muttered in Spanish that he was sorry and he would send a cleaner. 10-minutes after that a woman arrived with a mop and bucket and dried everything up. I was asked if I wanted to change rooms but I was too tired. Anyway, most of the room was still dry and I was only going to be sleeping and checking out. Slept 'til 7.30 when the mobi began pinging birthday messages.

Wednesday 14 May *Buenos Aires – Santiago*

Happy Birthday! Spent most of it on a plane.

Friday 16 May *Santiago Caupolican*

Woke around 10.00 and decided to brave the breakfast room. Poured myself some muesli and drank "coffee" (which was very weak and tasted of nothing much), while people wandered over to congratulate me on last night's performance and ask for autographs and photographs. In between spoonfuls of cereal I stood up and sat down patiently grinning for cameras. I don't mind doing it, but when you've just rolled out of bed and you're trying to have breakfast it gets a bit much after the first 2 or 3. Returned to my room to pack. Always a stressful time – I have a history of leaving stuff in hotel rooms and no amount of idiot checking seems to help. As I've probably already said here, an idiot-check is a flawed notion when it's an idiot who's doing the checking…

Left the Casino Monticelli hotel (with a sigh of relief – it's not exactly easy to stay here if you don't speak Spanish) at midday for the van-ride to Santiago. Was photographed and cuddled repeatedly while trying to make my way to the van. It was a beautiful morning and after about an hour along the distant-mountain-flanked freeway we arrived at the Crowne Plaza hotel Santiago and were met by a welcoming committee of managers and concierges all declaring it a great honour to have us in their hotel. At the reception desk, all the room keys were already prepared and I made my way in the elevator to room 2105. The key didn't open the door so had to return to reception to get another one. The duty manager let me in. I was to have trouble getting into my room for the rest of the day. I think the electric locks were past their sell-by date. My room was a suite with a lovely view of a palm-tree-lined square and church below. I had just enough time to unpack my laptop and gain access to the internet before promoter's rep, Werner, arrived at my door with a woman who was going to colour my roots. We hauled a chair into the bathroom and she promptly set about the task, leaving me to cook for 40-minutes before I showered off the colour and just made it back down to reception for the 3.30 departure to the show. Caupolican was the indigenous tribal king who stood up to the invading Spanish and later paid the ultimate unpleasant price. Went inside and straight up to the restaurant where we were given chicken and mashed-potato with bits of olive in. All very nice, if a bit chewy.

Soundcheck progressed without incident (in other words, took an hour instead of two) and we eventually returned to the hotel. By now I was very tired and couldn't wait to get back to my room to rest. 15 more minutes trying to gain access to my room wasn't what I needed. Ended up writing Sofi an email (to apologize for the one I'd sent her the other night) before lying on the bed relaxing but trying not to sleep. I didn't want my voice to close down. It has held up really well on this tour, but it's getting a little scratchy now. Arrived back at the gig at 7.50 for the 8 o'clock meet n'greet to discover that there has been a major problem all day with the lights. The local promoter has failed to supply our specified lights for the show and we don't have any follow-spots tonight. This is a disaster as I'm going to spend half the show running around in the dark.

Well, last-minute Latin American negotiations seemed, finally to have secured 1 follow-spot, so we were in business. We went on stage to huge applause and played *Gaza* after which I said good evening to receive an ecstatic crowd-response. The Santiago crowd lived up to our expectations after a very high benchmark last time. The band played well and technical troubles were thankfully absent for this, our last night of the tour. During the second encore I decided to do the walk through the crowd and eventually found myself at the back of the hall with Phil and Yens behind the sound and light desks. Beer rained down on us as the front row of the balcony leant over trying to see me below and spilling their drinks in the process. I took it into my head to step over the desks and back into the crowd, not realising that what I thought was a flat surface was, in fact, a hole which my leg went straight down. I landed on my backside on some sort of barrier. Fortunately, the damage was only minor bruising and I managed to return to the stage in one piece (minus microphone) to finish the song on a spare mic which Nick Todd magically produced. A great end to a successful tour, and no hospital visits!

Decompressed in the small dressing room before going to the cafe where the guests were assembled. Did the photographs and the autographs and returned to the Crowne Plaza to be given yet another room-key which, against all odds, opened my door! Hit the bed running, deciding not to shower until the morning. Too tired.

Saturday 17 May *Santiago – Rio – Heathrow*

Flew home from Santiago changing planes at Rio with a three-hour wait in a very warm club-lounge. Rio airport, like all the others, isn't finished and won't be in time for the World Cup. Flew home Business Class (ah, the luxury) so could lie down and kinda sleep during the overnight journey. Watched **The Best Exotic Marigold Hotel** and thoroughly enjoyed it.

Wednesday 9 July *Home – Montreal – Quebec*

Rose at 7.30 with Vibes and let L sleep for half an hour while he had breakfast. Today – Shreddies and I had coffee, feeling rough after a night of fitful sleep. This morning's going away has unsettled me. I am currently enduring a torn meniscus cartilage in my right knee. It locked up a couple of weeks ago in a meeting at - of all places - Beaconsfield motorway services, and I couldn't walk at all for a few days, although it has slowly eased up. An operation is scheduled at some point. In the meantime, it seems to be slowly sorting itself out. I can walk okay now but I'm worried about the forthcoming shows in Quebec and Loreley. I think that's what had kept me awake along with the knowledge that I must go away. By 8.40 we had the boy dressed, scrubbed and ready for school. He found an unusual fly on the window and wanted to take it with him - they're currently "doing bugs". I had helped him draw a few insects yesterday for homework. We put the fly in a tub and he carefully carried it into the car. For once, we weren't late. I did the school-run and we arrived in time for the whistle. He waved through the window at me after he arrived in his classroom and I mouthed an "I love you" to him. Exchanged pleasantries with the other dads and mums before returning home to pack. Always stressful – I always forget something. Still, if you've got your passport and money, everything else is a convenience.

The car came for me at 11.30 by which time I was ready. Decided to strap my knee for the flight so packed knee-straps in the hand-luggage. Said bye to my lovely L who seems okay about it – it's only 5 days. The taxi ride was uneventful. Chatted with the driver about Brazil's colossal 7-1 thrashing last night at the hands of Germany in the World Cup semi-final. Also chatted about Al Green, AC/DC, George Michael, Bob Harris, The Isley Brothers, Level 42, Earth Wind & Fire and the Travelling Wilburys all the way to Heathrow Terminal 2. Checked in without too much trouble; it's all getting hi-tech and I now have my boarding pass as a digital splodge on my iPhone, which gets scanned periodically - and somewhat uncertainly - by machines. Security was thorough. Despite wearing only thin cotton trousers and a t-shirt I managed to set off the beep and a man patted me down leaving nothing much unpatted…

Said hi to Rothers and we had brunch together in the new Terminal building at **The Perfectionists Café** (now that's just asking for trouble). In some regards we answered the description, but not in others. The eggs Benedict was, to be honest, perfect. The walk to the gate from Terminal 2 was miles along corridors, up and down escalators and along travelators until I was sure we were going to emerge in Beaconsfield or Brixton. I have a theory that it doesn't matter which Heathrow Terminal you fly from, by the time you've done the 2 mile trek to the gate – you end up at the same one.

Boarded the flight and was relieved to have been given quite a bit of leg room. I'm going to need it – it's a long way to Montreal with meniscus trouble. Strapped up my leg, settled down for the long flight, listened to Seal's **Dreaming in Metaphors** and Rufus Wainright's **I Don't Know What It Is**, and wrote this.

The stewardess made a great show of giving us menus so we could choose the meal, after which she informed us that, err, basically, it's pasta – the Thai curry has ran out. I ordered pasta. I've had worse, but it wouldn't have made it outta the kitchen at The Perfectionists Café.

Well, the flight passed quite quickly. Didn't sleep. Before we began the approach to Montreal the stewardess asked which hot snack I would prefer – chicken or vegetarian. I opted for the chicken. She came back and said they only had meatballs. I said just coffee would be fine. Air Canada doesn't look too rosy next to British Airways either. In Montreal there was a half hour wait for the bags. We had to clear customs before checking-in again for the onward flight to Quebec. Everyone was very friendly, as usual. As I walked towards the security queue to head back to yet another gate I noticed that the World cup semi-final between Holland and Argentina was approaching its 90th minute with a 0-0 score line. By the time I had cleared security, they were well into playing extra time and still 0-0. When I finally made gate A21, after another half-mile walk, extra time had finished and the match was going to be decided on penalties. Fortunately, there was a bar at the Gate and Rothers and I watched the penalties on a TV screen there. Holland missed the first penalty and never recovered. So the final will be Germany Argentina…

Waited a while more at the Gate to be told there was a technical fault on our plane and that we had to change Gates and wait while the luggage was transferred to another aeroplane. Just what you want after a transatlantic flight…

The flight up to Quebec was in one of those noisy prop planes that makes your brain vibrate in your skull. Mercifully it was only a 30 minute flight. I spent it re-reading Albert Camus' **The Outsider**.

In Quebec we were picked up in a van by a man called Calypso and taken the 20 minute drive to the Hilton. Checked-in and found room 1423. Nice view of the parliament building and BBC World on the telly. The Israeli's have decided it's a good idea to murder 80 Palestinians by bombing their homes in the Gaza strip in vengeance for the three Israeli kids kidnapped and murdered last month. Awful. I guess 25:1 is the usual ratio… Officially, of course, it's in retaliation for rockets fired out of Gaza – none of which seem to have injured anyone so far. That don't make it right, and I wouldn't want to sleep with the thought of a rocket - however crude - dropping on my house… but when you compare it to what those poor sods in Gaza have to contend with… And, of course, they are not allowed to leave – there's a wall round it. Went to bed at 10.00.

Thursday 10 July *Quebec*

Did well. Only got up briefly around 5.00 and slept 'til 8.00-ish. Hoorah. I have learned by now that it's the second and subsequent nights that are the tricky ones.

Facetimed home and chatted to L who sounds well. Went down to breakfast and had scrambled eggs and bacon. The coffee was that iffy stuff you get in

North America. Made a mental note to find better coffee.

After breakfast I went to reception and was recommended a hairdresser so I could get the grey roots done once again. At some point I'm going to have to shave my head and go grey... Went out and got said roots painted by a nice chap called Phillippe. Walked up the characterful Rue St Jean and nearly bought shoes but didn't bother. Returned with a slight limp as the right knee continues to remind me it may be called 'right' but it ain't.

Later was drawn to the sound of music coming from a stage in the Place d'Youville. When I arrived there I realised that this is where the Hotel and Theatre du Capitole is situated. This is the hotel with the theatre inside where we played on the **Marbles** tour when I ricked my neck, had the end-of-tour drinks and ended up missing the flight to Hawaii! Nice place though. I ordered seafood linguine and sat in bright sunshine at a terrace table on the street reading **The Hare with Amber Eyes** by Edmund de Waal, while a dub band soundchecked in the square. Quite blissful.

In the evening I went looking for a loudspeaker for my laptop so I could have a vibe going in my hotel room, but I never found one. Bumped into my old friend Kathleen Forcier (who'll be interviewing me tomorrow) along with Eric and Nathalie, (fans from Montreal who happened to be passing) so we all went for a beer outside on the street. Around 8.30 (1.30 in England) I could feel I'd had enough so returned to the Hilton. I really should have stayed up 'til at least 10.00, but, man of steel, caved in and went to bed at 9pm.

Friday 11 July *Quebec*

Awake at 4.00, 5.00, 6.00, 7.00, and got up at 8.30. Facetimed home. L and Vibes were back from school and sounded well. Vibes didn't say much, but drew me a snowflake and a love message. Walked round to Rue St Jean again and found a good coffee place where I bought cappucino and Chai tea. Returned to the hairdressers and bought Hipanema bracelet for L. She'd had her eye on one of these "for Christmas" but, having found them for sale yesterday at the hair salon, Christmas seemed destined to arrive early.

Had eggs benedict in a cafe on the corner before returning to the Hilton for my 11.00 appointment with Steeve and Kath who were to run me round to the Auberge Saint-Antoine Hotel where I was to be interviewed. Very nice hotel. Macca stayed here recently. Interview was v. relaxed. Jeff has been making a documentary about the fans for 2 years now and wanted to have my thoughts. I have known Steeve and Kath since the early nineties, so it was a coincidence that Jeff had met them through their children's sports clubs and he'd asked Kath to conduct the interview. Steeve and Kath dropped me back at the Hilton and invited me out for a spot of tea at 5.00.

Back to the Hilton around 1.30 to discover that Blondie will play tonight at 7.30. I wondered if Clem Burke was staying in the Hilton... As I was staring up at a TV screen in the lobby trying to find out who it was proudly welcoming to the

Hilton, "We have had the pleasure of welcoming Alice Cooper, David Bowie, Elton John etc.." to see if Blondie were on the list, Clem emerged from the lift! Said hello and that I'd love to come over this evening and see his show. He said he'd arrange it and that he was going to get some sleep.

Txted Frenchie and asked him if he fancied a half. He did, so we met up in the lobby again and bumped into Ian who came along too, back to the Capitole. Sat in the sunshine soaking up the atmosphere again and, when Phil Brown passed us, we shouted him over. At 3.30 Pete T and I were being picked up to go to a radio station (which turned out to be broadcasting from a pub on St Jean) so Frenchie and I walked back. The interview was friendly and fun. We were interviewed by Michel who I immediately recognized. No wonder – he says he's seen us over 70 times. He turns up all over the world. Amazing. …and such a considerate man – always affectionate but always respectful and never "in yer face".

Back to the Hilton where Clem had left me a message on my room-phone saying he would go over to the gig at 6.15 if I cared to join him. Sweet of him to bother. I'm sure he must have a lot of other stuff on his mind.

Back yet again to the Capitole Hotel cafe for a quick Caesar salad with Steeve and Kath before rushing back for the 6.15 rendezvous with Clem. Steeve and Kath tagged along and the four of us bundled into a van to the backstage of Blondie's huge gig. Kath knows the festival well and says there'll be 40,000 people out there tonight. Clem was very generous and wandered around trying to organise passes for the 3 of us. What a host. We said a brief hi to Chris Stein and Leigh Foxx before Clem invited us up to the stage when he went to check his kit. The stage was huge. I'm glad I'm not doing this one tonight with a bad leg. It'd be doubly frustrating not to be able to run around. Clem told us to help ourselves to beers from his dressing room. The dressing rooms were Portakabin things and they all had large signs on them saying "CLEMENT" much to Clem's amusement. I took a picture of him posing on the steps. After a while Frenchie, Ian and just about all our crew except Yens turned up and we were all milling about as Debbie H, Chris Stein and the boys appeared from their dressing rooms for the show. I wanted to get out of the way, but wasn't sure which direction to go to get out-front. We made our way out to the VIP area as the band struck up. Debbie was singing well and Clem played as only Clem can – punky, powerful, splashy and tight at the same time, and "for the song". They've written some killers. It was a great evening. Hung out for 5 mins after their set with Clem and all our crew. Billy Joel was next up - I'd seen him wander past in a low slung hat earlier backstage - but we all decided we needed to sleep, so returned to the hotel. In bed by half ten. Sent Clem a thanks email and attached the pic – a man and his wash-rooms.

Saturday 12 July *Quebec Festival d'Eté*

Soundcheck was a lobby call at 1.00. We bundled into a van which, basically, dropped us off across the road! Didn't realise the gig was quite so close. There were already a few people hanging around fishing for autographs. The gig is a grassy hill with a stage at one end and a makeshift fence round it. Rumour has it, the capacity is 5000+. It didn't look big enough to me to hold more than 3000, but outdoor spaces can be misleading. We had been allotted a generous sound check time of two hours – much longer than any of us had suspected, so we had plenty of time to get a sound. I gradually arrived at a good one. The hired AC30 sounded great. They often don't… Band sounded good and I reckoned we were in for a good night if anyone shows up. Spent the afternoon trying to relax and sleep. Couldn't sleep. I was in one of those weary jet-lagged states too tired to do anything but unable to rest. Spent the afternoon and early evening lolling on the bed, watching BBC World – which seems to alternate between reporting Gaza, where the Israelis are busy murdering hundreds of men, women and children, destroying homes and injuring thousands once again in so-called retaliation for Hamas's rockets which haven't killed anybody (does this sound like I'm one-sided? Check the facts yourself before writing to me) and reporting people warring and starving in Sudan and summary executions on street-corners in Syria and Iraq. Depressing in the extreme, especially in the middle of the night between sleep-phases of jet-lagged sensitive singers.

I'm glad we're opening the show with *Gaza*. That song cannot be sung enough.

At last, it was time to go. We journeyed across the street once again in the van to discover that the "arena" was packed and a band on-stage playing something arty and drone-y. I quite liked it. Phil Brown quipped "Let's hope all these people aren't here for them!" I had wondered myself if the throngs might depart along with the opening act…

They didn't. In fact I was to later learn that the place was full to capacity and that people were being turned away at the gate into another area where they could watch the show on a screen. I heard talk of between 5000 and 6000 people. Blimey… I'll never understand how this works. Perhaps we've had some airplay? Perhaps the promotion of our presence here has been unusually efficient/widespread? Who knows… Soundgarden are playing the big stage on the edge of town tonight, so one might have thought we'd have had a depleted crowd… Shit – I reckon we should move to Quebec!

Well, I hit the tequila and Red Bull (which Steeve says is "really bad for your heart, man, and actually illegal here, they are allowed to serve Red Bull separately at bars here, but can't mix it with alcohol". I am living proof that it can't be THAT bad for you – I've been drinking it for years!) and off we went…

Gaza was well received by the crowd stretching away onto the hill. I ran forward to the edge of the stage and screamed, "Quebec, Quebec, Quebec!" in celebration of being in front of this crowd. They knew what I meant. The crowd were great all night and - with the exception of a crap and wandering speech about the spectrum of our music before *No One Can* - I was very connected with the crowd. The band played well, and we all felt the love and bounced it around. A most enjoyable show and, at 90-minutes, no time for the set to flag anywhere.

The 90 passed like 45 and it was over. A great night. I sat on the grass for a while afterwards recovering and talking to people who came with their own histories which I endeavoured to process in the haze of aftershow adrenalin, Cuervo Gold tequila and Becks beer.

Back at the hotel, I ran a bath and wallowed in the water for a while before climbing into bed. I was fairly hammered and wondered if I, like Princess Margaret, might have the water too hot and have to go to hospital with 2nd degree burns before I realised and got out. This never happened, perhaps proving that Margaret was more rock n'roll than me. Not difficult…

Saw a txt had come in from Clem, wishing us a good one. What a nice chap. A few thousand gigs and twenty-million record sales don't appear to have had an adverse effect on him.

Sunday 13 July   *Quebec – Montreal – Home*

Finally managed a respectable lie-in, getting up at 10.00, but not without a few BBC World maim-and-murder sessions in the early hours. It can't be good for your subconscious…

Got up and txted home. L and V are out somewhere in Buckingham. Said we'd Facetime later before I check out.

Went out and found breakfast once again in the cafe of the Capitole Hotel. Read my book. I'm currently alternating between Edmund de Waal's **The Hare with the Amber Eyes** and Eduardo Galiano's **Mirrors** (although I'm supposed to be reading **Cider with Rosie** (Laurie Lee) for the book club in the village).

Returned to the hotel to pack (and managed to leave my phone-charger + mains adaptor in the wall! Now how many times have I done that?!) and Ftimed L who said the open garden thing was a let-down. Vibes didn't want to talk. He told L to tell me he was at Tescos in Brackley.

Checked out at 2.00 for a 2.30 departure. In the lobby I chatted to a couple who said they'd never heard of us until the Cruise To The Edge where they caught our show and were "transfixed".

"We never even looked at each other for the 90-minutes you were on stage – just at the band. When you played the last song we looked at each other and we were both in tears. We thought, 'Where have we been all these years!?' We flew up from Montreal to see you."

We arrived at Quebec airport and everything progressed at a snail's pace. Check-in took half an hour while Security took as long again. Bad enough, except that we were missing the World Cup Final between Argentina and Germany the whole time. Finally got through Security and into a bar with the match on TV half-way-through the second half. 0-0 at 90 minutes and we were running out of time for the call to the flight to Montreal. Mark "I hate football" Kelly sat at the bar seemingly riveted to the match, despite his many protestations whenever any of us talk about football. Maybe he's getting the bug… Just before final call, and 2-minutes before the end of extra-time, Germany scored and won the World Cup.

Rushed to Gate 25, limping along travelators and up flights of stairs, past broken escalators on the dodgy knee, and boarded the prop-plane to Montreal. Noisy, cramped and unpleasant, but mercifully only 30-minutes long. Didn't have a lot of time to change planes. Popped into a shop and bought Vibes a little killer-whale cuddly toy before boarding the plane back to London, marvelling at Phil Brown's silver 'mixing hat', a present from Robert (Norwegian drum-tech and excellent drummer) – which makes him look like Jay Kay after being exposed to radiation.

The flight home was luxurious ("Business"), I guess, and I shouldn't moan, but I will. We stood on the runway for over an hour owing to the pilots being late onto the plane from a late incoming Toronto flight. Once airborne, it took so long to be served the meal (which was excellent) that when I lay down after it to sleep, there was only 3 hours flying time before they put all the lights on and served breakfast (which may have been excellent too – I only had coffee). Despite the late take off we landed on time at 7.30 am and made the obligatory 1 mile walk, after 3 hours fitful sleep, to passport control which was mercifully empty. Made my way to the carousel and waited half an hour with everybody else for the bags. When the bags finally appeared, mine wasn't amongst them. The man at luggage services said he used to play drums with The Clash and Elvis Costello. That was cool, but unfortunately it was only his second day on the job and it took much head-scratching for him to register my bag as missing. It was eventually located in Heathrow at Terminal 1 where it had gone by mistake thanks to the "new system".

"Can I just go and get it?" I asked.

No, I couldn't. I was assured that could take up to 3 hours and that I would be better having it couriered home. I dug in my heels and said I want to take it with me. Another lady in Lost Baggage tried and failed to get hold of anyone at T1.

"The problem is... they don't care," she confided. I had to admire her honesty.

Gave up and was taken home by taxi. The bag showed up teatime the following day. What a waste of time (mine) and money (theirs). Mercifully, the bottle of Jack Daniels hadn't exploded all over my clothes, although I could tell someone had been in the case - probably the Customs men of Quebec, Montreal or London - probably all three.

Friday 18 July *Home – Kamp Bornhofen*

Up at 7.20 when little Vibes appeared at the bedroom door. I had been awake since 5.00 anyway, failing to coax my mind and body back into sleep so I left Linette sleeping. Got the day off to a stressful start – Vibes is refusing to read his school reading-books this morning and no amount of coaxing seems to help. He's been a good boy lately and I really thought he was growing up... but I guess I have overestimated him. It's the end of term and he's probably tired. Sadly, this doesn't lead to him sleeping any later. Took him to school and waved bye-bye from all three school windows, as he likes to do. Returned home and had just enough time for another coffee and to pack before the cab came to take me to Heathrow T5. At least I got my suitcase back before I had to leave again!

The journey was uneventful and I was dropped at the terminal at area B1 where I caught sight of the long blonde locks of Nick Beggs. Went over and said hello. He too is en-route to Germany for a show, somewhere near Berlin, with Kim Wilde. Nick introduced me to his band and I said hi to Kim as she arrived. Wandered over to where our crew were already checking in and waited AGES. I have never seen T5 quite so busy. Frenchie now seems to have acquired Silver status on his air miles and took me to the Exec Lounge as a guest. Drank cappuccino and rum and Coke while being joined by Lucy and Ian. Yesterday, a Malaysian passenger jet out of Schipol was shot down over Ukraine. Half the passengers were Dutch and there were allegedly 9 Brits and 23 Americans. All strewn across a field in the Russian-rebel-held part of Ukraine after being shot down from a height of 33000 feet! That's a guided missile then. After a week of hearing of Palestinian children murdered in Gaza, the thought of babies and children's smashed body-parts in a far-off field in Eastern Europe is almost more than I can live with. What a week.

The old head of the liberals, David Steele, came and sat at the next table, helping himself to a glass of red. I guess he's one of those people who knows what's REALLY going on in the world. I think I'd be starting the day with a glass of red too... We sat with Ian and Lucy for a while. Mosley said "I used to like the news – it was my favourite programme. But I've gone off it."

I feel the same. Night after night a load of horror, worry and injustice you can do nothing about. Exhausting. We wrote a song called *Gaza* to try to turn attention to the plight of those unfortunate people. It doesn't feel like much of a contribution but I suppose it's at least something.

I wandered around the gadget shops at Heathrow for a while looking at the laptop speakers. I could do with something to play music in the hotel rooms. Couldn't make my mind up though. After a delay of half an hour, a Gate was finally announced so I wandered over to A9 and was the last to board. It was hot on the runway and the warm air hit me in the face as I entered the boarding corridor. Europe's in the middle of a heatwave at the moment.

The flight was, happily, uneventful. At one point I glanced over at Rothers who was reading an article in **Sound-on-Sound** magazine about the making of Peter Gabriel's **So** album. There were a couple of pictures of Peter and also engineer, Kevin Killen, in Peter's old studio at the bottom of his garden at Ashcombe House, Swainswick, near Bath. I went there myself a couple of times back in the How We Live days. We used to borrow bits and pieces from Peter (we thought we were hiring them but, to this day, we never received and invoice). One morning I was taking back an Emu Emulator when he appeared at the door of the barn/control room and said, "We've just finished a mix – would you like to have a listen?"

I answered as nonchalantly as I could, "Yes please."

And so, I stood at the SSL desk with Peter G at my side listening to *Red Rain* as the unmistakable sound of Stewart Copeland's hi-hats came skittering in. I must have been the first person on earth to hear that mix apart from the musicians and engineers involved in its creation.

"What do you think?" he said

"Fabulous." Said I.

Thank you again, Peter.

We were met in Arrivals at Frankfurt by a couple of chaps who took us the 2 hour drive to Kamp Bornhofen a small village nestling in the hills of the Rhine. It's very beautiful round here. Halfway here we stopped at a petrol station for ice creams and Lucy and I ran into the shop and bought Magnums, orange lollies, rum and Coke's and Becks. That's better!

Arrived at the hotel in Kamp Bornhofen and was immediately given a drink by the affable owner, Werner, who speaks English with a Yorkshire accent. Apparently he gets a lot of tourists here from Yorkshire and he learned his English from them! His wife, Andrea, never stops smiling. They're both great hosts.

The weather here in Germany is roasting and, unfortunately, there's no air-conditioning in the hotel rooms. While I drank a beer and chatted to Werner, members of the band and crew began returning from their rooms looking hot and flushed. I decided to stay put in the air-conditioned cafe downstairs and, when Ian appeared and ordered a Strammer Max (Ham, fried eggs and bread) I ordered one myself and ate before going up to bed around 9.30. Sure enough, my room was like a sauna and it took until the small-hours before I managed to get to sleep. I got unfortunate deja vu again - drifting in and out of sleep in between TV reports of more Gazan dead and the horrors of the shot-down passenger jet.

Saturday 19 July *Loreley*

Up at 9.00 and into the shower. It had been such a hot night. Felt better after a shower and went down to breakfast and said hello to the Web Germany: Markus, Joerg, Alex, Dirk, Stefan. It was good to see them again and pass on congratulations for Germany's World Cup victory last Saturday. Was it only last week?! Everyone seemed well and happy.

We left for soundcheck around 9.40 and I jumped into a BMW with Steve R. Dirk drove, along the Rhine which cuts through the beautiful towering landscape of wooded hills dotted with old castles, churches and dreamlike old German houses. A railway runs in and out of tunnels alongside each bank of the river and whenever a train passes the entire vista takes on the feeling of a model railway perfectly laid out between hillsides and model buildings – except that it's 1:1 scale. We wound our way up the hillside roads and arrived at the top where the Loreley amphitheatre sits. A "Loreley" is the name given to a mermaid-like water spirit. An old German mythology no doubt inspired by the romantic notions of sexually-frustrated river-sailors.

We've played here before, a few years back. Last time the sound on and off stage was great - a combination of a good-sounding space and well designed and maintained German audio equipment - so I was looking forward to the experience. Soundcheck progressed well and everyone seemed happy with their gear so we returned to the hotel – this time I seemed to have Dirk to myself so I sat in the front and enjoyed the air-conditioning. The temperature outside was already in the high twenties and it was only 11.00 am. Back at the hotel I dropped my bag in my room (up four flights of stairs, not ideal for a man with a torn meniscus cartilage) and returned downstairs to ask Werner-with-the-Yorkshire-accent for a cup of coffee.

Phil Brown appeared and suggested a walk along the river so off we went, stopping briefly at the strange shop down the road (full of crucifixes and candles and ornaments no sane person would want) for an ice-cream – that's three Magnums I've consumed in under 24-hours. We walked along the river and sat on a bench for a while watching the passing barges and contemplating the number of trucks you'd have to put on the roads to move all that cargo. Germany - like Holland - seems to "just work" unlike Britain where we seem to just constantly "make do".

It was too hot to sit there for long, so we returned along the river and went looking for a bite of lunch. Decided to try a bar opposite our hotel which looked like the food might be good. It wasn't and neither was the service. Phil and I sat at the outside tables listening to bizarre German muzak playing from loudspeakers. At one point we heard *Delilah* - the Tom Jones hit - sung with great gusto in German while watching a German tourist photographing a cigarette machine on a wall. I was just commenting that I haven't seen a cigarette machine for years, when a monk walked past us and into the bar. He was a perfect Benedictine monk in dark brown habit tied at the waist with a rope, sandals etc. Went back up to my rooftop room to lie perspiring on the bed in the dark. Sent txts to Linette to say I was back if she wanted to call me.

Telly continued to be depressing and I eventually nodded off for a while.

We'd arranged to leave the hotel at 7.30 to go back up to the amphitheatre and check out the opening band Anathema. When we arrived they were already on stage. Watched from the side of stage for a little while. They were singing well.

Wandered down to the bar overlooking the river. A fabulous spot to watch the sunset over the valley of the Rhine stretching out below. This bar is open to the public so I posed for photographs and allowed myself to feel famous for a half an hour. Joined soon after by Pete and Fiona T, Lucy and Stephanie B and Phil B and Nick Todd. Lucy showed me a photograph of a banner she'd spotted in the crowd. It said "Marillion. Frankfurt Air-Traffic-Controllers!" on it. We have fans in high places – I wonder if they'd known which plane we were on?

Showtime beckoned so we returned backstage to get changed and ready. Said hello to old roadie Smick (now living and working in Sweden) who had happened along to see us. He's in Germany to watch the Grand Prix and thought he'd drive over. It was good to see him. He's split up with wife Helen who he'd met during our long spell at Stanbridge Farm, near Brighton, writing **Holidays in Eden** back in 1990. A shame. He looked well, bearded and tanned. I don't think he'd have looked out of place in the Swedish royal family.

Hit the stage at 10.00 and began with *Gaza* trying to contain my anger at what I was singing. 330 dead in a week and rising at a rate of 50 a day. Many children. So far, one Israeli soldier and three young men kidnapped and murdered by, according to Israel, Hamas, although Hamas have denied responsibility for it. "The world does nothing," says the song, and - apart from UN public declarations deploring Israel's actions -that's about it.

I felt good tonight and I was singing well. My sound was good and the crowd and I were "up for it". The evening had cooled to comfortable-mid-twenties for the crowd - perfect really. The two "sit-down" songs, *Fantastic Place* and *STCBM* went well. During *Cover my Eyes* I ran out into the crowd and sang the song from out front, taking a walk up to the mixing desks. Phil B had been badgering me to do it all day, so off I went. Unfortunately, the follow-spot operators weren't psychic and lost me so I performed the song in the dark among the crowd. It was kinda cool though, that I'd vanished. Mark later told me that he couldn't see me from the stage but could follow my progress by the camera flashes in the crowd and then when I returned to the stage, walking down the central division of the amphitheatre, he said it looked like Moses parting the Red Sea. When I got to the front I was prevented from returning to stage by the crowd crash-barriers. In my current state awaiting a right-knee operation I decided against trying to climb over, so I looked at the crowd and made a gesture with my thumb. They promptly hauled me into the air, over the barrier and set me down gently on the other side. Bless 'em. That shit makes you feel VERY powerful, and very loved. *Kayleigh*, *Lavender* and *Heart of Lothian* followed and, naturally the crowd loved it. I sang the whole set with soul tonight and was very pleased with it as a vocal performance. I can't often say that. It's so hard to remain in that place, but tonight I was there more-or-less throughout. Plans to encore with *This Strange Engine* before *Neverland* were abandoned as we were going to overrun the midnight curfew, so we returned for the encore and played only *Neverland*. This song suits my range and spirit about as well as anything we've ever written and again I felt good about every aspect of it, remaining "connected" to the words and the crowd throughout. Thank you Loreley. Really lovely.

Didn't stay long afterwards – the dressing room was too hot to hang out so I got changed quickly and staggered back down the fire-escape-style staircase where everyone seemed happy with the show. The editor of the influential German **Eclipsed** magazine said, "Tonight, Steve Hogarth conquered Loreley!". Well, I'm glad he thought so. It can't do any harm.

Back to the hotel, down the winding roads to the river wishing we could slow down a bit what-with all the Tequila and Red Bull sloshing around inside me... At the hotel I asked if there was anything to eat and Werner provided meatballs and a pickle. I ate this with bread and a mug of hot chocolate – a strange combo, guaranteeing indigestion before bed. Didn't stay up long. Went to bed and slept well in-between bouts of raging heartburn.

Saturday 9 August *Cropredy Festival UK*

Shortly after Loreley I developed a strange pain in my left arm. No, not a heart attack but an inflamed nerve in my neck. I went to the doctor who said the recovery time was 6 to 8 weeks. Bloody hell – 2 months! I had a kind of sleeve of pain – like a "dead leg" in my left arm. It got worse when I lay on either shoulder at night. I sleep on my side, so it made sleeping very uncomfortable. Not sure where it all came from, but I think it might have been a load of muscle spasm brought on by walking around and playing shows with this knee problem for a few weeks. I managed to find a good physiotherapist in Banbury just before Cropredy but she could only fit me in on the show day at 7.30 in the morning! And so..

I was up at 6.30 to get over to Banbury by 7.30 for an hour on the table being tractioned, pulled, pushed and stretched. Returned home feeling slightly better to pick up Phil, who had stayed over last night. Soundcheck was set for 9.00am.

I drove to Cropredy and Phil followed in his car. At some point he vanished from my rear-view mirror, so I waited for him for a few minutes before turning round and going back to look for him. He'd vanished. Tried calling him but he didn't answer. I thought he might have crashed. In the end I called Frenchie at the festival site to let him know I had lost Phil. Frenchie said, "He's standing next to me!"

I turned round again and made my way there. We had been given a decent amount of time to soundcheck, and the backstage atmosphere was relaxed and good-natured. I could tell that this is all passed down from Fairport Convention themselves. It's their gig and they employ everyone and therefore are ultimately responsible for the easy temperature of things.

Soundcheck seemed to go well and everything seemed to be working fine. Grabbed a bit of breakfast in catering and said hello to Dave Pegg and Simon Nicol as they passed.

Returned home and got back around midday. I was a bit weary after the dawn departure, so I went back to bed for an hour. Linette and young Vibes went on ahead to Cropredy to groove around and enjoy the festival. My old mate Dave Crawshaw arrived around 2.00 from Sheffield and we decided that it would be a good idea if he drive me to Cropredy in his car as I was unlikely to be sober after the show. In all the distraction of this plan, I left the Mini outside the house. This is not a good idea on a Saturday as we have cricket on the village green and there's always a chance of a cricket ball bouncing off your car.

Got back to the festival with Dave around 4.00 and dropped my bags. Was interviewed by the lovely Bob Harris for the BBC and said hello to his equally-lovely wife, Trudie. Was further interviewed by local press while little Vibes sat on my knee. I think he was missing the attention and not used to me getting it all. That's not the way it should be when you're six!

By the time they'd done with me it was time to get ready. We were on at 6pm. Got changed in our tent and hit the stage feeling pretty good. We were hoping the rain would miss us although it was forecast for late afternoon. It did rain around the midpoint of the set, but didn't last long and had fined-up again before the end.

I really enjoyed the show – I thought the band played well and I felt comfortable singing to the 20,000 sold-out crowd. It was one of my all-time best festival memories and lived up to the fabulous Quebec Festival d'Eté earlier in the year. Bigger by a factor of 4 though, and with much greater potential of picking up new fans. Got a txt from Fenella (one of the locals) who'd never seen us before which said, "Was blown away by your performance. You absolutely stole the show this weekend." Let's hope a good proportion of the crowd felt the same way.

Afterwards, we'd agreed to do an autograph session, so we were hurried to a trestle-table where I endured the pain in my left arm for a further (long) hour. The line seemed unending and the onset of darkness had made the air chilly. It's always good to meet the fans, but tonight I was tired and hurting, and it was a relief when the end of the line finally came into view and everyone had what they wanted.

Dave drove me home and I poured him a malt whisky while L and I relaxed and talked about the afternoon we'd had.

The Mini was still parked outside, complete with cricket-ball-shaped dint in the front wing. Doh!

Postscript

Well, I guess that concludes Volume II. At the time of signing this off to the publishers, I'm sitting on the sofa in the control-room of our studio, the Racket Club. The band have been jamming new ideas for the next album and interesting music is being born… I'm also occasionally performing solo this Autumn and I spoke and sang at Blenheim Palace Literary Festival last Saturday. The arm's better, and the knee has been operated upon with, so far, great results.

Stay tuned for Volume III – you might have to wait a decade or so for it.

Love and handstands,

h

ALSO AVAILABLE FROM **MIWK PUBLISHING**

Steve Hogarth

The *Invisible* Man

diaries 1991–1997

ISBN 978-1-908630-99-5

find a better way of life

MARILLION

www.marillion.com

www.miwk.com/

www.facebook.com/MiwkPublishingLtd

www.twitter.com/#!/MiwkPublishing